2004

by

Jack Gillis

Assisted by

Amy Curran
Ben Hardaway

Foreword by

Clarence Ditlow
Center for Auto Safety

A Center for Auto Safety Publication

ACKNOWLEDGMENTS

This 24th edition of *The Car Book* is the result of the hard work of Amy Curran, Ben Hardaway and Evan Shurak. Thanks to their efforts, the complex process of compiling the information you need to make a smart, sensible new car choice was expertly accomplished. Longtime *Car Book* veteran Amy Curran placed, as she has for thirteen years, all of this information in an easy-to-use format with her usual calm and grace. In addition, she helped considerably with the overall management of the project. This year, Ben Hardaway took the lead and marshaled the thousands of data points needed to develop the book. Rounding out the team was the hard working and skillful Stephanie Ackerman, who, as always, provided invaluable good spirits and sound advice.

This year's edition would not have been possible without essential contributions from many talented individuals. Most significant was Clarence Ditlow and the staff of the Center for Auto Safety. In addition, valuable insight and information was provided by Susan Tiffany, *Home and Family Finance*; Rick Morgan, The George Washington University; and, the staff of the National Highway Traffic Safety Administration.

As always, the most important factor in being able to bring this information to the American car buyer for 24 years is the encouragement, support, and love from my brilliant and beautiful wife, Marilyn Mohrman-Gillis.

—J.G.

As Always,

for Marilyn &
Katie, John, Brian, and Brennan

THE CAR BOOK (2004 edition). Copyright © 2003, 2002, 2001, 2000, 1999, 1998, 1997, 1996, 1995, 1994, 1993, 1992, 1991, 1990, 1989, 1988, 1987, 1986, 1985, 1984, 1983, 1982, 1981 by Jack Gillis. All rights reserved. Printed in the United States of America. No part of this book may be used or reproduced in any manner whatsoever without written permission except in the case of brief quotations embodied in critical articles and reviews. For information, address Gillis Publishing Group, 1518 K Street, NW, Suite 306, Washington, DC 20005.

The Car Book may be purchased for educational, business, or sales promotional use. For information, please write: Gillis Publishing Group, 1518 K Street, NW, Suite 306, Washington, DC 20005.

ISBN: 0-9727460-1-3

Printed in Canada

CONTENTS

BY CLARENCE DITLOW

There's good news and bad news in buying a new car in 2004. The good news is that overall cars are safer thanks to government regulation, product liability lawsuits and consumer advocates. The bad news is that many cars are still unsafe and neither the government nor the car companies will tell you which ones and why. By the time the government releases its first safety information on 2004 models, over 5 million consumers will have bought new cars from auto salesmen who have never seen a bad car.

The auto industry makes a lot of good cars and a lot of bad cars. For every Honda Civic or Chevrolet Prizm, there's a Ford Focus or BMW X5. Even the quality of the legendary Mercedes has dropped in recent years. The auto companies don't provide solid comparative information by make and model to separate the lemons from the peaches because they make a lot of money selling safety and economic lemons. The industry certainly doesn't want to disclose that a luxury SUV like the $50,000 Hummer H2 is nothing more than a gussied up $35,000 Chevrolet Tahoe which itself is based on a $20,000 Chevrolet Silverado pickup.

Congress' passage of the Motor Vehicle Safety Act in 1966 and the many amendments to the law since then have not stopped the sale of unsafe vehicles that have slipped through loopholes in the safety laws and regulations. Traffic deaths in 2002 increased to 42,815, the highest since 1990 with 10,666 people dying in rollover crashes led by a 14% increase in SUV rollover deaths.

Here are some of the safety and economic lemons consumers unknowingly bought:

- ☑ 2000-02 Ford Focus with 11 safety recalls
- ☑ 1973-87 GM C/K pickups that killed over 2000 people in fire crashes
- ☑ 1994-95 Nissan Altima with airbags that can blind passengers on deployment
- ☑ 1984-95 Chrysler minivans that killed over 40 people when tailgates opened in crashes.
- ☑ 1997-2002 Toyota and Lexus with engines that self destruct from oil sludge or gel.
- ☑ 2001 BMW X5 with 9 safety recalls in its debut model year

That's where the *Car Book* and the Center for Auto Safety (CAS) come in. The Car Book helps you buy the safest vehicles sold. *The Car Book* was the first to publish rollover ratings for every vehicle to help you avoid rollover prone SUVs; the first to publish crashworthiness ratings to help you buy vehicles that sacrifice themselves to save you in a crash; and the first to develop consumer complaints into a rating system to help you buy a more reliable vehicle.

The Center for Auto Safety is your voice for vehicle safety. On a shoe string budget, half what an auto company pays for one Super Bowl commercial, CAS has won many victories for consumers, not the least of which was saving the *Car Book* when the auto industry wanted to keep its vital information out of consumers' hands. Other CAS accomplishments for you include:

- ☑ Lemon laws in every state
- ☑ Airbags in every vehicle
- ☑ Citizen right to petition for safety recalls and standards.
- ☑ Exposed secret warranties saving consumers billions of dollars and got states to enact secret warranty disclosure laws
- ☑ Mandatory free repairs in safety recall law
- ☑ Sued and won landmark case upholding Clean Air Act recalls
- ☑ Exposed the Ford Pinto, Firestone 500 tire, GM side saddle gas tank, Ford ignition switch, Evenflo One Step child seat
- ☑ Passage of Mobile Home Construction and Safety Act
- ☑ Sued to obtain mandatory bridge inspections
- ☑ Saved tire treadwear grading standards
- ☑ Testified before Congress in 2000 to finally put criminal penalties in the Vehicle Safety Act so executives have to think twice about making and selling unsafe vehicles

And the list goes on. Since our founding in 1970 by Ralph Nader and Consumers Union, CAS has also taken on the oil, insurance and trucking companies and won on leadfree gasoline prices, wrecked vehicle disclosure laws and big trucks safety. If it were not for CAS, auto companies would run roughshod over the consumer. If we hadn't had a CAS these past 30 years, we would have more corporate lawlessness, consumer ripoffs, dirtier air, more lemons, fewer recalls and more deaths and injuries on the highway. No wonder the auto and highway lobbies would be much happier if CAS were not on the job watching our for consumers.

By reading the *Car Book*, you have taken an important first step toward your personal vehicle safety. The next step is to support the Center for Auto Safety which works every day on your behalf to ensure that all Americans ride in safe and reliable vehicles. To find out more about what CAS does for you and how you can support CAS, turn to pages 69-70 or go to our Website, www.autosafety.org.

BY JACK GILLIS

For 24 years *The Car Book* has helped consumers make wise and informed choices in the increasingly complex task of buying a car. This year, as the economy sputters back to life, more of us will be venturing back into the showroom. Armed with *The Car Book*, you can feel confident that your next car purchase can be you best one.

While the choices get better each year and safety is improved, it's still a challenge to separate the lemons from the peaches. There are notable differences in how cars protect you in a crash, how much they cost to maintain and how far they'll go on a gallon of very expensive gasoline. So, thanks to the Center for Auto Safety, we again bring you all the information you need to make a smart, safe and sensible choice among one of the most expensive products you'll ever purchase. In fact, if you use the information in *The Car Book*, there is no reason why your next car shouldn't last at least 150,000 miles.

Because more of us are understanding that most cars don't change much each year, we've included the stats on last year's models. Now you'll be able to quickly compare if there have been enough improvements to warrant spending the extra dollars on a brand-new car, versus a 2003 model that may look almost the same.

While car dealers have become much more sensitive to meeting consumer needs, don't be lulled into complacency. Buying a car means you have to stay on your toes, and *The Car Book* will help you do just that. In spite of all the new car technology and the Internet, the fundamentals of buying a good, safe, reliable car remain the same: do your homework; shop around; and remember that car dealers need you more than you need them!

So how do you buy for safety? Many consumers mistakenly believe that handling and performance are the key elements in the safety of a car. While an extremely unresponsive car could cause an accident, most new cars meet basic handling requirements. In fact, many people actually feel uncomfortable driving high performance cars because the highly responsive steering, acceleration, and suspension systems can be difficult to get used to. But the main reason handling is overrated as a safety measure is that automobile collisions are, by nature, accidents. Once they've begun, they are beyond human capacity to prevent, no matter how well your car handles. So the key to protecting yourself is to purchase a car that offers a high degree of crash protection.

Consumers are learning that they can get better-performing and safer cars by buying the ones with good safety records, low maintenance costs, long warranties, and insurance discounts. This is the most powerful signal you can send to let the car makers know what's going to make you buy.

Our exclusive car-by-car ratings at the end of the book provide a detailed review of each of the new cars, minivans, sport utilities, and pickups. These pages provide, at a glance, an overview of all the criteria you need to make a good choice. Here, you'll be able to quickly assess key features and see how the car you're interested in stacks up against its competition so you can make sure your selection is the best car for you. Car prices have more than doubled since 1980, so we've also included the percentage of dealer markup to help you negotiate the very best price. In addition, we've added information on the last model year, so you can decide if buying new is really best for you.

The information in *The Car Book* is based on data collected and developed by our staff, the U.S. Department of Transportation, and the Center for Auto Safety. With all of these data in hand, you'll find some great choices for 2004. Just let *The Car Book* guide you through the trade-offs, promises, facts, and myths to the car that will best meet your needs.

Safe shopping and buckle up!

—*Jack Gillis*

Use this page to keep some notes on the choices you are considering. Include any comments your friends make, statements made by the dealer that may be important later, and your own personal reactions to the car and the test drive. After you've looked at 4 or 5 cars, it's easy to mix up the details.

MAKE/MODEL: ____________ **PRICE RANGE:** ____________ **PAGE:** ______

PROS:	CONS:

NOTES:

MAKE/MODEL: ____________ **PRICE RANGE:** ____________ **PAGE:** ______

PROS:	CONS:

NOTES:

MAKE/MODEL: ____________ **PRICE RANGE:** ____________ **PAGE:** ______

PROS:	CONS:

NOTES:

IN THIS CHAPTER

INTRODUCTION

The "Buying Guide" provides an overall comparison of the 2004 cars in terms of warranty, safety, fuel economy, complaint ratings, and price range. The cars are arranged by size class based on weight. Based on these comparisons, we have developed *The Car Book* Best Bets for 2004—these vehicles rated tops when comparing all the key categories.

USING THE BUYING GUIDE

The "Buying Guide" provides a quick comparison of the 2004 models.

To fully understand these summary charts, it is important to read the appropriate section of the book. You will note that here and throughout the book, some of the charts contain empty boxes. This indicates that data were unavailable at the time of printing.

Here's how to understand what's included in the "Buying Guide."

Page Reference: The page in the back of the book where you'll find all the details for this car.

Overall Rating: This is the "bottom line." It shows how well this car stacks up on a scale of 1 to 10 when compared to all others on the market. The overall rating considers safety, maintenance, fuel economy, warranty, insurance costs, and complaints. Due to the importance of safety, cars with no crash test results as of our publication date cannot be given an overall rating.

Car Book Crash Test Rating: This indicates how well the car performed in the U.S. government's 35-mph frontal crash test program using a combined rating. We have analyzed and compared all of the crash test results to date and have given them a rating from very good to very poor. These ratings allow you to compare the test results of one car with another. A car with a poor rating may have done well according to government injury ratings but still be among the worst performers of cars being offered in 2004.

Important Note: Recently, the government began a side crash test program. If a vehicle has been side crash tested and the results are not good, we will not give that vehicle an overall "Best Bet" rating regardless of its other results. The crash test tables on pages 21-28 and the car rating pages in the back of the book provide side crash test results.

Fuel Economy: This is the EPA-rated fuel economy for city and highway driving measured in miles per gallon. A single model may have a number of fuel economy ratings because of different engine and transmission options. We have included the figure for what is expected to be the most popular model.

Warranty Rating: This is an overall assessment of the car's warranty when compared to all other warranties. The rating considers the important features of each warranty, with emphasis on the length of the basic and power train warranties.

Complaint Rating: This rating is based on the number of complaints about that car on file at the U.S. Department of Transportation. The complaint index will give you a general idea of experiences others have had with models which are essentially unchanged for this model year. Vehicles all-new in 2002 and 2004 are given an average complaint rating, as it is unknown how many complaints they will receive.

Price Range: This price range will give you a general idea of the "sticker," or asking price of a car. It is based on the lowest to highest retail price of the various models, and it does not include options or the discount that you should be able to negotiate using a service such as CarBargains (see the Showroom Strategies Chapter).

BEST BETS

Following the Buying Guide and based on information in *The Car Book*, is our list of the highest-rated cars in each of the size categories. Ratings are based on expected performance in ten important categories (crash tests, safety features, fuel economy, rollover, overall, maintenance and repair costs, warranties, insurance costs, and complaints), with the heaviest emphasis on safety. The Best Bets are on pages 14-18.

Vehicle	Page #	Overall Rating	Frontal Crash Tests	Warranty	Fuel Economy	Complaints	Price Range
Subcompact							
BMW Z4	107	9	Good	Average	21/28		$33-40,000
Chevrolet Aveo	121			Very Poor	26/35		$9-12,000
Honda Insight	164	2	Good	Very Poor	57/56	Good	$19-21,000
Honda S2000	167	7	Very Good	Very Poor	20/26	Poor	$32-32,000
Hyundai Accent	168	10	Very Good	Very Good	27/35	Good	$9-12,000
Hyundai Tiburon	172			Very Good	23/30		$17-19,000
Kia Rio	184	7	Good	Very Good	25/32		$9-11,000
Kia Spectra	187	9	Very Good	Very Good	22/30		$11-14,000
Mazda MX-5 Miata	200	4	Very Good	Very Poor	22/28		$21-24,000
Mini Cooper	206	10	Good	Poor	25/32		$16-19,000
Mitsubishi Lancer	210	7	Very Good	Average	24/29		$13-19,000
Nissan Sentra	221	8	Very Good	Poor	28/35	Good	$13-17,000
Scion xA	236			Poor	32/38		$12-13,000
Scion xB	237			Poor	31/35		$13-14,000
Subaru Impreza	240	4	Very Good	Poor	19/26	Very Poor	$17-24,000
Suzuki Aerio	243			Average	26/31	Very Good	$14-17,000
Toyota ECHO	253	7	Good	Poor	33/39	Very Good	$10-11,000
Toyota MR2 Spyder	255			Poor	26/32	Good	$24-25,000
Volkswagen Beetle	263	8	Very Good	Good	23/29		$16-25,000
Compact							
Acura RSX	98	7	Very Good	Good	24/33	Poor	$20-23,000
Audi A4	101	10	Good	Very Good	23/29	Very Good	$27-32,000
BMW 3 Series	104	9	Very Good	Average	19/28	Average	$30-43,000
Chev. Cavalier/Pont. Sunfire	123	3	Very Good	Very Poor	24/33	Average	$14-17,000
Chrysler Crossfire	135			Good	18/27		$33-33,000
Chrysler PT Cruiser	137	9	Good	Good	19/25	Good	$17-25,000
Chrys. Sebring/Ddg. Stratus*	139	7	Good	Good	21/28	Very Good	$20-23,000
Dodge Neon	144	8	Average	Good	25/32	Very Poor	$13-17,000
Ford Focus	152	8	Good	Very Poor	27/33	Very Poor	$12-15,000
Ford Mustang	155	7	Very Good	Very Poor	19/27	Poor	$17-27,000
Ford Thunderbird	158	5	Very Good	Very Poor	17/23		$36-43,000
Honda Civic	161	10	Very Good	Very Poor	29/38	Average	$13-18,000
Hyundai Elantra	169	10	Very Good	Very Good	24/33	Good	$13-15,000
Infiniti G35	175			Very Good	19/26		$27-31,000
Kia Optima	183	8	Good	Very Good	22/30		$15-19,000
Mazda RX-8	201			Very Poor	18/25		$25-26,000

*Sebring Coupe and Stratus Coupe.

Vehicle	Page #	Overall Rating	Frontal Crash Tests	Warranty	Fuel Economy	Complaints	Price Range
Compact (cont.)							
Mitsubishi Eclipse	207	5	Good	Average	21/28	Very Poor	$18-28,000
Mitsubishi Galant	209			Average	19/27		$18-24,000
Nissan 350Z	213	7	Very Good	Poor	19/26		$26-37,000
Pontiac GTO	229			Very Poor	16/21		$31-31,000
Pontiac Vibe/Toyota Matrix	230	9	Very Good	Very Poor	28/33		$16-19,000
Saab 9-3	231			Good	22/31		$26-39,000
Saturn ION	233	9	Very Good	Very Poor	24/32		$10-16,000
Subaru Legacy	241	8	Very Good	Poor	22/27	Poor	$21-26,000
Subaru Outback	242	9	Very Good	Poor	22/28	Average	$24-30,000
Suzuki Forenza	244			Average	22/30		$12-16,000
Toyota Celica	251	7	Very Good	Poor	29/36	Good	$17-22,000
Toyota Corolla	252	7	Very Good	Poor	29/38		$13-15,000
Volkswagen Golf/Jetta	264	9	Very Good	Good	23/29	Average	$15-18,000
Volvo 40 Series	267			Average	22/30		$24-29,000
Intermediate							
Acura TL	99	10	Good	Good	19/29	Good	$32-32,000
Acura TSX	100			Good	22/31		$26-28,000
Audi A6	102			Very Good	20/27	Very Poor	$35-49,000
Audi Allroad Quattro	103			Very Good	16/22	Very Good	$39-46,000
BMW 5 Series	105			Average	19/25		$39-57,000
Buick Century	108	6	Average	Very Poor	20/29	Good	$21-21,000
Buick Regal	112	6	Average	Very Poor	19/29	Average	$24-28,000
Chevrolet Malibu	126			Very Poor	23/33		$18-22,000
Chrys. Sebring/Conv./Stratus	138	10	Very Good	Good	22/30	Very Good	$18-21,000
Ford Taurus/Mercury Sable	157	9	Very Good	Very Poor	20/28	Average	$19-23,000
Honda Accord	160	8	Very Good	Very Poor	24/33		$15-26,000
Hyundai Sonata	171	10	Good	Very Good	22/30	Very Poor	$16-19,000
Hyundai XG350	173			Very Good	17/26	Very Good	$23-25,000
Infiniti I35	176	10	Very Good	Very Good	20/26	Very Good	
Lexus ES 330	190			Very Good	18/24		$31-31,000
Lexus IS 300	192			Very Good	18/24	Very Good	$29-30,000
Mazda 6	198	7	Very Good	Very Poor	23/29		$18-21,000
Mercedes-Benz C-Class	202	9	Good	Very Poor	19/25	Very Good	$28-39,000
Nissan Altima	214	9	Very Good	Poor	23/29	Very Good	$17-23,000
Nissan Maxima	216	9	Very Good	Poor	20/28		$26-28,000
Oldsmobile Alero	224	6	Very Good	No Index	24/33	Poor	$18-22,000
Pontiac Grand Am	227	4	Very Good	Very Poor	24/33		$17-23,000
Saab 9-5	232	10	Very Good	Good	20/29	Average	$32-39,000

Vehicle	Page #	Overall Rating	Frontal Crash Tests	Warranty	Fuel Economy	Complaints	Price Range
Intermediate (cont.)							
Saturn L/LW	234	9	Very Good	Very Poor	24/32		$16-22,000
Suzuki Verona	246			Average	20/28		$16-19,000
Toyota Avalon	249	10	Very Good	Poor	21/29	Average	$26-30,000
Toyota Camry	250	10	Very Good	Poor	23/32	Very Good	$22-25,000
Toyota Prius	256			Poor	59/51		$19-19,000
Toyota Solara	260			Poor	20/29		$19-25,000
Volkswagen Passat	265	8	Very Good	Good	19/26	Very Poor	$21-32,000
Volvo 60 Series	268	10	Good	Average	22/31		$29-36,000
Volvo 70 Series	269			Average	20/26		$31-38,000
Large							
Acura RL	97	7	Good	Good	18/24	Poor	$43-45,000
Buick LeSabre	109	7	Very Good	Very Poor	20/29	Poor	$25-31,000
Buick Park Avenue	110	7	Good	Very Poor	20/29	Poor	$34-39,000
Cadillac CTS	114	7	Good	Average	18/26		$30-30,000
Cadillac DeVille	115	9	Very Good	Average	18/27	Average	$44-49,000
Cadillac Seville	118			Average	18/27	Poor	$45-45,000
Chev. Impala/Monte Carlo	125	7	Very Good	Very Poor	21/32	Average	$21-27,000
Chrys. 300M/Concorde/Intrepid	134	10	Good	Good	18/27	Average	$29-32,000
Ford Cr. Vic./Gr. Marq./Marauder	146	10	Very Good	Very Poor	18/26	Good	$23-26,000
Kia Amanti	182			Very Good	17/25		$25-25,000
Lexus GS 300/GS 430	191			Very Good	18/25	Good	$38-38,000
Lexus LS 430	193			Very Good	18/25	Very Good	$55-55,000
Lincoln LS	196			Average	18/25	Poor	$31-39,000
Lincoln Town Car	197	10	Very Good	Average	17/25	Average	$41-44,000
Mercedes-Benz E-Class	203	9	Very Good	Very Poor	19/27		$48-60,000
Pontiac Bonneville	226	7	Very Good	Very Poor	17/27	Good	$26-29,000
Pontiac Grand Prix	228	6	Good	Very Poor	20/30	Poor	$21-25,000
Volvo 80 Series	270	9	Very Good	Average	20/28		$37-48,000
Minivan							
Chevrolet Astro/GMC Safari	120	2	Average	Very Poor	17/23	Poor	$24-27,000
Chev. Vent./Pont. Mont./Olds Silh.	133	6	Very Good	Very Poor	19/26	Very Poor	$21-33,000
Chrys. T&C/Ddg. Gr. Caravan	140	10	Good	Good	18/24	Good	$26-37,000
Dge. Caravan/Chrys. T&C SWB	141	10	Good	Good	21/27	Very Poor	$18-22,000
Ford Freestar	153	4	Very Good	Very Poor	17/23		$26-32,000
Honda Odyssey	165	8	Very Good	Very Poor	18/25	Poor	$24-30,000
Kia Sedona	185	6	Very Good	Very Good	15/20		$19-22,000
Mazda MPV	199	7	Very Good	Very Poor	18/25	Good	$23-28,000
Mercury Monterey	205	4	Very Good	Very Poor	16/22		$29-35,000

Vehicle	Page #	Overall Rating	Frontal Crash Tests	Warranty	Fuel Economy	Complaints	Price Range
Minivan (cont.)							
Nissan Quest	220	6	Very Good	Poor	18/25		$24-32,000
Toyota Sienna	259	7	Very Good	Poor	19/27		$23-36,000
Compact Pickup							
Chev. Colorado/GMC Canyon	124			Very Poor	19/24		$16-26,000
Chev. S Ser./GMC Sonoma	127	1	Poor	Very Poor	19/25	Very Poor	$24-24,000
Dodge Dakota	142	7	Good	Good	14/19	Very Poor	$16-21,000
Ford Ranger/Mazda Truck	156	6	Good	Very Poor	23/26	Poor	$13-22,000
Nissan Frontier	215	4	Good	Poor	20/23	Very Good	$15-24,000
Toyota Tacoma	261	3	Good	Poor	22/25	Average	$12-20,000
Standard Pickup							
Chev. Silverado/GMC Sierra	128	3	Average	Very Poor	15/20	Average	$19-28,000
Dodge Ram Pickup	145	2	Very Good	Good	15/20		$18-29,000
Ford F-Series	154			Very Poor	16/19		$24-34,000
Nissan Titan	222			Poor	14/19		$24-34,000
Toyota Tundra	262	4	Very Good	Poor	16/19	Average	$15-31,000
Small SUV							
Chevrolet Blazer	122	1	Poor	Very Poor	17/23	Very Poor	$20-26,000
Chev. Tracker/Suzuki Vitara	131	1	Good	Very Poor	19/21	Average	$19-22,000
Ford Escape/Mazda Tribute	147	8	Very Good	Very Poor	19/25	Very Poor	$18-24,000
Honda CR-V	162	9	Very Good	Very Poor	22/26		$19-22,000
Honda Element	163	4	Very Good	Very Poor	22/26		$16-20,000
Hyundai Santa Fe	170	9	Good	Very Good	20/27	Very Good	$17-25,000
Infiniti FX	174			Very Good	15/19		$34-44,000
Jeep Wrangler	181	7	Good	Good	19/20	Poor	$16-25,000
Land Rover Freelander	189			Good	17/21	Very Good	$25-28,000
Mitsubishi Montero Sport	211	4	Average	Average	15/19		$23-33,000
Subaru Forester	239	6	Very Good	Poor	19/26	Poor	$20-24,000
Suzuki Grand Vitara	245	2	Good	Average	19/21	Poor	$17-22,000
Toyota RAV4	257	7	Good	Poor	24/29	Good	$18-20,000
Mid-Size SUV							
Acura MDX	96	10	Very Good	Good	17/23	Very Good	$36-39,000
BMW X5	106	8	Very Good	Average	15/20	Poor	$40-51,000
Buick Rendezvous	113	5	Poor	Very Poor	19/26		$25-29,000
Cadillac SRX	119			Average	18/23		$37-46,000
Ford Explorer/Merc. Mountain.	150	8	Very Good	Very Poor	15/19		$26-36,000
Honda Pilot	166	6	Very Good	Very Poor	17/22		$27-32,000
Isuzu Axiom	177	6	Good	Good	17/21		$24-30,000
Isuzu Rodeo	178	4	Average	Good	18/23	Very Poor	$20-25,000
Jeep Grand Cherokee	179	8	Poor	Good	16/21	Very Poor	$26-38,000

Vehicle	Page #	Overall Rating	Frontal Crash Tests	Warranty	Fuel Economy	Complaints	Price Range
Mid-Size SUV (cont.)							
Jeep Liberty	180	10	Good	Good	19/23	Average	$18-24,000
Kia Sorento	186	5	Good	Very Good	15/20		$18-24,000
Land Rover Discovery	188	1	Very Good	Good	13/17	Very Poor	$34-41,000
Lexus RX 330	194	9	Very Good	Very Good	18/24		$35-36,000
Lincoln Aviator	195			Average	13/19		$39-42,000
Mercedes-Benz M-Class	204			Very Poor	17/21	Average	$38-46,000
Mitsubishi Outlander	212	6	Very Good	Average	21/26		$18-22,000
Nissan Murano	217	7	Good	Poor	20/25		$28-31,000
Nissan Pathfinder	218	7	Average	Poor	16/21	Good	$26-34,000
Nissan Xterra	223	5	Good	Poor	15/19	Good	$20-26,000
Pontiac Aztek	225	5	Good	Very Poor	19/26	Average	$20-23,000
Saturn VUE	235	9	Very Good	Very Poor	22/28		$16-23,000
Subaru Baja	238			Poor	21/26		
Suzuki XL-7	247			Average	17/22	Very Good	$20-27,000
Toyota 4Runner	248	6	Very Good	Poor	16/20		$27-36,000
Toyota Highlander	254	9	Good	Poor	22/27	Good	$25-31,000
Volkswagen Touareg	266			Good	15/20		$34-45,000
Volvo XC90	271	8	Very Good	Average	18/24		$34-40,000
Large SUV							
Buick Rainier/Olds Bravada	111	4	Average	Very Poor	16/21		$35-38,000
Cad. Escalade/Escalade ESV	116	3	Average	Average	14/18		$51-54,000
Cad. Escd. EXT/Chev. Avalanche	117	2	Average	Average	12/16		$52-52,000
Chev. Suburban/GMC Yukon XL	129	2	Average	Very Poor	14/18	Poor	$37-41,000
Chevrolet Tahoe/GMC Yukon	130	3	Average	Very Poor	14/18	Good	$34-37,000
Chev. T. Blazer/Envoy/Ascender*	132	2	Average	Very Poor	16/22		$27-29,000
Chrysler Pacifica	136	8	Very Good	Good	17/23		$30-32,000
Dodge Durango	143			Good	15/21		$25-27,000
Ford Excursion	148			Very Poor		Very Poor	$36-44,000
Ford Exped./Lincoln Navigator	149	4	Very Good	Very Poor	14/19		$31-37,000
Ford Explorer Sport Trac	151			Very Poor	16/20		$23-27,000
GMC Envoy XL/XUV/Ascender**	159			Very Poor	15/20		$31-35,000
Mitsubishi Endeavor	208	5	Very Good	Average	17/23		$27-33,000
Nissan Pathfinder Armada	219			Poor	13/19		$33-40,000
Toyota Sequoia	258	4	Very Good	Poor	14/18	Very Good	$31-44,000

*5-pass. Isuzu Ascender
**7-pass. Isuzu Ascender

HYUNDAI ACCENT — SUBCOMPACT

10

Front Crash Test	9	Warranty	10
Side Crash Test	5	Fuel Rating	9
Safety Features	2	Rollover	9
Preventive Maint.	8	Complaints	10
Repair Costs	10	Insurance Costs	5

MINI COOPER — SUBCOMPACT

10

Front Crash Test	8	Warranty	4
Side Crash Test	6	Fuel Rating	8
Safety Features	9	Rollover	9
Preventive Maint.	10	Complaints	
Repair Costs	7	Insurance Costs	1

BMW Z4 — SUBCOMPACT

9

Front Crash Test	7	Warranty	6
Side Crash Test	5	Fuel Rating	6
Safety Features	7	Rollover	10
Preventive Maint.	10	Complaints	
Repair Costs		Insurance Costs	5

KIA SPECTRA — SUBCOMPACT

9

Front Crash Test	9	Warranty	10
Side Crash Test	7	Fuel Rating	7
Safety Features	1	Rollover	9
Preventive Maint.	7	Complaints	
Repair Costs	9	Insurance Costs	1

AUDI A4 — COMPACT

10

Front Crash Test	7	Warranty	10
Side Crash Test	10	Fuel Rating	7
Safety Features	7	Rollover	9
Preventive Maint.	5	Complaints	1
Repair Costs	1	Insurance Costs	10

HONDA CIVIC — COMPACT

10

Front Crash Test	10	Warranty	1
Side Crash Test	9	Fuel Rating	10
Safety Features	5	Rollover	9
Preventive Maint.	10	Complaints	5
Repair Costs	10	Insurance Costs	1

HYUNDAI ELANTRA — COMPACT

10

Front Crash Test	10	Warranty	10
Side Crash Test	9	Fuel Rating	8
Safety Features	2	Rollover	8
Preventive Maint.	7	Complaints	10
Repair Costs	10	Insurance Costs	1

BMW 3 SERIES — COMPACT

9

Front Crash Test	10	Warranty	6
Side Crash Test	9	Fuel Rating	5
Safety Features	9	Rollover	9
Preventive Maint.	10	Complaints	7
Repair Costs	1	Insurance Costs	5

CHRYSLER PT CRUISER — COMPACT

9

Front Crash Test	7	Warranty	8
Side Crash Test	9	Fuel Rating	4
Safety Features	3	Rollover	7
Preventive Maint.	10	Complaints	5
Repair Costs	8	Insurance Costs	1

PONTIAC VIBE/TOYOTA MATRIX — COMPACT

9

Front Crash Test	10	Warranty	2
Side Crash Test	10	Fuel Rating	9
Safety Features	4	Rollover	7
Preventive Maint.	10	Complaints	
Repair Costs	6	Insurance Costs	5

SATURN ION — COMPACT

9

Front Crash Test	10	Warranty	2
Side Crash Test	4	Fuel Rating	8
Safety Features	7	Rollover	8
Preventive Maint.	8	Complaints	
Repair Costs	9	Insurance Costs	5

SUBARU OUTBACK — COMPACT

9

Front Crash Test	9	Warranty	3
Side Crash Test	10	Fuel Rating	7
Safety Features	5	Rollover	7
Preventive Maint.	7	Complaints	7
Repair Costs	5	Insurance Costs	10

VOLKSWAGEN GOLF/JETTA — COMPACT

8

Front Crash Test	10	Warranty	7
Side Crash Test	9	Fuel Rating	7
Safety Features	4	Rollover	8
Preventive Maint.	6	Complaints	4
Repair Costs	5	Insurance Costs	1

ACURA TL — INTERMEDIATE

10

Front Crash Test	8	Warranty	7
Side Crash Test	10	Fuel Rating	5
Safety Features	5	Rollover	9
Preventive Maint.	9	Complaints	3
Repair Costs	3	Insurance Costs	10

CHRYSLER SEBRING/CONV./DODGE STRATUS — INTERMEDIATE

10

Front Crash Test	10	Warranty	8
Side Crash Test	5	Fuel Rating	7
Safety Features	5	Rollover	10
Preventive Maint.	8	Complaints	10
Repair Costs	10	Insurance Costs	1

HYUNDAI SONATA — INTERMEDIATE

10

Front Crash Test	8	Warranty	10
Side Crash Test	9	Fuel Rating	7
Safety Features	3	Rollover	10
Preventive Maint.	7	Complaints	10
Repair Costs	8	Insurance Costs	1

INFINITI I35 — INTERMEDIATE

10

Front Crash Test	9	Warranty	9
Side Crash Test	10	Fuel Rating	5
Safety Features	7	Rollover	8
Preventive Maint.	8	Complaints	1
Repair Costs	2	Insurance Costs	10

SAAB 9-5 — INTERMEDIATE

10

Front Crash Test	10	Warranty	7
Side Crash Test	10	Fuel Rating	5
Safety Features	8	Rollover	8
Preventive Maint.	5	Complaints	8
Repair Costs	2	Insurance Costs	10

TOYOTA AVALON — INTERMEDIATE

10

Front Crash Test	10	Warranty	3
Side Crash Test	9	Fuel Rating	6
Safety Features	6	Rollover	9
Preventive Maint.	10	Complaints	6
Repair Costs	4	Insurance Costs	10

TOYOTA CAMRY — INTERMEDIATE

10

Front Crash Test	10	Warranty	3
Side Crash Test	9	Fuel Rating	8
Safety Features	8	Rollover	9
Preventive Maint.	10	Complaints	9
Repair Costs	3	Insurance Costs	5

VOLVO 60 SERIES — INTERMEDIATE

10

Front Crash Test	8	Warranty	6
Side Crash Test	10	Fuel Rating	7
Safety Features	10	Rollover	10
Preventive Maint.	3	Complaints	
Repair Costs	5	Insurance Costs	5

CHRYSLER 300M/CONCORDE/INTREPID — LARGE

10

Front Crash Test	8	Warranty	8
Side Crash Test	9	Fuel Rating	4
Safety Features	4	Rollover	9
Preventive Maint.	9	Complaints	7
Repair Costs	8	Insurance Costs	5

FORD CR. VIC./MERCURY GR. MARQUIS/MARAUDER — LARGE

10

Front Crash Test	10	Warranty	2
Side Crash Test	9	Fuel Rating	4
Safety Features	7	Rollover	10
Preventive Maint.	7	Complaints	10
Repair Costs	9	Insurance Costs	10

LINCOLN TOWN CAR — LARGE

10

Front Crash Test	10	Warranty	6
Side Crash Test	10	Fuel Rating	3
Safety Features	7	Rollover	10
Preventive Maint.	5	Complaints	8
Repair Costs	9	Insurance Costs	10

CADILLAC DEVILLE — LARGE

9

Front Crash Test	9	Warranty	6
Side Crash Test	8	Fuel Rating	4
Safety Features	9	Rollover	10
Preventive Maint.	6	Complaints	8
Repair Costs	1	Insurance Costs	10

MERCEDES-BENZ E-CLASS — LARGE

9

Front Crash Test	9	Warranty	1
Side Crash Test	10	Fuel Rating	5
Safety Features	10	Rollover	10
Preventive Maint.		Complaints	
Repair Costs		Insurance Costs	10

VOLVO 80 SERIES — LARGE

9

Front Crash Test	10	Warranty	6
Side Crash Test	10	Fuel Rating	5
Safety Features	10	Rollover	10
Preventive Maint.	2	Complaints	
Repair Costs	3	Insurance Costs	10

CHRYS. TOWN AND COUNTRY/DODGE GR. CARAVAN — MINIVAN

10

Front Crash Test	7	Warranty	8
Side Crash Test	10	Fuel Rating	3
Safety Features	4	Rollover	6
Preventive Maint.	10	Complaints	5
Repair Costs	9	Insurance Costs	10

DODGE CARAVAN/CHRYS. TOWN AND COUNTRY SWB — MINIVAN

10

Front Crash Test	7	Warranty	8
Side Crash Test	10	Fuel Rating	6
Safety Features	4	Rollover	6
Preventive Maint.	10	Complaints	2
Repair Costs	9	Insurance Costs	5

DODGE DAKOTA — COMPACT PICKUP

7

Front Crash Test	7	Warranty	8
Side Crash Test	10	Fuel Rating	1
Safety Features	1	Rollover	6
Preventive Maint.	9	Complaints	3
Repair Costs	8	Insurance Costs	1

HONDA CR-V — SMALL SUV

9

Front Crash Test	10	Warranty	1
Side Crash Test	10	Fuel Rating	6
Safety Features	5	Rollover	5
Preventive Maint.	10	Complaints	
Repair Costs	7	Insurance Costs	10

HYUNDAI SANTA FE — SMALL SUV

9

Front Crash Test	8	Warranty	10
Side Crash Test	7	Fuel Rating	5
Safety Features	2	Rollover	6
Preventive Maint.	7	Complaints	10
Repair Costs	7	Insurance Costs	5

ACURA MDX — MID-SIZE SUV

Rating: 10

Front Crash Test	10	Warranty	7
Side Crash Test	10	Fuel Rating	2
Safety Features	9	Rollover	7
Preventive Maint.	8	Complaints	9
Repair Costs	5	Insurance Costs	10

JEEP LIBERTY — MID-SIZE SUV

Rating: 10

Front Crash Test	8	Warranty	8
Side Crash Test	10	Fuel Rating	4
Safety Features	3	Rollover	5
Preventive Maint.	9	Complaints	2
Repair Costs	8	Insurance Costs	10

LEXUS RX330 — MID-SIZE SUV

Rating: 9

Front Crash Test	10	Warranty	9
Side Crash Test	10	Fuel Rating	3
Safety Features	10	Rollover	6
Preventive Maint.		Complaints	
Repair Costs		Insurance Costs	5

SATURN VUE — MID-SIZE SUV

Rating: 9

Front Crash Test	9	Warranty	2
Side Crash Test	10	Fuel Rating	7
Safety Features	6	Rollover	6
Preventive Maint.	7	Complaints	
Repair Costs	7	Insurance Costs	10

TOYOTA HIGHLANDER — MID-SIZE SUV

Rating: 9

Front Crash Test	8	Warranty	3
Side Crash Test	10	Fuel Rating	7
Safety Features	6	Rollover	6
Preventive Maint.	9	Complaints	8
Repair Costs	4	Insurance Costs	10

CHRYSLER PACIFICA — LARGE SUV

Rating: 8

Front Crash Test	10	Warranty	8
Side Crash Test	10	Fuel Rating	2
Safety Features	8	Rollover	7
Preventive Maint.		Complaints	
Repair Costs		Insurance Costs	5

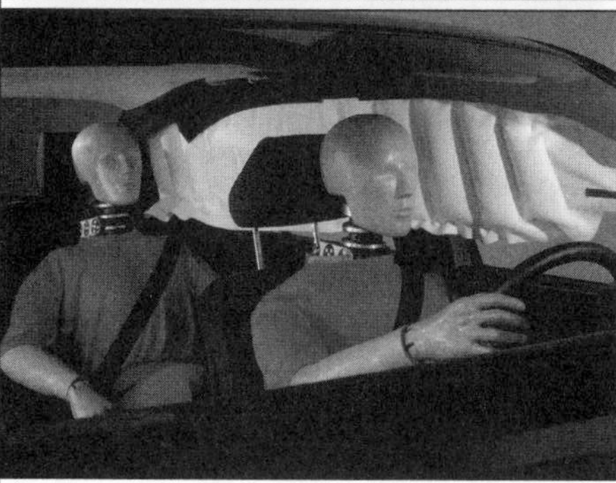

IN THIS CHAPTER

CRASH TESTS

Safety is likely the most important factor that most of us consider when choosing a new car. In the past, evaluating safety was difficult. Now, thanks to the information in *The Car Book*, it's much easier to pick a safe car. To provide the greatest possible protection, a car should have a variety of safety features including dual inflation airbags, side and head airbags, safety belt load limiters and pretensioners, four-wheel anti-lock brakes, built-in child safety seats, and occupant position sensors.

Crash Test Program:

A key factor in occupant protection is how well the car protects you in a crash. This depends on the car's ability to absorb the force of impact rather than transfer it to the occupant. In the government's frontal crash test program, an automobile is sent into a concrete barrier at 35 mph, causing an impact similar to two identical cars crashing head-on at 35 mph. The car contains electronically monitored dummies in the driver and passenger seats which measures the impact of such a collision on the head, chest, and legs of the occupants.

For the side crash tests, a moving barrier is smashed into the side of the vehicle at 38.5 mph. This simulates a typical intersection collision between two vehicles. The dummies in the side crash tests measure the impact on the pelvis and chest of front and back seat passengers. *The Car Book Side Crash Text Index* (CTI) combines the results of both passengers. If there are test results for only one occupant, as when there is no back seat, then the *Index* is based on a single occupant. In addition, when test results are missing, the index is based on a single occupant.

Note that in both crash tests the dummies are securely belted. Therefore, these test results do not apply to unbelted occupants.

To make it easy for you to compare vehicles, we have presented the results using our *Car Book Crash Test Index* which enables you to easily compare the crash tests of various vehicles.

It is best to compare the results within the same weight class, such as compacts to compacts. Do not compare cars with differing weights. For example, a subcompact that is rated "Good" may not be as safe as a large car with the same rating. We rate the crash test results of each car, relative to all of the cars ever crash tested.

How the Cars are Rated:

The tables on the following pages indicate how this year's cars can be expected to perform in crash tests. We only included a vehicle if its design has not changed enough to significantly alter previous results or if it had actually been tested. Twins (such as the Ford Taurus and the Mercury Sable) that are structurally similar can be expected to perform similarly.

The first column provides *The Car Book*'s overall *Crash Test Index*. This number represents all the forces measured by the test. Lower CTI numbers are better. The CTI is best used to compare cars within the same size and weight class.

The second column provides an overall rating of *Very Good*, *Good*, *Average*, *Poor*, or *Very Poor*. These reflect the car's performance compared to all other models ever tested.

The next two columns indicate the likelihood of each occupant sustaining a life-threatening injury, based on the front test head and chest scores and the side test chest scores. Lower percentages mean a lower likelihood of being seriously injured. This information is taken directly from the government's analysis of the crash test results.

The last two columns indicate how the dummy's legs faired in the frontal crash test or how the pelvis faired in the side crash test. Results labeled *Poor* did not meet the government's standards. Those that did meet the standards are rated *Moderate*, *Good*, and *Very Good*, reflecting performance relative to all other cars ever tested. The leg or pelvic injury ratings are not weighted as heavily as the head and chest in determining overall CTI performance.

Crash test results may vary due to differences in the way cars are manufactured, in how models are equipped, and in test conditions. There is no absolute guarantee that a car which passed the test will adequately protect you in an accident. Some 2-door models may not perform exactly like their 4-door counterparts.

Crash Test Performance		Crash Test Index	Car Book Rating	Likelihood of Life Threatening Injury				Leg or Pelvis Injury Rating	
				Front: Driver	Side: Fr. Occup.	Front: Passger.	Side: Rr. Occup.	Front: Driver Side: Fr. Occup.	Front: Passenger Side: Rear Occup.
Subcompact									
BMW Z4	FRONT	3160	Good	20%		16%		Very Good	Very Good
	SIDE	2994	Average		33%			Very Good	
Honda Insight	FRONT	3032	Good	12%		21%		Good	Good
	SIDE	2915	Average		32%			Good	
Honda S2000	FRONT	2376	Very Good	14%		12%		Very Good	Very Good
	SIDE	2362	Good		26%			Very Good	
Hyundai Accent 4-dr.	FRONT	2402	Very Good	11%		14%		Good	Very Good
	SIDE	2973	Average		14%		22%	Very Good	Good
Kia Rio	FRONT	2746	Good	16%		12%		Good	Good
	SIDE	3535	Poor		22%		22%	Moderate	Good
Kia Spectra	FRONT	2355	Very Good	13%		11%		Good	Good
	SIDE	2403	Good		17%		11%	Very Good	Very Good
Mazda MX-5 Miata	FRONT	2293	Very Good	12%		10%		Good	Good
	SIDE	3177	Poor		35%			Very Good	
Mini Cooper	FRONT	2705	Good	17%		14%		Very Good	Very Good
	SIDE	2550	Average		28%			Very Good	
Mitsubishi Lancer	FRONT	2386	Very Good	12%		12%		Good	Good
	SIDE	2641	Average		22%		9%	Good	Good
Nissan Sentra	FRONT	2267	Very Good	12%		11%		Very Good	Good
	SIDE	4093	Very Poor		45%			Moderate	
Subaru Impreza	FRONT	2152	Very Good	11%		10%		Very Good	Good
	SIDE	2452	Average		27%			Very Good	
Toyota ECHO	FRONT	2816	Good	18%		13%		Very Good	Very Good
	SIDE	1941	Good		14%		8%	Moderate	Good
Volkswagen Beetle	FRONT	2388	Very Good	12%		13%		Very Good	Good
	SIDE	1750	Good		5%		15%	Good	Very Good
Compact									
Acura RSX w/SAB	FRONT	1485	Very Good	9%		7%		Very Good	Very Good
	SIDE	2648	Average		29%			Good	
Audi A4 w/SAB	FRONT	3139	Good	16%		18%		Good	Very Good
	SIDE	1026	Very Good		3%		8%	Very Good	Very Good
BMW 3 Series	FRONT	1912	Very Good	11%		9%		Very Good	Very Good
w/SAB	SIDE	1520	Very Good		12%		4%	Moderate	Very Good
Chevrolet Cavalier	FRONT	2451	Very Good	11%		13%		Good	Good
2-dr.	SIDE	5492	Very Poor		49%		22%	Moderate	Good
4-dr.	SIDE	3853	Poor		31%		15%	Poor	Moderate
Chrysler PT Cruiser	FRONT	3205	Good	20%		12%		Moderate	Moderate
w/SAB	SIDE	1251	Very Good		8%		6%	Very Good	Very Good
Chrysler Sebring Coupe	FRONT	2951	Good	17%		14%		Good	Good
	SIDE	2047	Good		18%		5%	Good	Very Good

*Vehicle to be tested in 2004. Results expected to be the same or better.

CRASH TEST RESULTS

Crash Test Performance		Crash Test Index	Car Book Rating	Likelihood of Life Threatening Injury				Leg or Pelvis Injury Rating	
				Front: Driver	Side: Fr. Occup.	Front: Passger.	Side: Rr. Occup.	Front: Driver Side: Fr. Occup.	Front: Passenger Side: Rear Occup.
Dodge Neon	*FRONT*	3903	Average	22%		22%		Good	Good
	SIDE	2587	Average		14%		16%	Good	Moderate
Dodge Stratus Coupe	*FRONT*	2951	Good	17%		14%		Good	Good
	SIDE	2047	Good		18%		5%	Good	Very Good
Ford Focus 2-dr.	*FRONT*	2260	Very Good	11%		11%		Good	Good
	SIDE	3826	Poor		9%		36%	Good	Good
4-dr.	*FRONT*	2598	Good	10%		16%		Good	Good
	SIDE	2021	Good		13%		10%	Good	Very Good
Ford Mustang	*FRONT*	1981	Very Good	8%		9%		Good	Good
	SIDE	2558	Average		18%		12%	Good	Very Good
Convertible	*SIDE*	3499	Poor		24%		18%	Very Good	Very Good
Ford Thunderbird	*FRONT*	2045	Very Good	12%		8%		Very Good	Very Good
	SIDE	3351	Poor		37%			Good	
Honda Civic 2-dr.	*FRONT*	1631	Very Good	8%		9%		Very Good	Very Good
	SIDE	1606	Good		12%		6%	Very Good	Very Good
Hatchback	*SIDE*	1803	Good		10%		10%	Very Good	Good
w/SAB	*SIDE*	1042	Very Good		6%		6%	Very Good	Very Good
Honda Civic 4-dr.	*FRONT*	1463	Very Good	8%		6%		Very Good	Good
	SIDE	1391	Very Good		7%		8%	Very Good	Good
w/SAB	*SIDE*	1536	Very Good		7%		10%	Very Good	Very Good
Hyundai Elantra	*FRONT*	2007	Very Good*	11%		10%		Good	Very Good
	SIDE	1361	Very Good		6%		9%	Good	Good
Kia Optima	*FRONT*	2679	Good	15%		11%		Good	Good
Mitsubishi Eclipse	*FRONT*	2712	Good	15%		13%		Good	Good
	SIDE	2907	Average		32%			Very Good	
Nissan 350Z	*FRONT*	2111	Very Good	10%		12%		Very Good	Very Good
	SIDE	2276	Good		25%			Very Good	

*Vehicle to be tested in 2004. Results expected to be the same or better.

How to Read the Charts:

1234	**Crash Test Index** is the overall numerical injury rating for front occupants in a frontal and side crash. *Lower numbers mean better performance.*
Very Good	**Car Book Rating** shows how the vehicle compares among all vehicles tested to date. The range is very good, good, moderate, poor, and very poor.
00%	**Likelihood of Life Threatening Injury** is the chance that the occupants would be seriously injured in a frontal and side crash. *Lower percentages mean better performance.*
Good	**Leg Injury Rating** compares occupant leg protection in a frontal and side crash for all cars tested to date.

CRASH TEST RESULTS

Crash Test Performance		Crash Test Index	Car Book Rating	Likelihood of Life Threatening Injury				Leg or Pelvis Injury Rating	
				Front: Driver	Side: Fr. Occup.	Front: Passgr.	Side: Rr. Occup.	Front: Driver Side: Fr. Occup.	Front: Passenger Side: Rear Occup.
Pontiac Sunfire	FRONT	2451	Very Good	11%		13%		Good	Good
	SIDE	5492	Very Poor		49%		22%	Moderate	Good
Pontiac Vibe	FRONT	1810	Very Good	9%		10%		Very Good	Very Good
	SIDE	1038	Very Good		5%		6%	Very Good	Very Good
Saturn ION	FRONT	1513	Very Good	9%		6%		Very Good	Very Good
	SIDE	3266	Poor				36%		Very Good
Subaru Legacy	FRONT	2269	Very Good	14%		9%		Good	Good
4-dr.	SIDE	1678	Good		11%		8%	Very Good	Very Good
Wagon	SIDE	1217	Very Good		8%		6%	Very Good	Very Good
Subaru Outback	FRONT	2269	Very Good	14%		9%		Good	Good
	SIDE	708	Very Good*		2%		5%	Very Good	Very Good
Toyota Celica	FRONT	2383	Very Good	12%		15%		Very Good	Very Good
	SIDE	3815	Poor		42%			Good	
Toyota Corolla	FRONT	1753	Very Good	10%		9%		Very Good	Very Good
	SIDE	1808	Good		10%		10%	Good	Very Good
Toyota Matrix	FRONT	1810	Very Good	9%		10%		Very Good	Very Good
	SIDE	1038	Very Good		5%		6%	Very Good	Very Good
Volkswagen Golf	FRONT	1888	Very Good	9%		9%		Good	Good
	SIDE	1444*	Very Good		6%		10%	Very Good	Good
Volkswagen Jetta	FRONT	1888	Very Good	9%		9%		Good	Good
	SIDE	1444	Very Good		6%		10%	Very Good	Good
Intermediate									
Acura TL	FRONT	2751	Good*	13%		16%		Good	Good
w/SAB	SIDE	1092	Very Good*		6%		5%	Very Good	Very Good
Buick Century 4-dr.	FRONT	4037	Average	12%		33%		Good	Good
	SIDE	2763	Average		15%		18%	Moderate	Good
w/SAB	SIDE	2458	Average		18%		11%	Poor	Good
Buick Regal	FRONT	4037	Average	12%		33%		Good	Good
	SIDE	2763	Average		15%		18%	Moderate	Good
w/SAB	SIDE	2458	Average		18%		11%	Poor	Good
Chrysler Sebring	FRONT	1976	Very Good	10%		9%		Good	Good
	SIDE	2913	Average		18%		16%	Good	Very Good
Chrysler Sebring Convertible	SIDE	1835	Good		14%		7%	Very Good	Very Good
Dodge Stratus	FRONT	1976	Very Good	10%		9%		Good	Good
Ford Taurus	FRONT	1958	Very Good	11%		8%		Good	Very Good
	SIDE	2426	Good		11%		17%	Good	Good
w/SAB	SIDE	2783	Average		16%		16%	Moderate	Very Good
Honda Accord 4-dr.	FRONT	1511	Very Good	8%		8%		Very Good	Good
	SIDE	1262	Very Good		8%		5%	Very Good	Very Good

*Vehicle to be tested in 2004. Results expected to be the same or better.

CRASH TEST RESULTS

Crash Test Performance		Crash Test Index	Car Book Rating	Likelihood of Life Threatening Injury				Leg or Pelvis Injury Rating	
				Front: Driver	Side: Fr. Occup.	Front: Passger.	Side: Rr. Occup.	Front: Driver Side: Fr. Occup.	Front: Passenger Side: Rear Occup.
Honda Accord Coupe	FRONT	1496	Very Good	8%		8%		Very Good	Very Good
	SIDE	931	Very Good		5%		5%	Very Good	Very Good
Hyundai Sonata	FRONT	2679	Good	15%		11%		Good	Good
	SIDE	1242	Very Good		8%		6%	Good	Good
Hyundai XG350 w/SAB	SIDE	1392	Very Good		7%		9%	Very Good	Very Good
Infiniti I35	FRONT	2524	Very Good	13%		14%		Very Good	Good
w/SAB	SIDE	1144	Very Good		6%		6%	Good	Very Good
Lexus IS 300 w/SAB	SIDE	871	Very Good		4%		5%	Good	Very Good
Mazda 6	FRONT	1516	Very Good	9%		7%		Very Good	Very Good
	SIDE	2037	Good		14%		9%	Good	Good
Mercedes-Benz C-Class	FRONT	2989	Good	15%		18%		Good	Very Good
w/SAB	SIDE	878	Very Good		4%		5%	Very Good	Very Good
Mercury Sable	FRONT	1958	Very Good	11%		8%		Good	Very Good
	SIDE	2426	Good		11%		17%	Good	Good
w/SAB	SIDE	2783	Average		16%		16%	Moderate	Very Good
Nissan Altima	FRONT	2098	Very Good	12%		12%		Very Good	Very Good
	SIDE	2373	Good		7%		10%	Moderate	Good
Nissan Maxima	FRONT	2102	Very Good	9%		14%		Very Good	Very Good
	SIDE	1351	Very Good		6%		9%	Good	Good
Oldsmobile Alero 2-dr.	FRONT	2184	Very Good	11%		10%		Good	Good
	SIDE	3816	Poor		36%		9%	Good	Good
4-dr.	FRONT	2469	Very Good	13%		11%		Good	Good
	SIDE	2807	Average		15%		18%	Very Good	Good
Pontiac Grand Am 2-dr.	FRONT	2184	Very Good	11%		10%		Good	Good
	SIDE	3816	Poor		36%		9%	Good	Good
4-dr.	FRONT	2469	Very Good	13%		11%		Good	Good
	SIDE	2807	Average		15%		18%	Good	Moderate
Saab 9-5	FRONT	1887	Very Good	9%		10%		Good	Very Good
w/SAB	SIDE	1060	Very Good		5%		6%	Good	Very Good
Saturn L/LW	FRONT	2015	Very Good	11%		10%		Very Good	Good
	SIDE	2140	Good		19%		5%	Good	Good
Toyota Avalon	FRONT	2066	Very Good	11%		10%		Good	Very Good
w/SAB	SIDE	1216	Very Good		8%		5%	Good	Very Good
Toyota Camry	FRONT	1896	Very Good*	9%		11%		Very Good	Very Good
	SIDE	1446	Very Good*		11%		5%	Very Good	Very Good
Volkswagen Passat	FRONT	1905	Very Good	10%		8%		Good	Good
w/SAB	SIDE	1642	Good		8%		10%	Good	Good
Volvo 60 Series	FRONT	2602	Good	16%		12%		Good	Very Good
w/SAB	SIDE	921	Very Good		4%		6%	Very Good	Very Good
Large									
Acura RL w/SAB	FRONT	3226	Good	21%		18%		Very Good	Very Good

*Vehicle to be tested in 2004. Results expected to be the same or better.

CRASH TEST RESULTS

Crash Test Performance		Crash Test Index	Car Book Rating	Likelihood of Life Threatening Injury				Leg or Pelvis Injury Rating	
				Front: Driver	Side: Fr. Occup.	Front: Passger.	Side: Rr. Occup.	Front: Driver Side: Fr. Occup.	Front: Passenger Side: Rear Occup.
Buick LeSabre	*FRONT*	2442	Very Good	15%		10%		Good	Good
w/SAB	*SIDE*	1509	Very Good		9%		8%	Very Good	Very Good
Buick Park Avenue	*FRONT*	2758	Good	13%		16%		Good	Good
w/SAB	*SIDE*	1446	Very Good		6%		10%	Very Good	Very Good
Cadillac CTS	*FRONT*	3073	Good	13%		21%		Good	Very Good
w/SAB	*SIDE*	1114	Very Good		8%		4%	Very Good	Very Good
Cadillac DeVille	*FRONT*	2513	Very Good	13%		12%		Good	Good
w/SAB	*SIDE*	1562	Good		9%		9%	Very Good	Very Good
Chrysler 300M	*FRONT*	2849	Good	17%		12%		Moderate	Good
	SIDE	1505	Very Good		6%		11%	Very Good	Moderate
Chrysler Concorde	*FRONT*	2849	Good	17%		12%		Moderate	Good
	SIDE	2161	Very Good		8%		17%	Good	Good
Chrysler Concorde Ltd.	*FRONT*	2849	Good	17%		12%		Moderate	Good
	SIDE	2161	Very Good		8%		17%	Good	Good
Chevrolet Impala	*FRONT*	1678	Very Good	6%		8%		Good	Good
4-dr.	*SIDE*	1398	Very Good		7%		8%	Good	Good
4-dr. w/SAB	*SIDE*	1723	Good		9%		10%	Good	Good
Chevrolet Monte Carlo 2-dr.	*FRONT*	1992	Very Good	10%		9%		Moderate	Very Good
	SIDE	2027	Good		16%		7%	Moderate	Good
Dodge Intrepid	*FRONT*	2849	Good	17%		12%		Moderate	Good
	SIDE	2232	Good		8%		18%	Very Good	Moderate
Ford Crown Victoria	*FRONT*	1706	Very Good	10%		7%		Good	Very Good
4-dr.	*SIDE*	1271	Very Good		8%		5%	Very Good	Good
4-dr. w/SAB	*SIDE*	832	Very Good		6%		3%	Very Good	Very Good
Lincoln LS w/SAB	*SIDE*	1281	Very Good		9%		4%	Very Good	Good
Lincoln Town Car	*FRONT*	1721	Very Good	10%		7%		Good	Very Good
w/SAB	*SIDE*	830	Very Good		6%		3%	Very Good	Very Good
Mercedes-Benz E-Class	*FRONT*	2487	Very Good	14%		13%		Very Good	Good
w/SAB	*SIDE*	635	Very Good		3%		4%	Very Good	Very Good
Mercury Grand Marquis	*FRONT*	1721	Very Good	10%		7%		Good	Very Good
4-dr.	*SIDE*	1271	Very Good		8%		5%	Very Good	Good
4-dr. w/SAB	*SIDE*	832	Very Good		6%		3%	Very Good	Very Good
Mercury Marauder	*FRONT*	1721	Very Good	10%		7%		Good	Very Good
	SIDE	1271	Very Good		8%		5%	Very Good	Good
Pontiac Bonneville	*FRONT*	2442	Very Good	15%		10%		Good	Good
	SIDE	1509	Very Good		9%		8%	Very Good	Very Good
Pontiac Grand Prix	*FRONT*	3315	Good	23%		11%		Moderate	Good
	SIDE	2582	Average		13%		17%	Good	Good
Volvo 80 Series	*FRONT*	1994	Very Good	10%		10%		Very Good	Good
	SIDE	975	Very Good		5%		5%	Very Good	Very Good

*Vehicle to be tested in 2004. Results expected to be the same or better.

CRASH TEST RESULTS

Crash Test Performance		Crash Test Index	Car Book Rating	Likelihood of Life Threatening Injury				Leg or Pelvis Injury Rating	
				Front: Driver	Side: Fr. Occup.	Front: Passger.	Side: Rr. Occup.	Front: Driver Side: Fr. Occup.	Front: Passenger Side: Rear Occup.
Minivan									
Chevrolet Astro	FRONT	4168	Average	30%		14%		Moderate	Moderate
	SIDE	220	Very Good		1%		1%	Very Good	Very Good
Chevrolet Venture	FRONT	2543	Very Good	11%		13%		Moderate	Good
	SIDE	978	Very Good		4%		6%	Very Good	Good
Chrys. Town and Cntry. LX	FRONT	3418	Good	18%		19%		Good	Good
	SIDE	1035	Very Good		5%		6%	Very Good	Good
w/SAB	SIDE	924	Very Good		4%		6%	Very Good	Good
Chrys. Town and Cntry. SWB	FRONT	3061	Good	15%		20%		Very Good	Very Good
	SIDE	1147	Very Good		7%		6%	Very Good	Very Good
Dodge Caravan	FRONT	3061	Good	15%		20%		Very Good	Very Good
	SIDE	1147	Very Good		7%		6%	Very Good	Very Good
Dodge Grand Caravan	FRONT	3418	Good	18%		19%		Good	Good
	SIDE	1035	Very Good		5%		6%	Very Good	Good
w/SAB	SIDE	924	Very Good		4%		6%	Very Good	Good
Ford Freestar	FRONT	1169	Very Good	5%		6%		Very Good	Poor
GMC Safari	FRONT	4168	Average	30%		14%		Moderate	Moderate
	SIDE	220	Very Good		1%		1%	Very Good	Very Good
Honda Odyssey	FRONT	1554	Very Good	8%		7%		Very Good	Good
	SIDE	448	Very Good		2%		2%	Very Good	Very Good
Kia Sedona	FRONT	1694	Very Good	9%			6%	Very Good	Very Good
	SIDE	814	Very Good		5%		3%	Good	Moderate
Mazda MPV	FRONT	1889	Very Good	10%		8%		Good	Very Good
	SIDE	625	Very Good		3%		3%	Very Good	Good
Mercury Monterey	FRONT	1169	Very Good	5%		6%		Very Good	Poor
Nissan Quest	FRONT	1752	Very Good	7%		10%		Very Good	Very Good
Oldsmobile Silhouette	FRONT	2543	Very Good	11%		13%		Moderate	Good
	SIDE	978	Very Good		4%		6%	Very Good	Good
Pontiac Montana	FRONT	2543	Very Good	11%		13%		Moderate	Good
	SIDE	978	Very Good		4%		6%	Very Good	Good
Toyota Sienna	FRONT	1898	Very Good	8%		10%		Good	Good
	SIDE	989	Very Good		5%		5%	Very Good	Good
Compact Pickup									
Chevrolet S Series	FRONT	6022	Poor	48%		24%		Moderate	Moderate
	SIDE	3361	Poor		37%			Very Good	
Dodge Dakota Ext. Cab	FRONT	4165	Average	35%		10%		Good	Good
	SIDE	2381	Good		26%			Good	
Quad Cab	FRONT	3189	Good	21%		11%		Good	Moderate
	SIDE	499	Very Good		2%		3%	Very Good	Very Good

*Vehicle to be tested in 2004. Results expected to be the same or better.

CRASH TEST RESULTS

Crash Test Performance		Crash Test Index	Car Book Rating	Likelihood of Life Threatening Injury				Leg or Pelvis Injury Rating	
				Front: Driver	Side: Fr. Occup.	Front: Passgr.	Side: Rr. Occup.	Front: Driver Side: Fr. Occup.	Front: Passenger Side: Rear Occup.
Ford Ranger	FRONT	2910	Good	17%		14%		Good	Good
	SIDE	2190	Good		24%			Good	
Ext. Cab 4x2	FRONT	3047	Good	19%		13%		Moderate	Good
	SIDE	2742	Average		30%			Moderate	
GMC Sonoma	FRONT	6022	Poor	48%		24%		Moderate	Moderate
	SIDE	3361	Average		37%			Very Good	
Mazda Truck	FRONT	2910	Good	17%		14%		Good	Good
	SIDE	2190	Good		24%			Good	
Ext. Cab 4x2	FRONT	3047	Good	19%		13%		Moderate	Good
	SIDE	2742	Average		30%			Moderate	
Nissan Frontier	FRONT	3105	Good	18%		18%		Very Good	Very Good
	SIDE	685	Very Good		3%		4%	Good	Very Good
Ext. Cab 4x2	FRONT	2279	Very Good	14%		10%		Very Good	Very Good
	SIDE	2652	Average		29%			Moderate	
Toyota Tacoma Double Cab	FRONT	3366	Good	17%		20%		Good	Good
	SIDE	568	Very Good		3%		3%	Good	Very Good
Ext. Cab 4x2	FRONT	3799	Average	24%		19%		Good	Good
	SIDE	3479	Poor		38%			Poor	
Standard Pickup									
Chevrolet Silverado	FRONT	3909	Average	16%		28%		Good	Good
Dodge Ram Pickup	FRONT	2277	Very Good	15%		9%		Good	Very Good
GMC Sierra	FRONT	3906	Average	16%		28%		Good	Good
Toyota Tundra	FRONT	2513	Very Good	13%		13%		Good	Good
	SIDE	1811	Good			20%			Very Good
Small SUV									
Chevrolet Blazer 2-dr.	FRONT	4536	Average	37%		14%		Good	Good
	SIDE	688	Very Good		5%		2%	Very Good	Very Good
4-dr.	FRONT	4822	Poor	36%		19%		Moderate	Good
	SIDE	828	Very Good		5%		3%	Very Good	Very Good
Chevrolet Tracker 4-dr.	FRONT	3408	Good	19%		17%		Moderate	Good
	SIDE	845	Very Good		7%		2%	Good	Very Good
Ford Escape	FRONT	2275	Very Good	9%		13%		Good	Good
	SIDE	846	Very Good		5%		4%	Good	Very Good
Honda CR-V	FRONT	1624	Very Good	7%		9%		Very Good	Good
	SIDE	535	Very Good		2%		4%	Very Good	Very Good
w/SAB	SIDE	636	Very Good		3%		4%	Very Good	Very Good
Honda Element	FRONT	1646	Very Good	7%		8%		Very Good	Good
	SIDE	1151	Very Good[%]		3%		9%	Very Good	Very Good
Hyundai Santa Fe	FRONT	2613	Good	10%		13%		Good	Poor
	SIDE	1910	Good		21%			Very Good	

[*]Vehicle to be tested in 2004. Results expected to be the same or better.
[%]Higher likelihood of head injury.

Crash Test Performance		Crash Test Index	Car Book Rating	Likelihood of Life Threatening Injury				Leg or Pelvis Injury Rating	
				Front: Driver	Side: Fr. Occup.	Front: Passgr.	Side: Rr. Occup.	Front: Driver Side: Fr. Occup.	Front: Passenger Side: Rear Occup.
Jeep Wrangler	FRONT	3387	Good	20%		16%		Good	Good
Mazda Tribute	FRONT	2275	Very Good	9%		13%		Good	Good
	SIDE	846	Very Good		5%		4%	Good	Very Good
Mitsubishi Montero Sport	FRONT	3939	Average	21%		24%		Good	Good
	SIDE	603	Very Good		5%		1%	Very Good	Very Good
Subaru Forester	FRONT	1893	Very Good	11%		8%		Very Good	Good
	SIDE	741	Very Good		4%		3%	Very Good	Very Good
Suzuki Grand Vitara	FRONT	3408	Good	19%		17%		Moderate	Good
	SIDE	602	Very Good[%]		4%		12%	Good	Very Good
Suzuki Vitara	FRONT	3408	Good	19%		17%		Moderate	Good
	SIDE	845	Very Good		7%		2%	Good	Very Good
Toyota RAV4	FRONT	3096	Good*	16%		19%		Good	Very Good
	SIDE	936	Very Good		4%		5%	Very Good	Very Good
Mid-Size SUV									
Acura MDX	FRONT	2098	Very Good	9%		12%		Good	Good
w/SAB	SIDE	431	Very Good		1%		3%	Very Good	Very Good
BMW X5	FRONT	1864	Very Good	11%		11%		Very Good	Very Good
	SIDE	938	Very Good		9%		1%	Very Good	Very Good
Buick Rendezvous	FRONT	4713	Poor	25%		28%		Good	Moderate
	SIDE	688	Very Good		3%		4%	Moderate	Good
Ford Explorer	FRONT	2401	Very Good	14%		10%		Good	Good
	SIDE	452	Very Good[@]		2%		2%	Very Good	Very Good
Honda Pilot	FRONT	1661	Very Good	7%		10%		Very Good	Good
	SIDE	416	Very Good		2%		2%	Very Good	Very Good
Isuzu Axiom	FRONT	3377	Good	17%		19%		Good	Good
	SIDE	426	Very Good		2%		2%	Very Good	Very Good
Isuzu Rodeo	FRONT	4335	Average	31%		18%		Good	Good
	SIDE	579	Very Good		4%		2%	Good	Very Good
Jeep Grand Cherokee	FRONT	5011	Poor	33%		23%		Moderate	Moderate
	SIDE	1066	Very Good		7%		5%	Good	Good
Jeep Liberty	FRONT	2785	Good	9%		20%		Good	Good
	SIDE	592	Very Good		3%		3%	Very Good	Very Good
Kia Sorento	FRONT	2997	Good	16%		14%		Moderate	Moderate
	SIDE	399	Very Good		3%		1%	Very Good	Very Good
Land Rover Discovery	FRONT	2390	Very Good	13%		11%		Good	Good
Lexus RX330 w/SAB	FRONT	1964	Very Good	8%		11%		Good	Good
	SIDE	629	Very Good		2%		5%	Very Good	Very Good
Mercury Mountaineer	FRONT	2401	Very Good	14%		10%		Good	Good
	SIDE	452	Very Good		2%		2%	Very Good	Very Good
Mitsubishi Outlander	FRONT	2479	Very Good	12%		16%		Very Good	Very Good
	SIDE	1042	Very Good		5%		6%	Very Good	Very Good

*Vehicle to be tested in 2004. Results expected to be the same or better.
[%]Higher likelihood of head injury. [@]Door became unlatched.

Crash Test Performance		Crash Test Index	Car Book Rating	Likelihood of Life Threatening Injury				Leg or Pelvis Injury Rating	
				Front: Driver	Side: Fr. Occup.	Front: Passger.	Side: Rr. Occup.	Front: Driver Side: Fr. Occup.	Front: Passenger Side: Rear Occup.
Nissan Murano	*FRONT*	2580	Good	12%		16%		Very Good	Very Good
	SIDE	1007	Very Good		4%		7%	Good	Good
Nissan Pathfinder	*FRONT*	2501	Average	13%		15%		Very Good	Very Good
	SIDE	421	Very Good		3%		1%	Very Good	Very Good
Nissan Xterra	*FRONT*	3182	Good	17%		21%		Very Good	Very Good
	SIDE	715	Very Good		6%		1%	Good	Very Good
Pontiac Aztek	*FRONT*	3098	Good	24%		13%		Very Good	Very Good
w/SAB	*SIDE*	1313	Very Good		3%		11%	Very Good	Moderate
Saturn VUE	*FRONT*	2450	Very Good*	9%		16%		Good	Good
	SIDE	707	Very Good		4%		4%	Good	Very Good
Toyota 4Runner	*FRONT*	2268	Very Good*	14%		11%		Very Good	Very Good
	SIDE	390	Very Good		2%		2%	Very Good	Very Good
Toyota Highlander	*FRONT*	2664	Good*	15%		14%		Good	Very Good
	SIDE	637	Very Good*		2%		4%	Very Good	Moderate
Volvo XC90	*FRONT*	2296	Very Good	10%		12%		Moderate	Good
	SIDE	332	Very Good		1%		2%	Very Good	Very Good
SUV Large									
Buick Rainier w/SAB	*FRONT*	4348	Average	27%		22%		Moderate	Good
	SIDE	428	Very Good**		3%		2%	Very Good	Very Good
Cadillac Escalade w/SAB	*FRONT*	3959	Average	21%		20%		Moderate	Good
Cad. Escalade ESV w/SAB	*FRONT*	3992	Average	16%		26%		Moderate	Good
Cad. Escalade EXT w/SAB	*FRONT*	3804	Average	22%		19%		Moderate	Good
Chevrolet Avalanche w/SAB	*FRONT*	3804	Average	22%		19%		Moderate	Good
Chevrolet Suburban w/SAB	*FRONT*	3992	Average	16%		26%		Moderate	Good
Chevrolet Tahoe w/SAB	*FRONT*	3959	Average	21%		20%		Moderate	Good
Chevrolet Trail Blazer	*FRONT*	4348	Average	27%		22%		Moderate	Good
w/SAB	*SIDE*	428	Very Good**		3%		2%	Very Good	Very Good
Chrysler Pacifica	*FRONT*	1278	Very Good	6%		5%		Good	Good
	SIDE	428	Very Good		3%		2%	Very Good	Very Good
Ford Expedition	*FRONT*	1751	Very Good	8%		10%		Very Good	Very Good
GMC Envoy	*FRONT*	4450	Average	27%		22%		Moderate	Moderate
w/SAB	*SIDE*	428**	Very Good**		3%		2%	Very Good	Very Good
GMC Yukon	*FRONT*	3959	Average	21%		20%		Moderate	Good
GMC Yukon XL	*FRONT*	3992	Average	16%		26%		Moderate	Good
Lincoln Navigator	*FRONT*	1751	Very Good	8%		10%		Very Good	Very Good
Mitsubishi Endeavor	*FRONT*	2094	Very Good	9%		12%		Very Good	Good
	SIDE	632	Very Good		4%		3%	Good	Good
Oldsmobile Bravada	*FRONT*	4348	Average	27%		22%		Moderate	Good
w/SAB	*SIDE*	428	Very Good**		3%		2%	Very Good	Very Good
Toyota Sequoia	*FRONT*	1765	Very Good	10%		8%		Good	Good

**Version without SAB to be tested.

AUTOMATIC CRASH PROTECTION

The concept of automatic safety protection is not new—automatic fire sprinklers in public buildings, release of oxygen masks in airplanes, purification of drinking water, and pasteurization of milk are all commonly accepted forms of automatic safety protection. Airbags provide automatic crash protection in cars.

The idea behind automatic crash protection is to protect people from what is called the "second collision," when the occupant comes forward and collides with the interior of their own car. Because the "second collision" occurs within milliseconds, providing automatic rather than manual protection dramatically improves the chances of escaping injury.

Depowered Airbags: In an effort to lower the number of out-of-position occupants killed by deploying airbags, some auto makers with poor airbags began depowering in their 1999 models, while auto makers with good designs did not have to depower. A depowered airbag comes out with less force than earlier designs. It is not clear that this will improve the situation for children; however, it may reduce airbag effectiveness for adults.

Sit Correctly: Drivers should note that the ideal position when driving is belted with your chest approximately 10 inches from the center of the steering wheel. If it isn't possible for you to get at least 10 inches away from the wheel, you can try pedal extenders. For more information about pedal extenders, you can contact the National Mobility Equipment Dealers Association at 800-833-0427.

Smart Airbags: The solution to airbag concerns lies with smart airbags. Most automakers are developing smart airbag systems which will differentiate between an adult, a child, a rear-facing child seat, or an empty seat using various heat, ultrasonic sound wave, and infrared sensors. Not only will smart airbags save lives, but by preventing the passenger-side airbag from deploying when the seat is empty, they will save thousands in repair costs. We expect these safer airbags to become increasingly available in the next few years.

AIRBAG TYPES

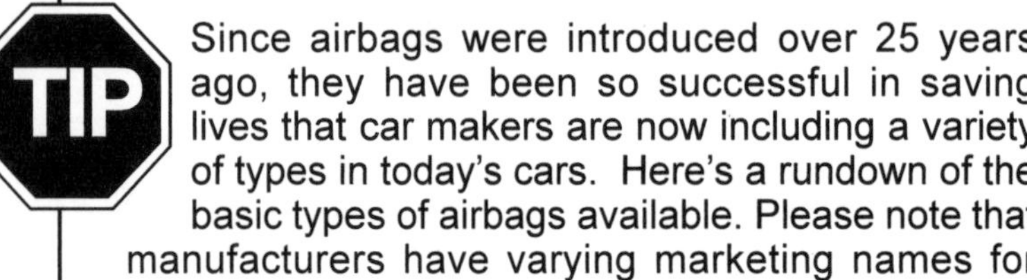

Since airbags were introduced over 25 years ago, they have been so successful in saving lives that car makers are now including a variety of types in today's cars. Here's a rundown of the basic types of airbags available. Please note that manufacturers have varying marketing names for these airbags.

Front: These airbags deploy toward the occupant and protect both the driver and front passenger. They are now standard in all vehicles. Many vehicles now have de-powered airbags, which deploy with less force.

Side: These airbags deploy from the side of a seat or from the door and are designed to protect the body in a side impact. They can be placed to protect both the front and rear passengers. Bags mounted in seats offer protection in a wider range of seating positions.

Head: These airbags deploy from above the front doors or the front roof pillars. In many cars, there is one head curtain that stretches from the front to the back of the vehicle. They serve as a shield from spraying glass and protection in rollovers and can protect your side and chest area. Some designs such as Audi's "side guard," remain inflated for five seconds in the event of a sustained rollover.

CHILDREN AND AIRBAGS

While airbags have saved thousands of lives, a deploying airbag can be deadly to an unrestrained child. Properly buckling your child has never been more important now that all new vehicles offer airbags on the passenger's side. While some studies of actual crashes indicate that older children can be protected by airbags, it's only if they are properly buckled up! Your best bet is to keep kids in the back seat whenever possible.

Over 100 children have been killed by passenger airbags. To protect an occupant, an airbag must inflate in a fraction of a second before the occupant hits the dashboard. For a full-sized adult, the result is coming forward into a cushion of air. For a child who isn't properly restrained, it can be deadly, especially if the child is standing up or leaning on the dashboard.

Remember—most children killed by airbags are not properly belted. Almost 60 percent of all children killed by passenger airbags are either unrestrained or improperly restrained at the time of the crash.

Use caution if your vehicle has side airbags. The best way to protect your child is to make sure they are seated and buckled up properly. The safest spot for your child is in the middle of the back seat.

Airbag On/Off Switches: Some light trucks and vehicles without a rear seat may have an on/off switch pre-installed. Otherwise, these switches may be installed at the request of the owners who meet criteria specified by the federal government. To qualify for a waiver that would allow you to install an on/off switch in your vehicle, you must be an individual 1) with a medical condition where risk of injury from a deploying airbag is greater than the risk of impacting the steering wheel, 2) who is unable to position themself at least 10 inches back from the center of the airbag's cover, 3) who must transport an infant in a rear-facing seat because the vehicle has no back seat, or 4) who routinely transports children younger than 12 in carpools in a vehicle without enough seats in the rear to accommodate all the children.

HOW TO BEST PROTECT YOUR CHILD (AND YOURSELF)

Never place a rear-facing child seat in front of a passenger-side airbag. Even front-facing child seats should be used on a rear seat. The best spot for your children is in the center of the back seat. If you do not have a back seat, here are some tips for keeping your child (and yourself) safe while seated in an airbag seat:

☑ Push the seat as far back as it will go.

☑ Make sure your child is sitting up straight with the safety belt across the center of his or her chest and not leaning forward against the dash.

☑ If you are an adult, sit at least 10–12 inches away from the steering wheel. In the passenger side, slide the seat back as far as it will go.

☑ Use caution if your vehicle has side airbags. Just like frontal airbags, the best way to protect your child is to make sure they are seated and buckled up properly. Again, the safest spot for your child in an accident is the middle of the back seat.

! REAR-FACING CHILD SAFETY SEATS !

Never use a rear-facing child safety seat in a seating position that has an airbag. To deploy fast enough to protect adult occupants, an airbag inflates with enough force to potentially cause serious head and chest injuries to a child in a rear-facing safety seat. And remember, airbags do not take the place of child safety seats.

CHILD SAFETY SEATS

Probably the most important purchase you will make to protect your child is a child safety seat. While we often go out of our way to prevent our children from being injured by poisons, watching carefully as they swim, or keeping a good grip on their hand while crossing the street, many of us ignore the biggest danger of all when we allow our children to lie down in the back of a minivan or roam unrestrained in a car. Ironically, it's your automobile that poses the greatest threat to your child's health.

Never place a child in your lap! At 30 mph, a crash or sudden stop will wrench a 10-pound child from your arms with a force of nearly 300 pounds! If you aren't wearing a seat belt, then your own body will be thrown forward with enough force to crush your child against the dashboard or the back of the front seat.

To make child safety seats more effective, the government now requires all vehicles to have anchor points to attach a strap that will tether the top of a child seat to the vehicle. This will help keep the child seat in place and reduce the distance a child's head is thrown forward in a crash, which reduces the chances of head injury.

Buying Tips: Child seats with an automatic retracting harness and a shield are typically the easiest to use. Here are more buying tips for a child safety seat:

☑ Try before you buy. Your car's seat belts and the shape of its seats will determine which child seats fit your car so make sure it can be properly installed. Some seats will not fit in certain cars.

☑ Determine how many straps or buckles must be fastened to use a child seat. The less complicated the seat, the less chance for misuse. The easiest seats require only one strap or buckle after fastening the seat belt around the child seat.

☑ Make sure the seat is wide enough for growth and bulky winter clothes. If possible, let your child sit in the seat to measure for fit.

☑ Is the child seat light and easy to install if you have more than one car?

☑ Make sure you fill out and mail the owner registration card. This is the best way to find out if your seat is ever recalled.

The incorrect use of child safety seats has reached epidemic proportions. A stunning 85 percent of parents misuse their child's safety seat. Problems fall into two categories: incorrect installation of the seat and incorrect use of the seat's straps to secure the child. In most cases, the car's safety belt was improperly routed through the seat.

Safe Use: In addition to following your seat's installation instructions, here are some important usage tips:

☑ The safest place for the seat is the center of the back seat.

☑ Use a locking clip when needed. Check the instructions that come with your seat and those in your car owner's manual.

☑ Keep your child rear-facing for at least a year.

☑ Regularly check the seat's safety harness and the car's seat belt for a tight, secure fit because the straps will stretch on impact.

☑ Don't leave sharp or heavy objects or groceries loose in the

BUCKLED UP = BETTER BEHAVIOR

Medical researchers have concluded that belted children are better behaved. When not buckled up, children squirm, stand up, complain, fight, and even pull at the steering wheel. When buckled into safety seats, however, they displayed 95 percent fewer incidents of bad behavior.

When buckled up, children feel secure. In addition, being in a seat can be more fun because most safety seats are high enough to allow children to see out the window. Also, children are less likely to feel carsick and more likely to fall asleep in a car seat.

Make the car seat your child's own special place, so he or she will enjoy being in it. Pick out some special soft toys or books that can be used only in the car seat to make using the seat a positive experience. Finally, set a good example for your child by using your own safety belt *every* time you get in the car.

car. Anything loose can be deadly in a crash.

☑ In the winter, dress your baby in a legged suit to allow proper attachment of the harness. If necessary, drape an extra blanket over the seat after your baby is buckled.

☑ Keep all doors locked.

☑ Do not allow lollipops or ice cream on a stick while riding. A bump or swerve could jam the stick into his or her throat.

☑ If your baby is very small, you may want to roll up a towel or purchase an infant head support and place it around the baby's head for extra comfort.

Seat Belts for Kids: How long should children use car seats? For school-age children, a car seat is twice as effective in preventing injury as an adult lap and shoulder harness—use a booster as long as possible. Most children can start using seat belts at 65 pounds and when tall enough for the shoulder belt to cross the chest, not the neck. The lap section of the belt should be snug and as low on the hips as possible. If the shoulder belt does cross the face or neck, use a booster.

Never:

☒ Use the same belt on two children.

☒ Move a shoulder belt behind a child's back or under an arm.

☒ Buckle in a pet or any large toys with the child.

☒ Recline a seat with a belted child.

☒ Use a twisted seat belt. The belt must be straight and flat.

☒ Use pillows or cushions to boost your child.

☒ Place a belt around you with a child in your lap. In an accident or sudden stop, your child would absorb most of the crash force.

Correct Installation: Surveys show up to 85 percent of parents do not install their child seats properly. Incorrect installation of a child safety seat can deny the child the lifesaving protection offered by the seat and may even contribute to further injuring the child. It is very important to read the installation instructions carefully. If you have any questions about the correct installation in your particular car, contact the National Highway Traffic Safety Administration's website at www.nhtsa.dot.gov. They can direct you to the nearest child seat inspection station that will check to see if you have installed your child seat correctly and instruct you on the proper way to install the seat if you have any questions.

Following are some common mistakes parents make in child safety seat installation.

☒ Infant is in safety seat facing forward, rather than to the rear.

☒ Child safety seat in front with an airbag.

☒ Child is not secured by safety seat harness and is sitting loose in safety seat.

☒ Safety belt is not used to secure safety seat in vehicle. The safety seat loose on vehicle seat.

☒ Safety belt is fastened to or around wrong part of safety seat.

☒ Tether strap is not used, missing, or at wrong angle of attachment, when required.

☒ Use of incompatible safety belts.

☒ Booster seat used without a shield or a shoulder belt.

☒ Harness strap adjustment slides are not securely locked, permitting straps to release in a crash.

Warning: After an accident, rescue experts suggest that the entire seat be removed from the car, rather than unbuckling the child first.

! CHILD SAFETY SEAT RECALLS !

Manufacturers are required to put address cards in child seat packages. Mail the registration card as soon as you open the box! This is the only way you will receive notification of a seat recall.

Keep a copy of the manufacturer's address and contact the manufacturer if you move. To find out if the seat you are using has ever been recalled go to www.nhtsa.dot.gov/people/injury/childps/recall/canister.htm. You can also contact the Auto Safety Hotline at 800-424-9393, (D.C. call 202-366-0123.)

CHILD SAFETY SEAT TYPES

There are six general types of child seats: *infant-only, convertible, toddler-only, child/booster, booster, and built-in.*

Infant-Only Seats: Infant-only seats can be used from birth until your baby reaches a weight of 17–20 pounds. This type of seat must be installed facing the rear. In a collision, the crash forces are spread over the baby's back, the strongest body surface.

One benefit of an infant-only seat is that you can easily install and remove the seat with the baby in place. Most infant car seats can also be used as household baby seats. Caution: Some household baby seats look remarkably similar to infant safety seats. These are not crashworthy and should never be used as car safety seats.

Convertible Seats: Buying a convertible seat can save you the expense of buying both an infant and toddler seat. Most convertible seats can be used from birth until the child reaches four years or 40 pounds. When used for an infant, the seat faces rearward. When the child reaches 20 pounds, you reverse the seat so the child faces forward.

Convertible seats come in three basic types:

The *five-point harness* consists of two shoulder and two lap straps that converge at a buckle connected to a crotch strap.

The *T-shield style* has a small pad joining the shoulder belts. With only one buckle, this is the simplest type of convertible seat, but it will not fit newborns properly.

The *tray shield* has a safety harness is attached to a large safety shield. As the shield comes down in front of the child, the harness comes over the child's shoulders. This seat will not fit small infants.

Toddler-Only Seats: Toddler-only seats are forward-facing and they may take the place of convertible seats when a child is 20 pounds and over 1 year of age. Some convert to a belt-positioning booster for children over 40 pounds which allows the seat to be used longer.

! NEW CHILD SAFETY SEAT DESIGNS !

One reason 70–80 percent of children are improperly buckled up in cars is because many child safety seats are difficult to properly install and adjust. In fact, some seats simply don't fit in certain cars. To overcome this problem, a new federal law requires car makers and child seat manufactures to produce seats and cars with special attachment systems that make properly installing a car seat a simple task.

The new system requires car makers to install two 6mm metal bars (anchors) in the crevice between the rear seat and a tether attachment higher on the backrest. This allows specially designed child safety seats to attach directly to the anchors, eliminating the need to use the safety belt to secure child seats. This system was phased in and must be in all cars manufactured after September 1, 2002. All child safety seats manufactured after September 1, 2002 must have connection systems.

Currently, child safety seat manufacturers are using two different methods of connecting to the car's anchors. One is the Britax system, used in Europe, which involves rigid metal attachment pieces that slide perfectly into the anchors. This design is easy to use and very secure.

In the U.S., child seat manufacturers are using flexible straps with hooks or buckles rather than the rigid European system. The hooks or buckles attach to the seat anchors and the top tether. This system is easier to produce because manufacturers can add them to the seats without redesigning the seat. However, they don't always allow for a secure installation and are difficult to tighten effectively. Studies conducted by the Insurance Institute for Highway Safety, reveal the flexible attachment system allowed the child seat to move over an inch from the car's seat. That's too much movement according to the National Highway Traffic Safety Administration.

Combination Child/Booster Seats: Some manufacturers make a variety of combination child booster seats. For example, one model can be converted from a 5-point harness to a high-backed, belt-positioning booster seat. They can be used for children ranging from 20 to 40 pounds with the harness and from 30 to 80 pounds without the harness, making them a very economical choice.

Booster Seats: Booster seats are used when your child is too big for a convertible seat, but too small to use safety belts. Most car lap/shoulder belts do not adequately fit children with a seating height less than 28 inches. Booster seats can be used for children over 30 pounds and come in three different types:

Belt-positioning booster seats raise the child for a better fit with the car's safety belts. If your child is under three years old, do not use belt-positioning booster seats because your child may be able to unbuckle him or herself.

The *removable-shield booster* can be used with a lap/shoulder belt with the shield removed, or with a lap belt with the shield on.

The *shield-type booster* seat has a small plastic shield with no straps and can be used only with lap belts. Typically, the safety belt fastens in front of the shield, anchoring it to the car. Most safety experts recommend using these seats until a child is four years old and 40 pounds.

Built-in Seats: Chrysler, Ford, GM, Volvo, and other auto companies offer the option of a fold-out toddler seat on some of their models. These seats are only for children older than one and come as either a five-point harness or a booster with three-point belt; however, the three-point booster is not recommended for children under three years old. This built-in seat is an excellent feature because it is always in the car and does not pose the problem of compatability that often occurs with separate child seats.

ANTI-LOCK BRAKES

After airbags, one of the best safety features available is an anti-lock braking system (ABS). ABS shortens stopping distance on dry, wet, and even icy roads by preventing wheel lockup and keeps you from skidding out of control when you "slam" on the brakes.

The ABS works by sensing the speed of each wheel. If one or more of the wheels begins to lock up or skid, it releases that wheel's brakes, allowing the wheel to roll normally again, thus stopping the skid. When the wheel stops skidding, the hydraulic pressure is reapplied instantly. This cycle can be repeated several times per second, keeping each wheel at its optimum braking performance even while your foot keeps pushing on the brake pedal. Although ABS is typically connected to all four wheels, in some light trucks and vans it is connected to only the rear wheels.

The ABS is only active when it senses that the wheels are about to lock up. When an ABS is active, you may notice that the brake pedal pulsates slightly. This pulsation is normal and it indicates that the brakes are being released and reapplied. *Don't pump your brakes*—the ABS is doing it for you. If there is a failure in the ABS, the vehicle reverts to its conventional braking system and a warning light indicates that the ABS needs repair.

ROLLOVER

The risk of rollover is a significant safety issue, especially with sport utility vehicles. Because of their relatively high center of gravity, they don't hug the road like smaller, lower automobiles and trucks. As a result, they are more likely to turn over on sharp turns or corners. Not only does a rollover increase the likelihood of injuries, but it also increases the risk of the occupant being thrown from the vehicle. In fact, the danger of rollover with sport utilities is so severe that manufacturers are now required to place a sticker where it can be seen by the driver every time the vehicle is used. Each year, approximately 10,000 people died in rollover-related accidents.

To understand the concept behind these vehicles' propensity to roll over, consider this: place a section of 2x4 lumber on its 2-inch side. It is easily tipped over by a force pushing against the side. But if you place it on its 4-inch side, the same force will cause it to slide rather than tip over. Similarly, in a moving vehicle, the forces generated by a turn can cause a narrow, tall vehicle to roll over.

Congress has required the United States Department of Transportation to develop a dynamic (moving) rating system to accompany the static (stationery) rating system by the 2004 model year.

Following are rollover ratings for many 2004 vehicles. We have been publishing these ratings for a number of years and last year, the National Highway Traffic Safety Administration adopted this rating system.

A rollover rating is called the Static Stability Factor (SSF) and consists of a formula that uses the track width of the vehicle (tire to tire) and height to determine which vehicles are more or less likely to roll over when compared to each other. You can't use this information to exactly predict rollovers. However, all things being equal, if two vehicles are in the same situation where a rollover could occur, the one with a high SSF is more likely to roll over than a vehicle with a low SSF. Because this formula doesn't consider such things as driver behavior and the weight of the vehicle, among other factors, some experts do not believe it tells the whole story. We agree, and urged the government to provide an even better rollover rating system.

In the meantime, knowing how the vehicles rate using the SSF can be a key consideration in your evaluation of the vehicle.

YAW CONTROL SYSTEMS

Yaw Control Systems are electronic systems that are designed to control a vehicle's response when the driver's emergency steering and braking efforts may be hazardous. Just as anti-lock brakes partially take over a vehicle's braking to prevent wheel lockup, yaw control systems reduce the likelihood that a vehicle will oversteer in response to the driver's emergency steering and braking efforts. When a vehicle oversteers it will begin to slide sideways it can roll over easier or experience a dangerous side impact. Yaw control systems selectively apply or reduce braking to individual wheels in such a manner that keeps a vehicle about to go out of control, continuing to travel forward.

STATIC STABILITY FACTOR

Vehicle	SSF (Higher=Better)	Rollover Rating
Acura MDX	1.29	Low
Acura RL	1.43	Very Low
Acura RSX	1.39	Low
Acura TL	1.44	Very Low
Acura TSX*	1.39	Low
Audi A4	1.42	Very Low
Audi A6*	1.43	Very Low
Audi Allroad Quattro*	1.34	Low
BMW 3 Series	1.41	Very Low
BMW 5 Series*	1.42	Very Low
BMW X5	1.14	Moderate
BMW Z4*	1.57	Very Low
Buick Century	1.41	Very Low
Buick LeSabre	1.45	Very Low
Buick Park Avenue	1.43	Very Low
Buick Rainier*	1.13	Moderate
Buick Regal	1.41	Very Low
Buick Rendezvous	1.21	Moderate
Cadillac CTS	1.4	Very Low
Cadillac DeVille	1.48	Very Low
Cadillac Escalade	1.14	Moderate
Cadillac Escalade EXT	1.12	High
Cadillac Seville	1.14	Moderate
Cadillac SRX*	1.19	Moderate
Chevrolet Astro	1.13	Moderate
Chevrolet Aveo*	1.27	Low
Chevrolet Blazer	1.09	High
Chevrolet Cavalier	1.39	Low
Chevrolet Colorado*	1.15	Moderate
Chevrolet Impala	1.36	Low
Chevrolet Malibu*	1.38	Low
Chevrolet S Series	1.14	Moderate
Chevrolet Silverado	1.27	Low
Chevrolet Suburban	1.14	Moderate
Chevrolet Tahoe	1.14	Moderate
Chevrolet Tracker	1.15	Moderate
Chevrolet Trail Blazer	1.18	Moderate
Chevrolet Venture	1.18	Moderate
Chrysler 300M	1.43	Very Low
Chrysler Crossfire*	1.51	Very Low
Chrysler Pacifica*	1.32	Low
Chrysler PT Cruiser	1.26	Low
Chrysler Sebring	1.49	Very Low
Chrysler Town and Country	1.23	Moderate
Dodge Caravan	1.2	Moderate
Dodge Dakota	1.23	Moderate
Dodge Durango*	1.13	High
Dodge Neon	1.41	Very Low
Dodge Ram Pickup	1.19	Moderate
Dodge Stratus	1.49	Very Low
Ford Crown Victoria	1.51	Very Low
Ford Escape	1.21	Moderate
Ford Excursion*	1.11	High
Ford Expedition*	1.12	High
Ford Explorer	1.14	Moderate
Ford Explorer Sport Track*	1.08	High
Ford Focus	1.33	Low
Ford Freestar*	1.2	Moderate
Ford F-Series*	1.2	Moderate
Ford Mustang	1.45	Very Low
Ford Ranger	1.14	Moderate
Ford Taurus	1.43	Very Low
Ford Thunderbird	1.51	Very Low
GMC Envoy XUV*	1.06	Very High
Honda Accord	1.42	Very Low
Honda Civic	1.4	Very Low
Honda CR-V	1.16	Moderate
Honda Element	1.12	High
Honda Insight*	1.36	Low
Honda Odyssey	1.32	Low
Honda Pilot	1.3	Low
Honda S2000	1.57	Very Low
Hyundai Accent	1.42	Very Low
Hyundai Elantra	1.38	Low
Hyundai Santa Fe	1.2	Moderate
Hyundai Sonata	1.45	Very Low
Hyundai Tiburon*	1.5	Very Low
Hyundai XG350*	1.44	Very Low
Infiniti FX*	1.27	Low
Infiniti G35*	1.47	Very Low
Infiniti I35	1.38	Low
Isuzu Axiom	1.2	Moderate
Isuzu Rodeo	1.18	Moderate
Jeep Grand Cherokee	1.11	High
Jeep Liberty	1.15	Moderate
Jeep Wrangler	1.13	Moderate
Kia Optima	1.45	Very Low
Kia Rio	1.36	Low

*Calculated

STATIC STABILITY FACTOR

Vehicle	SSF (Higher=Better)	Rollover Rating
Kia Sedona	1.25	Low
Kia Sorento	1.16	Moderate
Kia Spectra	1.42	Very Low
Land Rover Discovery	1.05	Very High
Land Rover Freelander*	1.14	Moderate
Lexus ES 330*	1.24	Moderate
Lexus GS 300	1.41	Very Low
Lexus IS 300	1.47	Very Low
Lexus LS 430*	1.4	Very Low
Lexus RX 330*	1.21	Moderate
Lincoln Aviator*	1.12	High
Lincoln LS	1.51	Very Low
Lincoln Town Car	1.48	Very Low
Mazda 6	1.46	Very Low
Mazda MPV	1.21	Moderate
Mazda MX-5 Miata	1.59	Very Low
Mazda RX-8*	1.49	Very Low
Mercedes-Benz C-Class	1.35	Low
Mercedes-Benz E-Class	1.45	Very Low
Mercedes-Benz M-Class*	1.09	High
Mercury Monterey*	1.21	Moderate
Mini Cooper	1.44	Very Low
Mitsubishi Eclipse	1.46	Very Low
Mitsubishi Endeavor*	1.18	Moderate
Mitsubishi Galant	1.43	Very Low
Mitsubishi Lancer	1.42	Very Low
Mitsubishi Montero*	1.12	High
Mitsubishi Outlander	1.22	Moderate
Nissan 350Z	1.57	Very Low
Nissan Altima	1.44	Very Low
Nissan Frontier	1.14	Moderate
Nissan Maxima*	1.41	Very Low
Nissan Murano	1.3	Low
Nissan Pathfinder	1.16	Moderate
Nissan Pathfinder Armada*	1.14	Moderate
Nissan Quest*	1.3	Low
Nissan Sentra	1.38	Low
Nissan Titan*	1.17	Moderate
Nissan Xterra	1.12	High
Oldsmobile Alero	1.41	Very Low
Pontiac Aztek	1.26	Low
Pontiac Bonneville	1.45	Very Low
Pontiac Grand Am	1.41	Very Low
Pontiac Grand Prix*	1.48	Very Low
Pontiac GTO*	1.5	Very Low
Pontiac Vibe	1.27	Low
Saab 9-3*	1.41	Very Low
Saab 9-5	1.37	Low
Saturn ION	1.38	Low
Saturn L/LW	1.42	Very Low
Saturn VUE	1.22	Moderate
Scion xA*	1.26	Low
Scion xB*	1.17	Moderate
Subaru Baja*	1.23	Moderate
Subaru Forester*	1.33	Low
Subaru Impreza	1.37	Low
Subaru Legacy	1.42	Very Low
Subaru Outback	1.26	Low
Suzuki Aerio*	1.25	Low
Suzuki Forenza*	1.37	Low
Suzuki Grand Vitara	1.15	Moderate
Suzuki Verona*	1.42	Very Low
Suzuki XL-7*	1.14	Moderate
Toyota 4Runner	1.16	Moderate
Toyota Avalon	1.42	Very Low
Toyota Camry	1.4	Very Low
Toyota Celica	1.47	Very Low
Toyota Corolla	1.34	Low
Toyota ECHO	1.32	Low
Toyota Highlander	1.2	Moderate
Toyota MR2 Spyder*	1.58	Very Low
Toyota Prius*	1.36	Low
Toyota RAV4	1.22	Moderate
Toyota Sequoia	1.14	Moderate
Toyota Sienna*	1.25	Moderate
Toyota Solara*	1.44	Very Low
Toyota Tacoma*	1.16	Moderate
Toyota Tundra	1.16	Moderate
Volkswagen Beetle	1.39	Low
Volkswagen Golf*	1.39	Low
Volkswagen Passat	1.41	Very Low
Volvo 40 Series	1.38	Low
Volvo 60 Series	1.49	Very Low
Volvo 70 Series*	1.43	Very Low
Volvo 80 Series	1.47	Very Low
Volvo XC90*	1.19	Moderate

*Calculated

Land Rover Freelander

Acura TSX

Chevrolet Colorado

Chevrolet Aveo

IN THIS CHAPTER

INTRODUCTION

The important fuel economy gains over the past years have been offset by the dramatic increase in heavier, less fuel-efficient vehicles—namely, the popular sport utility vehicles. The increasing market share of these more fuel-inefficient vehicles is bringing the overall averages down.

Using EPA ratings is an excellent way to incorporate fuel efficiency in selecting a new car. By comparing these ratings, even among cars of the same size, you'll find that fuel efficiency varies greatly. One compact car might get 36 miles per gallon (mpg) while another gets only 22 mpg. If you drive 15,000 miles a year and you pay $1.50 per gallon for fuel, the 36 mpg car will save you $319 a year over the "gas guzzler."

Octane Ratings: Once you've purchased your car, you'll be faced with choosing the right gasoline. Oil companies spend millions of dollars trying to get you to buy so-called higher performance or high octane fuels. Because high octane fuel can add considerably to your gas bill, it is important that you know what you're buying.

The octane rating of a gasoline is not a measure of power or quality. It is simply a measure of the gas's resistance to engine knock, which is the pinging sound you hear when the air and fuel mixture in your engine ignites prematurely during acceleration.

The octane rating appears on a yellow label on the fuel pump. Octane ratings vary with different types of gas (premium or regular), in different parts of the country (higher altitudes require lower octane ratings), and even between brands (Texaco's gasolines may have a different rating than Exxon's).

Determining the Right Octane for Your Car: Using a lower-rated gasoline saves money. Most cars are designed to run on a posted octane rating of 87. Check your owner's manual. The following procedure can help you select the lowest octane level for your car.

1 Have your engine tuned to exact factory specifications by a competent mechanic, and make sure it is in good working condition.

2 When the gas in your tank is very low, fill it up with your usual gasoline. After driving 10 to 15 miles, find a safe place to come to a complete stop and then accelerate rapidly. If your engine knocks during acceleration, switch to a higher octane rating. If there is no knocking sound, wait until your tank is very low and fill up with a lower- rated gasoline. Repeat the test. When you determine the level of octane that causes your engine to knock during the test, use gasoline with the next highest rating.

Your engine may knock when accelerating a heavily loaded car uphill or when the humidity is low. This is normal and does not call for a higher-octane gasoline.

FUEL ECONOMY

Get up-to-date information about fuel economy at www.fueleconomy.gov, a joint website created by the U.S. Department of Energy and the EPA. The EPA's entire Fuel Economy Guide can be found there, allowing you to compare fuel economy among several 2004 model year vehicles. You'll also find out the latest on technological advances pertaining to fuel efficiency. The site's information is extremely useful and easy to navigate. We've added the fuel economy ratings to our car rating pages as well.

FACTORS AFFECTING FUEL ECONOMY

Fuel economy is affected by a number of factors that you can consider before you buy.

Transmission: Manual transmissions are generally more fuel-efficient than automatic transmissions. In fact, a 5-speed manual transmission can add up to 6.5 miles per gallon over a 3-speed automatic. However, the incorrect use of a manual transmission wastes gas, so choose a transmission that matches your preference. Many transmissions now feature an overdrive gear, which can improve a vehicle's fuel economy by as much as 9 percent for an automatic transmission and 3 percent for a manual transmission.

Engine: The size of your car's engine greatly affects your fuel economy. The smaller your engine, the better your fuel efficiency. A 10 percent increase in the size of an engine can increase fuel consumption by 6 percent.

Cruise Control: Cruise control can save fuel because driving at a constant speed uses less fuel than changing speeds frequently.

Air Conditioning: Auto air conditioners add weight and require additional horsepower to operate. They can cost up to 3 miles per gallon in city driving. At highway speeds, however, an air conditioner has about the same effect on fuel economy as the air resistance created by opening the windows.

Trim Package: Upgrading a car's trim, installing soundproofing, and adding undercoating can increase the weight of a typical car by 150 pounds. For each 10 percent increase in weight, fuel economy drops 4 percent.

Power Options: Power steering, brakes, seats, windows, and roofs reduce your mileage by adding weight. Power steering alone can cause a 1 percent drop in fuel economy.

Here are some tips for after you buy.

Tune-up: If you have a 2 to 3 mpg drop over several fill-ups that is not due to a change of driving pattern or vehicle load, first check tire pressure, then consider a tune-up. A properly tuned engine is a fuel saver.

Tire Inflation: For maximum fuel efficiency, tires should be inflated to the pressure range found on the label in your door well. The tire's maximum pressure may not be suitable for your car. Be sure to check the tire pressure when the tires are cold before you've driven a long distance. Note: Inflated tires improve gas mileage by 6 percent.

Short Trips: Short trips can be expensive because they usually involve a "cold" vehicle. For the first mile or two before the engine gets warmed up, a cold vehicle only gets 30 to 40 percent of the mileage it gets at full efficiency.

Line up: Periodic wheel alignments improve gas mileage by 10%.

Unnecessary Weight: Every 200 pounds shaves 1 mpg off fuel mileage.

Don't Speed: A car moving at 55 mph gets 15 percent better fuel economy than the same car at 65 mph.

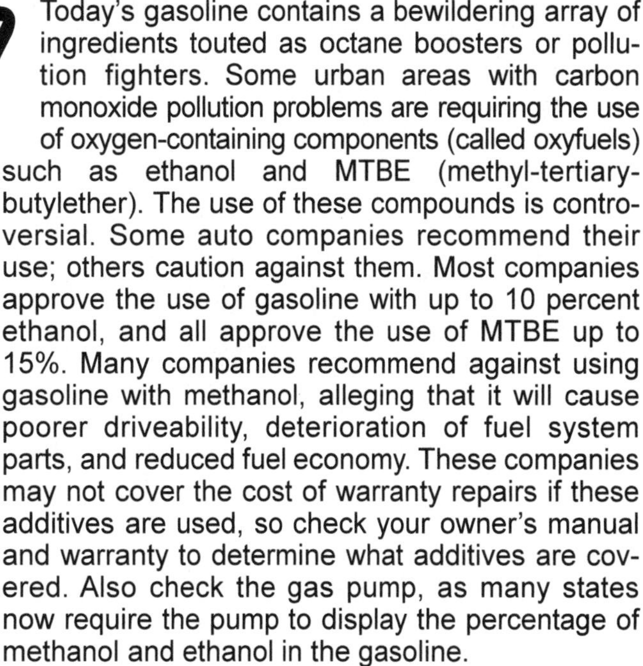

USING OXYFUELS

Today's gasoline contains a bewildering array of ingredients touted as octane boosters or pollution fighters. Some urban areas with carbon monoxide pollution problems are requiring the use of oxygen-containing components (called oxyfuels) such as ethanol and MTBE (methyl-tertiary-butylether). The use of these compounds is controversial. Some auto companies recommend their use; others caution against them. Most companies approve the use of gasoline with up to 10 percent ethanol, and all approve the use of MTBE up to 15%. Many companies recommend against using gasoline with methanol, alleging that it will cause poorer driveability, deterioration of fuel system parts, and reduced fuel economy. These companies may not cover the cost of warranty repairs if these additives are used, so check your owner's manual and warranty to determine what additives are covered. Also check the gas pump, as many states now require the pump to display the percentage of methanol and ethanol in the gasoline.

FUEL ECONOMY MISERS AND GUZZLERS

Every year the Department of Energy publishes the results of the Environmental Protection Agency's (EPA) fuel economy tests in a comparative guide. Because the success of the EPA program depends on consumers' ability to compare the fuel economy ratings easily, we have included key mileage figures in our ratings page and listed below this year's misers and guzzlers. The complete EPA fuel economy guide is available at www.fueleconomy.gov.

FUEL ECONOMY MISERS AND GUZZLERS

EPA Rank	Vehicle	MPG (city/hwy)	Annual Fuel Cost
	THE BEST		
1	Honda Insight, Manual (M5)	60/66	$334
2	Honda Insight, Auto (AV)	57/56	$376
3	Toyota Prius, Auto (AV)	60/51	$382
4	Honda Civic Hybrid, Manual (M5)	46/51	$437
4	Honda Civic Hybrid, Auto (AV)	48/47	$437
5	Honda Civic Hybrid, Manual (M5)	45/51	$447
5	Honda Civic Hybrid, Auto (AV)	47/48	$447
6	Volkswagen Golf, Manual (M5)	38/46	$494
6	Volkswagen Jetta, Manual (M5)	38/46	$494
6	Volkswagen Jetta Wagon, Manual (M5)	36/47	$494
6	Volkswagen New Beetle, Manual (M5)	38/46	$494
7	Honda Civic, Manual (M5)	36/44	$538
8	Toyota ECHO, Manual (M5)	35/43	$552
8	Volkswagen New Beetle, Auto (S6)	36/42	$533
9	Honda Civic, Auto (AV)	35/40	$567
10	Volkswagen Golf, Auto (S5)	33/44	$547
10	Volkswagen Jetta, Auto (S5)	33/44	$547
10	Volkswagen Jetta Wagon, Auto (S5)	33/44	$547
	THE WORST		
1	Lamborghini L-147/148 Murcielago, Manual (M6)	9/13	$2,400
2	Lamborghini L-140/141 Gallardo, Manual (M6)	9/15	$2,182
3	Chevrolet C2500 HD Silverado 2WD, Auto (L4)	10/12	$1,227
4	Chevrolet K1500 Silverdo 4WD, Auto (L4)	10/13	$2,045
5	Bentley Bentley Arnage, Auto (L4)	10/14	$1,999
5	Bentley Bentley Arnage LWB, Auto (L4)	10/14	$1,999
5	Chevrolet C1500 Avalanche 2WD, Auto (L4)	10/14	$1,874
5	Chevrolet C1500 Suburban 2WD, Auto (L4)	10/14	$1,874
5	GMC C1500 Yukon XL 2WD, Auto (L4)	10/14	$1,874
5	Chevrolet K1500 Avalanche AWD, Auto (L4)	10/14	$1,874
5	Chevrolet K1500 Suburban AWD, Auto (L4)	10/14	$1,874
5	Chevrolet K1500 Tahoe AWD, Auto (L4)	10/14	$1,874
5	GMC K1500 Yukon AWD, Auto (L4)	10/14	$1,874
5	GMC K1500 Yukon XL AWD, Auto (L4)	10/14	$1,874
6	Lamborghini L-147/148 Murcielago, Auto (S6)	10/15	$1,999
7	Ferrari 360 Modena/Spider/Challenge, Auto (S6)	10/16	$1,999
7	Ferrari Ferrari 575 M Maranello, Manual (M6)	10/16	$1,999
8	Ferrari Ferrari 575 M Maranello, Auto (S6)	10/17	$1,999
8	Lamborghini L-140/141 Gallardo, Auto (S6)	10/17	$1,999
9	GMC C1500 Sierra 2WD, Auto (L4)	11/14	$1,874
9	Chevrolet C1500 Silverado 2WD, Auto (L4)	11/14	$1,874
9	Chevrolet C1500 Tahoe 2WD, Auto (L4)	11/14	$1,874
9	GMC C1500 Yukon 2WD, Auto (L4)	11/14	$1,874
9	Ford F150 Pickup 4WD, Auto (L4)	11/14	$1,125
10	Ford F150 Pickup 2WD, Manual (M6)	11/15	$1,038
10	Land RoverDiscovery Series II	12/16	$1443

WARRANTIES, MAINTENANCE AND TIRES

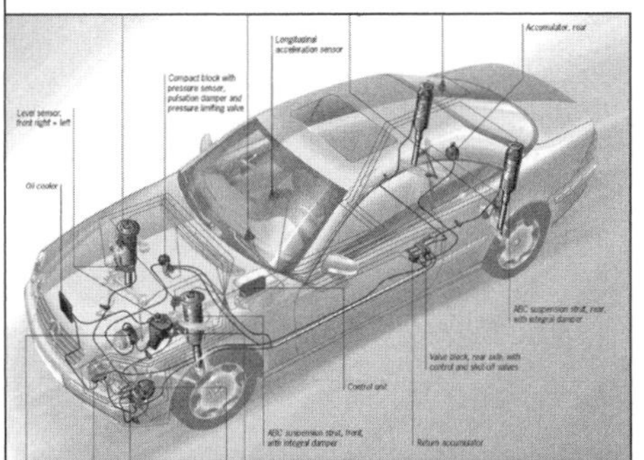

IN THIS CHAPTER

INTRODUCTION

After buying your car, maintenance will be a significant portion of your operating costs. The strength of your warranty and the cost of repairs after the warranty expires will determine these costs. Comparing warranties and repair costs, before you buy can save you thousands of dollars down the road. This chapter takes a look at warranties, allows you to compare potential repair costs, and offers tips on tires.

Along with your new car comes a warranty which is a promise from the manufacturer that the car will perform as it should. Most of us never read the warranty—until it is too late. In fact, because warranties are often difficult to read and understand, most of us don't really know what our warranties offer. Here's what to look for in a new car warranty.

There are two types of warranties: one provided by the manufacturer and one implied by law.

Manufacturers' warranties are either "full" or "limited." The best warranty you can get is a full warranty because by law, it must cover all aspects of the product's performance. Any other guarantee is called a limited warranty, which is what most car manufacturers offer. Limited warranties must be clearly marked as such, and you must be told exactly what is covered.

Warranties implied by law are warranties of merchantability and fitness. The "warranty of merchantability" ensures that your new car will be fit for the purpose for which it is used—that means safe, efficient, and trouble-free transportation. The "warranty of fitness" guarantees that if the dealer says a car can be used for a specific purpose, it will perform that purpose.

Many claims made by the salesperson are also considered warranties. They are called expressed warranties and you should have them put in writing if you consider them to be important. If the car does not live up to promises made to you in the showroom, you may have a case against the seller.

The manufacturer can restrict the amount of time the limited warranty is in effect. And in most states, the manufacturer can also limit the time that the warranty implied by law is in effect. This period of time is usually measured in both months and miles, whichever comes first is the limit.

While the warranty is in effect, the manufacturer will perform, at no charge, repairs that are necessary because of defects in materials or in the way the car was manufactured.

Implied warranties, including the warranties of merchantability and fitness, can at most be limited to the length of the written warranty. Manufacturer warranties try to disclaim responsibility for other problems caused by repairs, such as the loss of time or use of your car, or any expenses they might cause. In at least nine states, such limitations on your warranty rights are invalid.

In addition to the rights granted to you in the warranty, you may have other rights under your state laws.

To keep your warranty in effect, you must operate and maintain your car according to the instructions in your owner's manual. Remember, it is important to keep a record of all maintenance performed on your car.

Be careful not to confuse your warranty with a service contract. The service contract must be purchased separately while the warranty is yours at no extra cost when you buy the car.

Corrosion Warranty: All manufacturers warrant against corrosion. The typical corrosion warranty lasts for six years or 100,000 miles, whichever comes first.

Some dealers offer extra rust protection at an additional cost. Before you purchase this option, compare the extra protection offered to the corrosion warranty already included in the price of the car—it probably already provides sufficient protection against rust.

Emission System Warranty: The emission system is warranted by federal law. Any repairs required during the first two years or 24,000 miles will be paid for by the manufacturer if an original engine part fails because of a defect in materials or workmanship and the failure causes your car to exceed federal emissions standards. Major components are covered for eight years or up to 80,000 miles.

SECRET WARRANTIES

If dealers report a number of complaints about a certain part and the manufacturer determines that the problem is due to faulty design or assembly, the manufacturer may permit dealers to repair the problem at no charge to the customer even though the warranty is expired. In the past, this practice was often reserved for customers who made a big fuss. The availability of the free repair was never publicized, which is why we call these "secret warranties."

Manufacturers deny the existence of secret warranties. They call these free repairs "policy adjustments" or "goodwill service." Whatever they are called, most consumers never hear about them.

Many secret warranties are disclosed in service bulletins that the manufacturers send to dealers. These bulletins outline free repair or reimbursement programs, as well as other problems and their possible causes and solutions.

Service bulletins from many manufacturers may be on file at the National Highway Traffic Safety Administration. Visit their website at www.nhtsa.dot.gov to access NHTSA's Service Bulletin database.

If you find that a secret warranty is in effect and repairs are being made at no charge after the warranty has expired, contact the Center for Auto Safety, 1825 Connecticut Ave., NW, #330, Washington, DC 20009. They will publish the information so others can benefit.

Disclosure Laws: Spurred by the proliferation of secret warranties and the failure of the FTC to take action, California, Connecticut, Virginia, and Wisconsin have passed legislation that requires consumers to be notified of secret warranties on their cars. Several other states have introduced similar warranty bills.

Typically, the laws require the following: direct notice to consumers within a specified time after the adoption of a warranty adjustment policy; notice of the disclosure law to new car buyers; reimbursement within a number of years after payment to owners who paid for covered repairs before they learned of the extended warranty service; and dealers must inform consumers who complain about a covered defect that it is eligible for repair under warranty.

If you live in a state with a secret warranty law already in effect, write your state attorney general's office (in care of your state capital) for information. To encourage passage of such a bill, contact your state representative (in care of your state capital).

Some state lemon laws require dealers and manufacturers to give you copies of Technical Service Bulletins on problems affecting your vehicle. These bulletins may alert you to a secret warranty on your vehicle or help you make the case for a free repair if there isn't a secret warranty. Go to www.autosafety.org to view your states' lemon laws.

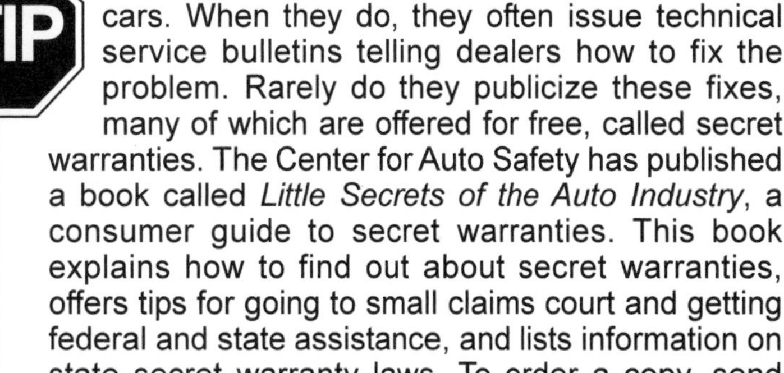

LITTLE SECRETS OF THE AUTO INDUSTRY

Every auto company makes mistakes building cars. When they do, they often issue technical service bulletins telling dealers how to fix the problem. Rarely do they publicize these fixes, many of which are offered for free, called secret warranties. The Center for Auto Safety has published a book called *Little Secrets of the Auto Industry*, a consumer guide to secret warranties. This book explains how to find out about secret warranties, offers tips for going to small claims court and getting federal and state assistance, and lists information on state secret warranty laws. To order a copy, send $17.50 to: Center for Auto Safety, Pub. Dept. CB, 1825 Connecticut Ave., NW, Suite 330, Washington, DC 20009.

COMPARING WARRANTIES

Warranties are difficult to compare because they contain lots of fine print and confusing language. The following table will help you understand this year's new car warranties. Because the table does not contain all the details about each warranty, you should review the actual warranty to make sure you understand its fine points. Remember, you have the right to inspect a warranty before you buy—it's the law.

The table provides information on five areas covered by a typical warranty:

The Basic Warranty covers most parts of the car against manufacturer's defects. The tires, batteries, and items you may add to the car are covered under separate warranties. The table describes coverage in terms of months and miles. For example, 36/36,000 means the warranty is good for 36 months or 36,000 miles, whichever comes first. This is the most important part of your warranty.

The Powertrain Warranty usually lasts longer than the basic warranty. Because each manufacturer's definition of the powertrain is different, it is important to find out exactly what your warranty will cover. Powertrain coverage should include parts of the engine, transmission, and drivetrain. The warranty on some luxury cars will often cover some additional systems such as steering, suspension, and electrical systems.

The Corrosion Warranty usually applies only to actual holes due to rust. Read this section carefully, because many corrosion warranties do not apply to what the manufacturer may describe as cosmetic rust or bad paint.

The Roadside Assistance column indicates whether or not the warranty includes a program for helping with problems on the road. Typically, these programs cover such things as lockouts, jump starts, flat tires, running out of gas, and towing. Most of these are offered for the length of the basic warranty. Some have special limitations or added features, which we have pointed out. Because each one is different, check yours out carefully.

The last column, the **Warranty Rating Index**, provides an overall assessment of this year's warranties. **The higher the Index number, the better the warranty.** The Index number incorporates the important features of each warranty. In developing the Index, we gave the most weight to the basic and powertrain components of the warranties. The corrosion warranty was weighted somewhat less, and the roadside assistance features received the least weight. We also considered special features such as whether you had to bring the car in for corrosion inspections, or if rental cars were offered when warranty repairs were being done.

After evaluating all the features of the warranties, here are this year's best and worst ratings. The best are in **BOLD**.

Manufacturer	Basic Warranty	Power Train Warranty	Corrosion Warranty	Roadside Assistance	Index	Warranty Rating
Acura	48/50000	48/50000	72/Unlimited	48/50000	1229	Good
Audi	48/50000	48/50000	144/Unlimited	36/30000	1577	Very Good
BMW	48/50000	48/50000	72/100000	48/50000^	1177	Average
Buick	36/36000	36/36,000	72/100000	36/36000	956	Very Poor
Cadillac	48/50000	48/50000	72/100000	48/50000	1177	Average
Chevrolet	36/36000	36/36,000	72/100000	36/36000	956	Very Poor
Chrysler	36/36000	84/70000*	60/100000	84/70000	1301	Good
Dodge	36/36000	84/70000*	60/100000	84/70000	1301	Good
Ford	36/36000	36/36000**	60/Unlimited	36/36000	942	Very Poor
GMC	36/36000	36/36,000	72/100000	36/36000	956	Very Poor

WARRANTY COMPARISON

Manufacturer	Basic Warranty	Power Train Warranty	Corrosion Warranty	Roadside Assistance	Index	Warranty Rating
Honda	36/36000	36/36,000	60/100000	Optional	824	Very Poor
Hummer	36/36000	36/36,000	72/100000	36/36000	956	Very Poor
Hyundai	60/60000	120/100000	60/100000	60/Unlimited	1706	Very Good
Infiniti	48/60000	72/70000	84/Unlimited	48/60000	1482	Very Good
Isuzu	36/50000	84/75000	72/100000	84/75000	1404	Good
Jaguar	48/50000	48/50000	72/Unlimited	48/50000	1229	Good
Jeep	36/36000	84/70000*	60/100000	84/70000	1301	Good
Kia	60/60000	120/100000	60/100000	60/Unlimited	1706	Very Good
Land Rover	48/50000	48/50000	72/Unlimited	48/50000	1229	Good
Lexus	48/50000	72/70000	72/Unlimited	48/Unlimited	1412	Very Good
Lincoln	48/50000	48/50000	60/Unlimited	48/50000	1163	Average
Mazda	36/50000	36/50000	36/50000	36/50000	903	Very Poor
Mercedes-Benz	48/50000	48/50000	48/50000	Unlimited	882	Very Poor
Mercury	36/36000	36/36,000	60/Unlimited	36/36000	942	Very Poor
Mini	48/50000	48/50000	72/Unlimited	Optional	1082	Poor
Mitsubishi	36/36000	60/60000	84/100000	36/36000	1124	Average
Nissan	36/36000	60/60000	60/Unlimited	36/36000	1086	Poor
Oldsmobile***	36/36000	36/36,000	72/100000	36/36000	956	Very Poor
Pontiac	36/36000	36/36,000	72/100000	36/36000	956	Very Poor
Saab	48/50000	48/50000	72/Unlimited****	48/50000	1229	Good
Saturn	36/36000	36/36000	72/100000	36/36000	956	Very Poor
Scion	36/36000	60/60000	60/Unlimited		978	Poor
Subaru	36/36000	50/50000	50/Unlimited	36/36000*****	971	Poor
Suzuki	36/36000%	84/100000@	36/36000	36/36000	1092	Average
Toyota	36/36000	60/60000	60/Unlimited		978	Poor
Volkswagen	48/50000	60/60000	144/12000	48/50000	1211	Good
Volvo	48/50000	48/50000	60/Unlimited	48/50000	1163	Average

^Covers Trip Interruption costs; *Powertrain Warranty is transferable to subsequent owners at no extra cost. Roadside assistance administered by Cross Country Motor Club, Inc., Boston, MA 02155. You must call 1800/521-2779 for prior authorization to receive these benefits; **Ford Focus offers a 5-year/100,000 mile powertrain warranty that is fully transferable to future owners at no extra cost. The Focus warranty also includes a 5-year roadside assistance and towing plan; ***A limited, 60-month/100,000-mile powertrain warranty applies to Florida buyers; ****9-3 has 120/100,000 mile; *****Subaru Roadside; Assistance covers towing only;%Soft tops have 24/24000 basic warranty on the soft tops; @Suzuki's warranty is transferable.

KEEPING IT GOING

Comparing maintenance costs before you buy can help decide which car to purchase. These costs include preventive maintenance servicing—such as changing the oil and filters—as well as the cost of repairs after your warranty expires. On the following pages, we enable you to compare the costs of preventive maintenance and nine likely repairs for the 2004 models.

Preventive maintenance is the periodic servicing, specified by the manufacturer, that keeps your car running properly. For example, regularly changing the oil and oil filter. Every owner's manual specifies a schedule of recommended servicing for at least the first 60,000 miles, and the tables on the following pages estimate the cost of following this preventive maintenance schedule.

Typical Repairs: The tables also list the costs for nine repairs that typically occur during the first 100,000 miles. There is no precise way to predict exactly when a repair will be needed. But if you keep a car for 75,000 to 100,000 miles, it is likely that you will experience most of these repairs at least once. The last column provides a relative indication of how expensive these nine repairs are for many cars. Repair cost is rated as Very Good if the total for nine repairs is in the bottom fifth of all the cars rated, and Very Poor if the total is in the top fifth.

Most repair shops use "flat-rate manuals" to estimate repair costs. These manuals list the approximate time required for repairing many items. Each automobile manufacturer publishes its own manual and there are several independent manuals as well. For many repairs, the time varies from one manual to another. Some repair shops even use different manuals for different repairs. To determine a repair bill, a shop multiplies the time listed in its manual by its hourly labor rate and then adds the cost of parts.

Some dealers and repair shops create their own maintenance schedules which call for more frequent (and thus more expensive) servicing than the manufacturer's recommendations. If the servicing recommended by your dealer or repair shop doesn't match what the car maker recommends, make sure you understand and agree to the extra items. Our cost estimates are based on flat-rate manual repair times multiplied by a nationwide average labor rate of $50 per hour. All estimates also include the cost of replaced parts and related adjustments, which are based on 2002 figures.

Prices in the following tables may not predict the exact costs of these repairs. For example, the labor rate for your area may be more or less than the national average. However, the prices will provide you with a relative comparison of maintenance costs for various automobiles.

TIP: TURBOCHARGING

A turbocharger is an air pump that forces more air into the engine for combustion. Most turbochargers consist of an air compressor driven by a small turbine wheel that is powered by the engine's exhaust. The turbine takes advantage of energy otherwise lost and forces increased efficiency from the engine. Turbochargers are often used to increase the power and sometimes the fuel efficiency of small engines. Engines equipped with turbochargers are more expensive than standard engines. The extra power may not be necessary when you consider the added expense and the fact that turbocharging adds to the complexity of the engine.

MAINTENANCE COSTS

	PM Costs to 60,000 Miles	Water Pump	Alternator	Front Brake Pads	Starter	Fuel Injection	Fuel Pump	Struts/ Shocks	Timing Belt/ Chain	Power Steer. Pump	Relative Maint. Cost
Subcompact											
Honda S2000	310	216	605	91	313	134	417	239	417	NA	Good
Hyundai Accent	515	215	273	88	335	104	146	115	117	386	Vry. Gd.
Kia Rio	560	332	409	80	317	156	233	188	223	363	Good
Kia Spectra	560	315	312	72	325	201	193	188	216	232	Vry. Gd.
Mazda MX-5 Miata	570	262	490	98	240	311	501	158	179	636	Poor
Mini Cooper	154	229	397	107	193	190	272	189	234	504	Good
Mitsubishi Lancer	430	294	295	123	303	138	556	195	220	724	Avg.
Nissan Sentra	330	143	327	91	246	158	288	225	392	374	Good
Subaru Impreza	565	227	499	118	265	155	355	275	190	495	Average
Suzuki Aerio	975	173	330	146	445	263	357	236	327	460	Poor
Toyota ECHO	570	131	495	105	213	207	283	212	354	484	Avg.
Toyota MR2 Spyder	525	173	411	106	290	202	343	208	404	742	Poor
Volkswagen Beetle	685	205	476	213	412	232	403	224	182	207	Avg.
Compact											
Acura RSX	290	238	915	91	574	133	240	132	281	521	Vry. Pr.
Audi A4	655	362	979	182	537	216	465	184	249	532	Vry. Pr.
BMW 3 Series	154	230	740	112	350	160	262	255	730	505	Vry. Pr.
Chev. Cavalier/Pont. Sunfire	655	362	295	168	321	418	433	272	451	499	Vry. Pr.
Chrysler PT Cruiser	395	293	368	176	132	115	314	165	287	226	Good
Chrys. Sebring/Dge. Stratus (Cpe.)	465	376	1,012	147	917	174	381	180	213	114	Vry. Pr.
Dodge Neon	450	243	365	171	163	101	341	186	230	340	Good
Ford Focus	725	176	249	138	220	92	330	157	190	270	Vry. Gd.
Ford Mustang	535	226	228	169	260	160	337	150	246	199	Vry. Gd.
Ford Thunderbird	685	183	267	124	197	152	316	145	714	283	Good
Honda Civic	295	211	405	96	365	93	259	161	156	261	Vry. Gd.
Hyundai Elantra	540	212	273	95	262	116	267	142	149	411	Vry. Gd.
Kia Optima	540	282	559	104	306	210	203	174	173	325	Good
Mitsubishi Eclipse	465	348	328	128	545	173	296	147	183	331	Avg.
Pontiac Vibe/Toyota Matrix	295	233	585	125	470	256	138	222	185	282	Avg.
Saturn ION	500	278	422	120	265	169	244	143	302	45	Vry. Gd.
Subaru Legacy	565	220	505	109	325	145	320	245	300	457	Avg.
Subaru Outback	565	220	505	109	325	145	320	245	230	457	Avg.
Toyota Celica	520	182	406	94	368	207	283	208	384	441	Avg.
AVERAGE	**624**	**257**	**402**	**138**	**308**	**197**	**362**	**182**	**327**	**374**	

*Estimate based on averages.

MAINTENANCE COSTS

	PM Costs to 60,000 Miles	Water Pump	Alternator	Front Brake Pads	Starter	Fuel Injection	Fuel Pump	Struts/ Shocks	Timing Belt/ Chain	Power Steer. Pump	Relative Maint. Cost
Compact (cont.)											
Volkswagen Golf/Jetta	640	205	736	218	351	192	388	173	178	207	Avg.
Volvo 40 Series	800	372	409	100	192	187	314	198	223	469	Avg.
Intermediate											
Acura TL	415	547	265	106	368	333	352	202	276	370	Poor
Audi A6	530	373	568	182	281	245	443	246	216	526	Vry. Pr.
Buick Century	610	143	357	133	329	259	449	180	358	174	Good
Buick Regal	610	158	342	151	334	231	449	163	336	179	Good
Chrys. Sebring Conv. /Dge. Stratus	465	308	335	160	126	84	248	154	210	193	Vry. Gd.
Ford Taurus/Mercury Sable	570	240	297	190	202	106	325	150	258	234	Vry. Gd.
Hyundai Sonata	540	207	384	106	363	110	178	146	122	574	Good
Hyundai XG350	540	305	491	86	368	185	178	148	295	328	Good
Infiniti I35	465	300	353	109	292	263	323	368	454	506	Vry. Pr.
Lexus IS 300	690	386	552	99	393	235	330	147	166	503	Poor
Mercedes-Benz C-Class	320	481	1,005	124	660	272	354	238	260	685	Vry. Pr.
Nissan Altima	570	168	292	118	329	203	200	169	355	354	Good
Oldsmobile Alero	725	301	305	169	336	207	410	342	279	446	Poor
Pontiac Grand Am	725	205	360	168	319	214	476	241	283	302	Avg.
Saab 9-5	675	220	545	133	300	140	380	233	607	506	Vry. Pr.
Saturn L/LW	460	255	342	127	280	116	395	195	320	362	Good
Toyota Avalon	390	259	577	89	389	287	293	238	179	419	Poor
Toyota Camry	370	257	530	89	374	297	293	220	414	458	Poor
Volkswagen Passat	790	229	561	182	628	112	328	234	311	485	Vry. Pr.
Volvo 60 Series	920	322	409	108	333	248	322	182	153	543	Avg.
Volvo 70 Series	680	312	429	144	333	243	362	182	278	543	Poor
Large											
Acura RL	450	547	440	182	215	149	362	200	311	598	Vry. Pr.
Buick LeSabre	725	229	367	143	331	184	497	228	287	482	Poor
Buick Park Avenue	630	261	344	143	331	171	517	276	307	468	Poor
Cadillac CTS	540	230	483	175	334	330	567	223	160	431	Vry. Pr.
Cadillac DeVille	610	188	605	161	403	130	527	249	773	392	Vry. Pr.
Cadillac Seville	720	141	598	131	453	170	517	192	798	392	Vry. Pr.
Chev. Impala/Monte Carlo	835	150	312	121	329	276	459	272	340	174	Good
Chrys. 300M/Concorde/Intrepid	430	231	343	159	289	128	344	170	222	248	Good
AVERAGE	**624**	**257**	**402**	**138**	**308**	**197**	**362**	**182**	**327**	**374**	

*Estimate based on averages.

MAINTENANCE COSTS

	PM Costs to 60,000 Miles	Water Pump	Alternator	Front Brake Pads	Starter	Fuel Injection	Fuel Pump	Struts/ Shocks	Timing Belt/ Chain	Power Steer. Pump	Relative Maint. Cost
Large (cont.)											
Ford Cr. Vic. /Gr. Marq./Marauder	570	213	252	158	233	134	362	132	300	201	Vry. Gd.
Lexus GS 300/GS 430	690	386	567	115	408	340	343	162	186	498	Vry. Pr.
Lexus LS 430	590	330	610	115	265	305	345	162	244	632	Vry. Pr.
Lincoln LS	750	187	254	149	195	205	316	120	528	260	Good
Lincoln Town Car	680	168	262	163	233	187	347	147	366	196	Vry. Gd.
Pontiac Bonneville	725	199	405	123	331	161	497	177	277	482	Avg.
Volvo 80 Series	950	437	409	108	342	222	307	213	278	543	Poor
Minivan											
Chev. Astro/GMC Safari	1,505	295	307	201	322	197	331	137	305	456	Avg.
Chev. Venture/Pont. Montana	600	143	468	138	329	261	472	281	426	426	Vry. Pr.
Chrys. T&C/Grand Caravan	395	281	254	140	166	126	332	174	295	243	Vry. Gd.
Dodge Caravan	395	203	266	151	267	93	334	168	295	243	Vry. Gd.
Honda Odyssey	505	333	512	96	445	333	419	141	276	271	Poor
Kia Sedona	650	414	538	158	311	195	283	211	367	315	Poor
Mazda MPV	580	181	412	124	468	441	337	117	503	286	Poor
Compact Pickup											
Chev. S Series/GMC Sonoma	940	178	299	168	339	289	577	165	295	331	Avg.
Dodge Dakota	440	203	343	156	361	119	520	89	221	281	Good
Ford Ranger/Mazda Truck	510	149	260	148	240	135	330	83	273	208	Vry. Gd.
Nissan Frontier	765	168	322	120	283	153	280	160	563	337	Good
Toyota Tacoma	630	187	533	92	377	237	425	242	743	504	Vry. Pr.
Standard Pickup											
Chev. Silverado/GMC Sierra	1,085	263	308	225	320	187	449	133	266	356	Avg.
Dodge Ram Pickup	970	206	418	174	317	92	364	165	552	156	Avg.
Toyota Tundra	690	255	523	86	269	297	343	124	161	443	Avg.
Small SUV											
Chev. Blazer	940	297	296	168	332	263	559	102	340	468	Poor
Chev. Tracker/Suzuki Vitara	1,050	222	431	164	348	353	704	295	470	592	Vry. Pr.
Ford Escape/Mazda Tribute	505	200	317	156	256	105	286	130	350	275	Good
Honda CR-V	310	278	347	100	315	133	268	176	282	454	Good
Hyundai Santa Fe	540	283	504	86	368	164	189	171	210	255	Good
Jeep Wrangler	390	169	245	192	120	130	362	122	168	322	Vry. Gd.
Land Rover Freelander	540	269	476	123	532	185	556	262	270	403	Vry. Pr.
AVERAGE	**624**	**257**	**402**	**138**	**308**	**197**	**362**	**182**	**327**	**374**	

*Estimate based on averages.

MAINTENANCE COSTS

	PM Costs to 60,000 Miles	Water Pump	Alternator	Front Brake Pads	Starter	Fuel Injection	Fuel Pump	Struts/ Shocks	Timing Belt/ Chain	Power Steer. Pump	Relative Maint. Cost
Small SUV (cont.)											
Suzuki Grand Vitara	970	624	710	127	446	368	561	228	726	516	Vry. Pr.
Toyota RAV4	435	177	572	87	292	197	323	252	414	441	Poor
Mid-Size SUV											
Acura MDX	465	358	439	106	435	333	345	169	276	195	Avg.
BMW X5	154	230	382	146	285	165	118	268	980	395	Vry. Pr.
Buick Rendezvous	624	154	364	163	319	276	535	276	408	416	Poor
Ford Explorer/Merc. Mountaineer	660	180	259	183	215	133	336	117	388	238	Vry. Gd.
Isuzu Axiom	1,530	287	423	98	240	207	347	100	160	657	Good
Isuzu Rodeo	1,130	307	739	98	295	272	318	83	160	662	Poor
Jeep Grand Cherokee	395	200	383	231	120	80	352	99	189	287	Vry. Gd.
Jeep Liberty	410	175	410	177	156	117	309	113	536	215	Good
Land Rover Discovery	1,645	276	512	183	197	328	418	123	331	385	Poor
Lincoln Aviator	660	265	257	188	212	121	322	164	388	313	Good
Mercedes-Benz M-Class	750	456	950	182	585	277	291	125	110	601	Vry. Pr.
Mitsu. Montero/Montero Sport	1,230	356	346	128	223	203	395	210	355	634	Poor
Nissan Pathfinder	715	210	290	104	282	263	318	339	195	480	Avg.
Nissan Xterra	765	168	318	112	296	153	257	230	513	338	Good
Pontiac Aztek	624	154	364	193	319	206	535	298	408	416	Poor
Saturn VUE	535	258	438	149	338	176	434	246	260	NA	Good
Suzuki XL-7	970	624	587	127	446	327	561	228	726	516	Vry. Pr.
Toyota Highlander	435	177	567	95	289	197	308	267	414	441	Poor
Large SUV											
Cad. Escalade EXT/Chev. Avalanche	1,080	265	308	255	327	147	500	283	360	454	Poor
Cad. Escalade/Escalade ESV	915	265	308	255	327	147	450	197	297	438	Poor
Chev. Suburban/GMC Yukon XL	1,080	265	308	225	327	160	584	96	297	356	Avg.
Chev. Tahoe/GMC Yukon	1,080	265	308	225	327	160	450	106	297	356	Avg.
Chev. Trail Blazer/GMC Envoy	1,030	291	333	197	322	301	509	222	800	439	Vry. Pr.
Ford Excursion	1,055	253	274	161	192	181	327	74	495	230	Good
Ford Expedition/Lincoln Navigator	695	203	284	173	205	155	408	206	481	275	Good
Ford Explorer Sport Trac	660	180	257	169	215	162	353	74	403	248	Vry. Gd.
Toyota Sequoia	720	283	572	86	334	297	343	198	198	477	Poor
AVERAGE	**624**	**257**	**402**	**138**	**308**	**197**	**362**	**182**	**327**	**374**	

*Estimate based on averages.

SERVICE CONTRACTS

Service contracts are one of the most expensive options you can buy. In fact, service contracts are a major profit source for many dealers.

A service contract is not a warranty. It is more like an insurance plan that, in theory, covers repairs that are not covered by your warranty or that occur after the warranty runs out. They may also be referred to as an "extended warranty."

Service contracts are generally a poor value. The companies who sell contracts are very sure that, on average, your repairs will cost considerably less that what you pay for the contract—if not, they wouldn't be in business.

Tip: One alternative to buying a service contract is to deposit the cost of the contract into a savings account. If the car needs a major repair not covered by your warranty, the money in your account will cover the cost. Most likely, you'll be building up your down payment for your next car!

Here are some important questions to ask before buying a service contract:

How reputable is the company responsible for the contract? If the company offering the contract goes out of business, you will be out of luck. The company may be required to be insured but they may not. Find out if they are insured and by whom. Check with your Better Business Bureau or office of consumer affairs if you are not sure of a company's reputation. Service contracts from car and insurance companies are more likely to remain in effect than those from independent companies.

Exactly what does the contract cover and for how long? Service contracts vary considerably—different items are covered and different time limits are offered. This is true even among service contracts offered by the same company. For example, one company has plans that range from 4 years/36,000 miles maximum coverage to 6 years/100,000 miles maximum coverage, with other options for only power train coverage. Make sure you know what components are covered because if a breakdown occurs on a part that is not covered, you are responsible for the repairs.

If you plan to resell your car in a few years, you won't want to purchase a long-running service contract. Some service contracts automatically cancel when you resell the car, while others require a hefty transfer fee before extending privileges to the new owner.

Some automakers offer a "menu" format, which lets you pick the items you want covered in your service contract. Find out if the contract pays for preventive maintenance, towing, and rental car expenses. If not written into the contract, assume they are not covered.

Make sure the contract clearly specifies how you can reach the company. Knowing this before you purchase a service contract can save you time and aggravation in the future.

How will the repair bills be paid? It is best to have the service contractor pay bills directly. Some contracts require you to pay the repair bill, and reimburse you later.

Where can the car be serviced? Can you take the car to any mechanic if you have trouble on the road? What if you move?

What other costs can be expected? Most service contracts will have a deductible expense. Compare deductibles on various plans. Also, some companies charge the deductible for each individual repair while other companies pay per visit, regardless of the number of repairs being made.

TIPS FOR DEALING WITH A MECHANIC

Call around. Don't choose a shop simply because it's nearby. Calling a few shops may turn up estimates cheaper by half.

Don't necessarily go for the lowest price. A good rule is to eliminate the highest and lowest estimates; the mechanic with the highest estimate is probably charging too much, and the lowest may be cutting too many corners.

Check the shop's reputation. Call your local consumer affairs agency and the Better Business Bureau. They don't have records on every shop, but unfavorable reports on a shop disqualify it.

Look for certification. Mechanics can be certified by the National Institute for Automotive Service Excellence, an industry-wide yardstick for competence. Certification is offered in eight areas of repair and shops with certified mechanics are allowed to advertise this fact. However, make sure the mechanic working on your car is certified for the repair.

Take a look around. A well-kept shop reflects pride in workmanship. A skilled and efficient mechanic would probably not work in a messy shop.

Don't sign a blank check. The service order you sign should have specific instructions or describe your vehicle's symptoms. Avoid signing a vague work order. Be sure you are called for final approval before the shop does extra work. Many states require a written estimate signed by you and require that the shop get your permission for repairs that exceed the estimate by 10%.

Show interest. Ask about the repair. But don't act like an expert if you don't really understand what's wrong. Express your satisfaction. If you're happy with the work, compliment the mechanic and ask for him or her the next time you come in. You will get to know each other and the mechanic will get to know your vehicle.

Take a test-drive. Before you pay for a major repair, you should take the car for a test-drive. The few extra minutes you spend checking out the repair could save you a trip back to the mechanic. If you find that the problem still exists, there will be no question that the repair wasn't properly completed.

REPAIR PROTECTION BY CREDIT CARD

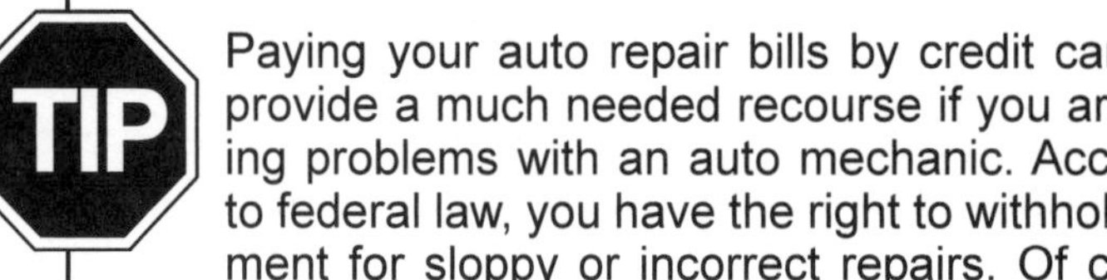

Paying your auto repair bills by credit card can provide a much needed recourse if you are having problems with an auto mechanic. According to federal law, you have the right to withhold payment for sloppy or incorrect repairs. Of course, you may withhold no more than the amount of the repair in dispute.

In order to use this right, you must first try to work out the problem with the mechanic. Also, unless the credit card company owns the repair shop (this might be the case with gasoline credit cards used at gas stations), two other conditions must be met. First, the repair shop must be in your home state (or within 100 miles of your current address), and second, the cost of repairs must be over $50. Until the problem is settled or resolved in court, the credit card company cannot charge you interest or penalties on the amount in dispute.

If you decide to take action, send a letter to the credit card company and a copy to the repair shop, explaining the details of the problem and what you want as settlement. Send the letter by certified mail with a return receipt requested.

Sometimes the credit card company or repair shop will attempt to put a "bad mark" on your credit record if you use this tactic. Legally, you can't be reported as delinquent if you've given the credit card company notice of your dispute, but a creditor can report that you are disputing your bill, which goes in your record. However, you have the right to challenge any incorrect information and add your side of the story to your file.

For more information, write to the Federal Trade Commission, Credit Practices Division, 601 Pennsylvania Avenue, NW, Washington, DC 20580.

TIRE RATINGS

Buying tires has become an infrequent task because today's radial tires last much longer than the tires of the past. Suprisingly, a tire has to perform more functions simultaneously than any other part of the car (steering, bearing the load, cushioning the ride, and stopping). And because there are nearly 1,800 tire lines to choose from, and only a few tire manufacturers, the difference in many tires may only be the brand name.

Because comparing tires is so difficult, many consumers mistakenly use price and brand name to determine quality. But there is help. The U.S. government requires tires to be rated according to their safety and expected mileage.

Treadwear, traction, and heat resistance grades are printed on the sidewall and are attached to the tire on a paper label. Ask the dealer for the grades of the tires they sell. Using this rating system, a sampling of top rated tires follows on page 58.

Treadwear: The treadwear grade gives you an idea of the mileage you can expect from a tire. It is shown in numbers—300, 310, 320, 330, and so forth. Higher numbers mean longer tire life. A tire with a grade of 200 should give you twice as much mileage as one rated 100. Driving on underinflated tires will wear out the tread faster, in addition to reducing your car's fuel economy. Because driving habits vary and tire wear is affected by regional differences in road surfaces, use the treadwear as a relative basis of comparison.

Traction: Traction grades of AA, A, B, and C describe the tire's ability to stop on wet surfaces. Tires graded AA will stop on a wet road in a shorter distance than tires graded B or C. Tires rated C have poor traction. It is also important to remember that underinflation of tires does not improve traction, as one might think. In fact, underinflation will cause the tire to run hot, which can damage the tire and increase its chances of blowing out. Drivers should refer to the vehicle owner's manual and the tire information placard on the vehicle for proper tire pressure information.

Heat Resistance: Heat resistance is also graded A, B, and C. Hot-running tires can result in blowouts or tread separation. An A rating means the tire will run cooler than one rated B or C, and it is less likely to fail if driven over long distances at highway speeds. Tires that run cooler tend to be more fuel-efficient.

BUYING TIRES

There are two important considerations in selecting the best tire: how long you plan to keep your car and whether the majority of your driving is highway or local. Remember, higher prices do not necessarily mean better tires.

Snow and all-season are two subcategories of tires. Snow tires have an open tread pattern with deep grooves. A snow tire will wear out rapidly on dry roads. Because of this wear and the inconvenience of seasonally changing tires, all-season tires are becoming popular. They are effective in snow, have good traction on wet roads, and outlast snow tires on dry roads.

You can also buy a retread. Adding the tread is the last step to building a tire. A retreader takes undamaged used tires, strips off the remaining tread and repeats this last step of the original manufacturing process.

Tread Design: Look for a tread design that is made up of independent blocks arranged in a staggered fashion. These designs have grooves that run from side to side in order to displace more water for better traction on wet

SPEED RATINGS

All passenger car tires meet government standards up to 85 mph. Some tires are tested at higher speeds because certain cars require tires that perform at higher speeds. Consult your owner's manual for the right speed rating for your car. See the tire size: P215/60 SR15. The "S" indicates the tire is tested for speeds up to 112 mph. Other letters include: "T" for up to 118 mph, "H" for up to 130 mph, "V" for up to 149 mph and "Z" for 150 mph or higher.

roads. Most all-season tires have this tread pattern.

Load Range: Check the load range to ensure that the tires are adequate for your driving needs. The maximum load is printed on each tire—the higher the load range, the more weight you can carry. To ensure that the tires are adequate, add your vehicle's weight (you'll find it in your owner's manual) and the weight of your average payload (passengers and baggage) and divide by four. This number should never exceed the tire's maximum load range.

Where to Buy: Most tires are sold at one of four outlets: independent dealers (large national chains and small stores which carry a number of brands), department stores (Sears, JC Penney), tire company stores (Goodyear, Uniroyal), and service stations.

The price of the same tire can vary depending on where you shop. Shopping around is vital to finding a good buy. Most tire ads are grouped together in the sports section of your Wednesday and Saturday daily newspaper.

You are most likely to find the best prices at independent tire dealers who carry a variety of tire brands.

Tire Care

Pump 'em Up: An estimated one-third of us are driving on underinflated tires. Because even good tires lose air, it is important to check your tire pressure at least once a month. Underinflated tires can be dangerous, use more fuel and cause premature tire failure. When checking your tires, be sure to use an accurate guage and inflate to the pressure indicated in your owner's manual, not the maximum pressure printed on your tire.

When to Replace: If any part of Lincoln's head is visible when you insert the top of a penny into a tread groove, it's time to replace the tire. While this old rule of thumb is still valid, today's tires also have a built-in wear indicator. A series of horizontal bars appear across the surface when the tread depth reaches the danger zone.

Getting the Best Price

The price of a tire is based on its size, and tires come in as many as nine sizes. For example, the list price of the same tire can range from $74.20 to $134.35, depending on its size.

The following tips can help you get the best buy.

1. Check to see which manufacturer makes the least expensive "off brand." Only twelve manufacturers produce the over 1,800 types of tires sold in the U.S.

2. Don't forget to inquire about balancing and mounting costs when comparing tire prices. In some stores, the extra charges for balancing, mounting, and valve stems can add up to more than $25. Other stores may offer them as a customer service at little or no cost.

3. Never pay list price for a tire. A good rule of thumb is to pay at least 30–40 percent off the suggested list price.

4. Use the treadwear grade the same way you would the "unit price" in a supermarket. The tire with the lowest cost per grade point is the best value. For example, if tire A costs $100 and has a treadwear grade of 300, and tire B costs $80 and has a treadwear grade of 200:

Tire A: $100÷300=$.33 per point

Tire B: $80÷200=$.40 per point

Since 33 cents is less than 40 cents, tire A is the better buy even though its initial cost is more.

TIRE PRESSURE MONITORS

TIP

Tire pressure monitors are sensors that measure the air pressure in your tires to determine if they are under-inflated. There are two types of monitors available: direct and indirect. Direct tire pressure monitors have sensors on each of the four wheels that measure rotation rates to determine if any particular tire is under-inflated. Indirect systems use a sensor in the antilock braking system to measure tire rotation rates. Indirect systems are not as accurate as direct systems and NHTSA is currently reevaluating regulations regarding these sensors. An accurate tire pressure monitor can enable you to lengthen the life of your tires, improve fuel economy and keep you safe.

HOW LONG WILL THEY LAST?

Mileage is an important factor for most of us when we purchase tires. However, few of us realize that where we live is a key factor in how long tires last. In addition to construction and design, tire wear is affected by the level of abrasive material in the road surface. Generally, the road surfaces of the West Coast, Great Lakes region, and northern New England are easiest on tires. The Appalachian and Rocky Mountain areas are usually hardest on tires.

To estimate a tire's treadlife, look at the accompanying map to determine if you live in a high, medium, or low mileage area. Then use the treadwear grade of the tires you are considering to estimate their treadlife for your area. For example, if you are considering tires with a treadwear grade of 300, you can expect those tires to get about 90,000 miles in a high mileage area, 60,000 miles in a medium mileage area, and 45,000 miles in a low mileage area.

Of course, actual mileage depends not only on where you drive but also on how you drive and whether you keep your tires properly inflated and your wheels aligned.

WHAT CAN YOU EXPECT FROM YOUR TIRES?

Treadwear Grade	High Mileage Area	Medium Mileage Area	Low Mileage Area
300	90,000	60,000	45,000
310	93,000	62,000	46,500
320	96,000	64,000	48,000
330	99,000	66,000	49,500
340	102,000	68,000	51,000
350	105,000	70,000	52,500
360	108,000	72,000	54,000
370	111,000	74,000	55,500
380	114,000	76,000	57,000
390	117,000	78,000	58,500
400	120,000	80,000	60,000
410	123,000	82,000	61,500
420	126,000	84,000	63,000
430	129,000	86,000	64,500
440	132,000	88,000	66,000
450	135,000	90,000	67,500
460	138,000	92,000	69,000
470	141,000	94,000	70,500
480	144,000	96,000	72,000
490	147,000	98,000	73,500
500	150,000	100,000	75,000
510	153,000	102,000	76,500
520	156,000	104,000	78,000
530	159,000	106,000	79,500
540	162,000	108,000	81,000
550	165,000	110,000	82,500
560	168,000	112,000	84,000

High Mileage Area

Medium Mileage Area

Low Mileage Area

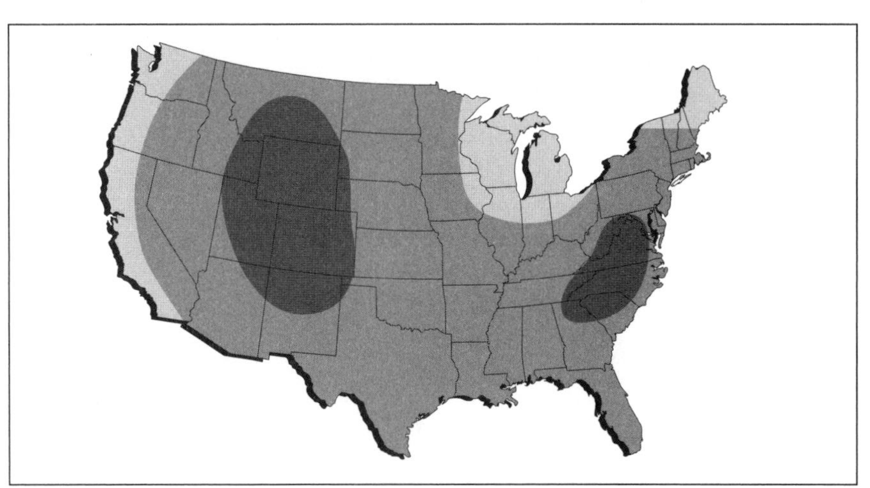

A Sampling of Top Rated Tires

Brand Name	Model	Description	Grades: Traction	Grades: Heat	Grades: Treadwear
BIG-O	LEGACY TOUR PLUS	P185,195,205 & 215/70R14 T	A	B	700
BIG-O	LEGACY TOUR PLUS	P195/65R14 T	A	B	700
BIG-O	LEGACY TOUR PLUS	P195/65R15 T	A	B	700
BIG-O	LEGACY TOUR PLUS	P205,215,225 & 235/70R15 T	A	B	700
BIG-O	LEGACY TOUR PLUS	P205,215/65R15 T	A	B	700
BIG-O	LEGACY TOUR PLUS	P215/65R16 T	A	B	700
BIG-O	LEGACY TOUR PLUS	P255 & 215/60R16 T	A	B	700
COOPER	LIFELINER STE	ALL	A	B	700
MASTERCRAFT	TOURING LX	ALL	A	B	700
MENTOR	VANTAGE TOURING LE	ALL	A	B	700
MICHELIN	X ONE with DURABLACK	ALL	A	B	700
MICHELIN	X RADIAL PLUS with DURABLACK	ALL	A	B	700
TOYO	800 ULTRA	ALL	A	B	700
BIG-O	LEGACY TOUR PLUS 60/65/70 SR	14-16	A	B	660
CAVALIER	PRIMERA 70/75 SER.	P205+	A	B	660
RIKEN	RAPTOR TOURING EDITION 70/75 SR	P205+	A	B	660
TRIVANT	PRIMERA 70/75 SER.	P205 +	A	B	660
VOGUE		S-RATED	A	B	660
AMERICAN	GOLD TOUR PLUS 70/75 ser.	THRU P195	A	B	640
AMERICAN	GOLD TOUR PLUS 70/75 ser.	THRU P195	A	B	640
CAVALIER	PRIMERA 70/75 SER.	THRU P195	A	B	640
COOPER	LIFELINER STE	13	A	B	640
CORDOVAN	GRAND PRIX TOURING LXE	ALL OTHERS	A	B	640
DOUGLAS	TOURING	ALL	A	B	640
GOODYEAR	AQUATRED 3	ALL OTHERS	AA	B	640
HALLMARK	ULTRA TOURING GT	ALL	A	B	640
KELLY	AQUA TOUR	ALL	A	B	640
LEE	ULTRA TOURING GT	ALL	A	B	640
MASTERCRAFT	TOURING LX	13 ONLY	A	B	640
MULTIMILE	GRAND AM TOURING LSS	ALL OTHERS	A	B	640
RIKEN	RAPTOR TOURING EDITION 70/75 SR	THRU P195	A	B	640
SIGMA	SUPREME TOURING SSR	ALL OTHERS	A	B	640
TRIVANT	PRIMERA 70/75 SER.	THRU P195	A	B	640
CONTINENTAL	CONTI TOURING CONTACT CT85	ALL	A	B	620
CONTINENTAL	TOURING GT8000	ALL	A	B	620
COOPER	LIFELINER TOURING SLE T-RATED	ALL	A	B	620
DAYTON	DAYTONA PREM GT	ALL	A	B	620
DEAN	TOURING EDITION	ALL	A	B	620
GENERAL	AMERI'TOUR	ALL	A	B	620
GOODYEAR	AQUATRED 3	13	AA	B	620
HANKOOK	MILEAGE PLUS GT	ALL	AA	A	620
HERCULES	MEGA TOURING LXT (SR)	ALL	A	B	620
MENTOR	VANTAGE TOURING	ALL	A	B	620
MICHELIN	X ONE	ALL	A	B	620
MICHELIN	X ONE ZP	ALL	A	B	620
MICHELIN	X RADIAL PLUS	ALL	A	B	620
MULTIMILE	WILD COUNTRY XRT	ALL	B	C	620
PIRELLI	P-3000 CINTURATO 55/60/65	ALL	A	A	620
PIRELLI	P-3000 CINTURATO 70/75	ALL	A	B	620
ROAD KING	PREMIUM GT	ALL	A	B	620
STARFIRE	MENTOR VANTAGE TOURING	ALL	A	B	620
AMERICAN	GOLD TOUR PLUS 60/65 series	ALL	A	B	600
AURORA	H715	ALL	A	B	600
BIG-O	LEGACY TOUR PLUS 75/80 SR	14-16	A	B	600
CAVALIER	PRIMERA 60/65 SER.	ALL	A	B	600
CORDOVAN	GRAND PRIX TOURING LXE	75 SR	A	B	600
FISK	FISK CLASSIC 60/65 SER.	ALL	A	B	600
MULTIMILE	GRAND AM TOURING LSS	75 (SR)	A	B	600
RIKEN	RAPTOR TOURING EDITION 60/65 SR	ALL	A	B	600
SIGMA	SUPREME TOURING SSR	75 SR	A	B	600
TRIVANT	PRIMERA 60/65 SER.	ALL	A	B	600
VANDERBILT	TURBO TECH TOURING A/S	ALL			

For a complete listing of all the tires on the market, you can call the Auto Safety Hot Line toll free, at 800-424-9393 or 800-424-9153(TTY). (In Washington, DC, the number is 202-366-7800.) Or, go to www.nhtsa.dot.gov.

IN THIS CHAPTER

INTRODUCTION

Insurance is a big part of ownership expenses, yet it's often forgotten in the showroom. As you shop, remember that the car's design and accident history may affect your insurance rates. Some cars cost less to insure because experience has shown that they are damaged less, less expensive to fix after a collision, or stolen less. This chapter provides you with the information you need to make a wise insurance purchase. We discuss the different types of insurance, offer special tips on reducing this cost, and include information on occupant injury, theft, and bumper ratings—all factors that can affect your insurance.

Shop Around: More and more consumers are saving hundreds of dollars by shopping around for insurance. In order to be a good comparison shopper, you need to know a few things about automobile insurance.

A number of factors determine what these coverages will cost you. A car's design can affect both the chances and severity of an accident. A car with a well-designed bumper may escape damage altogether in a low-speed crash. Some cars are easier to repair than others or may have less expensive parts. Cars with four doors tend to be damaged less than cars with two doors.

The reason one car may get a discount on insurance while another receives a surcharge also depends upon the way it is traditionally driven. Sports cars, for example, are usually surcharged due, in part, to the typical driving habits of their owners. Four-door sedans and station wagons generally merit discounts.

Insurance companies use this and other information to determine whether to offer a discount on insurance premiums for a particular car or whether to levy a surcharge.

Not all companies offer discounts or surcharges, and many cars receive neither. Some companies offer a discount or impose a surcharge on collision premiums only. Others apply discounts and surcharges on both collision and comprehensive coverage. Discounts and surcharges usually range from 10–30 percent. Remember that one company may offer a discount on a particular car while another may not. Check with your insurance company to find out whether they have a rating program.

TIP

TYPES OF COVERAGE

Collision Insurance: This pays for the damage to your car after an accident.

Comprehensive Physical Damage Insurance: This pays for damages when your car is stolen or damaged by fire, flood, or other perils.

Property Damage Liability: This pays claims and defense costs if your car damages someone else's property.

Medical Payments Insurance: This pays for your car's occupants' medical expenses resulting from an accident.

Bodily Injury Liability: This provides money to pay claims against you and to pay for the cost of your legal defense if your car injures or kills someone.

Uninsured Motorists Protection: This pays for injuries caused by an uninsured or a hit-and-run driver.

Reducing Insurance Costs

After you have shopped around and found the best deal by comparing the costs of different coverages, there are some other factors you can consider that will affect your insurance bill.

Your Annual Mileage: The more you drive, the more your vehicle will be "exposed" to a potential accident. The insurance cost for a car rarely used will be less than the cost for a frequently used car. For some companies, 7,500 miles is the cutoff for low use.

Where You Drive: If you regularly drive and park in the city, you will most likely pay more than if you drive in rural areas.

Youthful Drivers: Usually the highest premiums are paid by male drivers under the age of 25. Whether or not the under-25-year-old male is married also affects insurance rates. (Married males pay less.) As the driver gets older, rates are lowered.

In addition to shopping around, take advantage of certain discounts to reduce your insurance costs. Most insurance companies offer discounts of 5 to 30 percent on various parts of your insurance bill. The availability of discounts varies among companies and often depends on where you live. Many consumers do not benefit from these discounts simply because they don't ask about them.

To determine whether you are getting all the discounts that you're entitled to, ask your insurance company for a complete list of the discounts that it offers.

Here are some of the most common insurance discounts:

Driver Education/Defensive Driving Courses: Many insurance companies offer discounts to young people who have successfully completed a state-approved driver education course. Typically, this can mean a $40 reduction in the cost of coverage. Also, a discount of 5–15 percent is available in some states to those who complete a defensive driving course.

Good Student Discounts: Many insurance companies offer discounts of up to 25 percent on insurance to full-time high school or college students who are in the upper 20 percent of their class, on the dean's list, or have a B or better grade point average.

Good Driver Discounts: Many companies will offer discounts to drivers with an accident and violation-free record, (or no incidents in 3 years).

Mature Driver Credit: Drivers ages 50 and older may qualify for up to a 10 percent discount or a lower price bracket.

Sole Female Driver: Some companies offer discounts of 10 percent for females, ages 30 to 64, who are the only driver in a household.

Non-Drinkers and Non-Smokers: A limited number of companies offer incentives ranging from 10–25 percent to those who abstain.

Farmer Discounts: Many companies offer farmers either a discount of 10–30 percent or a lower price bracket.

Car Pooling: Commuters sharing driving may qualify for discounts of 5–25 percent or a lower price bracket.

Insuring Driving Children: Children away at school don't drive the family car very often, so it's usually less expensive to

! DON'T SPEED !

Besides endangering the lives of your passengers and other drivers, speeding tickets will increase your insurance premium. It only takes one speeding ticket to lose your "preferred" or "good driver" discount, which requires a clean driving record. Two or more speeding tickets or accidents can increase your premium by 40% to 200%. Some insurers may simply drop your coverage. According to the Insurance Institute for Highway Safety (IIHS), you are 17% more likely to be in an accident if you have just one speeding ticket. Insurance companies know this and will charge you for it.

insure them on the parents' policy rather than separately. If you do insure them separately, discounts of 10–40 percent or a lower price bracket are available.

Desirable Cars: Premiums are usually much higher for cars with high collision rates or that are the favorite target of thieves.

Anti-Theft Device Credits: Discounts of 5 to 15 percent are offered in some states for cars equipped with a hood lock and an alarm or a disabling device (active or passive) that prevents the car from being started.

Multipolicy and Multicar Policy Discount: Some companies offer discounts of up to 10–20 percent for insuring your home and auto with the same company, or more than one car.

Long-Term Policy Renewal: Although not available in all states, some companies offer price breaks of 5–20 percent to customers who renew a long-term policy.

First Accident Allowance: Some insurers offer a "first accident allowance," which guarantees that if a customer achieves five accident-free years, his or her rates won't go up after the first at-fault accident.

Deductibles: Opting for the largest reasonable deductible is the obvious first step in reducing premiums. Increasing your deductible to $500 from $200 could cut your collision premium about 20 percent. Raising the deductible to $1,000 from $200 could lower your premium about 45 percent. The discounts may vary by company.

Collision Coverage: The older the car, the less the need for collision insurance. Consider dropping collision insurance entirely on an older car. Regardless of how much coverage you carry, the insurance company will only pay up to the car's "book value." For example, if your car requires $1,000 in repairs, but its "book value" is only $500, the insurance company is required to pay only $500.

Uninsured Motorist Coverage/Optional Coverage: The necessity of both of these policies depends upon the extent of your health insurance coverage. In states where they are not required, consumers with applicable health insurance may not want uninsured motorist coverage. Also, those with substantial health insurance coverage may not want an optional medical payment policy.

Rental Cars: If you regularly rent cars, special coverage on your personal auto insurance can cover you while renting for far less than rental agencies offer.

Organizations: If you are a member of AARP, AAA, the military, a union, a professional group, an alumni association, or similar organization, you may be able to get a discount. Often insurance companies will enter joint ventures with organizations.

AUTO THEFT

The Highway Loss Data Institute regularly compiles statistics on motor vehicle thefts. Using the frequency of theft and the loss resulting from the theft, HLDI publishes an index based on "relative average loss payments per insured vehicle year." The list below includes the most and least stolen cars among the 2003 models.

Most Stolen		Least Stolen	
Cadillac Escalade	1099	Buick LeSabre	10
Chevrolet Corvette Conv.	492	Buick Park Avenue	10
Lincoln Navigator 4x4	464	Volvo 70 Series	12
BMW X5	438	Mercury Grand Marquis	17
BMW 3 Series Conv.	416	Mazda Tribute	19
Lincoln Navigator 4x2	409	Saturn L/LW	20
Lexus LX 470	403	Honda Odyssey	24
Chevrolet Corvette Coupe	390	Oldsmobile Silhouette	25
Lexus IS 300	387	Buick Century	28
Audi A4	361	Saturn L/LW	28

BUMPERS

The main purpose of the bumper is to protect your car in low-speed collisions. Despite this intention, most of us have been victims of a $200 to $400 repair bill resulting from a seemingly minor impact. Since most bumpers offered little or no damage protection in low-speed crashes, the federal government used to require that automakers equip cars with bumpers capable of withstanding up to 5 mph crashes with no damage. Unfortunately, this is no longer the case.

In the early eighties, while under pressure from car companies, the government rolled back the requirement that bumpers protect cars in collisions up to 5 mph. Now, car companies only build bumpers to protect cars in 2.5 mph collisions—about the speed at which we walk. This rollback has cost consumers millions of dollars in increased insurance premiums and repair costs. While the rollback satisfied car companies, most car owners were unhappy.

To let consumers know that today's bumpers offer widely varying amounts of protection in 5-mph collisions, each year the Insurance Institute for Highway Safety tests bumpers to see how well they prevent damage. Thankfully, some automobile manufacturers are betting that consumers still want better bumpers on at least some of their models.

These results are rather startling when you consider that the sole purpose of a bumper is to protect a car from damage in low-speed collisions. Only about one-third of the cars tested to date have bumpers which actually prevented damage in front and rear 5 mph collisions. As the Institute's figures show, there is no correlation between the price of the car and how well the bumper worked.

Unfortunately, we can't simply look at a bumper and determine how good it will be at doing its job—protecting a car from inevitable bumps. The solution to this problem is quite simple—simply require carmakers to tell the consumer the highest speed at which their car could be crashed with no damage.

Following are the results of the IIHS bumper crash tests. We have included some of the best and worst from recent models. This will give you an indication of the huge differences in repair costs from the exact same accident. For more test results, you can visit the Insurance Institute for Highway Safety on the internet at www.highwaysafety.org.

BUMPER BASHING—DAMAGE REPAIR COSTS FOR RECENT MODELS IN 5 MPH CRASH TESTS

Source: Insurance Institute for Highway Safety	Front into Flat Barrier	Rear into Flat Barrier	Front into Angle Barrier	Rear into Pole	Total
The Best					
2002 Audi A4	$0	$0	$494	$371	$865
2003 Toyota Corolla	$289	$234	$337	$322	$1,182
2003 Mazda 6	$151	$521	$398	$297	$1,367
2003 Subaru Forester	$359	$110	$717	$271	$1,457
2003 Honda Pilot	$325	$404	$449	$438	$1,616
2002 Lexus ES 300	$234	$557	$522	$553	$1,866
2002 Toyota Camry	$243	$384	$725		$2,112
2003 Honda Element	$512	$346	$697	$594	$2,149
The Worst					
2002 Kia Sedona	$4,382	$1,304	$1,271	$3,025	$9,982
2002 Jaguar X-Type	$1,254	$739	$2,539	$2,502	$7,034
2002 Honda CR-V	$505	$2,505	$870	$2,727	$6,607
2003 Kia Sorento	$1,125	$1,325	$1,860	$2,273	$6,583
2004 Cadillac SRX	$388	$985	$2,390	$2,814	$6,577
2002 Land Rover Freelander	$932	$2,727	$719	$2,096	$6,474
2002 Buick Rendezvous	$246	$865	$1,219	$3,957	$6,287
2002 Jeep Liberty	$833	$1,878	$1,727	$1,627	$6,065
2003 Infiniti G35	$679	$1,824	$1,431	$1,988	$5,922

SAFETY BELT MYTHS

Myth: *"I don't want to be trapped by a seat belt. It's better to be thrown free in an accident."*

Fact: The chance of being killed is 25 times greater if you're ejected. A safety belt will keep you from plunging through the windshield, smashing into trees, rocks, or other cars, scraping along the ground, or getting run over by your own or anothers vehicle. If you are wearing your belt, you're far more likely to be conscious after an accident to free yourself and other passengers.

Myth: *"Pregnant women should not wear safety belts."*

Fact: According to the American Medical Association, "Both the pregnant mother and the fetus are safer, provided the lap belt is worn as low on the pelvis as possible."

Myth: *"I don't need it. In case of an accident, I can brace myself with my hands."*

Fact: At 35 mph, the impact of a crash on you and your passengers is brutal. There's no way your arms and legs can brace you against that kind of collision—the speed and force are just too great. The force of impact at only 10 mph is roughly equivalent to the force of catching a 200-pound bag of cement dropped from a first-floor window.

Myth: *"I just don't believe it will ever happen to me."*

Fact: Every one of us can expect to be in a crash once every 10 years. For 1 out of 20 of us, it will be a serious crash. For 1 out of 60 born today, it will be fatal.

TIP

YOUNG DRIVERS

Each year, teenagers account for about 15 percent of highway deaths. According to the Insurance Institute for Highway Safety (IIHS), the highest driver death rate per 100,000 people is among 18-year-olds. Clearly, parents need to make sure their children are fully prepared to be competent, safe drivers before letting them out on the road. All states issue learner's permits. However, only 35 states and the District of Columbia require permits before getting a driver's license. It isn't difficult for teenagers to get a license and only 14 states prohibit teenagers from driving during night and early morning. Call your MVA for your state's young driver laws.

COMPLAINTS

Chevrolet Monte Carlo

Audi A4 Cabriolet

Volkswagen Beetle

Cadillac Escalade ESV

IN THIS CHAPTER

INTRODUCTION

Americans spend billions of dollars on motor vehicle repairs every year. While many of those repairs are satisfactory, there are times when getting your vehicle fixed can be a very difficult process. In fact, vehicle defects and repairs are the number one cause of consumer complaints in the U.S., according to the Federal Trade Commission. This chapter is designed to help you resolve your complaint, whether it's for a new vehicle still under warranty or for one you've had for years. In addition, we offer a guide to arbitration, the names and addresses of consumer groups, federal agencies, and the manufacturers themselves. Finally, we tell you how to take the important step of registering your complaint with the U.S. Department of Transportation.

No matter what your complaint, keep accurate records. Copies of the following items are indispensable in helping to resolve your problems:

☑ your service invoices

☑ bills you have paid

☑ letters you have written to the manufacturer or the repair facility owner

☑ written repair estimates from your independent mechanic.

RESOLVING COMPLAINTS

If you are having trouble, here are some basic steps to help you resolve your problem:

1 First, return your vehicle to the repair facility that did the work. Bring a written list of the problems and make sure that you keep a copy of the list. Give the repair facility a reasonable opportunity to examine your vehicle and attempt to fix it. Speak directly to the service manager (not to the service writer who wrote up your repair order), and ask him or her to test drive the vehicle with you so that you can point out the problem.

2 If that doesn't resolve the problem, take the vehicle to a diagnostic center for an independent examination. This may cost $45 to $60. Get a written statement defining the problem and outlining how it may be fixed. Give your repair shop a copy. If your vehicle is under warranty, do not allow any warranty repair by an independent mechanic; you may not be reimbursed by the manufacturer.

3 If your repair shop does not respond to the independent assessment, present your problem to a mediation panel. These panels hear both sides of the story and try to come to a resolution.

If the problem is with a new vehicle dealer, or if you feel that the manufacturer is responsible, you may be able to use one of the manufacturer's mediation programs.

If the problem is solely with an independent dealer, a local Better Business Bureau (BBB) may be able to mediate your complaint. It may also offer an arbitration hearing. In any case, the BBB should enter your complaint into its files on that establishment.

When contacting any mediation program, determine how long the process takes, who makes the final decision, whether you are bound by that decision, and whether the program handles all problems or only warranty complaints.

4 If there are no mediation programs in your area, contact private consumer groups, local government agencies, or your local "action line" newspaper columnist, newspaper editor, or radio or TV broadcaster. A phone call or letter from them may persuade a repair facility to take action. Send a copy of your letter to the repair shop.

5 One of your last resorts is to bring a lawsuit against the dealer, manufacturer, or repair facility in small claims court. The fee for filing such an action is usually small, and you generally act as your own attorney, saving attorney's fees. There is a monetary limit on the amount you can claim, which varies from state to state. Your local consumer affairs office, state attorney general's office, or the clerk of the court can tell you how to file such a suit.

6 Finally, talk with an attorney. It's best to select an attorney who is familiar with handling automotive problems. Call the lawyer referral service listed in the telephone directory and ask for the names of attorneys who deal with automobile problems. If you can't afford an attorney, contact the Legal Aid Society.

WARRANTY COMPLAINTS

If your vehicle is under warranty or you are having problems with a factory-authorized dealership, here are some special guidelines:

1 Have the warranty available to show the dealer. Make sure you call the problem to the dealer's attention before the end of the warranty period.

2 If you are still dissatisfied after giving the dealer a reasonable opportunity to fix your vehicle, contact the manufacturer's representative (also called the zone representative) in your area. This person can authorize the dealer to make repairs or take other steps to resolve the dispute. Your dealer will have your zone representative's name and telephone number. Explain the problem and ask for a meeting and a personal inspection of your vehicle.

3 If you can't get satisfaction from the zone representative, call or write the manufacturer's owner relations department. Your owner's manual contains this phone number and address. In each case, as you move up the chain, indicate the steps you have already taken.

4 Your next option is to present your problem to a complaint handling panel or to the arbitration program in which the manufacturer of your vehicle participates.

If you complain of a problem during the warranty period, you have a right to have the problem fixed even after the warranty runs out. If your warranty has not been honored, you may be able to "revoke acceptance," which means that you return the vehicle to the dealer. If you are successful, you may be entitled to a replacement vehicle or to a full refund of the purchase price and reimbursement of legal fees under the Magnuson-Moss Warranty Act. Or, if you are covered by one of the state lemon laws, you may be able to return the vehicle and receive a refund or replacement from the manufacturer.

NEED HELP?

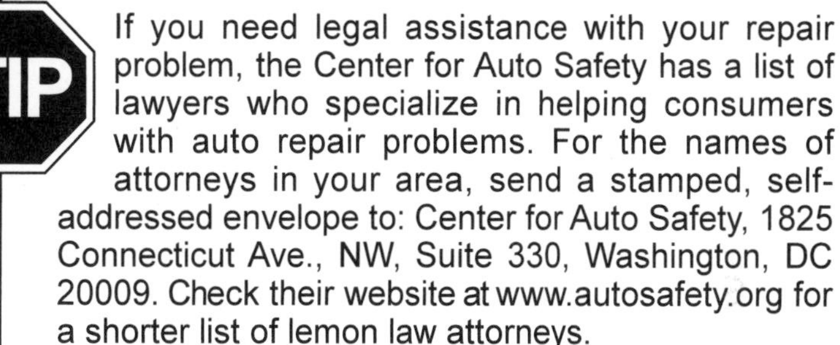

If you need legal assistance with your repair problem, the Center for Auto Safety has a list of lawyers who specialize in helping consumers with auto repair problems. For the names of attorneys in your area, send a stamped, self-addressed envelope to: Center for Auto Safety, 1825 Connecticut Ave., NW, Suite 330, Washington, DC 20009. Check their website at www.autosafety.org for a shorter list of lemon law attorneys.

In addition, the Center has published *The Lemon Book*, a detailed 368-page guide to resolving automobile complaints. The book is available for $17.50 directly from the Center.

Attorneys Take Note: For information on litigation assistance provided by the Center for Auto Safety, including *The Lemon Law Litigation Manual*, please contact the Center for Auto Safety at the above address.

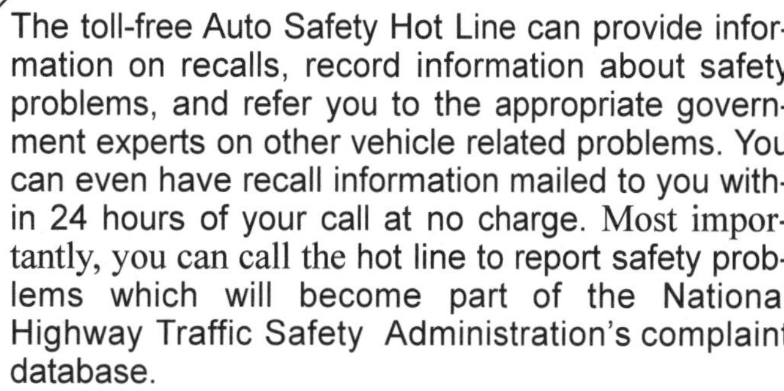

AUTO SAFETY HOT LINE
800-424-9393
IN WASHINGTON, DC: 202-366-0123
TTY FOR HEARING IMPAIRED:
800-424-9153 OR DC: 202-366-7800

The toll-free Auto Safety Hot Line can provide information on recalls, record information about safety problems, and refer you to the appropriate government experts on other vehicle related problems. You can even have recall information mailed to you within 24 hours of your call at no charge. Most importantly, you can call the hot line to report safety problems which will become part of the National Highway Traffic Safety Administration's complaint database.

COMPLAINT INDEX

Thanks to the efforts of the Center for Auto Safety, we are able to provide you with the vehicle complaints on file with the National Highway Traffic Safety Administration (NHTSA). Each year, thousands of Americans call the government in order to register complaints about their vehicles. The federal government collects this information but has never released it to the public.

The complaint index is the result of our analysis of these complaints. It is based on a ratio of the number of complaints for each vehicle to the sales of that vehicle. In order to predict the expected complaint performance of the 2004 models, we have examined the complaint history of that car's series. The term series refers to the fact that when a manufacturer introduces a new model, that vehicle remains essentially unchanged, on average, for four to six years. For example, the Ford Crown Victoria was redesigned in 1998 and remains essentially the same car for 2004. As such, we have compiled the complaint experience for that series in order to give you some information to use in deciding which car to buy. For those vehicles just introduced, we do not yet have enough data to develop a complaint index.

The following table presents the projected best and worst complaint ratings for the 2004 models for which we can develop ratings. Higher index numbers mean the vehicle generated a greater number of complaints. Lower numbers indicate fewer complaints. We can only rate vehicles whose models haven't changed since 2001. New cars do not have enough data to be rated.

2004 PROJECTED COMPLAINT RATINGS

THE BEST	
Chrysler Sebring Convertible	211
GMC Yukon XL	318
Suzuki XL-7	451
Lexus IS 300	508
Toyota Sequoia	642
Toyota Land Cruiser	872
Mercedes-Benz C-Class	981
Mitsubishi Montero Sport	1015
Lexus GS 300	1165
Lexus LS 430	1175
Acura MDX	1351
Ford Crown Victoria	1564
Buick Century	1595
Nissan Sentra	1753
Nissan Pathfinder	1834
Toyota Tacoma	1856
Buick Regal	1917
Pontiac Sunfire	1965
Chevrolet Cavalier	2034
Mercedes-Benz M-Class	2077
Chevrolet Tahoe	2081
Toyota Avalon	2083
Lincoln Town Car	2160
Chevrolet Tracker	2186
Mercury Grand Marquis	2351

THE WORST	
Subaru Impreza	27952
Infiniti I35	21372
Audi A4	18943
Ford Escape	14441
Ford Focus	13436
Acura RSX	11657
Pontiac Aztek	11537
Ford Excursion	10277
Mitsubishi Eclipse	9691
Jeep Liberty	9450
Chevrolet Corvette	9214
Chevrolet Blazer	7938
Suzuki Grand Vitara	7385
Volkswagen Passat	6687
Honda Insight	6496
Volkswagen Jetta	6152
Acura TL	6058
Suzuki Vitara	5913
Land Rover Freelander	5589
Audi A6	5571
Dodge Caravan	5561
Jeep Grand Cherokee	5235
Honda S2000	5162
GMC Yukon	5094
Dodge Neon	5045

CENTER FOR AUTO SAFETY

Every year automobile manufacturers spend millions of dollars making their voices heard in government decision making. For example, General Motors and Ford have large staffs in Detroit and Washington that work solely to influence government activity. But who looks out for the consumer?

For over 30 years, the non-profit Center for Auto Safety (CAS) has told the consumer's story to government agencies, to Congress, and to the courts. Its efforts focus on all consumers rather than only those with individual complaints.

CAS was established in 1970 by Ralph Nader and Consumers Union. As consumer concerns about auto safety issues expanded, so did the work of CAS. It became independent of its founders in 1972. CAS' activities include:

Initiating Safety Recalls: CAS analyzes over 50,000 consumer complaints each year. By following problems as they develop, CAS requests government investigations and recalls of defective vehicles. CAS was responsible for the Ford Pinto faulty gas tank recall, the Firestone 500 steel-belted radial tire recall, and the record recall of over three million Evenflo One Step child seats.

Representing the Consumer in Washington: CAS follows the activities of federal agencies and Congress to ensure that they carry out their responsibilities to the American taxpayer. CAS brings a consumer's point of view to vehicle safety policies and rule-making. Since 1970, CAS has submitted more than 500 petitions and comments on federal safety standards.

One major effort on safety standards has been the successful fight to get airbags in every car. After opposing airbags for decades, the auto industry now can't get enough lifesaving airbags in cars with some models having eight airbags. With airbags to protect consumers in front and side crashes, CAS is now working to strengthen weak roofs that cannot support a vehicle's own weight and crush in rollovers that result in 27,000 deaths and serious injuries each year.

In 1992, CAS uncovered a fire defect that dwarfed the highly publicized flammability of the Ford Pinto. It had to do with the side saddle gas tanks on full size 1973–87 GM pickups and 1988–90 crew cabs that tend to explode on impact. Over 2,000 people have been killed in fire crashes involving these trucks. After mounting a national campaign to warn consumers to steer clear of these GM fire hazards, the U.S. Department of Transportation granted CAS' petition and conducted one of its biggest defect investigations in history. The result—GM was asked to recall its pickups. GM, sadly, denied this request.

Exposing Secret Warranties: CAS played a prominent role in the disclosure of secret warranties, "policy adjustments," as they are called by manufacturers. These occur when an automaker agrees to pay for repair of certain defects beyond the warranty period but refuses to notify consumers.

Lemon Laws: CAS' work on Lemon Laws aided in the enactment of state laws which make it easier to return a defective new automobile and get money back.

Tire Ratings: After a suspension between 1982 and 1984, consumers have reliable treadwear ratings to help them get the most miles for their dollar. CAS's lawsuit overturned DOT's revocation of this valuable tire information program.

Initiating Legal Action: When CAS has exhausted other means of obtaining relief for consumer problems, it will initi-

CENTER FOR AUTO SAFETY ONLINE

The Center for Auto Safety has a website at www.autosafety.org to provide information to consumers and to organize consumer campaigns against auto companies on safety defects. Detailed packages of information and advice on defects in specific makes and models are on CAS's website. Consumers with lemons and safety defects can file electronic complaints with CAS and get referred to lemon lawyers.

www.autosafety.org

ate legal action. For example, in 1978 when the Department of Energy attempted to raise the price of gasoline four cents per gallon without notice or comment, CAS succeeded in stopping this illegal move through a lawsuit, thus saving consumers $2 billion for the six-month period that the action was delayed.

A 1985 CAS lawsuit against the Environmental Protection Agency (EPA) forced the EPA to recall polluting cars, rather than let companies promise to make cleaner cars in the future. As part of the settlement, GM (which was responsible for the polluting cars) funded a $7 million methanol bus demonstration program in New York City.

CAS' latest legal victory came in 2003 when they overturned a Department of Transportation (DOT) rule that allowed auto makers to install indirect tire pressure monitors in cars that were accurate half the time. Instead, DOT will have to require auto makers to use more accurate direct tire pressure monitors that identify, on the dash, when a particular tire has low pressure.

Help CAS help you: CAS depends on public support. Annual consumer membership is $20 with *The Lemon Book.* All contributions to this nonprofit organization are tax-deductible. Annual membership includes a quarterly newsletter called "Lemon Times." To join, send a check to:

Center for Auto Safety
1825 Connecticut Ave., NW, #330
Washington, DC
20009-5708

Consumer Groups and Government

Below are the names of additional consumer groups which you may find helpful:

Advocates for Highway and Auto Safety
750 First St., NE, Suite 901
Washington, DC 20002
(202) 408-1711/408-1699 fax
www.saferoads.org
An alliance of consumer, health and safety groups, and insurance companies.

Consumer Action/San Fran.
717 Market St., Suite 310
San Francisco, CA 94103
(415) 777-9635
www.consumer-action.org
General problems of California residents.

Consumers for Auto Reliability and Safety
926 J St., Suite 523
Sacramento, CA 95814
(530) 759-9440
www.carconsumers.com
Auto safety, airbags, and lemon laws.

SafetyBelt Safe, U.S.A.
P.O. Box 553
Altadena, CA 91003
(800) 745-SAFE or (310)222-6860
www.carseat.org
Excellent information and training on child safety seats and safety belt usage.

Kids N Cars
14413 Norwood
Leawood, KS 66224
(913) 851-0008/851-0086 fax
www.kidsncars.org
Safety and advocacy related to protecting children in and around cars.

Several federal agencies conduct automobile-related programs. Listed below is each agency with a description of the type of work it performs and how to contact them. Useful web sites are also listed.

National Highway Traffic Safety Administration
400 Seventh St., SW, Room 5232
Washington, DC 20590
(800) DASH-2-DOT
www.nhtsa.dot.gov
NHTSA issues safety and fuel economy standards for new motor vehicles; investigates safety defects and enforces recall of defective vehicles and equipment; conducts research and demonstration programs on vehicle safety, fuel economy, driver safety, and automobile inspection and repair; provides grants for state highway safety programs in areas such as police traffic services, driver education and licensing, emergency medical services, pedestrian safety, and alcohol abuse.

Environmental Protection Agency
401 M St., SW
Washington, DC 20460
(202) 260-2090
www.epa.gov
EPA's responsibilities include setting and enforcing air and noise emission standards for motor vehicles and measuring fuel economy in new vehicles (EPA Fuel Economy Guide).

Federal Trade Commission
CRC-240
Washington, DC 20580
(877) FTC-HELP
www.ftc.gov
The FTC regulates advertising and credit practices, marketing abuses, and professional services and ensures that products are properly labeled (as in fuel economy ratings). The commission covers unfair or deceptive trade practices in motor vehicle sales and repairs, as well as in non-safety defects.

U.S. Department of Justice
Office of Consumer Litigation
P.O. Box 386
Washington, DC 20044
(202) 307-0092
www.usdoj.gov
The DOJ enforces the federal law that requires manufacturers to label new automobiles and forbids removal or alteration of labels before delivery to consumers. Labels must contain make, model, vehicle identification number, dealer's name, suggested base price, manufacturer option costs, and manufacturer's suggested retail price.

AUTOMOBILE MANUFACTURERS

Acura Automobile Division
Mr. Richard Colliver
Exec.V. P. of Sales
1919 Torrance Blvd.
Torrance, CA 90501-2746
(310) 783-2000

Audi of America
Mr. Len Hunt
Vice President
3800 Hamlin Road
Auburn Hills, MI 48326
(248) 340-5000

BMW of North America, Inc.
Mr. Tom Purves
Chairman and CEO
300 Chestnut Ridge Road
Woodcliff Lake, NJ 07677

DaimlerChrysler Corporation
Dieter Zetsche
President and CEO
1000 Chrysler Drive
Auburn Hills, MI 48326-2766
(248) 576-5741

Ford Motor Company
Mr. William Clay Ford, Jr.
Chairman
The American Road
Dearborn, MI 48126
(313) 322-3000

General Motors Corporation
Mr. G. Richard Wagoner, Jr.
Chairman and CEO
100 Renaissance Center
Detroit, MI 48243
(313) 556-5000

American Honda Motor Co.
Mr. Koichi Amemiya
President and Chairman
1919 Torrance Blvd.
Torrance, CA 90501-2746
(310) 783-2000

Hyundai Motor America
Mr. Finbarr O'Neill
President and CEO
10550 Talbert Avenue
Fountain Valley, CA 92728
(714) 965-3000

Infiniti
Mr. Marc McNabb
Vice President and General Mgr.
18501 S. Figueroa St.
Gardena, CA 90248
(310) 532-3111

American Isuzu Motors Inc.
Mr. Gaku Nitta
President and CEO
13340 183rd St.
Cerritos, CA 90703
(562) 229-7000

Kia Motors America, Inc.
Mr. B.M. Ahn
President and CEO
P.O. Box 52410
Irvine, CA 92619-2410
(949) 470-7000

Land Rover of America
Mr. Mike O'Driscoll
President
One Premier Place
Irvine, CA 92618

Lexus/Toyota Motor Sales, U.S.A., Inc.
Mr. Denny Clements
Group Vice President & GM
19001 S. Western Ave.
Torrance, CA 90509-2991
(310) 328-2075

Mazda Motor of America, Inc.
Mr. Jim O'Sullivan
President and CEO
7755 Irvine Center Drive,
PO Box 19734
Irvine, CA 92623-9734
(800) 222-5500

Mercedes-Benz of N.A.
Mr. Paul Halata
President and CEO
1 Mercedes Drive
Montvale, NJ 07645
(800) 367-6372

Mitsubishi Motor Sales
Mr. Hiroshi Yajima
Chairman and CEO
6400 Katella Ave.
Cypress, CA 90630-0064
(714) 372-6000

Nissan Motor Corp. U.S.A.
Mr. Jed Connolly
Sr. V.P. of Sales and Marketing
18501 S. Figueroa St.
Gardena, CA 90248
(310) 532-3111

Saab Cars USA, Inc.
Mr. Daniel Chasins
President and CEO
4405-A International Drive
Norcross, GA 30093
(770) 279-0100

Subaru of America, Inc.
Mr. Takao Saito
Chairman and CEO
Subaru Plaza
Cherry Hill, NJ 08034-6000
(609) 488-8500

American Suzuki Motor Corp.
Mr. Rick Suzuki
President
3251 E. Imperial Hwy.
Brea, CA 92821
(714) 996-7040

Toyota Motor Sales, U.S.A., Inc.
Mr. Yoshimi Inaba
President and CEO
19001 S. Western Avenue
Torrance, CA 90509-2991
(310) 468-4000

Volkswagen of America, Inc.
Mr. Gerd Klauss
President and CEO
3800 Hamlin Road
Auburn Hills, MI 48326
(248) 340-5000

Volvo Cars of North America
Mr. Vic Doolan
President and CEO
7 Volvo Drive
Rockleigh, NJ 07647
(201) 768-7300

LEMON LAWS

Sometimes, despite our best efforts, we buy a vehicle that just doesn't work right. There may be little problem after little problem, or perhaps one big problem that never seems to be fixed. Because of the "sour" taste that such vehicles leave in the mouths of consumers who buy them, these vehicles are known as "lemons."

In the past, it's been difficult to obtain a refund or replacement if a vehicle was a lemon. The burden of proof was left to the consumer. Because it is hard to define exactly what constitutes a lemon, many lemon owners were unable to win a case against a manufacturer. And when they won, consumers had to pay for their attorneys giving them less than if they had traded in their lemon.

Thanks to "Lemon Laws" passed by all states, lemon-aide is available when consumers get stuck with a lemon. Although there are some important state-to-state variations, all of the laws have similarities: They establish a period of coverage, usually two years from delivery or the written warranty period, whichever is shorter; they may require some form of noncourt arbitration; and most importantly they define a lemon. In most states a lemon is a new car, truck, or van that has been taken back to the shop 3 to 4 times for the same problem or is out of service for a total of 30 days during the covered period. This time does not mean consecutive days and can be for different problems. 15 states have safety lemon provisions which presume a vehicle is a lemon after only 1 to 2 repairs of a defect likely to cause death or serious injury. Be sure to keep careful records of your repairs since some states now require only one of the repairs to be within the specified time period. 33 states provide for the award of attorney fees with the other 17 relying on the Federal lemon law for fees.

Specific information about laws in your state can be obtained from your state attorney general's office or at the Center for Auto Safety's website. The following table offers a general description of the Lemon Law in your state and what you need to do to set it in motion (Notification/Trigger). We indicate where state-run arbitration programs are available. State-run programs are the best type of arbitration. Be aware a few state lemon laws are so bad consumers should only rely on the Federal lemon law and state contract law. We have marked these bad laws with a ☒ while the best laws have a ☑.

☑ **The Best Lemon Laws**
☒ **The Worst Lemon Laws**

Alabama	Qualification: 3 unsuccessful repairs or 30 calendar days within shorter of 24 months or 24,000 miles, provided 1 repair attempt or 1 day out of service is within shorter of 1 year or 12,000 miles. Notice/Trigger: Certified mail to manufacturer + opportunity for final repair attempt within 14 calendar days.
Alaska	Qualification: 3 unsuccessful repairs or 30 business days out of service within shorter of 1 year or warranty. Notice/Trigger: Certified mail to manufacturer + dealer (or repair agent) that problem has not been corrected in reasonable number of attempts + refund or replacement demanded within 60 days. Manufacturer has 30 calendar days for final repair attempt.
Arizona	Qualification: 4 unsuccessful repairs or 30 calendar days out of service within warranty period or shorter of 2 years or 24,000 miles. Notice/Trigger: Written notice + opportunity to repair to manufacturer.
Arkansas ☑	Qualification: 3 unsuccessful repairs, 5 total repairs of any nonconformity, or 1 unsuccessful repair of problem likely to cause death or serious bodily injury within longer of 24 months or 24,000 miles. Notice/Trigger: Certified or registered mail to manufacturer who has 10 days to notify consumer of repair facility. Facility has 10 days to repair.

L—Law specifically applies to leased vehicles; S-C—State has certified guidelines for arbitration; S-R—State-run arbitration mechanism available

California ☑	Qualification: 4 repair attempts or 30 calendar days out of service or 2 repair attempts for defect likely to cause death or serious bodily injury within shorter of 18 months or 18,000 miles, or "reasonable" number of attempts during entire express warranty period. Notice/Trigger: Direct written notice to manufacturer at address clearly specified in owner's manual. Covers small businesses with up to 5 vehicles under 10,000 pounds GVWR.
Colorado ☒	Qualification: 4 unsuccessful repairs or 30 business days out of service within shorter of 1 year or warranty. Notice/Trigger: Prior certified mail notice + opportunity to repair for manufacturer.
Connecticut	Qualification: 4 unsuccessful repairs or 30 calendar days out of service within shorter of 2 years or 24,000 miles, or 2 unsuccessful repairs of problem likely to cause death or serious bodily injury within warranty period or 1 year. Notice/Trigger: Report to manufacturer, agent, or dealer. Written notice to manufacturer only if required in owner's manual or warranty. S-R
Delaware	Qualification: 4 unsuccessful repairs or 30 calendar days out of service within shorter of 1 year or warranty. Notice/Trigger: Written notice + opportunity to repair to manufacturer.
D.C.	Qualification: 4 unsuccessful repairs or 30 calendar days out of service or 1 unsuccessful repair of safety-related defect, within shorter of 2 years or 18,000 miles. Notice/Trigger: Report to manufacturer, agent, or dealer.
Florida	Qualification: 3 unsuccessful repairs or 15 calendar days within 24 months from delivery. Notice/Trigger: Certified or express mail notice to manufacturer who has 10 days to notify consumer of repair facility plus 10 more calendar days for final repair attempt after delivery to designated dealer. S-R
Georgia	Qualification: 3 unsuccessful repair attempts or 30 calendar days out of service within shorter of any 24,000 miles or 24 months period if 1 repair or 15 days out of service within shorter of 1 year or 12,000 miles; or 1 unsuccessful repair of serious safety defect in braking or steering within shorter of 1 year or 12,000, or 2 unsuccessful repairs of any other serious safety defect within shorter of any 24,000 miles or 24 months period if 1 repair within shorter of 1 year or 12,000 miles. Notice/Trigger: Certified mail return receipt requested. Manufacturer has 7 days to notify consumer of repair facility which has 14 calendar days to repair. S-R Note: Proceeding under lemon law may cause consumer to lose rights under other laws.
Hawaii	Qualification: 3 unsuccessful repair attempts, or 1 unsuccessful repair attempt of defect likely to cause death or serious bodily injury, or out of service for total of 30 days within shorter of 2 years or 24,000 miles. Notice/Trigger: Written notice + opportunity to repair to manufacturer. S-R
Idaho	Qualification: 4 repair attempts or 30 business days out of service within shorter of 2 years or 24,000 miles, or 1 repair of complete failure of braking or steering likely to cause death or serious bodily injury. Notice/Trigger: Written notice to manufacturer or dealer + one opportunity to repair to manufacturer. S-R.
Illinois	Qualification: 4 unsuccessful repairs or 30 business days out of service within shorter of 1 year or 12,000 miles. Notice/Trigger: Written notice + opportunity to repair to manufacturer.
Indiana ☒	Qualification: 4 unsuccessful repairs or 30 business days out of service within shorter of 18 months or 18,000 miles. Notice/Trigger: Written notice to manufacturer only if required in the warranty.

L—Law specifically applies to leased vehicles; S-C—State has certified guidelines for arbitration; S-R—State-run arbitration mechanism available

Iowa	Qualification: 3 unsuccessful repairs, or 1 unsuccessful repair of nonconformity likely to cause death or serious bodily injury, or 30 calendar days out of service within shorter of 2 years or 24,000 miles. Notice/Trigger: Certified registered mail + final opportunity to repair within 10 calendar days of receipt of notice to manufacturer.
Kansas	Qualification: 4 unsuccessful repairs or 30 calendar days out of service or 10 total repairs within shorter of 1 year or warranty. Notice/Trigger: Actual notice to manufacturer.
Kentucky	Qualification: 4 unsuccessful repairs or 30 calendar days out of service within shorter of 1 year or 12,000 miles. Notice/Trigger: Written notice to manufacturer.
Louisiana	Qualification: 4 unsuccessful repairs or 90 calendar days out of service within shorter of 1 year or warranty. Notice/Trigger: Report to manufacturer or dealer.
Maine	Qualification: 3 unsuccessful repairs (when at least 2 times same agent attempted repair) or 15 business days out of service within shorter of warranty or 2 years or 18,000 miles. Applies to vehicles within first 18,000 miles or 2 years regardless of whether claimant is original owner. Notice/Trigger: Written notice to manufacturer or dealer. Manufacturer has 7 business days after receipt for final repair attempt. S-R
Maryland	Qualification: 4 unsuccessful repairs, 30 calendar days out of service or 1 unsuccessful repair of braking or steering system within shorter of 15 months or 15,000 miles. Notice/Trigger: Certified mail return receipt requested + opportunity to repair within 30 calendar days of receipt of notice to manufacturer or factory branch.
Massachusetts	Qualification: 3 unsuccessful repairs or 10 business days out of service within shorter of 1 year or 15,000 miles. Notice/Trigger: Notice to manufacturer or dealer who has 7 business days to attempt final repair. S-R
Michigan	Qualification: 4 unsuccessful repairs within 2 years from date of first unsuccessful repair or 30 calendar days within shorter of 1 year or warranty. Notice/Trigger: Certified mail return receipt requested to manufacturer who has 5 business days to repair after delivery. Consumer may notify manufacturer after third repair attempt.
Minnesota	Qualification: 4 unsuccessful repairs or 30 business days or 1 unsuccessful repair of total braking or steering loss likely to cause death or serious bodily injury within shorter of 2 years or warranty. Notice/Trigger: Written notice + opportunity to repair to manufacturer, agent, or dealer.
Mississippi	Qualification: 3 unsuccessful repairs or 15 business days out of service within shorter of 1 year or warranty. Notice/Trigger: Written notice to manufacturer who has 10 business days to repair after delivery to designated dealer.
Missouri	Qualification: 4 unsuccessful repairs or 30 business days out of service within shorter of 1 year or warranty. Notice/Trigger: Written notice to manufacturer who has 10 calendar days to repair after delivery to designated dealer.
Montana	Qualification: 4 unsuccessful repairs or 30 business days out of service after notice within shorter of 2 years or 18,000 miles. Notice/Trigger: Written notice + opportunity to repair to manufacturer. S-R
Nebraska	Qualification: 4 unsuccessful repairs or 40 calendar days out of service within shorter of 1 year or warranty. Notice/Trigger: Certified mail + opportunity to repair to manufacturer.

L—Law specifically applies to leased vehicles; S-C—State has certified guidelines for arbitration; S-R—State-run arbitration mechanism available

Nevada	Qualification: 4 unsuccessful repairs or 30 calendar days out of service within shorter of 1 year or warranty. Notice/Trigger: Written notice to manufacturer.
New Hampshire	Qualification: 3 unsuccessful repairs by same dealer or 30 business days out of service within warranty. Notice/Trigger: Report to manufacturer, distributor, agent, or dealer (on forms provided by manufacturer) + final opportunity to repair before arbitration. S-R
New Jersey ☑	Qualification: 3 unsuccessful repairs or 20 calendar days out of service within shorter of 2 years or 18,000 miles. Notice/Trigger: Certified mail notice, return receipt requested to manufacturer who has 10 days to repair. Consumer may notify manufacturer any time after the second repair attempt.
New Mexico ☒	Qualification: 4 unsuccessful repairs or 30 business days out of service within shorter of 1 year or warranty. Notice/Trigger: Written notice + opportunity to repair to manufacturer, agent, or dealer.
New York	Qualification: 4 unsuccessful repairs or 30 calendar days out of service within shorter of 2 years or 18,000 miles. Notice/Trigger: Notice to manufacturer, agent, or dealer.
North Carolina	Qualification: 4 unsuccessful repairs within shorter of 24 months, 24,000 miles or warranty or 20 business days out of service during any 12 month period of warranty. Notice/Trigger: Written notice to manufacturer + opportunity to repair within 15 calendar days of receipt only if required in warranty or owner's manual.
North Dakota ☒	Qualification: 3 unsuccessful repairs or 30 business days out of service within shorter of 1 year or warranty. Notice/Trigger: Direct written notice + opportunity to repair to manufacturer. (Manufacturer's informal arbitration process serves as prerequisite to consumer refund or replacement.)
Ohio ☑	Qualification: 3 unsuccessful repairs of same nonconformity, 30 calendar days out of service, 8 total repairs of any nonconformity, or 1 unsuccessful repair of problem likely to cause death or serious bodily injury within shorter of 1 year or 18,000 miles. Notice/Trigger: Report to manufacturer, its agent, or dealer.
Oklahoma	Qualification: 4 unsuccessful repairs or 45 calendar days out of service within shorter of 1 year or warranty. Notice/Trigger: Written notice + opportunity to repair to manufacturer.
Oregon	Qualification: 4 unsuccessful repairs or 30 business days within shorter of 1 year or 12,000 miles. Notice/Trigger: Direct written notice + opportunity to repair to manufacturer.
Pennsylvania	Qualification: 3 unsuccessful repairs or 30 calendar days within shorter of 1 year, 12,000 miles, or warranty. Notice/Trigger: Delivery to authorized service + repair facility. If delivery impossible, written notice to manufacturer or its repair facility obligates them to pay for delivery.
Rhode Island	Qualification: 4 unsuccessful repairs or 30 calendar days out of service within shorter of 1 year or 15,000 miles. Notice/Trigger: Report to dealer or manufacturer who has 7 days for final repair opportunity.
South Carolina	Qualification: 3 unsuccessful repairs or 30 calendar days out of service within shorter of 1 year or 12,000 miles. Notice/Trigger: Certified mail + opportunity to repair (not more than 10 business days) to manufacturer only if manufacturer informed consumer of such at time of sale.

L—Law specifically applies to leased vehicles; S-C—State has certified guidelines for arbitration; S-R—State-run arbitration mechanism available

State	Requirements
South Dakota	Qualification: 4 unsuccessful repairs, 1 of which occurred during shorter of 1 year or 12,000 miles, or 30 calendar days out of service during shorter of 24 months or 24,000 miles. Notice/Trigger: Certified mail to manufacturer + final opportunity to repair + 7 calendar days to notify consumer of repair facility.
Tennessee	Qualification: 4 unsuccessful repairs or 30 calendar days out of service within shorter of 1 year or warranty. Notice/Trigger: Certified mail notice to manufacturer + final opportunity to repair within 10 calendar days.
Texas	Qualification: 4 unsuccessful repairs when 2 occurred within shorter of 1 year or 12,000 miles, + other 2 occur within shorter of 1 year or 12,000 miles immediately following second repair attempt; or 2 unsuccessful repairs of serious safety defect when 1 occurred within shorter of 1 year or 12,000 miles + other occurred within shorter of 1 year or 12,000 miles immediately following first repair; or 30 calendar days out of service within shorter of 2 years or 24,000 miles + at least 2 attempts were made within shorter of 1 year or 12,000 miles. Notice/Trigger: Written notice to manufacturer. S-R
Utah	Qualification: 4 unsuccessful repairs or 30 business days out of service within shorter of 1 year or warranty. Notice/Trigger: Report to manufacturer, agent, or dealer.
Vermont	Qualification: 3 unsuccessful repairs when at least first repair was within warranty, or 30 calendar days out of service within warranty. Notice/Trigger: Written notice to manufacturer (on provided forms) after third repair attempt, or 30 days. Arbitration must be held within 45 days after notice, during which time manufacturer has 1 final repair. S-R Note: Repairs must been done by same authorized agent or dealer, unless consumer shows good cause for taking vehicle to different agent or dealer.
Virginia	Qualification: 3 unsuccessful repairs, or 1 repair attempt of serious safety defect, or 30 calendar days out of service within 18 months. Notice/Trigger: Written notice to manufacturer. If 3 unsuccessful repairs or 30 days already exhausted before notice, manufacturer has 1 more repair attempt not to exceed 15 days.
Washington	Qualification: 4 unsuccessful repairs, 30 calendar days out of service (15 during warranty period), or 2 repairs of serious safety defect, first reported within shorter of warranty or 24 months or 24,000 miles. One repair attempt + 15 of 30 days must fall within manufacturer's express warranty of at least 1 year of 12,000 miles. Notice/Trigger: Written notice to manufacturer. S-R Note: Consumer should receive replacement or refund within 40 calendar days of request.
West Virginia ☑	Qualification: 3 unsuccessful repairs or 30 calendar days out of service or 1 unsuccessful repair of problem likely to cause death or serious bodily injury within shorter of 1 year or warranty. Notice/Trigger: Written notice + opportunity to repair to manufacturer.
Wisconsin	Qualification: 4 unsuccessful repairs or 30 calendar days out of service within shorter of 1 year or warranty. Notice/Trigger: Report to manufacturer or dealer. Note: Consumer should receive replacement or refund within 30 calendar days after offer to return title.
Wyoming	Qualification: 3 unsuccessful repairs or 30 business days out of service within 1 year. Notice/Trigger: Direct written notice + opportunity to repair to manufacturer. S-R State-run arbitration mechanism available.

L—Law specifically applies to leased vehicles; S-C—State has certified guidelines for arbitration; S-R—State-run arbitration mechanism available

Mitsubishi Galant

Cadillac SRX

Saturn ION

Nissan Quest

IN THIS CHAPTER

INTRODUCTION

Buying a car means matching wits with a seasoned professional. But if you know what to expect, you'll have a much better chance of getting a really good deal! This chapter offers practical advice on buying a car, tips on getting the best price and financing, information on buying versus leasing, and tips on avoiding lemons.

There's no question that buying a car can be an intimidating experience. But it doesn't have to be. First of all, you have in your hands all of the information you need to make an informed choice. Secondly, if you approach the purchase logically, you'll always maintain control of the decision. Start with the following basic steps:

1 Narrow your choice down to a particular class of car—sports, station wagon, minivan, sedan, large luxury, or economy car. These are general classifications and some cars may fit into more than one category. In most cases, *The Car Book* presents the vehicles by size class.

2 Determine what features are really important to you. Most buyers consider safety on the top of their list, which is why the "Safety" chapter is right up front in *The Car Book*. Airbags, power options, ABS, and the number of passengers, as well as "hidden" elements such as maintenance and insurance costs, should be considered at this stage in your selection process.

3 Find three or four cars that meet the needs you outlined above and your pocketbook. It's important not to narrow your choice down to one car because then you lose all your bargaining power in the showroom. (Why? Because you might lose the psychological ability to walk away from a bad deal!) In fact, because cars today are more similar than dissimilar, it's not hard to keep three or four choices in mind. In the car rating pages in the back of the book, we suggest some competitive choices for your consideration. For example, if you are interested in the Honda Accord, you should also consider the Toyota Camry and Ford Taurus.

4 Make sure you take a good, long test drive. The biggest car buying mistake most of us make is to overlook those nagging problems that seem to surface only after we've brought the car home. Spend at least an hour driving the car without a salesperson in the car. If a dealership won't allow you to testdrive a car without a salesperson, go somewhere else. The test-drive should include time on the highway, parking, taking the car in and out of your driveway or garage, sitting in the back seat, and using the trunk or storage area.

TIP: Whatever you do, don't talk price until you're ready to buy!

5 This is the stage most of us dread—negotiating the price. While price negotiation is a car buying tradition, a few carmakers and dealers are trying to break tradition by offering so-called "no-haggle pricing." Since they're still in the minority and because it's very hard for an individual to establish true competition between dealers, we offer a new means to avoid negotiating altogether by using the non-profit CarBargains pricing service.

Now that you have a quick guide to the steps necessary in making a good choice, use the tables that follow to quickly review the new cars and the pages in the back for a detailed critique of each model. See the showroom strategies on the next page for more details on getting the best price.

For most of us, the auto showroom can be an intimidating environment. We're matching wits with professional negotiators over a very complex product. Being prepared is the best way to turn a potentially intimidating showroom experience into a profitable one. Here's some advice on handling what you'll find in the showroom.

Beware of silence. Silence is often used to intimidate, so be prepared for long periods of time when the salesperson is "talking with the manager." This tactic is designed to make you want to "just get the negotiation over with." Instead of becoming a victim, do something that indicates you are serious about looking elsewhere. Bring the classified section of the newspaper and begin circling other cars or review brochures from other manufacturers. By sending the message that you have other options, you increase your bargaining power and speed up the process.

Don't fall in love with a car. Never look too interested in any particular car. Advise family members who go with you against being too enthusiastic about any one car. Tip: Beat the dealers at their own game—bring along a friend who tells you that the price is "too much compared to the other deal."

Keep your wallet in your pocket. Don't leave a deposit, even if it's refundable. You'll feel pressure to rush your shopping, and you'll have to return and face the salesperson again before you are ready.

Shop at the end of the month. Salespeople anxious to meet sales goals are more willing to negotiate a lower price at this time.

Buy last year's model. The majority of new cars are the same as the previous year, with minor cosmetic changes. You can save considerably by buying in early fall when dealers are clearing space for "new" models. The important trade-off you make using this technique is that the carmaker may have added airbags or anti-lock brakes to an otherwise unchanged vehicle.

Buying from stock. You can often get a better deal on a car that the dealer has on the lot. However, these cars often have expensive options you may not want or need. Do not hesitate to ask the dealer to remove an option (and its accompanying charge) or sell you the car without charging for the option. The longer the car sits there, the more interest the dealer pays on the car, which increases the dealer's incentive to sell.

Ordering a car. Cars can be ordered from the manufacturer with exactly the options you want. Simply offering a fixed amount over invoice may be attractive because it's a sure sale and the dealership has not invested in the car. All the salesperson has to do is take your order.

If you do order a car, make sure when it arrives that it includes only the options you requested. Don't fall for the trick where the dealer offers you unordered options at a "special price," because it was their mistake. If you didn't order an option, don't pay for it.

THE 180-DEGREE TURN

TIP

When buying a car, remember that you have the most important weapon in the bargaining process: the 180-degree turn. Be prepared to walk away from a deal, even at the risk of losing the "very best deal" your salesperson has ever offered, and you will be in the best position to get a real "best deal." Remember: Dealerships need you, the buyer, to survive.

! BEWARE OF MANDATORY ARBITRATION AGREEMENTS !

More and more dealers are adding mandatory binding arbitration agreements, which they often call "dispute resolution mechanisms," to your purchase contract. What this means is that you wave the right to sue or appeal any problem you have with the vehicle. Before you start negotiating the price, ask if the dealer requires Mandatory Binding Arbitration. If so, and they won't remove that requirement, you should buy elsewhere. Many dealers do not have this requirement.

Don't trade in. Although it is more work, you can usually do better by selling your old car yourself than by trading it in. To determine what you'll gain by selling the car yourself, check the NADA Official Used Car Guide at your credit union or library. On the web, the Kelly Blue Book website at kbb.com is a good source for invoice pricing. The difference between the trade-in price (what the dealer will give you) and the retail price (what you typically can sell it for) is your extra payment for selling the car yourself.

If you do decide to trade your car in at the dealership, keep the buying and selling separate. First, negotiate the best price for your new car, then find out how much the dealer will give you for your old car. Keeping the two deals separate ensures that you know what you're paying for your new car and simplifies the entire transaction.

Question everything the dealer writes down. Nothing is etched in stone. Because things are written down, we tend not to question them. This is wrong—always assume that anything written down is negotiable.

Test-drive without the salesperson. When you test-drive a car, go alone and take a good, long test-drive. If a dealership will not let you take a car without a salesperson, go to another dealership. Test-driving without the distraction of a salesperson is a necessity when trying out a new car.

! AVOIDING LEMONS !

One way to avoid the sour taste of a lemon after you've bought your car is to protect yourself before you sign on the dotted line. These tips will help you avoid problems down the road.

1 **Avoid new models.** Any new car in its very first year of production often turns out to have a lot of defects. Sometimes the manufacturer isn't able to remedy the defects until the second, third, or even fourth year of production. If the manufacturer has not worked out problems by the third model year, the car will likely be a lemon forever.

2 **Avoid the first cars off the line.** Most companies close down their assembly lines every year to make annual changes. In addition to adding hundreds of dollars to the price of a new car, these changes can introduce new defects. It can take a few months to iron out these bugs. Ask the dealer when the vehicle you are interested in was manufactured, or look on the metal tag found on the inside of the driver-side door frame to find the date of manufacture.

3 **Avoid delicate options.** Delicate options have the highest frequency-of-repair records. Power seats, power windows, power antennas, and special roofs are nice conveniences—until they break down. Of all the items on the vehicles, they tend to be the most expensive to repair.

4 **Inspect the dealer's checklist.** Request a copy of the dealer's pre-delivery service and adjustment checklist (also called a "make-ready list") at the time your new vehicle is delivered. Write the request directly on the new vehicle order. This request informs the dealer that you are aware of the dealer's responsibility to check your new car for defects.

5 **Examine the car on delivery.** Most of us are very excited when it comes time to take the vehicle home. A few minutes of careful inspection can save hours of misery later. Look over the body for any damage; check for the spare tire and jack equipment; make sure all electrical items work, and all the hubcaps and body molding are on. You may want to take a short test-drive. Finally, make sure you have the owner's manual, warranty forms, and all the legal documents.

DEPRECIATION

Over the past 20 years, new vehicle depreciation costs have steadily increased. A study conducted by Runzheimer International shows that depreciation and interest now account for just over 50 percent of the costs of owning and operating a vehicle. Recently, however, the increasing cost of depreciation has slowed down. This is due to the relatively stable prices of new vehicles and to the slow increase in finance rates. The higher cost of gasoline consumes a larger percentage of the automotive dollar than ever before. Other costs, including insurance, maintenance, and tires, have remained at relatively steady shares of the automotive dollar.

While there is no foolproof method for predicting retained vehicle value, your best bet is to purchase a popular vehicle model. Chances are it will also be a popular used vehicle model, meaning that the retained value may be higher when you go to sell it.

Most new cars are traded in within four years and are then available on the used car market. The priciest used cars may not be the highest quality. Supply and demand, as well as appearance, are important factors in determining used car prices.

The following table indicates which of the top-selling 2000 cars held their value the best and which did not.

2000 CARS WITH THE BEST AND WORST RESALE VALUE

THE BEST				THE WORST			
Model	2000 Price	2003 Price	Retain. Value	Model	2000 Price	2003 Price	Retain. Value
Jeep Wrangler	$18,415	$15,650	85%	Chevrolet Cavalier	$13,165	$2,676	20%
Toyota Tacoma	$15,318	$13,000	85%	Oldsmobile Intrigue	$23,720	$10,425	44%
Toyota Celica	$16,695	$13,750	82%	Dodge Stratus	$19,810	$8,825	45%
Honda Odyssey	$23,400	$19,025	81%	Chrysler Voyager	$23,250	$10,675	46%
BMW 3 Series	$26,990	$21,600	80%	Dodge Caravan	$23,085	$10,675	46%
Chevrolet Silverado	$16,250	$12,800	79%	Plymouth Voyager	$23,085	$10,675	46%
Nissan Xterra	$20,499	$16,050	78%	Mazda 626	$20,445	$9,500	46%
Toyota Tundra	$22,250	$17,250	78%	Buick Century	$19,602	$9,150	47%
Nissan Frontier	$19,890	$15,400	77%	Lincoln Town Car	$40,630	$19,000	47%
GMC Sierra	$24,176	$18,650	77%	Kia Sephia	$10,995	$5,150	47%
Honda CR-V	$19,050	$14,575	77%	Dodge Intrepid	$22,085	$10,350	47%
Lexus RX 300	$33,905	$25,900	76%	Chevrolet Malibu	$16,460	$7,825	48%
VW New Beetle	$16,850	$12,650	75%	Pontiac Grand Prix	$19,185	$9,225	48%
VW Jetta	$18,700	$14,025	75%	MercurySable	$21,245	$10,400	49%
Toyota 4Runner	$25,958	$19,075	73%	Pontiac Grand Am	$18,085	$8,975	50%
Volkswagen Passat	$21,200	$15,525	73%	Ford Explorer	$23,290	$11,600	50%
Toyota RAV4	$16,668	$12,150	73%	Buick Regal	$22,220	$11,150	50%
Chevrolet Tahoe	$27,845	$20,050	72%	Isuzu Rodeo	$23,435	$11,900	51%
Dodge Dakota	$16,750	$11,950	71%	Ford Taurus	$22,005	$11,175	51%
Toyota Sienna	$22,858	$15,875	69%	Oldsmobile Alero	$15,675	$7,975	51%
Toyota Avalon	$25,195	$17,450	69%	Mercury Gr. Marquis	$24,315	$12,425	51%
Chevrolet Suburban	$33,134	$22,800	69%	Dodge Neon	$12,460	$6,425	52%
Honda Civic	$14,730	$10,125	69%	Chevrolet Venture	$22,350	$11,575	52%
Subaru Forester	$20,095	$13,575	68%	Chevrolet Prizm	$13,816	$7,250	52%
GMC Yukon XL	$35,986	$24,300	68%				

GETTING THE BEST PRICE

One of the most difficult aspects of buying a new car is getting the best price. Most of us are at a disadvantage negotiating because we don't know how much the car actually cost the dealer. The difference between what the dealer paid and the sticker price represents the negotiable amount.

Until recently, the key to getting the best price was finding out the dealer cost. Many shoppers now ask to see the factory invoice, so some dealers promote their cars by offering to sell at only $49 or $99 over invoice. This sounds like a good deal, but these cars often have options you may not want and most invoice prices do not reveal the extra, hidden profit to the dealer.

Now that most savvy consumers know to check the so-called "dealer invoice," the industry has camouflaged this number. Special incentives, rebates, and kickbacks can account for $500 to $2,000 worth of extra profit to a dealer selling a car at "dealer invoice." The non-profit Center for the Study of Services recently discovered that in 37 percent of cases when dealers are forced to bid against each other for the sale, they offered the buyer a price below the "dealer invoice"—an unlikely event if the dealer was actually losing money. The bottom line is that "dealer invoice" doesn't really mean dealer cost.

Because the rules have changed, we believe that most consumers are ill-advised to try and negotiate with a dealer. This is because introducing competition is the best way to get the lowest price on a new car. To do this you have to convince three or four dealers that you are, in fact, prepared to buy a car; that you have decided on the make, model, and features; and that your decision now rests solely on which dealer will give you the best price. You can try to do this by phone, but often dealers will not give you the best price, or will quote you a price over the phone that they will not honor later. Instead, you should try to do this in person. As anyone knows who has ventured into an auto showroom simply to get the best price, the process can be lengthy as well as terribly arduous. Nevertheless, if you can convince the dealer that you are serious and are willing to take the time to go to a number of dealers, it will pay off. Otherwise, we suggest you use the CarBargains service listed on the next page.

Here are some other showroom strategies:

Shop away from home. If you find a big savings at a dealership far from your home or on the Internet, call a local dealer with the price. They may very well match it. If not, pick up the car from the distant dealer, knowing your trip has saved you hundreds of dollars. You can still bring it to your local dealer for warranty work and repairs.

Beware of misleading advertising. New car ads are meant to get you into the showroom. They usually promise low prices, big rebates, high trade-in, and spotless integrity—don't be deceived. Advertised prices are rarely the true selling price. They usually exclude transportation charges, service fees, or document fees. And always look out for the asterisk, both in advertisements and on invoices. It can be a signal that the advertiser has something to hide.

Don't talk price until you're ready to buy. On your first few trips to the showroom, simply look over the cars, decide what options you want, and do your test-driving.

Shop the corporate twins. Page 95 contains a list of corporate twins—nearly identical cars that carry different name plates. Check the price and options of the twins of the car you like. A higher-priced twin may have more options, so it may be a better deal than the lower-priced car without the options you want.

Watch out for dealer preparation overcharges. Before paying the dealer to clean your car, make sure that preparation is not included in the basic price. The price sticker will state: "Manufacturer's suggested retail price of this model includes dealer preparation."

If you must negotiate . . . negotiate up from the "invoice" price rather than down from the sticker price. Simply make an offer close to or at the "invoice" price. If the salesperson says that your offer is too low to make a profit, ask to see the factory invoice.

CarBargains' Best Price Service

Even with the information that we provide you in this chapter of *The Ultimate Car Book*, many of us still will not be comfortable negotiating for a fair price. In fact, as we indicated on the previous page, we believe it's really very difficult to negotiate the best price with a single dealer. The key to getting the best price is to get dealers to compete with each other.

CarBargains is a service of the non-profit Center for the Study of Services, a Washington, DC, consumer group, set up to provide comparative price information for many products and services.

CarBargains will "shop" the dealerships in your area and obtain at least five price quotes for the make and model of the car that you want to buy. The dealers who submit quotes know that they are competing with other area dealerships and have agreed to honor the prices that they submit. It is important to note that CarBargains is not an auto broker or "car buying" service; they have no affiliation with dealers.

Here's how the service works:

1. You provide CarBargains with the make, model, and style of car you wish to buy (Ford Taurus GL, for example) by phone or mail.

2. Within two weeks, CarBargains will send you dealer quote sheets from at least five local dealers who have bid against one another to sell you that car. Each dealer's offer is actually a commitment to a dollar amount above (or below) "factory invoice cost" for that model. You get the name and phone number of the manager responsible for handling the quote.

You will also receive a printout that enables you to figure the exact cost for each available option you might want on the vehicle.

3. Determine which dealer offers the best price using the dealer quote sheets. Add up the cost including the specific options you want. Contact the sales manager of that dealership and arrange to purchase the car.

If a car with the options you want is not available on the dealer's lot, you can, in many cases, have the dealer order the car from the factory or from another dealer at the agreed price.

When you receive your quotes, you will also get some suggestions on low-cost sources of financing and a valuation of your used car (trade-in).

The price for this service ($190) may seem expensive, but when you consider the savings that will result by having dealers bid against each other, as well as the time and effort of trying to get these bids yourself, we believe it's a great value. First of all, the dealers know they have a bona fide buyer (you've paid for the service) and they know they are bidding against five to seven of their competitors.

To obtain CarBargains' competitive price quotes, call them at 800-475-7283 or visit their website at www.carbargains.org. Or, you can send a check for $190 to CarBargains, 733 15th St., NW, Suite 820CB, Washington, DC 20005. Be sure to include your complete mailing address, phone number (in case of questions), and the exact make, model, and year of the car you want to buy. You should receive your bids within two to three weeks.

! AUTO BROKERS !

While CarBargains is a non-profit organization created to help you find the best price for the car you want to purchase, auto brokers are typically in the business to make money. As such, whatever price you end up paying for the car will include additional profit for the broker. While many brokers are legitimately trying to get their customers the best price, others have developed special relationships with certain dealers and may not do much shopping for you. As a consumer, it is difficult to tell which are which. This is why we recommend CarBargains. There have been cases where the auto broker makes certain promises, takes your money, and you never hear from him or her again. If CarBargains is not for you, then we suggest you consider using a buying service associated with your credit union or auto club, which can arrange for the purchase of a car at some fixed price over "dealer invoice."

FINANCING

You've done your test-drive, researched prices, studied crash tests, determined the options you want, and haggled to get the best price. Now you have to decide how to pay for the car.

If you have the cash, pay for the car right away. You avoid finance charges, you won't have a large debt haunting you, and the full value of the car is yours. You can then make the monthly payments to yourself to save up for your next car.

However, most of us cannot afford to pay cash for a car, which leaves two options: financing or leasing. While leasing may seem more affordable, financing will actually cost you less. When you finance a car, you own it after you finish your payments. At the end of a lease, you have nothing. We don't recommend leasing, but if you want more information, see page 86.

Here are some tips when financing your car:

Shop around for interest rates. Most banks and credit unions will knock off at least a quarter of a percent for their customers. Have these quotes handy when you talk financing with the dealer.

The higher your down payment, the less you'll have to finance. This will not only reduce your overall interest charges, but often qualifies you for a lower interest rate. Down payments are typically 10–20 percent of the final price.

Avoid long car loans. The monthly payments are lower, but you'll pay far more in overall interest charges. For example, a two-year, $15,000 loan at 9 percent will cost you $1,446.51 in interest; the same amount at five years will cost you $3,682.52—way over twice as much!

Check out manufacturer promotional rates—the 0.9–2.9 percent rates you see advertised. These low rates are usually only valid on two- to three-year loans.

Read everything you are asked to sign and ask questions about anything you don't fully understand.

Make sure that an extended warranty has not been added to the purchase price. Dealers will sometimes add this cost without informing the consumer. Extended warranties are generally a bad value. See the "Warranties" chapter for more information.

Credit Unions vs. Banks: Credit unions generally charge fewer and lower fees and offer better rates than banks. In addition, credit unions offer counseling services where consumers can find pricing information on cars or compare monthly payments for financing. You can join a credit union either through your employer, an organization or club, or if you have a relative who is part of a credit union.

Low Rate or Cash Back? Sometimes auto manufacturers offer a choice of below market financing or cash back. The following table will tell you if it is better to take the lower rate or

DON'T BE TONGUE-TIED

Beware of high-pressure phrases like "I've talked to the manager and this is really the best we can do. As it is, we're losing money on this deal." Rarely is this true. Dealers are in the business to make money and most do very well. Don't tolerate a take-it-or-leave-it attitude. Simply repeat that you will only buy when you see the deal you want and that you don't appreciate the dealer pressuring you. Threaten to leave if the dealer continues to pressure you to buy today.

Don't let the dealer answer your questions with a question. If you ask, "Can I get air conditioning with this car?" and the salesperson answers, "If I get you air conditioning in this car, will you buy today?" this response tries to force you to decide to buy before you are ready. Ask the dealer to just answer your question and say that you'll buy when you're ready. It's the dealer's job to answer questions, not yours.

If you are having a difficult time getting what you want, ask the dealer: "Why won't you let me buy a car today?" Most salespeople will be thrown off by this phrase as they are often too busy trying to use it on you. If they respond in frustration, "OK, what do you want?" then you can make straightforward answers to simple questions.

Get a price; don't settle for: "If you're shopping price, go to the other dealers first and then come back." This technique ensures that they don't have to truly negotiate. Your best response is: "I only plan to come back if your price is the lowest, so that's what I need today, your lowest price."

You've done your test-drive, researched prices, studied crash tests, determined the options you want, and haggled to get the best price. Now you have to decide how to pay for the car.

If you have the cash, pay for the car right away. You avoid finance charges, you won't have a large debt haunting you, and the full value of the car is yours. You can then make the monthly payments to yourself to save up for your next car.

However, most of us cannot afford to pay cash for a car, which leaves two options: financing or leasing. While leasing may seem more affordable, financing will actually cost you less. When you finance a car, you own it after you finish your payments. At the end of a lease, you have nothing. We don't recommend leasing, but if you want more information, see page 86.

Here are some tips when financing your car:

Shop around for interest rates. Most banks and credit unions will knock off at least a quarter of a percent for their customers. Have these quotes handy when you talk financing with the dealer.

The higher your down payment, the less you'll have to finance. This will not only reduce your overall interest charges, but often qualifies you

TYPICAL OPERATING COSTS

The table below shows the annual operating costs for some popular cars. Costs include operating expenses (fuel, oil, maintenance, and tires) and ownership expenses (insurance, depreciation, financing, taxes, and licensing) and are based on keeping the car for 3 years and driving 20,000 miles per year. (Source: Runzheimer International-2003.)

Vehicle	Operating	Ownership	Total
BMW 540I	$3,760	$12,840	$16,600
Cadillac DeVille	$3,760	$12,893	$16,653
Lincoln Town Car Exec.	$3,850	$12,652	$16,502
Buick Park Avenue Ultra S.C.	$3,610	$12,054	$15,664
Buick LeSabre Limited	$2,890	$9,386	$12,276
Mercury Grand Marquis GS	$3,340	$7,708	$11,048
Dodge Intrepid SE	$2,950	$7,373	$10,323
Buick Century Custom	$2,990	$7,223	$10,213
Pontiac Grand Prix SE	$3,140	$6,945	$10,085
Ford Taurus SE	$3,010	$6,951	$9,961
Chevrolet Impala	$2,950	$6,949	$9,899
Chevrolet Malibu LS	$2,990	$6,829	$9,819
Chevrolet Malibu	$2,990	$6,597	$9,587
Pontiac Grand AM SE	$2,620	$6,597	$9,217
Toyota Camry LE	$2,760	$6,073	$8,833
Honda Accord LX	$2,700	$6,023	$8,723
Chevrolet Cavalier	$2,560	$6,045	$8,605
Ford Focus SE	$2,450	$5,748	$8,198
Honda Civic LX	$2,300	$5,175	$7,475
Toyota Corolla CE	$2,330	$5,127	$7,457

REBATE VS. LOW RATES (FOUR YEAR LOAN)

Bank/C.U.			Dealer Rate					
Rate	1%	2%	3%	4%	5%	6%	7%	8%
6	95	76	58	39	19	*	*	*
6.5	103	85	67	48	29	10	*	*
7	112	94	76	57	38	19	*	*
7.5	121	103	85	66	48	29	10	*

Based on data from *Home and Family Finances*, a publication of the Credit Union National Association.

LEASING VS. BUYING

As car prices continue to rise, many car buyers continue to be seduced by heavily advertised low monthly lease payments. Don't be deceived—in general, leasing costs more than buying outright or financing. When you pay cash or finance a car, you own an asset; leasing leaves you with nothing except all the headaches and responsibilities of ownership with none of the benefits. In addition, leased cars are often not covered by lemon laws. When you lease you pay a monthly fee for a predetermined time in exchange for the use of a car. However, you also pay for maintenance, insurance, and repairs as if you owned the car. Finally, when it comes time to turn in the car, it has to be in top shape—otherwise, you'll have to pay for repairs or body work.

If you are considering a lease, here are some leasing terms you need to know and some tips to get you through the process:

Capitalized Cost is the price of the car on which the lease is based. Negotiate this as if you were buying the car. Capitalized Cost Reduction is your down payment.

Know the make and model of the vehicle you want. Tell the agent exactly how you want the car equipped. You don't have to pay for options you don't request. Decide in advance how long you will keep the car.

Find out the price of the options on which the lease is based. Typically, they will be full retail price. Their cost can be negotiated (albeit with some difficulty) before you settle on the monthly payment.

Make sure options like a sunroof or stereo are added to the Capitalized Cost. When you purchase dealer-added options, be sure they add the full cost of the option to the Capitalized Cost so that you only pay for the depreciated value of the option, not the full cost.

Find out how much you are required to pay at delivery. Most leases require at least the first month's payment. Others have a security deposit, registration fees, or other "hidden costs." When shopping around, make sure price quotes include security deposit and taxes—sales tax, monthly use tax, or gross receipt tax. Ask how the length of the lease affects your monthly cost.

Find out how the lease price was determined. Lease prices are generally based on the manufacturer's suggested retail price, less the predetermined residual value. The best values are cars with a high expected residual value. To protect themselves, lessors tend to underestimate residual value, but you can do little about this estimate.

Find out the annual mileage limit. Don't accept a contract with a lower limit than you need. Most standard contracts allow 15,000 to 18,000 miles per year. If you go under the allowance one year, you can go over it the next. Watch out for Excess Mileage fees. If you go over, you'll get charged per mile.

Avoid "capitalized cost reduction" or "equity leases." Here the lessor offers to lower the monthly payment by asking you for more money up front—in other words, a down payment.

Ask about early termination. Between 30 and 40 percent of two-year leases are terminated early and 40–60 percent of four-year leases terminate early—this means expensive early termination fees. If you terminate the lease before it is up, what are the financial penalties? Typically, they are very high so watch out. Ask the dealer exactly what you would owe at the end of each year if you wanted out of the lease. Remember, if your car is stolen, the lease will typically be

LEASEWISE

TIP

If you must lease, why haggle when you can let someone else do it for you? LeaseWise, a new service from the Center for the Study of Services, makes dealers bid for your lease. First, they get leasing bids from dealers on the vehicles you're interested in. Next, you'll receive a detailed report with all the bids, the dealer and invoice cost of the vehicle, and a complete explanation of the various bids. Then, you can lease from the lowest bidder or use the report as leverage with another dealer. The service costs $335. For more information, call 800-475-7283, or visit www.checkbook.org.

terminated. While your insurance should cover the value of the car, you still may owe additional amounts per your lease contract.

Avoid maintenance contracts. Getting work done privately is cheaper in the long run. And don't forget, this is a new car with a standard warranty.

Arrange for your own insurance. By shopping around, you can generally find less expensive insurance than what's offered by the lessor.

Ask how quickly you can expect delivery. If your agent can't deliver in a reasonable time, maybe he or she can't meet the price quoted.

Retain your option to buy the car at the end of the lease at a predetermined price. The price should equal the residual value; if it is more then the lessor is trying to make an additional profit. Regardless of how the end-of-lease value is determined, if you want the car, make an offer based on the current "Blue Book" value of the car at the end of the lease.

Residual Value is the value of your car at the end of the lease.

Here's what Runzheimer International estimates the residual values for a few 2003 cars will be after four years:

Cadillac DeVille	41%
Merc. Gr. Marquis GS	44%
Ford Taurus SE	42%
Chevrolet Cavalier	41%
Saturn L Sedan	55%

LEASING VS. BUYING

The following table compares the typical costs of leasing vs. buying the same car over three and six years. Your actual costs may vary, but you can use this format to compare the cars you are considering. Our example assumes the residual value to be about 54 percent after three years and 36 percent after six years.

3 Years	**Lease**	**Finance**
MSRP	$31,250.00	$31,250.00
Purchase Cost of Car	$28,125.00	$28,125.00
Down Payment	$750.00	$2,812.50
Monthly Payment	$425.00	$489.36
Total Payments	$15,300.00	$17,616.96[1]
Amount left on loan		$11,041.40
Less value of vehicle		$16,875.00
Overall Cost, first 3 years	$16,050.00	$14,595.86

6 Years		
MSRP	$31,250.00	$31,250.00
Cost of Car	$56,250.00[2]	$28,125.00
Down Payment	$1,500.00	$2,812.50
Monthly Payment	$425.00	$489.36
Total Payments	$30,600.00	$29,361.60[3]
Less value of vehicle		$11,250.00
Overall Cost, 6 years	$32,100.00	$20,924.10

[1] First 3 years of 5-year loan with 8 percent annual percentage rate.
[2] Two 3-year leases.
[3] Five-year loan with 8 percent annual percentage rate, no monthly payments in sixth year.

USING THE INTERNET

The Internet is changing the way car buyers research and shop for cars. But the Internet should be used with caution. Remember that anyone—and we mean *anyone*—can publish a website with no guarantee concerning the accuracy of the information on it. We advise that you only visit websites that have a familiar non-web counterpart. A good example is the Center for Auto Safety's website at www.autosafety.org where you'll find information on auto safety, including publications and newsletters which are typically mailed out to subscribers.

Use the Internet as an information resource. Unfortunately, most automaker websites are nothing more than sophisticated ads with little comparative information.

Good information, like pricing and features, *can* be found online. We've listed some useful websites on this page.

There are also several online car shopping services that have launched. We view most of them with skepticism. Many online car shopping services are tied to a limited, often non-competitive, group of dealers. They may claim the lowest price, but you'll most likely have a dealer calling you with a price that is not much better than what you'd get if you went into a dealership to haggle.

Auto insurance and financing sites are sometimes no better. Don't rely solely on these online services; getting quotes from other sources is the only way to make sure you truly have the best deal.

Finally, clicking a mouse is no substitute for going out and test-driving a car. If you are shopping for a used car, you must check out the actual car before signing on the dotted line. Do not rely on online photos. In fact, online classifieds for cars are no more reliable than looking in a newspaper.

If you do use an online car shopping service, be sure to shop around on your own. Visit dealerships, get quotes from several car shopping services, and research the value of your used car (see www.kbb.com on this page). Beware that if you give anyone online your phone number, or email address, you are opening yourself up to unwanted email, junk mail, and even sales calls.

ON THE WEB

autosafety.org
The Center for Auto Safety (CAS) provides consumers with a voice for auto safety and quality in Washington and to help lemon owners fight back across the country.

carfax.com
Used car buyers will want to visit Carfax. Carfax collects information from numerous sources to provide a vehicle history on a specific vehicle, based on the Vehicle Identification Number (VIN). Carfax can help uncover costly and potentially dangerous hidden problems or confirm the clean history of a vehicle.

consumer.checkbook.org
The Center for the Study of Services (CSS) is an independent, nonprofit consumer organization and the creator of Consumer Checkbook. One of the few car buying services worth using, CSS's CarBargains pits dealers against each other, keeping you from haggling.

edmunds.com/edweb/Incentives.html
Edmund's Car Buying Guide's website offers a page on dealer and consumer rebates. The dealer rebates are especially valuable as dealers will not openly tell you about them.

kbb.com
The Kelly Blue Book website is a valuable reference to dealer invoice and retail pricing. Remember that the dealer invoice price is not necessarily how much the dealer has paid for the car; about 2–3 percent is usually held back. So, even if a dealer sells a car "at cost," they'll still make a few hundred dollars in profit.

nhtsa.dot.gov
The National Highway Traffic Safety Administration (NHTSA) website contains useful information on safety standards, crash tests, recalls, technical service bulletins, child seats, and safety advisories.

Corporate Twins and Asian Cousins

"Corporate twins" refers to vehicles that have different nameplates but share the same mechanics, drivetrain, and chassis. In most cases the vehicles are identical, like the Dodge and Plymouth Neon. Sometimes the difference is in body style, price, or options as with the Ford Taurus and Mercury Sable. Additionally, there are also "Asian cousins," which are Asian vehicles marketed under a U.S. nameplate. As with corporate twins, Asian cousins are the same vehicle with different nameplates, styles, prices, or options.

CORPORATE TWINS AND ASIAN COUSINS

DaimlerChrysler
Chrysler 300M
Chrysler Concorde
Dodge Intrepid

Chrysler Sebring
Dodge Stratus

Chrysler Sebring Coupe
Dodge Stratus Coupe

Chrysler Town & Country
Dodge Grand Caravan

Chrysler Town & Country SWB
Dodge Caravan

General Motors
Buick Century
Buick Regal

Buick LeSabre
Cadillac Seville
Pontiac Bonneville

Buick Rainer
Chevrolet Trail Blazer
GMC Envoy
Isuzu Ascender-5 pass.*
Oldsmobile Bravada

Cadillac Escalade ESV
Chevrolet Suburban
GMC Yukon XL

Chevrolet Avalanche
Cadillac Escalade EXT

Chevrolet Astro
GMC Safari

Chevrolet Cavalier
Pontiac Sunfire

Chevrolet Colorado
GMC Canyon

General Motors (cont.)
Chevrolet Venture
Oldsmobile Silhouette
Pontiac Montana

Chevrolet Monte Carlo
Chevrolet Impala
Pontiac Grand Prix

Chevrolet Silverado
GMC Sierra

Pontiac Vibe
Toyota Matrix*

Chevrolet Trail Blazer EXT
Isuzu Ascender-7 pass.*
GMC Envoy XL/XUV

Chevrolet Tracker
Suzuki Vitara*

Chevrolet S Series
GMC Sonoma

Cadillac Escalade
Chevrolet Tahoe
GMC Yukon

Ford
Ford Crown Victoria
Mercury Marauder
Mercury Grand Marquis

Ford Escape
Mazda Tribute*

Ford Expedition
Lincoln Navigator

Jaguar Type S
Lincoln LS

Ford Explorer
Mercury Mountaineer

Ford Ranger
Mazda Truck*

Ford (cont.)
Ford Taurus
Mercury Sable

Honda
Acura TSX
Honda Accord Coupe

Isuzu
Buick Rainer
Chevrolet Trail Blazer
GMC Envoy
Isuzu Ascender-5 pass.*
Oldsmobile Bravada

Chevrolet Trail Blazer EXT
GMC Envoy XL/XUV
Isuzu Ascender-7 pass.*

Mazda
Mazda Truck*
Ford Ranger

Mazda Tribute*
Ford Escape

Suzuki
Suzuki Vitara*
Chevrolet Tracker

Toyota
Toyota Matrix*
Pontiac Vibe

Lexus LX 470
Toyota Land Cruiser

Volkswagen
Volkswagen Jetta
Volkswagen Golf

Audi A4
Audi S4

*Asian Cousins

HOW TO BUY A USED CAR

No longer is buying a used car "buying someone else's troubles." In fact, because it is very difficult for most of us to determine even what year a car was made, it is hard to tell a brand new car from a two- to three-year-old model. This is why *The Ultimate Car Book* includes the previous model year for each 2004 model.

Should you consider getting a used car? Absolutely. Thanks to better reliability and the millions of previously leased vehicles hitting the used car market every year, there are more good used cars available than ever before.

Always testdrive and carefully inspect a used car. Take it to an independent mechanic and get it checked out. Oftentimes, a trusted friend can be the best source for a used car. You'll always get an honest answer when you ask, "Why are you selling the car?"

Remember these tips when shopping for a used car:

Used cars of the same brand as the new cars that a new car dealer sells are your best bets.

The longer a used car dealer has been in the same location, the better your chances of getting help should a problem arise.

To get a good deal from a rental car company, know the car's fair market value and have it checked by an independent mechanic.

If you know a private owner who trades in a car regularly, contact them and ask if they will sell to you rather than trade in. They will get more selling to you based on wholesale price than they would get from trade-in price. And you'll pay less than retail price.

Visit the used car superstore on a clear, bright day and allow yourself an afternoon's worth of time to peruse. Many superstores will let you sort through their stock via their web page. Take a printout of the models you're interested in with you on your visit.

WHERE TO GET A USED CAR

1 **NEW CAR DEALERS Pros:** Dealers keep best vehicles to sell; available service facilities **Cons:** Higher price; weaker warranties; be sure to get everything in writing

2 **USED CAR DEALERS Pros:** Lower price **Cons:** Vehicle is sold "as is"; weak warranties; typically no service facilities; vehicles often from fleets

3 **RENTAL CAR COMPANIES Pros:** Vehicle history available; good selection; no-haggle pricing **Cons:** Unwanted options; higher mileage; higher price

4 **PRIVATE SALES Pros:** Lower price **Cons:** Time-consuming; beware of pros masquerading as private sellers

5 **USED CAR SUPERSTORES Pros:** No-haggle pricing; great selection; good warranty; non-commission salespeople **Cons:** Higher prices

IN THIS CHAPTER

INTRODUCTION

This chapter provides an overview of the most important features of the new 2004 cars. In this section of *The Car Book*, all the information you'll need to make a smart choice is concisely presented on one page. Here's what you'll find and how to interpret the data we've provided:

THE DESCRIPTION

The vast majority of information in *The Car Book* is purely objective—we research and present the facts so that you can make an informed choice among the models that fit your taste and pocketbook. This section, however, includes some general information to help you round out the hard facts. Much of the information in our vehicle description is subjective and you may not share our opinion. Nevertheless, like the photo, which gives you a general idea of what the car looks like, the description will give you a snapshot of some of the features we think are worth noting.

THE RATINGS

These are ratings in ten important categories, as well as an overall comparative rating. We have adopted the Olympic rating system with "10" being the best.

Front Crash Test Performance: This rating compares the 2004 models against all crash test results to date. We give the best performers a 10 and the worst a 1. Remember to compare crash test results relative to other cars in the same size class. For details, see the "Safety Chapter."

Side Crash Test: This rating compares the 2004 models against all the side tests of the other vehicles. In many cases there may have been two side tests conducted showing the performance with different equipment. We present the result here with the best available safety equipment among the test results. See the "Safety Chapter" for detailed results and more side test results.

Safety Features: This is an evaluation of how much extra safety is built into the car. We give credit for side and head airbags, ABS, daytime running lights, seat belt pretensioners, built-in child safety seats, systems that close moon roofs and lock doors when a crash is sensed, air bag deactivation systems and roll stability systems. We also include various components of "smart" air bag systems such as impact adjustors, position sensors, seat/height adjustors and weight sensors. For details, see the "Safety Checklist" box on each page.

Preventive Maintenance: Each manufacturer suggests a preventive maintenance schedule designed to keep the car in good shape and to protect your rights under the warranty. Those with the lowest estimated PM costs get a 10 and the highest a 1. See the "Maintenance Chapter" for the actual costs and more information.

Repair Costs: It is virtually impossible to predict exactly what any new car will cost you in repairs. As such, we take nine typical repairs that you are likely to experience after your warranty expires and compare those costs among this year's models. Those with the lowest cost get a 10 and the highest a 1. For details, see the "Maintenance Chapter."

Warranty: This is an overall assessment of the car's warranty when compared to all warranties. We give the highest-rated warranties a 10 and the lowest a 1. See the "Warranty" chapter for details.

Fuel Economy: Here we compare the EPA mileage ratings of each car. The gas misers get a 10 and the guzzlers get a 1. For the purposes of the overall rating we pick the fuel economy rating of what is expected to be the most popular engine/drive train configuration. For more information, see the "Fuel Economy Chapter."

Rollover: Many consumers are aware that vehicles with higher centers of gravity could be more likely to roll over. Comparing the tendency of a vehicle to roll over is very difficult, as there is no agreed upon comparative rating system. Recently, the U.S. government adopted the rating system that we have been using called the static stability formula (SSF). We have compiled the SSF for all of the vehicles. The government provide the SSF rating for some vehicles. We use the SSF formula to provide ratings for those vehicles not on the government list. This is by no means a comprehensive means of comparing the vehicles, and it is important to read the details behind the SSF that appear in the "Safety Chapter."

Complaints: This is where you'll find how your car stacks up against hundreds of others on the road, based on the U.S. government complaint data. If the car has not been around long enough to have developed a complaint history, it is given a 5 (average). The least complained about cars get a 10 and the most problematic a 1. See the "Complaints Chapter" for details.

Insurance Costs: Insurance companies have rated most of the cars on the road to determine how they plan to charge for insurance. Here, you'll find whether you can expect a discount or a surcharge for what we expect to be the most popular model. If the car is likely to receive neither, we label it regular. Those receiving a discount get a 10; any cars with a surcharge get a 1; any with neither get a 5. Different insurance companies have different rating programs, so it's best to compare between companies.

Overall Rating: This is the "bottom line." Using a combination of all of the key ratings, this tells how this car stacks up against the others on a scale of 1 to 10. Due to the importance of crash tests, cars with no frontal crash test results as of our publication date cannot be given an overall rating. In other categories, if information is unavailable, an "average" is included in order to develop an overall rating.

Price Range

This box contains sample price information. When available, we a variety of prices between the base and the most luxurious version of the car. The difference is often substantial. Usually the more expensive versions have fancy trim, larger engines, and lots of automatic equipment. The least expensive versions usually have manual transmissions and few extra features. In addition, some manufacturers try to sell popular options as part of a package. In addition to the price range, we provide the expected dealer markup. Be prepared for higher retail prices when you get to the showroom. Manufacturers like to load their cars with factory options, and dealers like to add their own items such as fabric protection and paint sealant. Remember, prices and dealer costs can change during the year. Use these figures for general reference and comparisons, not as a precise indication of exactly how much the car you are interested in will cost. See page 83 for a buying service designed to ensure that you get the very best price.

Safety Checklist

For most of us, safety is a critical consideration in buying a new car. This box will tell you, at a glance, whether or not the car has the safety features you care about.

Frontal Crash Tests: Here's where we tell you if the frontal crash test index was either very good, good, average, poor, or very poor. Not all vehicles have been tested.

Side Crash Test: We've also included the car's performance in side crash tests. Here we indicate whether the side crash test index was very good, good, average, poor, or very poor. Not all vehicles have been tested.

Airbags (Side/Head): All cars come with dual frontal airbags. Many new models have added side and/or head protection airbags. Here we'll tell you what's available. The box on page 29 will give you a good overview on the types of airbags currently available.

Pretensioners/Impact Adjustors: How snugly your seat belt fits is a critical factor in offering you protection in a crash. Some manufacturers offer special devices that, sensing a potential crash, tighten up and/or lock the safety belt. Impact adjustors can adjust the deployment of the airbag based on such things as the speed of the crash. Here we tell you which vehicles offer each of these devices.

Position/Weight Sensors: Another feature in what some people call "smart airbags" are position and weight sensors. These govern the deployment of the airbag. For example, position sensors can determine if the passenger is too far forward and a weight sensor may detect the presence of a small vs. large person. This information is used in the appropriate deployment of the airbag.

Seat & Headrest Adjustors: Many people position their seat and head rest according to their own body and comfort requirements. This may not be the best position to protect you in a crash. These adjustors, sensing a potential crash, will move the seat and headrest to the optimal position.

Roll Stability System: Some manufacturers have installed sophisticated systems that will automatically adjust the suspension, steering and brakes to help prevent a roll over if the computer senses one is immanent. Of course, these systems cannot totally prevent rollovers, but they can react faster than most drivers when dangerous conditions are present.

Child Seats Built-In: 85% of parents use child safety seats improperly. One reason is because they are so difficult to properly install in your vehicle. To overcome this problem a few manufacturers offer built-in seats.

Antilock Brakes/Day Lamps: Find out if this model has two- or four-wheel anti-lock brakes, and whether you'll have to pay extra for them. In addition, some cars offer daytime running lights which can reduce your chances of being in a crash by up to 40 percent by increasing the visibility of your vehicle. We indicate whether daytime running lights are standard, optional, or not available.

Tire Pressure Monitors: There are two types of monitors, direct and indirect. Direct tire pressure monitors have sensors on each of the four wheels. Indirect systems use a sensor in the antilock braking system and are not as accurate as direct systems. Accurate tire pressure monitors are an important safety feature.

General Information

2004 Status: Here we tell you the overall status of the vehicle: all-new, unchanged, or appearance change. All-new vehicles (the minority) are brand new from the ground up. Unchanged vehicles are essentially the same, but could have some different color or feature options. Vehicles with an appearance change are those whose internal workings stayed essentially the same, but have updated body panels.

Series Started: We generally recommend against buying a car during its first model year of production. Each year the model is made, the production process is usually improved and there are fewer defects. Therefore, the longer a car has been made, the less likely you are to be plagued with manufacturing and design defects. On the other hand, the newer a car is, the more likely it is to have the latest in features and safety.

Where Made: Here we tell you where the car was assembled. You'll find that traditional domestic companies often build their vehicles in other countries. Also, many foreign companies build their cars in the U.S.

Theft Rating: This rating is given by the Insurance Institute for Highway Safety. It predicts the likelihood of the car being stolen or broken into based on its past history. If the car has no rating, (it may be too new) then we give it an "average."

Twins: Often a car company will make numerous models on the same platform. This is a list of this car's twins.

Specifications

Here are the "nuts and bolts." In this section we have listed eight key specifications which enable you to evaluate how best that car meets your particular needs. We provide the information for what we expect to be the most popular model.

Fuel Economy: This is the EPA-rated fuel economy for city and highway driving measured in miles per gallon. Most models have a variety of fuel economy ratings because of different engine and transmission options. We've selected the combination expected to be most popular.

Driving Range: Given the car's expected fuel economy and gas tank size, this gives an idea of how far you can go on a full tank.

Bumpers: Here we indicate the damage-resistance of the car's bumpers. Weak bumpers meet only the basic government requirements at 2.5 mph. Strong bumpers are just as damage-resistant at 5 mph. This information is not available for all vehicles.

Parking Index: Using the car's length, wheelbase, and turning circle, we have calculated how easy it will be to maneuver this car in tight spots. This rating of "very easy" to "very hard" is an indicator of how much difficulty you may have parking.

Seating: This figure represents the maximum number of seating positions equipped with safety belts. When more than one number is listed (for example, 5/6) it means that different models have different seat configurations.

Tow Rating: Ratings of very low, low, average, high, and very high indicate the vehicle's relative ability to tow trailers or other loads. Some manufacturers do not provide a tow rating.

Head/Leg Room: This tells how roomy the front seat is.

Interior Space: This tells how roomy the car is. Many SUVs do not provide interior space specifications.

Cargo Space: This gives you the cubic feet available for cargo. For minivans, it's the back of the two front seats to the rear of the vehicle. In cars, it's the trunk space.

COMPETITION

Here we tell you how the car stacks up with its competition. Use this information to compare the overall rating of similar cars and broaden your choice of new car possibilities. This may help you select a more economical or better performing car than the one you were originally considering. We've added page references so you can easily check out the competition. This list is only a guideline, not an all-inclusive list of every possible alternative.

Last Year's Model: One of the special features of The Car Book is that we have included ratings of last year's models. By buying a used car you will save dramatically on the purchase price and may get protection from the new car warranty left on the car. Because cars today don't change that much from year to year, no one may know that you bought used! In this section we include a brief description of the last year's model and a photo. See page 90 for some tips on buying a used car.

TIP

DESTINATION CHARGES

There once was a time when you could go directly to the factory and buy a car, saving yourself a few hundred dollars in destination and freight charges. Today, destination charges are a non-negotiable part of buying a new car, no matter where you purchase it. They are, however, an important factor when comparing prices. You'll find the destination charges on the price sticker attached to the vehicle. According to automakers, destination charges are the cost of shipping a vehicle from its "final assembly point" to the dealership. The cost of shipping other components for final assembly is sometimes also added.

But, the following table illustrates that there is little correlation between destination charges and where the cars are assembled:

Vehicle	Dest. Charge	Assembly Country
Acura RSX	$500	Japan
Jeep Liberty	$610	U.S.
Saturn ION	$675	U.S.
Volvo XC90	$685	Sweden

Acura MDX — Mid-Size SUV

For 2004, the Acura MDX has a new vehicle stability system, an optional rear seat DVD entertainment system, and a 3.5-liter V6 engine with more horsepower. Dual stage front airbags, position sensing side airbags, and safety belt pretensioners are some of the standard safety features. Available options include, an advanced audio system and a rearview camera to help with backing up. There is also a DVD based navigation system. The MDX is one of the leaders of midsized SUVs. It has great crash test performance.

Acura MDX

Ratings—10 Best, 1 Worst	2004	2003
Front Crash Tests	10	9
Side Crash Tests	10	10
Safety Features	9	6
Preventive Maintenance	8	8
Repair Costs	5	4
Warranty	7	5
Fuel Economy	2	3
Rollover	7	7
Complaints	9	9
Insurance Costs	10	10
OVERALL RATING	10	9

Acura MDX

Price Range	Retail	Markup
Base	$36,400	11%
With Touring Package	$39,000	11%

Safety Checklist

Frontal Crash Test	Very Good
Side Crash Test	Very Good
Airbags (Side/Head)	Front Standard/Yes
Pretensioners/Impact Adjustors	Yes/Yes
Position/Weight Sensors	Yes/Yes
Seat/Head Adjustors	No
Roll Stability System	Yes
Child Seats Built-in	None
Antilock Brakes/Day Lamps	4-Wheel/None
Tire Pressure Monitor	None

Last Year's Model

The MDX was all-new in 2001 and went into 2003 unchanged. The inside is like a large European luxury sedan. Leather is standard and the dash is similar to the Acura TL. The suspension system offers a ride more like a sedan than an SUV and the engine has more power than your typical off-roader. Acura claims that the all-wheel drive transmission will provide a smoother ride on paved roads than most comparable systems.

Acura MDX

General Information

2004 Status	Unchanged
Series Started	2001
Where Made	Canada
Theft Rating	Very High
Twins	

Specifications

Fuel Econ. (city/hwy)	Very Poor-17/23
Driving Range (mi.)	Short-369.8
Bumpers	Strong
Parking Index	Average
Seating	7
Tow Rating	Average-4500
Head/Leg Room (in.)	Cramped-38.7/41.5
Int. Space (cu. ft.)	Very Roomy-161.5
Cargo Space (cu. ft.)	Cramped-14.8

How the Competition Rates

	Rating	Pg.
BMW X5	8	106
Volvo XC90	8	271
Lexus RX 330	9	194

Acura RL — Large

Acura's largest luxury car is the first sedan to come equipped with standard XM radio and a voice activation system. The all-new 2004 Acura RL has dual stage front passenger airbags and side airbags with sensors that deploy the airbags in different ways depending on the size and position of the passenger. The vehicle stability assist system helps control rollover problems resulting from road or weather conditions. The standard engine is a 24-valve 3.5L V-6 that delivers 225 horsepower. OnStar and leather seating are standard. The RL did well in government crash tests.

Acura RL

Ratings—10 Best, 1 Worst	2004	2003
Front Crash Tests	7	7
Side Crash Tests	—	—
Safety Features	4	5
Preventive Maintenance	9	8
Repair Costs	2	2
Warranty	7	5
Fuel Economy	3	4
Rollover	9	10
Complaints	6	9
Insurance Costs	10	10
OVERALL RATING	7	6

Acura RL

Safety Checklist

Frontal Crash Test	Good
Side Crash Test	
Airbags (Side/Head)	Front Standard
Pretensioners/Impact Adjustors	Yes/Yes
Position/Weight Sensors	No/No
Seat/Head Adjustors	No
Roll Stability System	No
Child Seats Built-in	None
Antilock Brakes/Day Lamps	4-Wheel/None
Tire Pressure Monitor	None

Price Range	Retail	Markup
3.5 RL	$45,600	12%
w/o Nav System	$43,225	12%

General Information

2004 Status	Major Appearance Change
Series Started	1996
Where Made	Japan
Theft Rating	Very High
Twins	

Last Year's Model

The Acura RL, one of Acura's most luxurious models, received only minor enhancements for 2003. Leather interiors, heated front seats, front and rear headrests, automatic climate control, and heated door mirrors are among the numerous features found on the RL. In terms of creature comforts and style, the RL competes with mid-sized European luxury sedans.

Acura RL 2003

Specifications

Fuel Econ. (city/hwy)	Poor-18/24
Driving Range (mi.)	Short-365.1
Bumpers	Strong
Parking Index	Average
Seating	5
Tow Rating	
Head/Leg Room (in.)	Cramped-38.8/42.1
Int. Space (cu. ft.)	Cramped-96.2
Cargo Space (cu. ft.)	Cramped-14.8

How the Competition Rates

	Rating	Pg.
Cadillac CTS	7	114
Infiniti I35	10	176
Toyota Avalon	10	249

Acura RSX — Compact

The 2004 RSX is only available as a front wheel drive hatchback coupe. The base RSX comes with a 2.0-liter, 160-horsepower engine. The Sportier Type S has a 200-hp engine and a tighter suspension. A CD player and six speakers are standard. The Type S includes a six-CD changer and a 7-speaker audio system. Dual stage front airbags, side impact airbags with passenger-side sensors, and front and rear crumple zones provide added safety to the RSX. A 5-speed manual or a 5-speed automatic transmission is available. Despite its size, the RSX has great crash test results.

Acura RSX

Ratings—10 Best, 1 Worst	2004	2003
Front Crash Tests	10	10
Side Crash Tests	6	—
Safety Features	6	7
Preventive Maintenance	10	—
Repair Costs	2	—
Warranty	7	5
Fuel Economy	8	8
Rollover	8	8
Complaints	2	—
Insurance Costs	1	1
OVERALL RATING	7	7

Acura RSX

Safety Checklist

Frontal Crash Test	Very Good
Side Crash Test	Average
Airbags (Side/Head)	Front Standard
Pretensioners/Impact Adjustors	Yes/Yes
Position/Weight Sensors	Yes/Yes
Seat/Head Adjustors	No
Roll Stability System	No
Child Seats Built-in	None
Antilock Brakes/Day Lamps	4-Wheel/None
Tire Pressure Monitor	None

Price Range	Retail	Markup
5 AT	$20,925	10%
5 MT	$20,025	10%
6MT	$23,320	10%

General Information

2004 Status	Unchanged
Series Started	2002
Where Made	Japan
Theft Rating	Average
Twins	

Last Year's Model

Introduced in 2002, the RSX was Acura's replacement for the Integra. This stylish coupe is offered in two variants and is powered by a 2.0-liter four-cylinder engine. Large, red-back-lit, sport gauges are angled toward the driver. Automatic climate control, keyless entry, and an anti-theft immobilizer are standard. Side-impact airbags and front seat belt pretensioners are also found on the RSX. The rear seats are a bit cramped, but the front is spacious.

Acura RSX 2003

Specifications

Fuel Econ. (city/hwy)	Good-24/33
Driving Range (mi.)	Short-361.1
Bumpers	Strong
Parking Index	Average
Seating	5
Tow Rating	
Head/Leg Room (in.)	Cramped-37.8/43.1
Int. Space (cu. ft.)	Very Cramped-79.2
Cargo Space (cu. ft.)	Average-17.8

How the Competition Rates

	Rating	Pg.
Infiniti G35		175
Audi A4	10	101
Chrysler Crossfire		135

Acura TL

Intermediate

The Acura TL is aimed at the luxury entry-level, Lexus ES300 buyer. Unchanged for 2004, the TL's main engine is a 3.2-liter V6, which gives plenty of power at the expense of fuel economy. Dual stage front airbags come standard. Side airbags with a passenger side sensor that prevent the airbag from deploying if the passenger is leaning to the side or is too small in stature are also available. Antilock brakes, vehicle stability systems, traction control, and wider tires all aid in preventing accidents. A navigation system is available. The TL scored well in government crash tests.

Acura TL

Acura TL

Ratings—10 Best, 1 Worst	2004	2003
Front Crash Tests	8	8
Side Crash Tests	10	10
Safety Features	5	6
Preventive Maintenance	9	8
Repair Costs	3	5
Warranty	7	5
Fuel Economy	5	5
Rollover	9	9
Complaints	3	9
Insurance Costs	10	10
OVERALL RATING	10	10

Price Range	Retail	Markup
Sedan	$32,650	10%

Safety Checklist

Frontal Crash Test . . . . . Good
Side Crash Test . . . . . Very Good
Airbags (Side/Head) . . . . . Front Standard
Pretensioners/Impact Adjustors. . . . . None/Yes
Position/Weight Sensors . . . . . Yes/Yes
Seat/Head Adjustors. . . . . No
Roll Stability System. . . . . No
Child Seats Built-in. . . . . None
Antilock Brakes/Day Lamps. 4-Wheel/None
Tire Pressure Monitor. . . . . None

General Information

2004 Status. . . . . Unchanged
Series Started 1999
Where Made . . . . . US
Theft Rating. . . . . Very High
Twins. . . . .

Specifications

Fuel Econ. (city/hwy). Average-19/29
Driving Range (mi.) Average-386.8
Bumpers . . . . . Strong
Parking Index. . . . . Average
Seating 5
Tow Rating . . . . .
Head/Leg Room (in.) Cramped-38.2/42.4
Int. Space (cu. ft.). Cramped-95.5
Cargo Space (cu. ft.) Cramped-14.3

Last Year's Model

The only modification for the 2003 Acura TL came in the form of a navigation system, OnStar, and an increase in horsepower. The TL has many standard features, but leather interior, automatic climate control, and side window defoggers are optional. The Acura TL has a higher starting price than other Acuras. The interior is spacious, and the ride is good.

Acura TL 2003

How the Competition Rates

	Rating	Pg.
BMW 5 Series		105
Volvo 60 Series	10	268
Saab 9-5	10	232

Acura TSX — Intermediate

Designed to compete with top European and Japanese sports sedans, the Acura TSX makes its debut with a 200 horsepower four-cylinder engine. This sports sedan is aimed at young drivers and is built to bridge the gap between the RSX sports coupe and the TL luxury sedan. The 2004 TSX comes with a number of safety features as standard equipment including side curtain airbags, side impact airbags with a passenger-sensing system, a vehicle stability assist system and a traction control system. The handing of the TSX is similar to the Honda Accord Coupe models.

Acura TSX

Ratings—10 Best, 1 Worst	2004	2003
Front Crash Tests	—	
Side Crash Tests	—	
Safety Features	8	
Preventive Maintenance	—	
Repair Costs	—	
Warranty	7	
Fuel Economy	7	
Rollover	8	
Complaints	—	
Insurance Costs	5	
OVERALL RATING	—	

Acura TSX

Price Range	Retail	Markup
5 auto.	$26,490	10%
5 auto. w/Navigation System	$28,090	8%
6 man.	$26,490	10%
6sp man. w/Navigation System	$28,090	8%

Last Year's Model

Model Not Produced in 2003

2003

Safety Checklist

Frontal Crash Test	
Side Crash Test	
Airbags (Side/Head)	Front Standard/Yes
Pretensioners/Impact Adjustors	Standard/Yes
Position/Weight Sensors	Yes/No
Seat/Head Adjustors	No
Roll Stability System	Yes
Child Seats Built-in	None
Antilock Brakes/Day Lamps	4-Wheel/None
Tire Pressure Monitor	None

General Information

2004 Status	All New
Series Started	No series indicated
Where Made	Japan
Theft Rating	Average
Twins	Honda Accord Coupe 2004

Specifications

Fuel Econ. (city/hwy)	Good-22/31
Driving Range (mi.)	Very Long-432.7
Bumpers	Weak
Parking Index	Hard
Seating	5
Tow Rating	
Head/Leg Room (in.)	Cramped-37.8/42.4
Int. Space (cu. ft.)	Cramped-91
Cargo Space (cu. ft.)	Cramped-13

How the Competition Rates

	Rating	Pg.
Audi A4	10	101
BMW 3 Series	9	104
Infiniti G35		175

Audi A4 — Compact

Audi's best selling vehicle gets a host of electronic improvements. All models will be equipped for satellite radio installation as a standard feature. A tire pressure monitoring system is also standard. There is a new 6-speed manual transmission option on the 1.8-liter model. An all-new S4 powered by a V8 engine has been added to the A4 family this year. Safety features include advance dual stage front airbags that can deactivate the passenger side air bag if the seat is empty. The A4 is seen as a competitor to the BMW 3 Series and scored well in government's crash tests.

Audi A4

Ratings—10 Best, 1 Worst	2004	2003
Front Crash Tests	7	7
Side Crash Tests	10	10
Safety Features	7	7
Preventive Maintenance	5	8
Repair Costs	1	2
Warranty	10	9
Fuel Economy	7	7
Rollover	9	9
Complaints	1	—
Insurance Costs	10	10
OVERALL RATING	10	10

Audi A4

Price Range	Retail	Markup
1.8 T	$27,250	10%
1.8T Wagon	$28,250	10%
3.0 Quattro	$32,740	10%
3.0 Sedan	$31,150	11%

Safety Checklist

Frontal Crash Test	Good
Side Crash Test	Very Good
Airbags (Side/Head)	Front Optional/Yes
Pretensioners/Impact Adjustors	Yes/Yes
Position/Weight Sensors	NA/NA
Seat/Head Adjustors	No
Roll Stability System	Yes
Child Seats Built-in	None
Antilock Brakes/Day Lamps	4-Wheel/None
Tire Pressure Monitor	None

General Information

2004 Status	Unchanged
Series Started	2002
Where Made	Germany
Theft Rating	Very High
Twins	Audi S4 2004

Last Year's Model

In 2003, the A4 introduced a convertible model, but otherwise remained unchanged since its redesign in 2002. A five-speed-manual gearbox is standard with the 1.8-liter engine, and the V6 has a six-speed automatic option. A more rigid body, a longer wheelbase and bigger tires will make for a more luxurious ride. The A4 has four-way power lumbar support, more seat room, and a four-position memory system for the driver's seat is optional.

Audi A4 2003

Specifications

Fuel Econ. (city/hwy)	Good-23/29
Driving Range (mi.)	Very Long-441.3
Bumpers	Strong
Parking Index	Easy
Seating	5
Tow Rating	
Head/Leg Room (in.)	Very Cramped-38.4/41.3
Int. Space (cu. ft.)	Cramped-90.1
Cargo Space (cu. ft.)	Roomy-27.8

How the Competition Rates

	Rating	Pg.
Acura TSX		100
BMW 3 Series	9	104
Infiniti G35		175

Audi A6 — Intermediate

For the 2004 model year, the Audi A6 remains unchanged. A new sunroof has been added as standard equipment on all A6 Quattro models. A power outlet for your cell phone has replaced the retractable cup holder in the front center console. A 2.7-liter turbo engine, a 3.0-liter V6, or a 4.2-liter V8 can power the A6. Interior spaciousness is average for its size class. The A6 provides a blend of luxury features, good handling, and solid performance.

Audi A6

Audi A6

Ratings—10 Best, 1 Worst	2004	2003
Front Crash Tests	—	—
Side Crash Tests	—	—
Safety Features	7	8
Preventive Maintenance	7	7
Repair Costs	2	1
Warranty	10	9
Fuel Economy	5	5
Rollover	9	9
Complaints	3	2
Insurance Costs	5	5
OVERALL RATING	—	—

Price Range	Retail	Markup
2.7T Quattro	$42,150	10%
3.0 Sedan	$35,950	11%
Avant	$40,150	10%
Quattro 4.2	$49,000	11%

Last Year's Model

Like the A4, the Audi A6 is available in a sedan or Avant wagon version. The 2003 model has an improved suspension system and new leather seating as standard features. Safety features include next generation dual front airbags, side impact airbags, and lockable head rests for the front passengers. The A6 can be equipped with front wheel drive, but most will have all-wheel drive. Leather seating is standard.

Audi A6

Safety Checklist

Frontal Crash Test. . . . .
Side Crash Test. . . . .
Airbags (Side/Head) . . . . Fr. Std. Rear Opt./Yes
Pretensioners/Impact Adjustors . . . . Yes/Yes
Position/Weight Sensors . . . . NA/NA
Seat/Head Adjustors. . . . . No
Roll Stability System . . . . Yes
Child Seats Built-in. . . . . None
Antilock Brakes/Day Lamps. 4-Wheel/None
Tire Pressure Monitor. . . . . None

General Information

2004 Status. . . . . Unchanged
Series Started 1998
Where Made. . . . . Germany
Theft Rating. . . . . Very High
Twins. . . . .

Specifications

Fuel Econ. (city/hwy). Average-20/27
Driving Range (mi.). Long-418.9
Bumpers . . . . Strong
Parking Index . . . . Hard
Seating 5
Tow Rating . . . .
Head/Leg Room (in.) Cramped-39.3/41.3
Int. Space (cu. ft.) Average-98.3
Cargo Space (cu. ft.) Cramped-15.4

How the Competition Rates

	Rating	Pg.
BMW 5 Series		105
Volvo 60 Series	10	268
Lexus GS 300		191

Audi Allroad Quattro — Intermediate

In 2004, the Allroad Quattro adds a 4.2-liter V8 model to its line up. The standard 2.7-liter turbo model remains unchanged this year. The new V8 produces well over 300 horsepower. You have a choice of XM or Sirius satellite radio options. A new HomeLink garage door opener is standard. Memory equipped seats can also be found on the new 4.2 model. A power adjustable steering wheel is standard. All wheel drive is also standard. Side curtain airbags are available in this all-wheel drive wagon.

Audi Allroad Quattro

Audi Allroad Quattro

Ratings—10 Best, 1 Worst	2004	2003
Front Crash Tests	—	—
Side Crash Tests	—	—
Safety Features	9	8
Preventive Maintenance	6	7
Repair Costs	—	1
Warranty	10	9
Fuel Economy	2	2
Rollover	7	7
Complaints	10	10
Insurance Costs	10	10
OVERALL RATING	—	—

Price Range	Retail	Markup
2.7 T 6sp	$39,950	10%
2.7 T Tip Quattro	$39,950	10%
4.2	$46,950	11%

Last Year's Model

There were a few modifications in the 2003 Audi Allroad Quattro. This vehicle lies between a wagon and a SUV. Powered by a 250 hp, 2.7 liter V6 engine, the Quattro has a five-speed automatic transmission or a six-speed manual option. AWD is standard. Interior volume is excellent for this wagon. The Allroad Quattro comes equipped with a host of options and is a competitor to the Volvo XC 70 wagon.

Audi Allroad Quattro 2003

Safety Checklist

Frontal Crash Test. . . . .
Side Crash Test. . . . .
Airbags (Side/Head). . . . . Front Standard/Yes
Pretensioners/Impact Adjustors . . . . Yes/Yes
Position/Weight Sensors . . . . Yes/Yes
Seat/Head Adjustors. . . . . No
Roll Stability System . . . . Yes
Child Seats Built-in. . . . . None
Antilock Brakes/Day Lamps. 4-Wheel/None
Tire Pressure Monitor. . . . . None

General Information

2004 Status. . . . . Unchanged
Series Started 2000
Where Made. . . . . Germany
Theft Rating. . . . . Average
Twins. . . . .

Specifications

Fuel Econ. (city/hwy) . . . . Very Poor-16/22
Driving Range (mi.) . . . . Very Short-337.4
Bumpers . . . . Strong
Parking Index . . . . Hard
Seating 5
Tow Rating . . . .
Head/Leg Room (in.). . . . . Very Cramped-37.5/41.3
Int. Space (cu. ft.) Average-99.3
Cargo Space (cu. ft.). . . . . Very Roomy-52.7

How the Competition Rates

	Rating	Pg.
Volvo 70 Series		269
Mercedes-Benz C-Class	9	202
BMW 5 Series		105

BMW 3 Series — Compact

For 2004, the BMW 3-Series gets a substantial appearance change, particularly around the headlights and the front grille. The 325, and 330 models dominate the 3-Series vehicles and come in a coupe, convertible or a sedan version. The base line engine is a 2.5-liter inline 6-cylinder. The 330 has a larger engine. Antilock brakes, traction control, and side impact airbags are some of the features found on the 3-Series. All-wheel drive is optional. The 3-Series has very good crash test results.

Ratings—10 Best, 1 Worst	2004	2003
Front Crash Tests	10	10
Side Crash Tests	9	9
Safety Features	9	8
Preventive Maintenance	10	9
Repair Costs	1	1
Warranty	6	6
Fuel Economy	5	6
Rollover	9	9
Complaints	7	5
Insurance Costs	5	5
OVERALL RATING	9	10

Price Range	Retail	Markup
2D 325i Coupe	$30,100	9%
325CIC Convertible	$37,300	9%
330CI Coupe	$36,300	9%
330CIC Convertible	$43,600	9%

Last Year's Model

BMW's entry-level 3-Series remained unchanged this year. You have a choice of three power trains, three different models and rear or all-wheel drive. A 2.5-liter inline 6-cylinder engine is standard on the 3-Series. A larger 2.8-liter version is available as an option in some models. The 1.8-liter 4-cylinder engine was dropped in 2003. Safety features include front and side airbags and traction control along with 4-wheel ABS and dual airbags.

BMW 3 Series — 2003

BMW 3 Series Convertible

BMW 325i Sports Wagon

Safety Checklist

Frontal Crash Test	Very Good
Side Crash Test	Very Good
Airbags (Side/Head)	Fr. Std. Rear Opt./Yes
Pretensioners/Impact Adjustors	Yes/Yes
Position/Weight Sensors	Yes/No
Seat/Head Adjustors	No
Roll Stability System	Yes
Child Seats Built-in	None
Antilock Brakes/Day Lamps	4-Wheel/Standard
Tire Pressure Monitor	None

General Information

2004 Status	Minor Appearance Change
Series Started	1999
Where Made	Germany
Theft Rating	Very High
Twins	

Specifications

Fuel Econ. (city/hwy)	Average-19/28
Driving Range (mi.)	Short-368.7
Bumpers	Weak
Parking Index	Very Easy
Seating	5
Tow Rating	
Head/Leg Room (in.)	Very Cramped-37.5/41.7
Int. Space (cu. ft.)	Very Cramped-84.4
Cargo Space (cu. ft.)	Very Cramped-9.5

How the Competition Rates

	Rating	Pg.
Audi A4	10	101
Volvo 40 Series		267
Nissan Altima	9	214

BMW 5 Series — Intermediate

The 5-Series has been redesigned giving the sedan a new appearance and platform. It features an all-new aluminum and steel body with an all-aluminum suspension and chassis. There is an active roll stabilization system and run-flat tires. Either a 2.5 or 3.0-liter inline 6-cylinder engine powers the 5-Series and there is an optional V8. The interior has the latest in driver oriented instrument displays and comfort. There is a heads-up display and automatic climate control. There is an active cruise control system, which uses radar to help maintain road speed and spacing on the highway.

Ratings—10 Best, 1 Worst	2004	2003
Front Crash Tests	—	—
Side Crash Tests	10	—
Safety Features	10	10
Preventive Maintenance	—	10
Repair Costs	—	3
Warranty	6	6
Fuel Economy	4	6
Rollover	9	—
Complaints	—	8
Insurance Costs	5	5
OVERALL RATING	—	—

Price Range	Retail	Markup
525i	$39,300	9%
530i	$44,300	9%
545i	$54,300	10%
545i 6-speed	$57,600	10%

Last Year's Model

The 2003 5-Series was unchanged. The roomy 5-Series is more luxurious and has more safety features than the 3-Series. You can choose between two different engines: a 2.8-liter inline 6-cylinder or the more powerful 4.4-liter V8 engine. Standard safety features include dual and side airbags and a head airbag for protection in a rollover. A dynamic stability control, which helps on slippery roads, is standard. A DVD navigation system is optional.

BMW 5 Series — 2003

BMW 525i

BMW 530i

Safety Checklist

Frontal Crash Test	
Side Crash Test	
Airbags (Side/Head)	Fr. Std. Rear Opt./Yes
Pretensioners/Impact Adjustors	Standard/Yes
Position/Weight Sensors	Yes/Yes
Seat/Head Adjustors	Yes
Roll Stability System	Yes
Child Seats Built-in	None
Antilock Brakes/Day Lamps	4-Wheel/Standard
Tire Pressure Monitor	None

General Information

2004 Status	All New
Series Started	No series indicated
Where Made	Germany
Theft Rating	Very High
Twins	

Specifications

Fuel Econ. (city/hwy)	Poor-19/25
Driving Range (mi.)	Average-394.1
Bumpers	Strong
Parking Index	Hard
Seating	5
Tow Rating	
Head/Leg Room (in.)	Cramped-39.1/41.5
Int. Space (cu. ft.)	Average-99.1
Cargo Space (cu. ft.)	Cramped-14

How the Competition Rates

	Rating	Pg.
Acura TL	10	99
Lexus ES 330		190
Toyota Avalon	10	249

BMW X5 — Mid-Size SUV

The X5 receives a new 4.4-liter V8 engine option and a new trim model. There is also a new computer controlled all-wheel drive system to improve road handling and braking. The standard 3.0-liter inline 6-cylinder has been improved as well. The 4.6i trim model has been dropped for 2004. The X5 is BMW's answer to rise of mid sized luxury SUVs. The standard 3.0-liter I6 provides excellent power and performance. Options include heated rear seats, heated steering wheel, moon roof and a DVD-based navigation system. Dual stage airbags, and side curtain airbags are standard.

BMW X5

BMW X5

Ratings—10 Best, 1 Worst	2004	2003
Front Crash Tests	10	10
Side Crash Tests	10	10
Safety Features	10	10
Preventive Maintenance	10	10
Repair Costs	2	1
Warranty	6	6
Fuel Economy	1	2
Rollover	5	2
Complaints	4	8
Insurance Costs	10	10
OVERALL RATING	8	10

Price Range	Retail	Markup
3.0i	$40,300	9%
4.4i	$51,500	10%

Last Year's Model

The X5 zipped into 2003 unchanged. In addition to the solid BMW feel and their brand of no-nonsense luxury, the X5 comes with options such as a high-pressure liquid headlight cleaning system and rain-sensing wipers. Other safety features include dual stage airbags and standard front side airbags. Rear side airbags are an option. The X5 also got the 5 Series' DVD Navigation system as an option in 2003.

BMW X5 2003

Safety Checklist

Frontal Crash Test	Very Good
Side Crash Test	Very Good
Airbags (Side/Head)	Fr. Std. Rear Opt./Yes
Pretensioners/Impact Adjustors	Yes/Yes
Position/Weight Sensors	Yes/Yes
Seat/Head Adjustors	Yes
Roll Stability System	Yes
Child Seats Built-in	None
Antilock Brakes/Day Lamps	4-Wheel/Standard
Tire Pressure Monitor	None

General Information

2004 Status	Unchanged
Series Started	2000
Where Made	US
Theft Rating	Very High
Twins	

Specifications

Fuel Econ. (city/hwy)	Very Poor-15/20
Driving Range (mi.)	Long-415.8
Bumpers	Weak
Parking Index	Hard
Seating	5
Tow Rating	High-5953
Head/Leg Room (in.)	Very Cramped-39.9/39.3
Int. Space (cu. ft.)	Average-97.6
Cargo Space (cu. ft.)	Average-23.8

How the Competition Rates

	Rating	Pg.
Acura MDX	10	96
Land Rover Discovery	1	188
Volvo XC90	8	271

BMW Z4

Compact

The 2004 edition of the Z4 is unchanged. There will be a new hard top version available later this year. First introduced last year, the Z4 provides the U.S. market with an Autobahn inspired roadster. A 2.5-liter 6-cylinder engine powers the Z4. There is also a more powerful 3.0-liter version available on the pricier 3.0i trim model. The interior is designed for two people, and there is limited cargo room. Side-impact airbags, knee airbags and antilock brakes are standard. A cutoff switch for the front passenger airbag is included. The Z4 has good crash test performance.

BMW Z4

Ratings—10 Best, 1 Worst	2004	2003
Front Crash Tests	7	—
Side Crash Tests	5	—
Safety Features	10	7
Preventive Maintenance	10	10
Repair Costs	—	1
Warranty	6	6
Fuel Economy	6	6
Rollover	10	10
Complaints	—	—
Insurance Costs	5	5
OVERALL RATING	9	—

Price Range	Retail	Markup
2.5i	$33,200	9%
3.0i	$40,350	9%

Last Year's Model

The 2003, Z4 was the successor the Z3 roadster. It is longer, and has a more powerful engine than its older sibling. The base engine is a powerful 2.5-liter inline 6-cylinder. There is a more powerful 3.0-liter option available. The roadster has a standard six-speed manual transmission. In the spring of 2003, a Sequential Manual Gearbox (SMG) became available.

BMW Z4 2003

BMW Z4

Safety Checklist

Frontal Crash Test	Good
Side Crash Test	Average
Airbags (Side/Head)	Front Standard
Pretensioners/Impact Adjustors	Yes/Yes
Position/Weight Sensors	Yes/No
Seat/Head Adjustors	No
Roll Stability System	Yes
Child Seats Built-in	None
Antilock Brakes/Day Lamps	4-Wheel/Standard
Tire Pressure Monitor	None

General Information

2004 Status	Unchanged
Series Started	2003
Where Made	US
Theft Rating	Average
Twins	

Specifications

Fuel Econ. (city/hwy)	Average-21/28
Driving Range (mi.)	Very Short-343.1
Bumpers	Weak
Parking Index	Very Easy
Seating	2
Tow Rating	
Head/Leg Room (in.)	Very Cramped-37.3/42
Int. Space (cu. ft.)	Very Cramped-57
Cargo Space (cu. ft.)	Very Cramped-8.5

How the Competition Rates

	Rating	Pg.
Chrysler Crossfire		135
Honda S2000	7	167
Nissan 350Z	7	213

Buick Century

Intermediate

The 2004 Century, Buick's entry-level sedan, has three different opinion packages. The standard package includes keyless entry, dual zone climate control, a CD player, and an air filtration system. The custom package offers cruise control, a six-way power driver's seat, and a trunk cargo net. The limited package includes steering wheel mounted radio controls, 15 in. chrome wheel covers, and leather appointed seating surfaces. The only engine is a 3.1-liter V6 engine that delivers nearly 175 horsepower. Despite its size, the Century has average performance in NHTSA's crash tests.

Buick Century

Ratings—10 Best, 1 Worst	2004	2003
Front Crash Tests	5	5
Side Crash Tests	6	6
Safety Features	3	4
Preventive Maintenance	6	7
Repair Costs	7	7
Warranty	2	3
Fuel Economy	5	6
Rollover	9	9
Complaints	9	9
Insurance Costs	10	10
OVERALL RATING	6	7

Buick Century

Safety Checklist

Frontal Crash Test . . . . . Average
Side Crash Test . . . . . Average
Airbags (Side/Head) . . . . . Front Optional Rear Optional
Pretensioners/Impact Adjustors . . . . . None/No
Position/Weight Sensors . . . . . No/No
Seat/Head Adjustors . . . . . No
Roll Stability System . . . . . No
Child Seats Built-in . . . . . Optional
Antilock Brakes/Day Lamps 4-Wheel/Standard
Tire Pressure Monitor . . . . . Indirect

Price Range	Retail	Markup
Custom	$21,520	9%

General Information

2004 Status . . . . . Unchanged
Series Started 1996
Where Made . . . . . Canada
Theft Rating . . . . . Very Low
Twins . . . . . Buick Regal 2004

Last Year's Model

The 2003 Buick Century received a minor appearance change both externally and internally. A new graphite and chrome grille was added as well as new door and side moldings. Additional padding was been added to the interior to improve head-impact protection. Only one engine is available on the Century: a 3.1-liter V6, which produces 175 hp. ABS, power windows and power door locks are all standard.

Buick Century 2003

Specifications

Fuel Econ. (city/hwy) Average-20/29
Driving Range (mi.) Average-395.2
Bumpers . . . . . Strong
Parking Index . . . . . Hard
Seating 6
Tow Rating . . . . . Very Low-1000
Head/Leg Room (in.) Average-39.4/42.4
Int. Space (cu. ft.) Average-101.8
Cargo Space (cu. ft.) Average-16.7

How the Competition Rates

	Rating	Pg.
Nissan Maxima	9	216
Volkswagen Passat	8	265
Nissan Altima	9	214

Buick LeSabre — Large

Little has changed for the Buick LeSabre. The doors, rear compartment, and quarter panels have enhanced soundproofing to reduce noise inside the cabin. The "custom package" offers a driver information display, rearview electrochromic mirror, six-speaker audio system, steering wheel controls, 15-inch wheels, traction control, illuminated vanity mirror, and a theft deterrent system. The "celebration edition" of the LeSabre comes with turn signals integrated onto the rearview mirrors. The LeSabre has very good crash test scores.

Buick LeSabre

Ratings—10 Best, 1 Worst	2004	2003
Front Crash Tests	9	9
Side Crash Tests	9	9
Safety Features	3	3
Preventive Maintenance	4	3
Repair Costs	4	4
Warranty	2	3
Fuel Economy	5	6
Rollover	10	10
Complaints	5	3
Insurance Costs	10	10
OVERALL RATING	7	7

Buick LeSabre

Price Range	Retail	Markup
Custom	$25,745	9%
Limited	$31,520	9%

Safety Checklist

Frontal Crash Test . . . . . Very Good
Side Crash Test . . . . . Very Good
Airbags (Side/Head) . . . . . Front Optional Rear Optional
Pretensioners/Impact Adjustors . . . . . None/No
Position/Weight Sensors . . . . . No/No
Seat/Head Adjustors . . . . . No
Roll Stability System . . . . . No
Child Seats Built-in . . . . . None
Antilock Brakes/Day Lamps 4-Wheel/Standard
Tire Pressure Monitor . . . . . Indirect

Last Year's Model

The 2003 Buick LeSabre was a carryover from 2002. Side-impact airbags left the LeSabre's standard-equipment list and are only optional. An XM Satellite Radio is optional in the "celebration edition" and the Limited model. New chrome wheels, GM's OnStar communication system, a heads up display on the windshield and StabiliTrak, are standard. The LeSabre is equipped with the powerful 3.8-liter V6 engine.

Buick LeSabre

General Information

2004 Status . . . . . Unchanged
Series Started 2000
Where Made . . . . . US
Theft Rating . . . . . Very Low
Twins . . . . . Cadillac Seville, Pontiac Bonneville 2004

Specifications

Fuel Econ. (city/hwy) Average-20/29
Driving Range (mi.) Long-430.1
Bumpers . . . . . Strong
Parking Index . . . . . Very Hard
Seating 5/6
Tow Rating . . . . . Very Low-1000
Head/Leg Room (in.) Average-38.8/42.4
Int. Space (cu. ft.) Roomy-107.6
Cargo Space (cu. ft.) Average-18

How the Competition Rates

	Rating	Pg.
Cadillac DeVille	9	115
Ford Crown Victoria	10	146
Lexus GS 300		191

Buick Park Avenue | Large

The 2004 Park Avenue remains essentially unchanged from last years model. There is a new stand-up hood ornament, along with an assortment of new interior and exterior colors. Buick offers the supercharged Park Avenue Ultra, which has a more prominent grille, 17-inch chrome wheels, "portholes" in each front fender, and heated rearview mirrors with integrated turn signals. It also offers a supercharged version of the 3.8-liter V6 engine shared with the base model Park Avenue. The Park Avenue scored well in government crash tests.

Ratings—10 Best, 1 Worst	2004	2003
Front Crash Tests	8	8
Side Crash Tests	9	9
Safety Features	3	3
Preventive Maintenance	6	3
Repair Costs	4	5
Warranty	2	3
Fuel Economy	5	4
Rollover	9	10
Complaints	7	6
Insurance Costs	10	10
OVERALL RATING	7	6

Price Range	Retail	Markup
Sedan	$34,750	10%
Ultra	$39,925	10%

Last Year's Model

For 2003, Buick introduced the supercharged Park Avenue Ultra, with its prominent grille, 17-inch chrome wheels and "portholes." Side airbags, ABS, daytime running lamps, power windows and doors and a high-end audio system are all standard features on the Park Avenue. The Park Avenue fared well in front and side crash tests. The Ultra model has a rear-parking assist system.

Buick Park Avenue — 2003

Buick Park Avenue Ultra

Buick Park Avenue

Safety Checklist

Frontal Crash Test	Good
Side Crash Test	Very Good
Airbags (Side/Head)	Front Standard
Pretensioners/Impact Adjustors	None/No
Position/Weight Sensors	No/No
Seat/Head Adjustors	No
Roll Stability System	No
Child Seats Built-in	None
Antilock Brakes/Day Lamps	4-Wheel/Standard
Tire Pressure Monitor	Indirect

General Information

2004 Status	Unchanged
Series Started	1996
Where Made	US
Theft Rating	Very Low
Twins	

Specifications

Fuel Econ. (city/hwy)	Average-20/29
Driving Range (mi.)	Long-427.7
Bumpers	Strong
Parking Index	Very Hard
Seating	5
Tow Rating	Very Low-1000
Head/Leg Room (in.)	Roomy-39.8/42.4
Int. Space (cu. ft.)	Roomy-112.1
Cargo Space (cu. ft.)	Average-19.1

How the Competition Rates

	Rating	Pg.
Ford Crown Victoria	10	146
Pontiac Bonneville	7	226
Lincoln LS		196

Buick Rainier/Oldsmobile Bravada — Large SUV

The all-new Buick Rainier and its twin the Bravada come with a standard 4.2L-liter/inline 6-cylinder or an optional 5.3-liter V-8. The Rainer/Bravada provides a smooth ride with independent front suspension and electronically controlled rear air suspension. An on-demand All-Wheel-Drive system is offered as an option. Duel-stage front airbags and optional side airbags are among the safety features found on the Rainer and Bravada. They both have a spacious interior. This will be the last year for the Bravada. The Bravada and Rainier have similar options.

Buick Rainier

Oldsmobile Bravada

Ratings—10 Best, 1 Worst	2004	2003
Front Crash Tests	5	5
Side Crash Tests	10	10
Safety Features	7	7
Preventive Maintenance	5	6
Repair Costs	5	2
Warranty	2	7
Fuel Economy	2	2
Rollover	5	5
Complaints		—
Insurance Costs	5	10
OVERALL RATING	4	5

Price Range	Retail	Markup
2WD CXL	$35,945	13%
2WD CXL Plus	$36,995	12%
4WD CXL	$37,895	12%
4WD CXL Plus	$38,945	12%

Last Year's Model

The 2003 Bravada added coil suspension to its all-wheel drive models and a traction assistance systems as standard on 2WD vehicles. It has a 4.2-liter 270 hp six-cylinder engine and electronically controlled suspension. Leather upholstery, OnStar, and a backseat DVD entertainment system are available. Two or four-wheel drive is available and all-disc antilock brakes, side-impact airbags and dual-stage front airbags are standard.

Oldsmobile Bravada 2003

Safety Checklist

Frontal Crash Test	Average
Side Crash Test	Very Good
Airbags (Side/Head)	Fr. Std. Rear Opt.
Pretensioners/Impact Adjustors	Standard/Yes
Position/Weight Sensors	Yes/No
Seat/Head Adjustors	No
Roll Stability System	Yes
Child Seats Built-in	None
Antilock Brakes/Day Lamps	4-Wheel/Standard
Tire Pressure Monitor	Indirect

General Information

2004 Status	All New
Series Started	No series indicated
Where Made	
Theft Rating	Average
Twins	Trail Blazer, Envoy, Bravada, Ascender 5-pass.

Specifications

Fuel Econ. (city/hwy)	Very Poor-16/21
Driving Range (mi.)	Average-394.2
Bumpers	
Parking Index	Average
Seating	7
Tow Rating	High-6300
Head/Leg Room (in.)	Very Roomy-40.2/44.6
Int. Space (cu. ft.)	
Cargo Space (cu. ft.)	Roomy-39.8

How the Competition Rates

	Rating	Pg.
Volkswagen Touareg		266
Volvo XC90	8	271
Ford Expedition	4	149

Buick Regal

Intermediate

For 2004, the Buick Regal now offers a new luxury options package that includes 16-inch aluminum wheels; steering wheel mounted radio controls, and illuminated vanity mirrors. Additional luxury packages add leather seating surfaces and dual-zone climate control. The LS model has a 3.8-liter V-6 engine. The interior pillars and roof rails are backed with energy absorbing foam for head impact protection. Remote keyless entry and a battery rundown protection system are standard on the Regal. The Regal scored only average in crash tests.

Buick Regal

Buick Regal

Ratings—10 Best, 1 Worst	2004	2003
Front Crash Tests	5	5
Side Crash Tests	6	6
Safety Features	3	3
Preventive Maintenance	6	5
Repair Costs	7	7
Warranty	2	3
Fuel Economy	5	4
Rollover	9	10
Complaints	9	8
Insurance Costs	10	10
OVERALL RATING	6	5

Price Range	Retail	Markup
GS	$28,685	9%
LS	$24,235	9%

Last Year's Model

The Buick Regal remained unchanged for 2003. The Regal offers special models with color and trim touches by Joseph Abound-available in both LS and GS models. The LS engine is a 3.8-liter V6 and the GS has a supercharged version of the same engine. Daytime running lamps, cruise control, and remote keyless entry are standard on the LS, while the GS also offers a leather interior and standard front and side impact airbags.

Buick Regal 2003

Safety Checklist

Frontal Crash Test	Average
Side Crash Test	Average
Airbags (Side/Head)	Front Standard
Pretensioners/Impact Adjustors	None/No
Position/Weight Sensors	No/No
Seat/Head Adjustors	No
Roll Stability System	No
Child Seats Built-in	None
Antilock Brakes/Day Lamps	4-Wheel/Standard
Tire Pressure Monitor	None

General Information

2004 Status	Unchanged
Series Started	1998
Where Made	Canada
Theft Rating	Very Low
Twins	Buick Century 2004

Specifications

Fuel Econ. (city/hwy)	Average-19/29
Driving Range (mi.)	Average-382.3
Bumpers	Strong
Parking Index	Hard
Seating	5
Tow Rating	
Head/Leg Room (in.)	Average-39.4/42.4
Int. Space (cu. ft.)	Average-101.8
Cargo Space (cu. ft.)	Average-16.7

How the Competition Rates

	Rating	Pg.
Nissan Altima	9	214
Toyota Camry	10	250
Volkswagen Passat	8	265

Buick Rendezvous — Mid-Size SUV

This year Buick adds the Rendezvous Ultra model. The Ultra comes with a standard 245 horsepower 3.6-liter V-6. An "Oil Life" system will notify the driver that an oil change is needed. The front and side airbags have advanced inflation characteristics. A heads up instrument display, OnStar, and the Ultrasonic Rear Park Assist system (warns the driver of objects behind the car) all come standard. A GPS navigation system and DVD entertainment system are optional.

Buick Rendezvous

Ratings—10 Best, 1 Worst	2004	2003
Front Crash Tests	4	4
Side Crash Tests	10	10
Safety Features	8	7
Preventive Maintenance	6	—
Repair Costs	3	3
Warranty	2	3
Fuel Economy	4	5
Rollover	6	5
Complaints	—	—
Insurance Costs	10	10
OVERALL RATING	6	4

Buick Rendezvous

Safety Checklist

Frontal Crash Test . . . Poor
Side Crash Test . . . Very Good
Airbags (Side/Head) . . . Front Opt. Rear Opt./Yes
Pretensioners/Impact Adjustors . . . None/Yes
Position/Weight Sensors . . . Yes/Yes
Seat/Head Adjustors . . . No
Roll Stability System . . . Yes
Child Seats Built-in . . . None
Antilock Brakes/Day Lamps . 4-Wheel (optional)/Standard
Tire Pressure Monitor . . . Indirect

Price Range	Retail	Markup
AWD	$29,045	10%
FWD	$25,895	10%

General Information

2004 Status . . . Unchanged
Series Started . . . 2002
Where Made . . . Mexico
Theft Rating . . . Average
Twins . . .

Last Year's Model

The Rendezvous continued into 2003 unchanged. Based on the Pontiac Aztek, Buick tones down the dramatic angles, but essentially offers the same platform. An independent suspension and optional Versatrak all-wheel drive provide a stable ride. The 185 hp 3.4-liter V6 engine with a 4-speed automatic transmission powers the Rendezvous. Side airbags and ABS are standard, but OnStar and rear park assist are optional on most models.

Buick Rendezvous 2003

Specifications

Fuel Econ. (city/hwy) . . . Poor-19/26
Driving Range (mi.) . . . Average-389.1
Bumpers . . . Strong
Parking Index . . . Average
Seating . . . 6/7
Tow Rating . . . Low-2000
Head/Leg Room (in.) . . . Average-40.9/40.5
Int. Space (cu. ft.) . . . Very Roomy-147.4
Cargo Space (cu. ft.) . . . Very Roomy-108.9

How the Competition Rates

	Rating	Pg.
Ford Explorer	8	150
Mitsubishi Outlander	6	212
Pontiac Aztek	5	225

Cadillac CTS

Large

For 2004, the CTS went through some minor maturing since its introduction last year. Targeted at a younger market, the CTS offers a blend of luxury and performance that propelled it to the top of the Cadillac line up. There is a new optional 3.6-liter V6 VVT engine added for cars with an automatic transmission, a new suspension system, and shock mounts. StabiliTrack traction control is now available. The interior is well equipped and styling is similar to that of more expensive imports. The CTS provides luxury and performance for under $35,000 and has very good crash test results.

Cadillac CTS

Cadillac CTS

Ratings—10 Best, 1 Worst	2004	2003
Front Crash Tests	7	7
Side Crash Tests	10	10
Safety Features	7	7
Preventive Maintenance	7	—
Repair Costs	2	—
Warranty	6	6
Fuel Economy	4	4
Rollover	9	9
Complaints	—	—
Insurance Costs	5	5
OVERALL RATING	7	7

Price Range	Retail	Markup
Base Sedan	$30,140	8%

Safety Checklist

Frontal Crash Test . . . . . Good
Side Crash Test . . . . . Very Good
Airbags (Side/Head) . . . . . Fr. Std. Rear Opt./Yes
Pretensioners/Impact Adjustors . . . . . Yes/Yes
Position/Weight Sensors . . . . . No/No
Seat/Head Adjustors . . . . . No
Roll Stability System . . . . . Yes
Child Seats Built-in . . . . . None
Antilock Brakes/Day Lamps 4-Wheel/Standard
Tire Pressure Monitor . . . . . Indirect

General Information

2004 Status . . . . . Unchanged
Series Started 2003
Where Made . . . . . US
Theft Rating . . . . . Average
Twins . . . . .

Last Year's Model

The 2003, CTS was created to replace the Catera and is the only Cadillac that offers a manual 5-speed transmission. A standard automatic transmission is offered on all models. This transmission allows the driver to choose between "sport," "winter" and "economy" performance modes. The engine is a very powerful 3.2-liter double overhead V6 that produces 220hp. The CTS offers XM radio, a DVD navigation system and dual stage airbags

Cadillac CTS 2003

Specifications

Fuel Econ. (city/hwy) Poor-18/26
Driving Range (mi.) Short-365.6
Bumpers . . . . . Strong
Parking Index . . . . . Easy
Seating 5
Tow Rating . . . . . Very Low-1000
Head/Leg Room (in.) Average-38.9/42.4
Int. Space (cu. ft.) Average-98
Cargo Space (cu. ft.) . . . . . Very Cramped-12.8

How the Competition Rates

	Rating	Pg.
Acura TL	10	99
Lexus LS 430		193
Toyota Avalon	10	249

Cadillac DeVille

Large

Cadillac's flagship received some minor improvements to its interior for 2004. The Deville comes equipped with heated and cooled front seats and a heated steering wheel. Night vision is now available on the base model Deville. There are three new exterior colors for 2004. A 4.6L Northstar V-8 powers the Deville. The DTS model is equipped with a computer assisted stability system for better handling. Leather and XM Satellite Radio are standard.

Cadillac DeVille

Ratings—10 Best, 1 Worst	2004	2003
Front Crash Tests	9	3
Side Crash Tests	8	8
Safety Features	9	3
Preventive Maintenance	6	5
Repair Costs	1	2
Warranty	6	6
Fuel Economy	4	4
Rollover	10	10
Complaints	8	7
Insurance Costs	10	10
OVERALL RATING	9	5

Price Range	Retail	Markup
Base	$44,650	9%
DHS	$49,800	9%
DTS	$49,800	9%

Last Year's Model

The DeVille's minor changes for 2003 included revised taillamps and a signal indicator on the rear view mirrors. Safety features include an optional night vision system, which uses thermal imaging to see objects out of headlight range, rear parking assist, and a stability control system, OnStar and a CD-based navigation system. The DeVille comes in three different trim levels: the base model, the DHS and the DTS.

Cadillac DeVille
2003

Cadillac DeVille

Safety Checklist

Frontal Crash Test	Very Good
Side Crash Test	Good
Airbags (Side/Head)	Fr. Std. Rear Opt./Yes
Pretensioners/Impact Adjustors	None/Yes
Position/Weight Sensors	Yes/No
Seat/Head Adjustors	No
Roll Stability System	Yes
Child Seats Built-in	None
Antilock Brakes/Day Lamps	4-Wheel/Standard
Tire Pressure Monitor	Direct

General Information

2004 Status	Unchanged
Series Started	2000
Where Made	US
Theft Rating	Very High
Twins	

Specifications

Fuel Econ. (city/hwy)	Poor-18/27
Driving Range (mi.)	Average-391.8
Bumpers	Strong
Parking Index	Very Hard
Seating	5
Tow Rating	Low-2000
Head/Leg Room (in.)	Average-39.1/42.4
Int. Space (cu. ft.)	Roomy-115.3
Cargo Space (cu. ft.)	Average-19.1

How the Competition Rates

	Rating	Pg.
Buick Park Avenue	7	110
Ford Crown Victoria	10	146
Lincoln LS		196

Cadillac Escalade/Escalade ESV

Large SUV

For 2004, the Escalade and Escalade ESV receive improvements to their option packages. The ESV receives the option of full time all-wheel-drive. XM Satellite Radio, a rear seat entertainment system, and a sunroof are some of the options found on these two SUV's. There are new color options as well. Both versions of the Escalade are powered by a massive 6.0-liter V8. Second row bucket seats, leather seating surfaces, and wood trim are some of the interior features. The ESV has a rear park assist system. The Escalade ESV is based on the Chevrolet Suburban.

Cadillac Escalade

Cadillac Escalade ESV

Ratings—10 Best, 1 Worst	2003	2002
Front Crash Tests	5	5
Side Crash Tests	—	—
Safety Features	7	7
Preventive Maintenance	3	2
Repair Costs	4	8
Warranty	6	6
Fuel Economy	1	1
Rollover	5	5
Complaints	—	—
Insurance Costs	10	10
OVERALL RATING	3	3

Price Range	Retail	Markup
2WD	$51,980	9%
AWD	$54,880	7%

Last Year's Model

The Escalade remained unchanged for 2003 after its redesign in 2002. A twin of the GMC Yukon, the Escalade provides the driver with extensive creature comforts and power. The standard engine is a 5.3-liter V8 with 285 hp. All-wheel drive models get a 6.0-liter V8 with 345hp. The towing capacity is impressive for this luxury SUV. Side impact airbags, antilock brakes, and all-speed traction control are standard safety features.

Cadillac Escalade
2003

Safety Checklist

Frontal Crash Test	Average
Side Crash Test	
Airbags (Side/Head)	Front Standard
Pretensioners/Impact Adjustors	None/Yes
Position/Weight Sensors	Yes/Yes
Seat/Head Adjustors	No
Roll Stability System	Yes
Child Seats Built-in	None
Antilock Brakes/Day Lamps	4-Wheel/Standard
Tire Pressure Monitor	Indirect

General Information

2004 Status	Unchanged
Series Started	2002
Where Made	US
Theft Rating	Average
Twins	Chevrolet Tahoe, GMC Yukon 2004

Specifications

Fuel Econ. (city/hwy)	Very Poor-14/18
Driving Range (mi.)	Long-404.4
Bumpers	Strong
Parking Index	Very Hard
Seating	6/8
Tow Rating	Very High-7800
Head/Leg Room (in.)	Average-40.7/41.3
Int. Space (cu. ft.)	Very Roomy-138.4
Cargo Space (cu. ft.)	Very Roomy-108.2

How the Competition Rates

	Rating	Pg.
Ford Expedition	4	149
Mercedes-Benz M-Class		204

*Ratings are for Cadillac Escalade.

Cadillac Escalade EXT/Chevrolet Avalanche — Large SUV

For 2004, both the Cadillac Escalade EXT and Chevrolet Avalanche remain unchanged. The Escalade EXT now groups its sunroof and rear seat entertainment system together as an option package. The Avalanche gets four new exterior colors this year. The Escalade EXT is powered by the same 6.0-liter V8 as the standard Escalade, but the Avalanche has a smaller 5.3-liter V8. Both vehicles offer the comfort of an SUV, with the practicality of a pickup truck.

Cadillac Escalade EXT

Chevrolet Avalanche

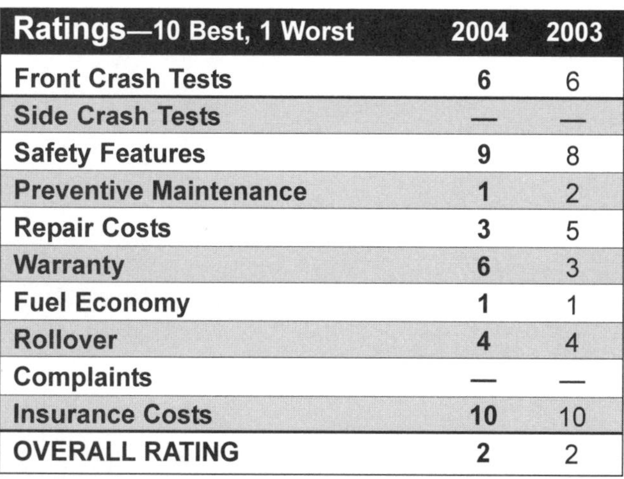

Ratings—10 Best, 1 Worst	2004	2003
Front Crash Tests	6	6
Side Crash Tests	—	—
Safety Features	9	8
Preventive Maintenance	1	2
Repair Costs	3	5
Warranty	6	3
Fuel Economy	1	1
Rollover	4	4
Complaints	—	—
Insurance Costs	10	10
OVERALL RATING	2	2

Price Range	Retail	Markup
Escalad EXT	$52,160	9%
Avalanche 1500 2WD	$33,100	17%
Avalanche 1500 4WD	$36,100	17%
Avalanche 2500 4WD	$37,935	17%

Last Year's Model

The Avalanche combo SUV/Pickup received minor improvements. Most are found in the cabin and in the suspension system. The Escalade EXT received minor refinements as well. A new StabiliTrack vehicle stability system improves handling on the road, in tight turns, and in the event of fishtailing. Dual-stage airbags have been installed. On either vehicle you have the choice of rear-wheel drive or the Autotrac four-wheel drive system.

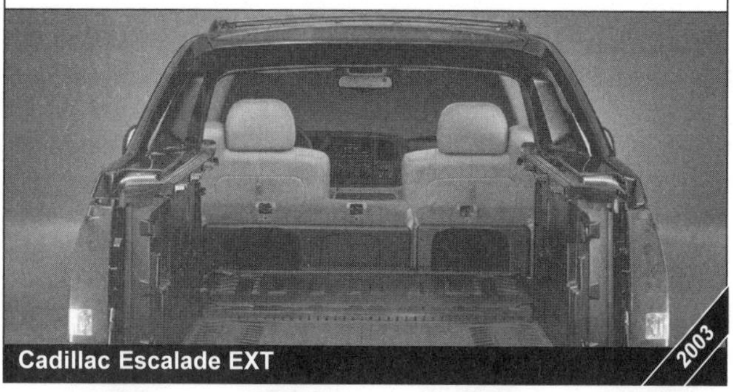

Cadillac Escalade EXT

Safety Checklist

Frontal Crash Test	Average
Side Crash Test	
Airbags (Side/Head)	Front Standard/Yes
Pretensioners/Impact Adjustors	None/Yes
Position/Weight Sensors	Yes/Yes
Seat/Head Adjustors	No
Roll Stability System	Yes
Child Seats Built-in	None
Antilock Brakes/Day Lamps	4-Wheel/Standard
Tire Pressure Monitor	None

General Information

2004 Status	Unchanged
Series Started	2002
Where Made	US
Theft Rating	Very High
Twins	Chevrolet Avalanche 2004

Specifications

Fuel Econ. (city/hwy)	Very Poor-12/16
Driving Range (mi.)	Long-417.8
Bumpers	
Parking Index	Very Hard
Seating	5
Tow Rating	Very High-7400
Head/Leg Room (in.)	Average-40.7/41.3
Int. Space (cu. ft.)	Very Roomy-120.2
Cargo Space (cu. ft.)	Very Roomy-97.6

How the Competition Rates

	Rating	Pg.
Ford Explorer Sport Trac		151
GMC Envoy XUV		159

Cadillac Seville

Large

For 2004, the Seville will slowly fade away into history as Cadillac gears up for the production of its replacement in the summer of 2004. The only version available this year is the SLS sedan, but there are two new colors. A Northstar 4.6-liter V8 engine powers the Seville. Technology is typical of a luxury sedan. Some of the features include: night vision, a GPS navigation system, a rear parking assist system, and XM satellite radio. Leather seats, and fine wood trim are some of the interior features found on this luxury sedan.

Cadillac Seville

Ratings—10 Best, 1 Worst	2004	2003
Front Crash Tests	—	—
Side Crash Tests	—	—
Safety Features	3	3
Preventive Maintenance	4	4
Repair Costs	1	1
Warranty	6	6
Fuel Economy	4	4
Rollover	5	10
Complaints	7	5
Insurance Costs	10	10
OVERALL RATING	—	—

Cadillac Seville

Safety Checklist

Frontal Crash Test. . . . .
Side Crash Test. . . . .
Airbags (Side/Head) . . . . Front Standard
Pretensioners/Impact Adjustors . . . . None/No
Position/Weight Sensors. No/No
Seat/Head Adjustors. . . . . No
Roll Stability System. . . . . No
Child Seats Built-in. . . . . None
Antilock Brakes/Day Lamps 4-Wheel/Standard
Tire Pressure Monitor . . . . Indirect

Price Range	Retail	Markup
SLS	$45,535	9%

General Information

2004 Status. . . . . Unchanged
Series Started 1998
Where Made . . . . US
Theft Rating. . . . . Very High
Twins . . . . Buick LeSabre, Pontiac Bonneville 2004

Last Year's Model

The 2003 Seville was unchanged. An enhanced sport package, DVD-based navigation and XM radio were options in 2003. The Seville comes with a 4.6-liter V8 engine. The OnStar communication system helps with directions and emergencies but is expensive. Dual airbags, traction control, and 4-wheel antilock brakes are standard. Luxury features include heated massaging seats, which adjust to the body and position of the occupant.

Specifications

Fuel Econ. (city/hwy). Poor-18/27
Driving Range (mi.) Average-391.8
Bumpers . . . . Strong
Parking Index . . . . Very Hard
Seating. 5/6
Tow Rating Low-2000
Head/Leg Room (in.) Cramped-38.2/42.5
Int. Space (cu. ft.). Roomy-104
Cargo Space (cu. ft.). Cramped-15

Cadillac Seville

2003

How the Competition Rates

	Rating	Pg.
Chrysler 300M	10	134
Mercedes-Benz E-Class	9	203
Toyota Avalon	10	249

Cadillac SRX — Mid-Size SUV

The all-new 2004 SRX gives Cadillac a contender in the midsize luxury SUV market. The new 3.6-liter V6 engine powers the SRX. There are two five-speed automatic transmissions available and the SRX comes in either rear-wheel or all-wheel drive. There is an optional third row seat, a DVD navigation system, and a rear seat entertainment system. XM satellite radio is available. OnStar is a standard feature. Legroom is ample in the front seats, but gets tight around the 3rd row seat. The SRX can seat up to seven passengers.

Cadillac SRX

Ratings—10 Best, 1 Worst	2004	2003
Front Crash Tests	—	
Side Crash Tests	—	
Safety Features	9	
Preventive Maintenance	—	
Repair Costs	—	
Warranty	6	
Fuel Economy	3	
Rollover	5	
Complaints	—	
Insurance Costs	5	
OVERALL RATING	—	

Cadillac SRX

Safety Checklist

Frontal Crash Test	
Side Crash Test	
Airbags (Side/Head)	Front Standard/Yes
Pretensioners/Impact Adjustors	Standard/Yes
Position/Weight Sensors	Yes/No
Seat/Head Adjustors	No
Roll Stability System	Yes
Child Seats Built-in	None
Antilock Brakes/Day Lamps	4-Wheel/Standard
Tire Pressure Monitor	Direct

General Information

2004 Status	All New
Series Started	No series indicated
Where Made	
Theft Rating	Average
Twins	

Price Range	Retail	Markup
V6	$37,995	8%
V8	$46,300	8%

Specifications

Fuel Econ. (city/hwy)	Poor-18/23
Driving Range (mi.)	Average-399.0
Bumpers	
Parking Index	Very Hard
Seating	7
Tow Rating	Very Low-1000
Head/Leg Room (in.)	Roomy-40.3/42.1
Int. Space (cu. ft.)	
Cargo Space (cu. ft.)	Average-20

Last Year's Model

Model Not Produced in 2003

2003

How the Competition Rates

	Rating	Pg.
Land Rover Discovery	1	188
Lexus RX 330	9	194
Infiniti FX		174

Chevrolet Astro/GMC Safari

Minivan

For 2004, the Chevrolet Astro and GMC Safari are unchanged. The Astro/Safari's main attribute is economy and practicality. The 4.3-liter V6 engine powers both vans. Dual airbags are standard, and there is a child safety lock on the sliding door. The PASSlock anti theft device is also standard. All-wheel drive is available, but most vans will be rear-wheel drive. Both vans have one of the highest towing capacities of any van on the market. Interior volume is ample, but fuel economy is low-especially with all-wheel drive.

Ratings—10 Best, 1 Worst	2004	2003
Front Crash Tests	5	5
Side Crash Tests	10	—
Safety Features	2	2
Preventive Maintenance	1	1
Repair Costs	6	6
Warranty	2	3
Fuel Economy	2	3
Rollover	5	5
Complaints	6	7
Insurance Costs	10	10
OVERALL RATING	2	1

Price Range	Retail	Markup
Base AWD	$26,395	13%
Base RWD	$24,395	13%
LS AWD	$27,640	10%
LS RWD	$25,640	10%

Last Year's Model

Chevy improved cabin safety and lowered the price of its base model Astro in 2003. A single 4.3-liter Vortec V6 engine, producing nearly 190 horsepower, powers the three trim models. Standard driver and passenger airbags and the PASSLock theft deterrent system are among the safety features found. Four-wheel antilock brakes are standard. The GMC Safari is the identical twin of the Astro and the changes for 2003 are similar.

Chevrolet Astro

Chevrolet Astro

GMC Safari

Safety Checklist

Frontal Crash Test	Average
Side Crash Test	Very Good
Airbags (Side/Head)	No Side
Pretensioners/Impact Adjustors	None/No
Position/Weight Sensors	No/No
Seat/Head Adjustors	No
Roll Stability System	No
Child Seats Built-in	None
Antilock Brakes/Day Lamps	4-Wheel/Standard
Tire Pressure Monitor	None

General Information

2004 Status	Unchanged
Series Started	1998
Where Made	US
Theft Rating	Very High
Twins	GMC Safari 2004

Specifications

Fuel Econ. (city/hwy)	Very Poor-17/23
Driving Range (mi.)	Very Long-520.0
Bumpers	Weak
Parking Index	Very Hard
Seating	7/8
Tow Rating	Average-5400
Head/Leg Room (in.)	Cramped-39.2/41.6
Int. Space (cu. ft.)	
Cargo Space (cu. ft.)	Very Roomy-170.4

How the Competition Rates

	Rating	Pg.
Chevrolet Venture	6	133
Ford Freestar	4	153
Honda Odyssey	8	165

Chevrolet Aveo — Subcompact

The 2004 Aveo is all-new this year. It marks Chevrolet's return to the world of subcompact, low priced vehicles. A 1.6-liter 4-cylinder engine powers the Aveo. The base model includes an AM/FM stereo, tinted glass, and folding rear seats as standard equipment. The LS model comes with a CD player with MP3 playback. A five-speed manual transmission is standard, but dual front airbags and antilock brakes are optional. The Aveo will be one of the lowest priced hatchbacks available. The Aveo is a result of GM's purchase of Daewoo.

Chevrolet Aveo

Chevrolet Aveo

Ratings—10 Best, 1 Worst	2004	2003
Front Crash Tests	—	
Side Crash Tests	—	
Safety Features	3	
Preventive Maintenance	—	
Repair Costs	—	
Warranty	2	
Fuel Economy	9	
Rollover	7	
Complaints	—	
Insurance Costs	5	
OVERALL RATING	—	

Price Range	Retail	Markup
Hatchback Special Value	$9,455	6%
Hatchback LS	$12,045	7%
Sedan Base	$11,150	7%
Sedan LS	$12,045	7%

Last Year's Model

Model Not Produced in 2003

2003

Safety Checklist

Frontal Crash Test. . . . .
Side Crash Test. . . . .
Airbags (Side/Head). . . . . No Side
Pretensioners/Impact Adjustors . . . . Standard/
Position/Weight Sensors . . . . /
Seat/Head Adjustors . . . .
Roll Stability System . . . .
Child Seats Built-in. . . . . None
Antilock Brakes/Day Lamps . . 2-Wheel (4-Whl. opt.)/Std.
Tire Pressure Monitor. . . . . None

General Information

2004 Status. . . . . All New
Series Started. . . . . No series indicated
Where Made . . . . Korea
Theft Rating . . . . Average
Twins. . . . .

Specifications

Fuel Econ. (city/hwy) . . . . Very Good-26/35
Driving Range (mi.) . . . . Very Short-349.9
Bumpers . . . .
Parking Index . . . . Very Easy
Seating 5
Tow Rating . . . .
Head/Leg Room (in.) Cramped-39.3/41.3
Int. Space (cu. ft.) Cramped-91
Cargo Space (cu. ft.) . . . . Very Cramped-11.7

How the Competition Rates

	Rating	Pg.
Kia Spectra	9	187
Suzuki Aerio		243
Scion xA		236

Chevrolet Blazer — Small SUV

For 2004, the Blazer is unchanged. A standard 4.3-liter V6 engine powers the two-door and four-door versions. Both models come with the options of either two-wheel drive or four-wheel drive. Antilock brakes, and standard dual front passenger airbags are some of the safety features found on this compact SUV. The Blazer ZR2 model has an improved suspension over the standard models. Cruise control, power door locks and heated mirrors round out some of the available features in this SUV.

Chevrolet Blazer

Ratings—10 Best, 1 Worst	2004	2003
Front Crash Tests*	4	5
Side Crash Tests*	10	10
Safety Features	2	2
Preventive Maintenance	2	6
Repair Costs	3	7
Warranty	2	3
Fuel Economy	2	3
Rollover	4	2
Complaints	2	2
Insurance Costs	5	5
OVERALL RATING	1	1

Price Range	Retail	Markup
LS 2D 2WD	$20,745	10%
LS 4D 2WD	$24,695	10%
LS 4D 4WD	$26,695	10%
Xtreme	$22,945	10%

Last Year's Model

There were no changes to the 2003 Blazer. As with most Chevy trucks, there are several variations to choose from. Models range from the two-door base model to the Blazer Xtreme. Each model has unique option packages available. The standard 4.3-liter V6 provides plenty of power with its redesigned fuel injector. Cloth seating surfaces are standard. A six-disc CD player is available in many of the options packages.

Chevrolet Blazer 2003

Chevrolet Blazer ZR2

Safety Checklist

Frontal Crash Test*	Poor
Side Crash Test*	Very Good
Airbags (Side/Head)	No Side
Pretensioners/Impact Adjustors	None/No
Position/Weight Sensors	No/No
Seat/Head Adjustors	No
Roll Stability System	No
Child Seats Built-in	None
Antilock Brakes/Day Lamps	4-Wheel/Standard
Tire Pressure Monitor	None

General Information

2004 Status	Unchanged
Series Started	1993
Where Made	US
Theft Rating	Very High
Twins	

Specifications

Fuel Econ. (city/hwy)	Very Poor-17/23
Driving Range (mi.)	Short-360.2
Bumpers	
Parking Index	Very Easy
Seating	5
Tow Rating	Average-5400
Head/Leg Room (in.)	Average-39.6/42.4
Int. Space (cu. ft.)	
Cargo Space (cu. ft.)	Roomy-29.8

How the Competition Rates

	Rating	Pg.
Jeep Liberty	10	180
Ford Escape	8	147
Nissan Murano	7	217

*Ratings based on 4-door models. For 2-door crash results, see page 27.

Chevrolet Cavalier/Pontiac Sunfire — Compact

For 2004, both the Sunfire and Cavalier have improvements to their audio systems in the form of an optional CD/MP3 radio. The Cavalier comes in either a coupe or a sedan, but the Sunfire is only available as a coupe. A 2.2 Inline 4-cylinder engine powers both vehicles. The Sunfire/Cavalier comes with standard dual airbags and OnStar is available. There are a number of option packages available on both cars. After 2004, the Cavalier nameplate will be dropped and replaced by the 2005 Cobalt compact car. Both have good crash test results.

Ratings—10 Best, 1 Worst	2004	2003
Front Crash Tests	9	9
Side Crash Tests*	1	1
Safety Features	3	3
Preventive Maintenance	5	5
Repair Costs	1	8
Warranty	2	3
Fuel Economy	8	8
Rollover	8	8
Complaints	9	8
Insurance Costs	1	1
OVERALL RATING	3	5

Price Range	Retail	Markup
Base Coupe	$14,045	7%
Base Sedan	$14,245	7%
LS Sedan	$15,815	7%
LS Sport Sedan	$17,220	7%

Last Year's Model

For 2003, the Cavalier received a new exterior with a redesigned front façade and headlights, as well as new safety features and options. The Sunfire also received a major appearance change. These compact cars are powered by a 2.2-liter 4-cylinder engine, which produces 140 horsepower. The OnStar vehicle safety system was an option for the LS and LS sport trim levels. XM Satellite radio is an option on all models.

Chevrolet Cavalier 2003

Chevrolet Cavalier

Pontiac Sunfire

Safety Checklist

Frontal Crash Test	Very Good
Side Crash Test*	Very Poor
Airbags (Side/Head)	Front Optional Rear Optional
Pretensioners/Impact Adjustors	None/No
Position/Weight Sensors	No/No
Seat/Head Adjustors	No
Roll Stability System	No
Child Seats Built-in	None
Antilock Brakes/Day Lamps	4-Wheel/Standard
Tire Pressure Monitor	None

General Information

2004 Status	Unchanged
Series Started	1995
Where Made	US
Theft Rating	Very High
Twins	Pontiac Sunfire 2004

Specifications

Fuel Econ. (city/hwy)	Good-24/33
Driving Range (mi.)	Average-385.7
Bumpers	Strong
Parking Index	Easy
Seating	5
Tow Rating	Very Low-1000
Head/Leg Room (in.)	Very Cramped-37.6/41.9
Int. Space (cu. ft.)	Roomy-105
Cargo Space (cu. ft.)	Cramped-13.2

How the Competition Rates

	Rating	Pg.
Ford Focus	8	152
Honda Civic	10	161
Volkswagen Golf	9	264

*Ratings are for 2-door Chevrolet Cavalier. For 4-door crash results, see page 22.

Chevrolet Colorado/GMC Canyon — Compact Pickup

Both the Chevrolet Colorado and the GMC Canyon are all new for 2004. They are a replacement for the S-Series/Sonoma pickup. A Vortec 2.8-liter Inline engine powers both trucks. You can upgrade to a more powerful in line five-cylinder engine. Dual stage front airbags with a passenger deactivation switch and side curtain airbags are some of the safety features found on the Colorado/Canyon. A restyled interior gives the Colorado/Canyon more room than most compact pickups. OnStar is available on both trucks.

Chevrolet Colorado

GMC Canyon

Ratings—10 Best, 1 Worst	2004	2003
Front Crash Tests	—	
Side Crash Tests	—	
Safety Features	3	
Preventive Maintenance	—	
Repair Costs	—	
Warranty	2	
Fuel Economy	4	
Rollover	5	
Complaints	—	
Insurance Costs	5	
OVERALL RATING	—	

Price Range	Retail	Markup
2WD Reg Cab ZQ8 LS	$18,915	3%
2WD Reg Z85	$16,200	4%
4WD Crew Cab Z71	$26,955	2%
4WD Reg Cab Z85	$18,760	4%

Last Year's Model

Model Not Produced in 2003

2003

Safety Checklist

Frontal Crash Test. . . . .
Side Crash Test. . . . .
Airbags (Side/Head). . . . . No Side
Pretensioners/Impact Adjustors . . . . Standard/No
Position/Weight Sensors. No/No
Seat/Head Adjustors. . . . . No
Roll Stability System. . . . . No
Child Seats Built-in. . . . . None
Antilock Brakes/Day Lamps 4-Wheel/Standard
Tire Pressure Monitor. . . . . None

General Information

2004 Status. . . . . All New
Series Started. . . . . No series indicated
Where Made . . . .
Theft Rating. . . . . Average
Twins . . . . GMC Canyon 2004

Specifications

Fuel Econ. (city/hwy). Poor-19/24
Driving Range (mi.). Long-410.9
Bumpers . . . .
Parking Index. . . . . Average
Seating 2
Tow Rating Low-1800
Head/Leg Room (in.). Average-40/42
Int. Space (cu. ft.) . . . .
Cargo Space (cu. ft.). . . . . Very Roomy-43.9

How the Competition Rates

	Rating	Pg.
Dodge Dakota	7	142
Toyota Tacoma	3	261
Nissan Frontier	4	215

Chevrolet Impala/Chevrolet Monte Carlo — Large

For 2004, SS models for both cars return. The base models of each remain essentially unchanged for 2004. The Impala does get new bucket seats and new environmental controls. The Monte Carlo receives new wheels and exterior colors. The Impala coupe and Monte Carlo are essentially the same vehicle, but with different options. The 3.4-liter V6 engine powers both models. Dual airbags and side impact airbags are standard safety equipment on these cars. The Impala has very good crash test results.

Chevrolet Impala

Ratings—10 Best, 1 Worst	2004	2003
Front Crash Tests*	10	10
Side Crash Tests*	8	8
Safety Features	3	3
Preventive Maintenance	3	3
Repair Costs	7	7
Warranty	2	3
Fuel Economy	7	7
Rollover	8	8
Complaints	8	4
Insurance Costs	5	5
OVERALL RATING	7	7

Chevrolet Monte Carlo

Price Range	Retail	Markup
Base	$21,240	9%
LS	$24,340	9%
SS	$27,335	9%

Safety Checklist

Frontal Crash Test*	Very Good
Side Crash Test*	Good
Airbags (Side/Head)	Fr. Std. Rear Opt.
Pretensioners/Impact Adjustors	None/No
Position/Weight Sensors	No/No
Seat/Head Adjustors	No
Roll Stability System	No
Child Seats Built-in	None
Antilock Brakes/Day Lamps	2-Wheel (4-Whl. opt.)/Std.
Tire Pressure Monitor	Indirect

Last Year's Model

The Impala/Monte Carlo remained unchanged for 2003. The standard engine on the on the base model is a 3.4-liter V6; the LS model comes with a 3.8-liter V6. The SS Impala has been dropped. XM Satellite radio is available. Comfortable seating and beefier engines bring this sedan and coupe to the forefront of the Chevrolet line. The Impala has one of the best mpg ratings of its class according to the EPA.

Chevrolet Impala 2003

General Information

2004 Status	Unchanged
Series Started	1999
Where Made	US
Theft Rating	Very High
Twins	Chevrolet Monte Carlo, Pontiac Grand Prix 2004

Specifications

Fuel Econ. (city/hwy)	Good-21/32
Driving Range (mi.)	Long-422.3
Bumpers	
Parking Index	Hard
Seating	5
Tow Rating	Very Low-1000
Head/Leg Room (in.)	Average-39.2/42.2
Int. Space (cu. ft.)	Roomy-104.5
Cargo Space (cu. ft.)	Average-18.6

How the Competition Rates

	Rating	Pg.
Buick Century	6	108
Ford Crown Victoria	10	146
Pontiac Bonneville	7	226

*Ratings are for Chevrolet Impala (4-dr.). For Monte Carlo crash results, see page 25.

Chevrolet Malibu — Intermediate

The Chevrolet Malibu is all-new for 2004. It has been completely redesigned to help Chevrolet compete in the very competitive intermediate class market. Power windows, mirrors and locks are standard. A factory installed remote starter is also available. The LS and LT trim models have power adjustable pedals as standard equipment. There is even a sport wagon model called the Malibu Maxx, which has a longer wheelbase for extra room. The base engine for the Malibu is a 2.2-liter inline 4-cylinder engine. A 3.5-liter V6 is engine optional.

Chevrolet Malibu

Ratings—10 Best, 1 Worst	2004	2003
Front Crash Tests	—	8
Side Crash Tests	—	7
Safety Features	5	2
Preventive Maintenance	—	3
Repair Costs	—	5
Warranty	2	3
Fuel Economy	8	6
Rollover	8	9
Complaints	—	4
Insurance Costs	5	5
OVERALL RATING	—	4

Chevrolet Malibu

Price Range	Retail	Markup
Base	$18,370	9%
LS	$20,370	9%
LT	$22,870	9%

Safety Checklist

Frontal Crash Test. . . . .
Side Crash Test. . . . .
Airbags (Side/Head) . . Front Optional Rear Optional/Yes
Pretensioners/Impact Adjustors . . . . Standard/No
Position/Weight Sensors. . . . . No/No
Seat/Head Adjustors. . . . . No
Roll Stability System. . . . . No
Child Seats Built-in. . . . . None
Antilock Brakes/Day Lamps 4-Wheel/Standard
Tire Pressure Monitor. . . . . None

Last Year's Model

In 2003, the LS model of the Malibu received new seats and two new color options but remained mechanically unchanged. The Malibu comes with a standard 3.1-liter V6 engine, good interior room and fine handling. The Malibu is Chevy's challenger to the best selling Taurus, Camry, and Accord trio. The LS comes with cruise control, power seats, and keyless entry. All Malibus have child seat attachment points in the rear seat.

Chevrolet Malibu 2003

General Information

2004 Status. . . . . All New
Series Started. . . . . No series indicated
Where Made . . . . US
Theft Rating. . . . . Very High
Twins. . . . .

Specifications

Fuel Econ. (city/hwy) Good-23/33
Driving Range (mi.) . . . . Very Long-442.1
Bumpers . . . . Strong
Parking Index . . . . Hard
Seating 5
Tow Rating . . . .
Head/Leg Room (in.). Average-39.6/41.9
Int. Space (cu. ft.) Average-101.4
Cargo Space (cu. ft.) Cramped-15.4

How the Competition Rates

	Rating	Pg.
Ford Taurus	9	157
Honda Accord	8	160
Toyota Camry	10	250

Chevrolet S Series/GMC Sonoma — Compact Pickup

2004 will be the last year of production for the S-Series/Sonoma pickup. Only the Crew Cab version, with a 122.9-inch wheelbase, is available for both models. A 4.3-liter V6 powers these pickups and air conditioning, dual airbags, and antilock brakes are some of the standard features. The Sonoma comes with a bed liner and front bucket seats as standard equipment. Both trucks offer similar option packages including the Insta-trac stability system.

Chevrolet S Series

Ratings—10 Best, 1 Worst	2004	2003
Front Crash Tests	3	4
Side Crash Tests	4	—
Safety Features	2	2
Preventive Maintenance	2	7
Repair Costs	5	5
Warranty	2	3
Fuel Economy	4	5
Rollover	5	5
Complaints	5	6
Insurance Costs	1	1
OVERALL RATING	1	1

GMC Sonoma

Safety Checklist

Frontal Crash Test	Poor
Side Crash Test	Poor
Airbags (Side/Head)	No Side
Pretensioners/Impact Adjustors	None/No
Position/Weight Sensors	No/No
Seat/Head Adjustors	No
Roll Stability System	No
Child Seats Built-in	None
Antilock Brakes/Day Lamps	4-Wheel/Standard
Tire Pressure Monitor	None

Price Range	Retail	Markup
Crew Cab LS	$24,460	10%

General Information

2004 Status	Unchanged
Series Started	1993
Where Made	US
Theft Rating	Very High
Twins	GMC Sonoma 2004

Last Year's Model

The S-Series line of Chevy pickups remained unchanged in 2003. Engine choices include the base line 2.2-liter L4 engine and the Vortec 4.3L V6 engine available on the Extended and Crew cab options. Two- and four-wheel drive options are available. The base transmission is a 5-speed manual with an automatic option available. The variety of option packages generate an equal variety in prices.

Chevrolet S10

2003

Specifications

Fuel Econ. (city/hwy)	Poor-19/25
Driving Range (mi.)	Average-383.4
Bumpers	
Parking Index	Hard
Seating	2/3
Tow Rating	Low-3100
Head/Leg Room (in.)	Average-39.5/42.4
Int. Space (cu. ft.)	
Cargo Space (cu. ft.)	Roomy-39.4

How the Competition Rates

	Rating	Pg.
Ford Ranger	6	156
Nissan Frontier	4	215
Dodge Dakota	7	142

Chevrolet Silverado/GMC Sierra — Standard Pickup

The 2004 model year brings many additions to the Chevrolet Silverado and GMC Sierra line-up. Both receive new cab and trim options. There are new exterior colors and 17-inch wheels. The base model Silverado now has an AM/FM/CD stereo, cruise control, power door locks, and chrome bumper as standard features. The Sierra has a rear underseat storage locker in its Extend Cab version. Quadrasteer is available on all models, and improves the truck's turning ability. The base engine for both trucks is a 4.3-liter V6.

Ratings—10 Best, 1 Worst	2004	2003
Front Crash Tests	6	6
Side Crash Tests	—	—
Safety Features	7	8
Preventive Maintenance	1	1
Repair Costs	6	5
Warranty	2	3
Fuel Economy	1	2
Rollover	7	7
Complaints	8	7
Insurance Costs	5	5
OVERALL RATING	3	3

Price Range	Retail	Markup
4x2 Extended Cab	$23,075	14%
4x2 Regular Cab	$19,020	10%
4x2 Regular Cab LS	$24,465	14%
4x4 Extended Cab	$28,450	14%

Last Year's Model

Chevy's full size pickup received a variety of major improvements in 2003, which both improved its styling and performance. The Silverado received GM's Quadrasteer system, which improves turning ability. Dual stage airbags are also standard. XM satellite radio is available on most models. With the standard 4.3-liter V6 engine the Silverado has ample power. You can also upgrade to a more powerful 6.0-liter V8 engine.

Chevrolet Silverado 2003

Chevrolet Silverado

GMC Sierra

Safety Checklist

Frontal Crash Test . . . . Average
Side Crash Test. . . . .
Airbags (Side/Head) . . . . . Front Optional Rear Optional
Pretensioners/Impact Adjustors. . . . . None/Yes
Position/Weight Sensors . . . . Yes/Yes
Seat/Head Adjustors. . . . . No
Roll Stability System . . . . Yes
Child Seats Built-in. . . . . None
Antilock Brakes/Day Lamps 4-Wheel/Standard
Tire Pressure Monitor. . . . . None

General Information

2004 Status. . . . . Unchanged
Series Started 1999
Where Made. . . . . Canada
Theft Rating. . . . . Very High
Twins. . . . . GMC Sierra 2004

Specifications

Fuel Econ. (city/hwy) . . . . Very Poor-15/20
Driving Range (mi.) . . . . Very Long-439.4
Bumpers . . . .
Parking Index . . . . Very Hard
Seating. 2/3
Tow Rating . . . . Very High-8400
Head/Leg Room (in.) Roomy-41/41.3
Int. Space (cu. ft.) . . . .
Cargo Space (cu. ft.). . . . . Very Roomy-43.5

How the Competition Rates

	Rating	Pg.
Dodge Ram Pickup	2	145
Ford F-Series		154
Nissan Titan		222

Chevrolet Suburban/GMC Yukon XL — Large SUV

For 2004, both the Chevrolet Suburban and its twin the GMC Yukon XL receive new braking systems, but remain essentially unchanged. The Suburban receives a tire pressure monitoring system. The Yukon XL now has the sunroof and DVD entertainment system grouped together in the same option package. Both SUV's are powered by a massive 5.3-liter V8, delivering nearly 290 horsepower. Quadrasteer is also available. Each model has different interior features, so explore both carefully as they will vary in price.

Chevrolet Suburban

Ratings—10 Best, 1 Worst	2004	2003
Front Crash Tests	5	5
Side Crash Tests	—	—
Safety Features	8	7
Preventive Maintenance	1	1
Repair Costs	5	5
Warranty	2	3
Fuel Economy	1	1
Rollover	5	5
Complaints	7	4
Insurance Costs	10	10
OVERALL RATING	2	2

GMC Yukon XL

Price Range	Retail	Markup
1500 2WD	$37,050	14%
1500 4WD	$39,850	14%
2500 2WD	$38,650	14%
2500 4WD	$41,550	14%

Safety Checklist

Frontal Crash Test	Average
Side Crash Test	
Airbags (Side/Head)	Fr. Std. Rear Opt./Yes
Pretensioners/Impact Adjustors	None/No
Position/Weight Sensors	Yes/Yes
Seat/Head Adjustors	No
Roll Stability System	Yes
Child Seats Built-in	None
Antilock Brakes/Day Lamps	4-Wheel/Standard
Tire Pressure Monitor	None

General Information

2004 Status	Unchanged
Series Started	2000
Where Made	US/Mexico
Theft Rating	Very High
Twins	Cadillac Escalade ESV, GMC Yukon XL 2004

Last Year's Model

With the exception of GM's StabiliTrak stability enhancement system and a Panasonic DVD entertainment system, the Suburban remained unchanged for 2003. A 5.3-liter V8 engine is standard, and there is a 6.0-liter V8 option. Antilock brakes, daytime running lights, and dual airbags are standard equipment on both the Suburban and Yukon XL. Front seat side airbags are also standard equipment. The towing capacity is excellent.

Chevrolet Suburban

Specifications

Fuel Econ. (city/hwy)	Very Poor-14/18
Driving Range (mi.)	Very Long-482.2
Bumpers	
Parking Index	Very Hard
Seating	8/9
Tow Rating	Very High-8100
Head/Leg Room (in.)	Average-40.7/41.3
Int. Space (cu. ft.)	
Cargo Space (cu. ft.)	Very Roomy-131.6

How the Competition Rates

	Rating	Pg.
Dodge Durango		143
Ford Expedition	4	149
Toyota Sequoia	4	258

Chevrolet Tahoe/GMC Yukon — Large SUV

The 2004 Chevrolet Tahoe and GMC Yukon Denali remain unchanged. Both SUVs receive a new braking system, 17-inch tires, and new color options. Riding a similar platform as the Cadillac Escalade, the Tahoe/Yukon provides excellent cargo and passenger room. Both are powered by a 4.8 -liter V8 engine. There are more option packages on the Tahoe than on the Yukon, so compare each carefully. Both are equipped with dual stage front airbags.

Chevrolet Tahoe

GMC Yukon

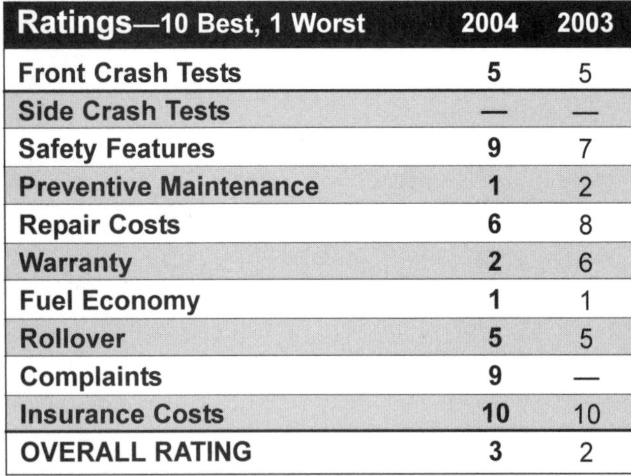

Ratings—10 Best, 1 Worst	2004	2003
Front Crash Tests	5	5
Side Crash Tests	—	—
Safety Features	9	7
Preventive Maintenance	1	2
Repair Costs	6	8
Warranty	2	6
Fuel Economy	1	1
Rollover	5	5
Complaints	9	—
Insurance Costs	10	10
OVERALL RATING	3	2

Price Range	Retail	Markup
2WD	$34,200	14%
4WD	$37,000	14%

Last Year's Model

For 2003, the Yukon and Tahoe remained unchanged. Dual airbags and antilock brakes are standard. Improvements were made in the suspension to reduce the heavy handling of the Tahoe/Yukon. Quadrasteer was introduced in 2003 as well. Both models are equipped with the OnStar emergency system. There is over 105-inches of possible cargo room in the Tahoe/Yukon.

Chevrolet Tahoe 2003

Safety Checklist

Frontal Crash Test	Average
Side Crash Test	
Airbags (Side/Head)	Front Standard/Yes
Pretensioners/Impact Adjustors	None/Yes
Position/Weight Sensors	Yes/Yes
Seat/Head Adjustors	No
Roll Stability System	Yes
Child Seats Built-in	None
Antilock Brakes/Day Lamps	4-Wheel/Standard
Tire Pressure Monitor	None

General Information

2004 Status	Unchanged
Series Started	2000
Where Made	US
Theft Rating	Very High
Twins	Cadillac Escalade, GMC Yukon 2004

Specifications

Fuel Econ. (city/hwy)	Very Poor-14/18
Driving Range (mi.)	Long-404.4
Bumpers	
Parking Index	Hard
Seating	8/9
Tow Rating	Very High-7400
Head/Leg Room (in.)	Average-40.7/41.3
Int. Space (cu. ft.)	
Cargo Space (cu. ft.)	Very Roomy-104.6

How the Competition Rates

	Rating	Pg.
Ford Expedition	4	149
Dodge Durango		143
Chevrolet Suburban	2	129

Chevrolet Tracker/Suzuki Vitara — Small SUV

This is expected to be the last year of production for the Chevrolet Tracker/Suzuki Vitara. They will be replaced by the new Equinox, which will go on sale in late 2004. There are no changes to the 2004 Tracker/Vitara which is available as a 4-door hardtop. Both are powered by a 2.5-liter V6. The base model Tracker/Vitara has air conditioning, an AM/FM/CD stereo and a folding rear seat as standard equipment. By upgrading to the LT trim model you get power door locks a as standard feature.

Chevrolet Tracker

Suzuki Vitara

Ratings—10 Best, 1 Worst	2004	2003
Front Crash Tests	7	7
Side Crash Tests	10	10
Safety Features	2	2
Preventive Maintenance	2	1
Repair Costs	1	1
Warranty	2	3
Fuel Economy	3	7
Rollover	5	5
Complaints	8	8
Insurance Costs	1	1
OVERALL RATING	1	2

Price Range	Retail	Markup
Base 2WD	$19,780	6%
Base 4WD	$20,880	6%
LT 2WD	$21,530	6%
LT 4WD	$22,630	6%

Last Year's Model

The Tracker/Vitara continued into 2003 unchanged, except for new paint options. The 2.0-liter 4-cylinder engine is standard on both the 2-door convertible and the 4 door hard top. There is also an optional 2.5-liter V6. 4-wheel antilock brakes are optional. Both vehicles are built on the same platform and have similar handling characteristics and crash test performance. They also have similar options and safety features.

Chevrolet Tracker — 2003

Safety Checklist

Frontal Crash Test	Good
Side Crash Test	Very Good
Airbags (Side/Head)	No Side
Pretensioners/Impact Adjustors	None/No
Position/Weight Sensors	No/No
Seat/Head Adjustors	No
Roll Stability System	No
Child Seats Built-in	None
Antilock Brakes/Day Lamps	2-Wheel (4-Whl. opt.)/Std.
Tire Pressure Monitor	None

General Information

2004 Status	Unchanged
Series Started	1998
Where Made	Canada
Theft Rating	Very High
Twins	Suzuki Vitara 2004

Specifications

Fuel Econ. (city/hwy)	Poor-19/21
Driving Range (mi.)	Very Short-345.4
Bumpers	
Parking Index	Very Easy
Seating	5
Tow Rating	Very Low-1000
Head/Leg Room (in.)	Average-39.9/41.4
Int. Space (cu. ft.)	Roomy-117.2
Cargo Space (cu. ft.)	Average-23.4

How the Competition Rates

	Rating	Pg.
Toyota RAV4	7	257
Subaru Forester	6	239
Jeep Wrangler	7	181

Chev. Trail Blazer/GMC Envoy/Isuzu Ascender 5-pass. Large SUV

The Trail Blazer/Envoy remains unchanged from last year. There are new exterior colors and new door locks. Built on the same platform, the Trail Blazer/Envoy provides the benefits of an SUV with feel of a car. A 4.2-liter Inline 6-cylinder engine powers both SUVs. The Trail Blazer EXT and Envoy XL are larger versions of these cars and we consider them different vehicles. Both are equipped with dual stage front airbags and side impact airbags. This year there will be an Isuzu version of this vehicle called the Ascender 5-passenger.

Chevrolet Trail Blazer

GMC Envoy

Ratings—10 Best, 1 Worst	2004	2003
Front Crash Tests	5	5
Side Crash Tests	10	10
Safety Features	6	7
Preventive Maintenance	2	—
Repair Costs	1	2
Warranty	2	3
Fuel Economy	2	2
Rollover	5	5
Complaints		—
Insurance Costs	10	10
OVERALL RATING	2	3

Price Range	Retail	Markup
LS 2WD	$27,145	10%
LS 4WD	$29,395	10%
LS EXT 2WD	$29,695	10%
LT 2WD	$29,645	10%

Last Year's Model

The Chevy Trailblazer/GMC Envoy received minor improvements in 2003. There were new option packages available, and the 4.2-liter inline 6-cylinder engine received a power boost. This midsize SUV has a rear seat DVD entertainment system. Four-wheel antilock brakes and side impact airbags are standard on both SUVs. If you want a larger version of these SUVs, check out the Envoy XL or Trail Blazer EXT.

Chevrolet Trail Blazer 2003

Safety Checklist

Frontal Crash Test	Average
Side Crash Test	Very Good
Airbags (Side/Head)	Front Standard
Pretensioners/Impact Adjustors	None/No
Position/Weight Sensors	Yes/Yes
Seat/Head Adjustors	No
Roll Stability System	Yes
Child Seats Built-in	None
Antilock Brakes/Day Lamps	4-Wheel/Standard
Tire Pressure Monitor	None

General Information

2004 Status	Unchanged
Series Started	2002
Where Made	US
Theft Rating	Very High
Twins	Rainier, Envoy, Ascender 5-pass., Bravada

Specifications

Fuel Econ. (city/hwy)	Very Poor-16/22
Driving Range (mi.)	Long-401.2
Bumpers	Strong
Parking Index	Average
Seating	5
Tow Rating	High-6200
Head/Leg Room (in.)	Roomy-40.2/42.9
Int. Space (cu. ft.)	
Cargo Space (cu. ft.)	Very Roomy-80.1

How the Competition Rates

	Rating	Pg.
Buick Rendezvous	5	113
Ford Explorer	8	150
Toyota 4Runner	6	248

Chev. Venture/Pont. Montana/Olds Silhouette — Minivan

The Chevrolet Venture/Pontiac Montana remain unchanged since last year. This year XM Satellite radio is available, as well as a new CD/MP3 player. A DVD entertainment system is now standard on the Venture LX and side impact airbags are now standard on the Pontiac Montana. Both are powered by the 3.4-liter V6 mated to a four-speed automatic transmission. All-wheel drive is available on all models. With all of these options, GM is attempting to compete with the Chrysler minivans. This is the last year for the upscale Oldsmobile Silhouette.

Chevrolet Venture

Pontiac Montana

Ratings—10 Best, 1 Worst	2004	2003
Front Crash Tests	9	9
Side Crash Tests	10	10
Safety Features	5	5
Preventive Maintenance	6	4
Repair Costs	2	3
Warranty	2	3
Fuel Economy	4	5
Rollover	5	5
Complaints	4	5
Insurance Costs	10	10
OVERALL RATING	4	5

Price Range	Retail	Markup
AWD Extended Van LT	$33,290	10%
Extended Van LS	$26,340	10%
Extended Van LT	$30,240	10%
Van Plus	$21,315	10%

Last Year's Model

There were few changes in 2003 for the Chevy Venture/Pontiac Montana which gives minivan buyers an alternative to the popular Chrysler minivans. All-wheel drive and a rear seat DVD entertainment system are available as are standard dual airbags, 4-wheel antilock brakes, and daytime running lamps. Side airbags are also available. The only engine choice is the 3.4-liter V6.

Chevrolet Venture 2003

Safety Checklist

Frontal Crash Test	Very Good
Side Crash Test	Very Good
Airbags (Side/Head)	Fr. Std. Rear Opt.
Pretensioners/Impact Adjustors	Yes/No
Position/Weight Sensors	No/No
Seat/Head Adjustors	No
Roll Stability System	No
Child Seats Built-in	Optional
Antilock Brakes/Day Lamps	4-Wheel/Standard
Tire Pressure Monitor	None

General Information

2004 Status	Unchanged
Series Started	1997
Where Made	US
Theft Rating	Very Low
Twins	Olds. Silhouette, Pontiac Montana

Specifications

Fuel Econ. (city/hwy)	Poor-19/26
Driving Range (mi.)	Very Long-540.5
Bumpers	Strong
Parking Index	Average
Seating	7/8
Tow Rating	Average-3500
Head/Leg Room (in.)	Very Cramped-39.9/39.9
Int. Space (cu. ft.)	
Cargo Space (cu. ft.)	Very Roomy-140.7

How the Competition Rates

	Rating	Pg.
Dodge Caravan	10	141
Ford Freestar	4	153
Kia Sedona	6	185

Chrysler 300M/Chrysler Concorde/Dodge Intrepid Large

All three of these sedans share the same platform and remain unchanged for 2004. Despite the age of the design, the 300M/Concorde/Intrepid still provides a good all-around vehicle. All are equipped with standard V6 engines. The 300M has a sport-tuned suspension, and the Intrepid has a more aggressive appearance than the Concorde. Seating for five is standard on all models. Side impact airbags, and antilock brakes with force distribution are optional. Each car offers a variety of option packages and trim models.

Chrysler Concorde

Ratings—10 Best, 1 Worst	2004	2003
Front Crash Tests	8	6
Side Crash Tests	9	7
Safety Features*	2	5
Preventive Maintenance	9	9
Repair Costs	8	8
Warranty	8	6
Fuel Economy	6	4
Rollover	10	9
Complaints	4	7
Insurance Costs	5	5
OVERALL RATING	10	7

Price Range	Retail	Markup
ES	$24,705	8%
SE	$21,385	8%
SXT	$24,235	8%

Last Year's Model

The flagships of the Chrysler and Dodge fleet received minor changes in 2003. Interior refinements include a Sirius Satellite Radio system or the standard CD player AM/FM radio. Luxury standard features include heated leather seats and wood trim on the 300M and Concorde. Safety features include a tire pressure sensor system and an improved child safety latch system. Dual-stage airbags are standard on all models.

Chrysler 300M 2003

Dodge Intrepid SXT

Safety Checklist

Frontal Crash Test	Good
Side Crash Test	Very Good
Airbags (Side/Head)	Front Optional/Rear Optional
Pretensioners/Impact Adjustors	None/No
Position/Weight Sensors	No/No
Seat/Head Adjustors	No
Roll Stability System	No
Child Seats Built-in	None
Antilock Brakes/Day Lamps	4-Wheel/Optional
Tire Pressure Monitor	None

General Information

2004 Status	Unchanged
Series Started	1999
Where Made	US/Canada
Theft Rating	Very High
Twins	Chrysler Concorde, Chrysler 300M

Specifications*

Fuel Econ. (city/hwy)	Average-21/29
Driving Range (mi.)	Long-407.6
Bumpers	Weak
Parking Index	Hard
Seating	5
Tow Rating	Low-1500
Head/Leg Room (in.)	Cramped-38.3/42.2
Int. Space (cu. ft.)	Roomy-104.0
Cargo Space (cu. ft.)	Average-16.8

How the Competition Rates

	Rating	Pg.
Nissan Maxima	9	216
Pontiac Bonneville	7	226
Acura TL	10	99

*Data based on the Intrepid. Safety features and specifications vary among different models.

Chrysler Crossfire — Compact

For 2004, the Crossfire is a new addition to the Chrysler line up and marks the start of an infusion of Mercedes parts and technology into the aging fleet. The Crossfire is based on components taken from the Mercedes SLK roadster. There is seating for two and cargo room is small. A 3.2-liter V6 engine generates nearly 215 horsepower. A six-speed manual or a five-speed automatic transmission is available. Side impact airbags, dual stage airbags and an electronic stability program are standard.

Chrysler Crossfire

Chrysler Crossfire

Ratings—10 Best, 1 Worst	2004	2003
Front Crash Tests	—	
Side Crash Tests	—	
Safety Features	9	
Preventive Maintenance	—	
Repair Costs	—	
Warranty	8	
Fuel Economy	4	
Rollover	10	
Complaints	—	
Insurance Costs	5	
OVERALL RATING	—	

Price Range	Retail	Markup
Base Coupe	$33,620	8%

Last Year's Model

Model Not Produced in 2003

2003

Safety Checklist

Frontal Crash Test. . . . .
Side Crash Test. . . . .
Airbags (Side/Head). . . . . Front Standard/Yes
Pretensioners/Impact Adjustors . . . . Standard/Yes
Position/Weight Sensors . . . . Yes/No
Seat/Head Adjustors. . . . . No
Roll Stability System . . . . Yes
Child Seats Built-in. . . . . None
Antilock Brakes/Day Lamps 4-Wheel/None
Tire Pressure Monitor . . . . Direct

General Information

2004 Status. . . . . All New
Series Started. . . . . No series indicated
Where Made . . . .
Theft Rating. . . . . Average
Twins. . . . .

Specifications

Fuel Econ. (city/hwy). Poor-18/27
Driving Range (mi.) . . . . Very Short-335.6
Bumpers . . . .
Parking Index . . . . Very Easy
Seating 2
Tow Rating . . . .
Head/Leg Room (in.). . . . . Very Cramped-36.9/42.7
Int. Space (cu. ft.) . . . . Very Cramped-48
Cargo Space (cu. ft.). . . . .

How the Competition Rates

	Rating	Pg.
BMW Z4	9	107
Nissan 350Z	7	213
Mazda RX-8		201

Chrysler Pacifica

Large SUV

The all-new 2004 Chrysler Pacifica falls in-between a minivan and a SUV. A 3.5-liter V6 engine powers the vehicle. The Pacifica has a wide stance and a high arch giving the vehicle the utility of a minivan, but the handling of a large car. A power sunroof and rear lift gate are standard equipment. Dual zone climate control and a leather wrapped steering wheel are also standard. A navigation system and a Sirius Satellite Radio are also available. Antilock brakes, side curtain airbags, and a tire pressure monitoring system are standard safety features.

Chrysler Pacifica

Chrysler Pacifica

Ratings—10 Best, 1 Worst	2004	2003
Front Crash Tests	10	
Side Crash Tests	10	
Safety Features	8	
Preventive Maintenance	—	
Repair Costs	—	
Warranty	8	
Fuel Economy	2	
Rollover	7	
Complaints	—	
Insurance Costs	5	
OVERALL RATING	8	

Price Range	Retail	Markup
AWD	$32,300	9%
FWD	$30,550	9%

Last Year's Model

Model Not Produced in 2003

2003

Safety Checklist

Frontal Crash Test	Very Good
Side Crash Test	Very Good
Airbags (Side/Head)	Fr. Std. Rear Opt./Yes
Pretensioners/Impact Adjustors	Standard/Yes
Position/Weight Sensors	Yes/No
Seat/Head Adjustors	No
Roll Stability System	Yes
Child Seats Built-in	None
Antilock Brakes/Day Lamps	4-Wheel/Standard
Tire Pressure Monitor	None

General Information

2004 Status	All New
Series Started	No series indicated
Where Made	
Theft Rating	Average
Twins	

Specifications

Fuel Econ. (city/hwy)	Very Poor-17/23
Driving Range (mi.)	Very Long-443.0
Bumpers	
Parking Index	Very Hard
Seating	6
Tow Rating	Average-3500
Head/Leg Room (in.)	Cramped-39.2/40.9
Int. Space (cu. ft.)	Very Roomy-143.3
Cargo Space (cu. ft.)	Average-20.2

How the Competition Rates

	Rating	Pg.
Cadillac Escalade	3	116
Ford Expedition	4	149
Chevrolet Tahoe	3	130

Chrysler PT Cruiser

Compact

Chrysler's "retro" hatchback remains unchanged for 2004. Safety features such as dual stage airbags and front seat belt pretensions are standard features, but four-wheel ABS and seat mounted side impact airbags are optional. Cargo room is ample for a car of this size especially with the folding rear seats. Additional storage bins are found on the rear and front doors. A 180 horsepower inline 4-cylinder engine powers the base model PT Cruiser. An AM/FM/CD player is standard, and so are 16-inch aluminum wheels. Cruise control, power door locks and power windows are optional.

Chrysler PT Cruiser

Chrysler PT Cruiser

Ratings—10 Best, 1 Worst	2004	2003
Front Crash Tests	7	7
Side Crash Tests	9	9
Safety Features	3	3
Preventive Maintenance	10	9
Repair Costs	8	10
Warranty	8	6
Fuel Economy	4	5
Rollover	7	7
Complaints	5	9
Insurance Costs	1	1
OVERALL RATING	9	9

Price Range	Retail	Markup
Base	$17,395	7%
GT	$25,365	8%
Limited	$21,410	7%
Touring	$19,170	7%

Last Year's Model

This "pop culture" car received a new trim level option in 2003—the Turbo. The Turbo offers improved performance with a turbocharged 2.4-liter engine rated at 215 horsepower. The introduction of 17-inch aluminum wheels improve the cruiser's handling. Dual front airbags, reclining bucket seats, and a large number of seating configurations help insure the Cruiser's popularity. Four-wheel antilock brakes and side airbags are optional.

Chrysler PT Cruiser 2003

Safety Checklist

Frontal Crash Test . . . . . Good
Side Crash Test . . . . . Very Good
Airbags (Side/Head) . . . . . Fr. Std. Rear Opt./Yes
Pretensioners/Impact Adjustors . . . . . None/No
Position/Weight Sensors . . . . . No/No
Seat/Head Adjustors . . . . . No
Roll Stability System . . . . . No
Child Seats Built-in . . . . . None
Antilock Brakes/Day Lamps . . . . 4-Wheel (optional)/None
Tire Pressure Monitor . . . . . None

General Information

2004 Status . . . . . Unchanged
Series Started 2000
Where Made . . . . . Mexico
Theft Rating . . . . . Very Low
Twins . . . . .

Specifications

Fuel Econ. (city/hwy) Poor-19/25
Driving Range (mi.) . . . . . Very Short-319.5
Bumpers . . . . .
Parking Index . . . . . Easy
Seating 5
Tow Rating . . . . . Very Low-1000
Head/Leg Room (in.) Average-40.4/40.6
Int. Space (cu. ft.) Average-101.2
Cargo Space (cu. ft.) . . . . . Very Roomy-64.2

How the Competition Rates

	Rating	Pg.
Ford Focus	8	152
Pontiac Vibe	9	230
Volkswagen Golf	9	264

Chrys. Sebring Sdn. & Conv./Dodge Stratus Intermediate

For 2004, the Chrysler Sebring sedan and convertible receives a minor restyling of the exterior. There is a new grille and front fascia on both vehicles. A new seatbelt alert system is now available in the convertible. Dodge's mid-size Stratus sedan also gets a facelift. Side curtain airbags are optional on the Sebring. The Stratus R/T version has a more powerful engine and improved suspension over other models. Dual stage front airbags, and antilock brakes are standard on both cars.

Chrysler Sebring

Ratings—10 Best, 1 Worst	2004	2003
Front Crash Tests	10	10
Side Crash Tests*	5	5
Safety Features	5	2
Preventive Maintenance	8	9
Repair Costs	10	8
Warranty	8	6
Fuel Economy	7	6
Rollover	10	10
Complaints	10	—
Insurance Costs	1	1
OVERALL RATING	10	8

Chrysler Sebring Convertible

Price Range	Retail	Markup
LX	$18,640	7%
Lxi	$21,215	8%

Safety Checklist

Frontal Crash Test . . . . . . Very Good
Side Crash Test* . . . . . . Average
Airbags (Side/Head). . . . . . Front Standard/Yes
Pretensioners/Impact Adjustors. . . . . . None/Yes
Position/Weight Sensors. . . . . . No/No
Seat/Head Adjustors. . . . . . No
Roll Stability System. . . . . . No
Child Seats Built-in. . . . . . None
Antilock Brakes/Day Lamps. . . . 4-Wheel (optional)/None
Tire Pressure Monitor. . . . . . None

General Information

2004 Status . . . . . . Minor Appearance Change
Series Started 1995
Where Made . . . . . . US
Theft Rating. . . . . . Very High
Twins. . . . . . Dodge Stratus 2004

Last Year's Model

The Sebring sedan remained unchanged in 2003 except for new colors and a new trim model. The Sebring sedan and convertible share the same platform and engine configurations. The Sebring sedan has side impact airbags and interior lights that turn off automatically. The Stratus sedan added the SXT trim model to its line-up. There are so many different engine choices and option packages on each car that 2003 prices will vary greatly.

Dodge Stratus

Specifications

Fuel Econ. (city/hwy) Good-22/30
Driving Range (mi.) Average-400.0
Bumpers . . . . . . Strong
Parking Index. . . . . . Average
Seating 5
Tow Rating . . . . . . Very Low-1000
Head/Leg Room (in.) . . . . . . Very Cramped-37.6/42.3
Int. Space (cu. ft.) Cramped-94
Cargo Space (cu. ft.). Cramped-16

How the Competition Rates

	Rating	Pg.
Chevrolet Malibu		126
Honda Accord	8	160
Suzuki Verona		246

*Ratings are for Chrysler Sebring Sedan. For Sebring Convertible crash results, see page 24.

Chrysler Sebring Coupe/Dodge Stratus Coupe — Compact

The 2004 Sebring and Stratus coupe are built on a different platform than the sedan, but remains unchanged this year. A 2.4-liter 4-cylinder engine powers the Sebring coupe. A V6 engine is optional. All cars come with antilock brakes, and dual stage airbags. Side curtain airbags are optional on the Sebring. Dual stage front airbags, and antilock brakes are standard. The R/T version of the Stratus coupe has a powerful V6 engine.

Chrysler Sebring

Dodge Stratus

Ratings—10 Best, 1 Worst	2004	2003
Front Crash Tests	**8**	8
Side Crash Tests	**8**	8
Safety Features	**1**	1
Preventive Maintenance	**8**	8
Repair Costs	**1**	6
Warranty	**8**	6
Fuel Economy	**6**	6
Rollover	**9**	10
Complaints	**10**	10
Insurance Costs	**1**	1
OVERALL RATING	**7**	8

Price Range	Retail	Markup
LX	$20,750	8%
Limited	$23,025	8%

Safety Checklist

Frontal Crash Test . . . . . Good
Side Crash Test . . . . . Good
Airbags (Side/Head). . . . . No Side
Pretensioners/Impact Adjustors . . . . . None/No
Position/Weight Sensors. . . . . No/No
Seat/Head Adjustors. . . . . No
Roll Stability System. . . . . No
Child Seats Built-in. . . . . None
Antilock Brakes/Day Lamps. . . . 4-Wheel (optional)/None
Tire Pressure Monitor. . . . . None

General Information

2004 Status. . . . . Unchanged
Series Started 1995
Where Made . . . . . US
Theft Rating. . . . . Very High
Twins . . . . . Dodge Stratus Coupe 2004

Specifications

Fuel Econ. (city/hwy). Average-21/28
Driving Range (mi.) Average-385.7
Bumpers . . . . . Strong
Parking Index . . . . . Very Hard
Seating 5
Tow Rating . . . . .
Head/Leg Room (in.) Cramped-38.5/42.3
Int. Space (cu. ft.) . . . . . Very Cramped-86.4
Cargo Space (cu. ft.) Cramped-16.3

Last Year's Model

For 2003, the Sebring/Stratus coupes received new front and rear fascias, new grilles, headlamps, and side moldings. There were new hood and trunk lid designs as well. A 2.4-liter 4-cylinder engine powers the base model of the Sebring/Stratus coupe. A V6 engine is optional on both. All cars come with antilock brakes and dual stage airbags. Side curtain airbags are optional on the Sebring. There are numberous option packages available on both.

Dodge Stratus

How the Competition Rates

	Rating	Pg.
Mitsubishi Galant	5	209
Hyundai Sonata	10	171
Honda Accord	8	160

Chrysler Town and Country/Dodge Gr. Caravan Minivan

For 2004, the Chrysler Town and Country/Dodge Grand Caravan are unchanged. There have been changes to the option packages and a short wheel base version of the Town and Country is now available. The standard engine for both models is a 3.0-liter V6. The Town and Country offers more in the way of luxury items, such as leather and wood trim, but the Grand Caravan does have a fine selection of options. A rear DVD entertainment system is available for both models.

Chrysler Town and Country

Ratings—10 Best, 1 Worst	2004	2003
Front Crash Tests	7	7
Side Crash Tests	10	10
Safety Features	4	4
Preventive Maintenance	10	9
Repair Costs	9	9
Warranty	8	6
Fuel Economy	3	6
Rollover	6	6
Complaints	5	6
Insurance Costs	10	10
OVERALL RATING	10	10

Price Range	Retail	Markup
AWD Touring	$32,665	9%
LWB Limited	$37,575	10%
LWB LX	$26,685	9%
LWB Touring	$30,340	9%

Last Year's Model

The 2003 Town and Country minivan received a powered sunroof and factory-installed DVD entertainment system. The Town and Country is the upscale version of the Chrysler minivans, featuring leather and suede interiors, heated power seats and lots of power equipment. New features also include adjustable pedals to help properly position them to various drivers, and a tire pressure monitor.

Chrysler Town and Country 2003

Dodge Grand Caravan

Safety Checklist

Frontal Crash Test	Good
Side Crash Test	Very Good
Airbags (Side/Head)	Fr. Std. Rear Opt.
Pretensioners/Impact Adjustors	None/Yes
Position/Weight Sensors	No/No
Seat/Head Adjustors	No
Roll Stability System	No
Child Seats Built-in	None
Antilock Brakes/Day Lamps	4-Wheel/Optional
Tire Pressure Monitor	Indirect

General Information

2004 Status	Unchanged
Series Started	2000
Where Made	US
Theft Rating	Very High
Twins	Dodge Grand Caravan 2004

Specifications

Fuel Econ. (city/hwy)	Poor-18/24
Driving Range (mi.)	Long-405.6
Bumpers	
Parking Index	Very Hard
Seating	7
Tow Rating	Low-2000
Head/Leg Room (in.)	Cramped-39.6/40.6
Int. Space (cu. ft.)	Very Roomy-163.5
Cargo Space (cu. ft.)	Average-17.8

How the Competition Rates

	Rating	Pg.
Honda Odyssey	8	165
Mercury Monterey	4	205
Nissan Quest	6	220

Dodge Caravan/Chrysler Town and Country SWB Minivan

For 2004, the Dodge Caravan remains unchanged. A capable 2.4-liter inline 4-cylinder engine powers the base model. A 3.3-liter V6 is available on certain models. A 4-speed automatic transmission is standard. A rear seat DVD entertainment system is available to help pass the time on long trips. Front seatbelt pretensioners, dual stage airbags and front disc brakes are standard. Seat mounted side airbags, and passenger head protection is optional. Keyless entry is available as an option. This is, essentially, a short version of the Grand Caravan.

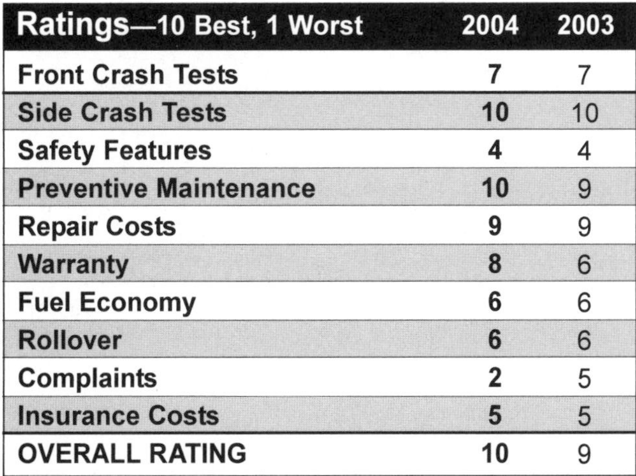

Ratings—10 Best, 1 Worst	2004	2003
Front Crash Tests	**7**	7
Side Crash Tests	**10**	10
Safety Features	**4**	4
Preventive Maintenance	**10**	9
Repair Costs	**9**	9
Warranty	**8**	6
Fuel Economy	**6**	6
Rollover	**6**	6
Complaints	**2**	5
Insurance Costs	**5**	5
OVERALL RATING	**10**	9

Price Range	Retail	Markup
ES	$21,835	8%
R/T	$22,370	8%
SE	$18,325	8%
SXT	$19,390	8%

Last Year's Model

The Dodge Caravan was unchanged in 2003. A 3.3-liter V6 engine is available on most models. Options include power door locks, 3-zone climate control, power lift gate and a rear organizer. Some of the new gadgets added for 2003 include a factory installed DVD entertainment system, a powered sunroof, and powered adjustable pedals. Safety features included dual stage front airbags, side impact airbags and side mounted curtain airbags.

Dodge Caravan

Dodge Caravan

Dodge Caravan

Safety Checklist

Frontal Crash Test	Good
Side Crash Test	Very Good
Airbags (Side/Head)	Front Optional Rear Optional
Pretensioners/Impact Adjustors	Yes/No
Position/Weight Sensors	No/No
Seat/Head Adjustors	No
Roll Stability System	No
Child Seats Built-in	Optional
Antilock Brakes/Day Lamps	4-Wheel/None
Tire Pressure Monitor	None

General Information

2004 Status	Unchanged
Series Started	1996
Where Made	US
Theft Rating	Very High
Twins	Chrysler Town and Country SWB

Specifications

Fuel Econ. (city/hwy)	Average-21/27
Driving Range (mi.)	Very Long-466.7
Bumpers	Strong
Parking Index	Hard
Seating	7
Tow Rating	Low-1800
Head/Leg Room (in.)	Cramped-39.7/40.6
Int. Space (cu. ft.)	Very Roomy-142.3
Cargo Space (cu. ft.)	Cramped-15.3

How the Competition Rates

	Rating	Pg.
Chevrolet Venture	6	133
Ford Freestar	4	153
Kia Sedona	6	185

Dodge Dakota — Compact Pickup

The Dodge Dakota is unchanged for 2004. The base engine is a 2.5-liter 4-cylinder engine, but there is an option to upgrade to a more powerful 210 horsepower V6. Rear wheel antilock brakes are standard, but 4-wheel antilock brakes are optional. The passenger airbag will deactivate if there is no one in the passenger seat. A full-size spare is also included. The Dakota has multiple cab, bed sizes and options. Front bucket seats, and an AM/FM/CD stereo are also available. The ride is smoother than most pickups.

Dodge Dakota SLT Quad Cab

Ratings—10 Best, 1 Worst	2004	2003
Front Crash Tests*	7	7
Side Crash Tests	10	10
Safety Features	1	1
Preventive Maintenance	9	9
Repair Costs	8	9
Warranty	8	6
Fuel Economy	1	2
Rollover	6	6
Complaints	3	3
Insurance Costs	1	1
OVERALL RATING	7	5

Price Range	Retail	Markup
Base	$16,940	9%
SLT	$17,785	9%
Sport	$17,785	9%
Sport/SXT	$21,810	9%

Last Year's Model

The Dakota was unchanged in 2003, but there were refinements in the option packages. The 2.5-liter 4-cylinder is the standard engine. There is also a 5.2-liter V8 option on some models. You'll have to choose between two- or four-wheel drive, cab size, and the type of transmission. The ride is smoother than typical compact trunks and the handling is responsive.

Dodge Dakota 2003

Dodge Dakota

Safety Checklist

Frontal Crash Test*	Good
Side Crash Test	Very Good
Airbags (Side/Head)	No Side
Pretensioners/Impact Adjustors	None/No
Position/Weight Sensors	No/No
Seat/Head Adjustors	No
Roll Stability System	No
Child Seats Built-in	None
Antilock Brakes/Day Lamps	4-Wheel (optional)/None
Tire Pressure Monitor	None

General Information

2004 Status	Unchanged
Series Started	1997
Where Made	US
Theft Rating	Very High
Twins	

Specifications

Fuel Econ. (city/hwy)	Very Poor-14/19
Driving Range (mi.)	Very Short-349.4
Bumpers	Strong
Parking Index	Average
Seating	5
Tow Rating	High-6600
Head/Leg Room (in.)	Average-40/41.9
Int. Space (cu. ft.)	Cramped-92.8
Cargo Space (cu. ft.)	Roomy-26

How the Competition Rates

	Rating	Pg.
Chevrolet Colorado		124
Ford Ranger	6	156
Nissan Frontier	4	215

*Ratings are for Quad Cab. For Extended Cab crash results, see page 26.

Dodge Durango

Large SUV

The Durango is all-new this year and much longer than last year's. It has a new 3.7-liter V6 as a standard engine. You can upgrade to a more powerful 4.7-liter magnum or 5.7 Hemi magnum V8 engine. The suspension has been refined for a smoother ride. Climate control is standard. A DVD entertainment system and a sunroof are available options. The Durango is equipped with dual stage airbags and passenger sensing technology to deactivate the passenger airbag if necessary. Side curtain airbags, and four-wheel ABS brakes are standard as well.

Dodge Durango

Ratings—10 Best, 1 Worst	2004	2003
Front Crash Tests	—	7
Side Crash Tests	—	—
Safety Features	8	3
Preventive Maintenance	—	9
Repair Costs	—	6
Warranty	8	6
Fuel Economy	1	1
Rollover	4	5
Complaints	—	5
Insurance Costs	5	5
OVERALL RATING	—	5

Dodge Durango

Safety Checklist

Frontal Crash Test . . . .
Side Crash Test . . . .
Airbags (Side/Head) . . . . Fr. Std. Rear Opt./Yes
Pretensioners/Impact Adjustors . . . . Standard/Yes
Position/Weight Sensors. Yes/No
Seat/Head Adjustors . . . . No
Roll Stability System. . . . . Yes
Child Seats Built-in . . . . None
Antilock Brakes/Day Lamps 4-Wheel/None
Tire Pressure Monitor . . . . None

Price Range	Retail	Markup
Base	$25,920	10%
SLT4X4	$27,420	10%

General Information

2004 Status . . . . All New
Series Started . . . . No series indicated
Where Made . . . . US
Theft Rating . . . . Very High
Twins . . . .

Last Year's Model

Based on the Dakota pickup platform, the Durango remained essentially unchanged for 2003 except for some new options. These include a DVD rear seat entertainment center. A new five-speed transmission was added to improve towing. 2-wheel ABS is standard. Supplemental side air bags for the front and second row seats are optional. The Durango competes with the Ford Expedition and the large GM SUVs.

Dodge Durango
2003

Specifications

Fuel Econ. (city/hwy) . . . . Very Poor-15/21
Driving Range (mi.) . . . .
Bumpers . . . . Strong
Parking Index . . . .
Seating 5/7
Tow Rating . . . . Very High-8900
Head/Leg Room (in.) . . . .
Int. Space (cu. ft.). . . . .
Cargo Space (cu. ft.) . . . . Very Roomy-67.3

How the Competition Rates

	Rating	Pg.
Chevrolet Tahoe	3	130
Ford Expedition	4	149
Nissan Pathfinder Armada		219

Dodge Neon Compact

For 2004, the Dodge Neon is unchanged. A 2.0-liter inline 4-cylinder engine rated at 132 horsepower powers the base model. An AM/FM cassette stereo is standard, but you can upgrade to a six-disc CD changer. Four-wheel ABS is optional. Supplemental front seat side airbags are available as part of an option package. A sport SRT version is available and powered by an improved turbo charged 4-cylinder engine. It has racing styled seats and a sporty suspension system. The Neon is aimed at young-first time buyers.

Dodge Neon SE

Dodge Neon SXT

Ratings—10 Best, 1 Worst	2004	2003
Front Crash Tests	6	6
Side Crash Tests	6	6
Safety Features	1	1
Preventive Maintenance	9	8
Repair Costs	8	9
Warranty	8	6
Fuel Economy	8	8
Rollover	9	9
Complaints	3	3
Insurance Costs	1	1
OVERALL RATING	8	7

Price Range	Retail	Markup
R/T	$17,275	7%
SE	$13,125	7%
SXT	$15,435	7%

Last Year's Model

The Neon under went a major appearance change in 2003. A new front end, rear fascias, headlamps and taillamps round out the Neon's updated exterior features. A new sportier trim level, the SRT-4was introduced this year. An all-new 2.4-liter turbocharged engine with 215hp powers the SRT-4 model. The base model Neon is powered by a 2-liter 4-cylinder with a manual transmission standard. ABS is optional.

Dodge Neon 2003

Safety Checklist

Frontal Crash Test	Average
Side Crash Test	Average
Airbags (Side/Head)	Front Optional Rear Optional
Pretensioners/Impact Adjustors	None/No
Position/Weight Sensors	No/No
Seat/Head Adjustors	No
Roll Stability System	No
Child Seats Built-in	None
Antilock Brakes/Day Lamps	4-Wheel (optional)/None
Tire Pressure Monitor	None

General Information

2004 Status	Unchanged
Series Started	2000
Where Made	US
Theft Rating	Very High
Twins	

Specifications

Fuel Econ. (city/hwy)	Good-25/32
Driving Range (mi.)	Very Short-346.6
Bumpers	Strong
Parking Index	Easy
Seating	5
Tow Rating	Very Low-1000
Head/Leg Room (in.)	Cramped-38.4/42.2
Int. Space (cu. ft.)	Average-102.3
Cargo Space (cu. ft.)	Cramped-13.1

How the Competition Rates

	Rating	Pg.
Honda Civic	10	161
Mitsubishi Galant		209
Nissan Sentra	8	221

Dodge Ram Pickup — Standard Pickup

For 2004, the Dodge Ram gets a new "racing" trim model called the SRT-10. The standard Regular Cab 1500 comes in either 2- or 4-wheel drive. A three- person bench seat is standard, but you can opt for captain's chairs. The standard engine is a V6, but you can upgrade to a more powerful version of the V6 or a V8. The SRT is powered by the same V10 as the Viper. Rear-wheel antilock brakes are a standard feature. Four-wheel antilock brakes are a separate feature that can be purchased. The Ram comes in a variety of bed lengths.

Dodge Ram 1500 Quad Cab

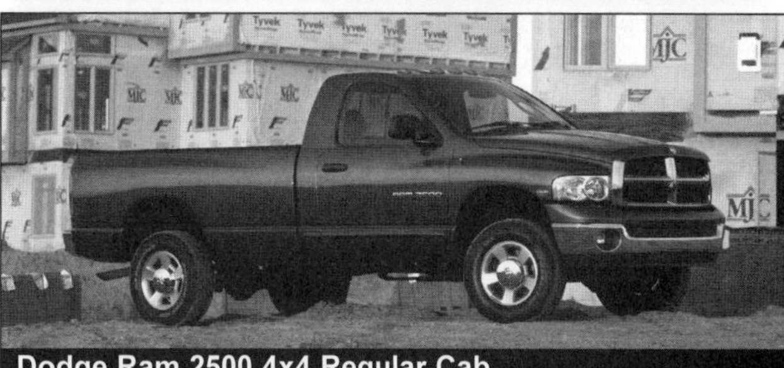

Dodge Ram 2500 4x4 Regular Cab

Ratings—10 Best, 1 Worst	2004	2003
Front Crash Tests	9	9
Side Crash Tests	—	—
Safety Features	2	2
Preventive Maintenance	2	2
Repair Costs	6	6
Warranty	8	6
Fuel Economy	1	2
Rollover	6	5
Complaints	—	3
Insurance Costs	1	1
OVERALL RATING	2	1

Price Range	Retail	Markup
4x2 Quad Cab	$26,085	13%
4x2 Regular Cab	$18,970	12%
4x2 Regular Cab SLT	$22,325	13%
4x4 Quad Cab SLT	$29,155	13%

Last Year's Model

This distinctive pickup received minor changes for 2003, but retained its rough and tough looks. The 3.7-liter Magnum V-6 engine is standard on the two-wheel drive Dodge Ram 1500 Regular Cab. The same V6 is also standard on two-wheel drive Quad Cab model. Dual zone climate control and 17-inch tires are standard on the SLT Plus model. The 2500 and 3500 models offer more powerful engines, longer bed options and cab selections.

Dodge Ram Pickup 2003

Safety Checklist

Frontal Crash Test	Very Good
Side Crash Test	
Airbags (Side/Head)	Front Optional Rear Optional
Pretensioners/Impact Adjustors	None/No
Position/Weight Sensors	No/No
Seat/Head Adjustors	No
Roll Stability System	No
Child Seats Built-in	None
Antilock Brakes/Day Lamps	4-Wheel (optional)/None
Tire Pressure Monitor	None

General Information

2004 Status	Unchanged
Series Started	2002
Where Made	US
Theft Rating	Very High
Twins	

Specifications

Fuel Econ. (city/hwy)	Very Poor-15/20
Driving Range (mi.)	Very Long-439.4
Bumpers	Strong
Parking Index	Very Hard
Seating	3
Tow Rating	Average-3500
Head/Leg Room (in.)	Average-40.9/41
Int. Space (cu. ft.)	Very Cramped-65.06
Cargo Space (cu. ft.)	

How the Competition Rates

Chevrolet Silverado	3	128
Ford F-Series		154
Toyota Tundra	4	262

Ford Cr. Victoria/Merc. Grand Marquis/Marauder — Large

For 2004, all three of these vehicles remain unchanged, but they do get new options, colors, improved suspensions and improved console designs. The Grand Marquis gets dual side airbags, a moon roof and heated front seats as options. The Marauder gets standard traction control. A 4.6-liter V8 engine powers the Crown Victoria and the Grand Marquis. The Marauder has the more powerful 300 horsepower version of the V8. All are equipped with dual stage airbags and optional side airbags on some models. All three models did very well in government crash tests.

Ford Crown Victoria

Mercury Marauder

Ratings—10 Best, 1 Worst	2004	2003
Front Crash Tests	10	10
Side Crash Tests	9	9
Safety Features	7	7
Preventive Maintenance	7	7
Repair Costs	9	9
Warranty	2	2
Fuel Economy	4	4
Rollover	10	10
Complaints	10	8
Insurance Costs	10	10
OVERALL RATING	10	10

Price Range	Retail	Markup
Base	$23,620	7%
Fleet	$23,740	7%
Fleet Ext	$25,760	7%
LX	$26,645	9%

Last Year's Model

For 2003, the Crown Victoria and Grand Marquis received major restyling changes. The Mercury Marauder was all new last year. All three have a new independent suspension system and improved structural frames. Side air bags are available on the LX models, as are improved headlights. A 4.6-liter V8 powers the Crown Victoria. There is a standard automatic transmission. Leather seating is standard on the Marauder and Grand Marquis.

Ford Crown Victoria

Safety Checklist

Frontal Crash Test	Very Good
Side Crash Test	Very Good
Airbags (Side/Head)	Front Optional Rear Optional
Pretensioners/Impact Adjustors	Yes/Yes
Position/Weight Sensors	Yes/Yes
Seat/Head Adjustors	Yes
Roll Stability System	NA
Child Seats Built-in	None
Antilock Brakes/Day Lamps	4-Wheel/None
Tire Pressure Monitor	None

General Information

2004 Status	Unchanged
Series Started	1998
Where Made	Canada
Theft Rating	Very High
Twins	Mercury Grand Marquis, Mercury Marauder 2004

Specifications

Fuel Econ. (city/hwy)	Poor-18/26
Driving Range (mi.)	Average-397.0
Bumpers	Strong
Parking Index	Very Hard
Seating	5/6
Tow Rating	Very Low-1500
Head/Leg Room (in.)	Average-39.3/42.5
Int. Space (cu. ft.)	Roomy-111.2
Cargo Space (cu. ft.)	Average-20.6

How the Competition Rates

	Rating	Pg.
Buick LeSabre	7	109
Chrysler 300M	10	134
Pontiac Bonneville	7	226

*Ratings are for Ford Crown Victoria.

Ford Escape/Mazda Tribute — Small SUV

Both the Ford Escape and its twin the Mazda Tribute remain unchanged for 2004. There have been some minor changes to the option packages and the Escape XLT gets new side cladding. The base engine for both of these small SUVs is a 2.0-liter inline 4-cylinder engine. A V6 is available on upgraded models. The front fascia of the Tribute is different than the Escape, but the options, power trains, and engines are the same. The Tribute offers an entertainment center with DVD capability as an option. The Escape can tow up to 3,500 lbs with the proper towing package.

Ford Escape

Ratings—10 Best, 1 Worst	2004	2003
Front Crash Tests	9	9
Side Crash Tests	10	10
Safety Features	3	3
Preventive Maintenance	8	9
Repair Costs	8	10
Warranty	2	2
Fuel Economy	4	5
Rollover	6	6
Complaints	1	1
Insurance Costs	10	10
OVERALL RATING	6	7

Mazda Tribute

Safety Checklist

Frontal Crash Test	Very Good
Side Crash Test	Very Good
Airbags (Side/Head)	Front Standard
Pretensioners/Impact Adjustors	Yes/No
Position/Weight Sensors	No/No
Seat/Head Adjustors	No
Roll Stability System	No
Child Seats Built-in	None
Antilock Brakes/Day Lamps	4-Wheel/None
Tire Pressure Monitor	None

Price Range	Retail	Markup
Limited FWD	$24,615	8%
XLS FWD	$18,710	8%
XLT 4WD	$24,180	8%
XLT FWD	$22,555	8%

General Information

2004 Status	Unchanged
Series Started	2001
Where Made	US
Theft Rating	Very Low
Twins	Mazda Tribute 2004

Last Year's Model

For 2003, the Escape added a new the Limited trim level and new fabrics, but otherwise remained unchanged. A 2.0-liter four-cylinder engine powers the Escape, but there is an optional 201-horsepower 3.0-liter V6 engine. The Escape offers reasonable room for a vehicle of its size. Two- and four-wheel drive options are available. Dual airbags are standard as are steel side impact door beams for added protection.

Ford Escape

Specifications

Fuel Econ. (city/hwy)	Poor-19/25
Driving Range (mi.)	Very Short-340.8
Bumpers	Strong
Parking Index	Easy
Seating	5
Tow Rating	Very Low-1000
Head/Leg Room (in.)	Roomy-40.4/42.7
Int. Space (cu. ft.)	Average-100.1
Cargo Space (cu. ft.)	Very Roomy-69.2

How the Competition Rates

	Rating	Pg.
Honda CR-V	9	162
Jeep Liberty	10	180
Hyundai Santa Fe	9	170

Ford Excursion — Large SUV

For 2004, the Ford Excursion remains unchanged. Wireless headphones are now available for the rear seat DVD entertainment center. The Excursion is powered by a 5.4-liter V8 engine and comes in either two-wheel or four-wheel drive. There is also a diesel engine option. There are four different trims you can select. Dual stage airbags and steel side door panels help product passengers. A reverse sensing system, to help you back up this 19 foot SUV, is available as an option.

Ford Excursion

Ford Excursion

Ratings—10 Best, 1 Worst	2004	2003
Front Crash Tests	—	—
Side Crash Tests	—	—
Safety Features	4	4
Preventive Maintenance	1	1
Repair Costs	8	9
Warranty	2	2
Fuel Economy	—	—
Rollover	4	4
Complaints	2	1
Insurance Costs	10	10
OVERALL RATING	—	—

Price Range	Retail	Markup
Eddie Bauer 2WD	$40,510	14%
Limited 4WD	$44,935	14%
XLS 2WD	$36,435	14%
XLT 2WD	$37,425	14%

Last Year's Model

The Excursion did not change in 2003. There was a new optional 6.0-liter diesel engine and a new Eddie Bauer trim level added. The Excursion is capable of seating up to nine adults and accommodating their luggage with ease. The two-wheel drive version comes with a 5.4-liter Triton V8. The four-wheel drive version has a larger 6.8-liter Triton V10. Towing capacity is great and the rear hatch's rear window opens separately.

Ford Excursion 2003

Safety Checklist

Frontal Crash Test	
Side Crash Test	
Airbags (Side/Head)	Front Optional Rear Optional
Pretensioners/Impact Adjustors	Yes/Yes
Position/Weight Sensors	NA/NA
Seat/Head Adjustors	No
Roll Stability System	No
Child Seats Built-in	None
Antilock Brakes/Day Lamps	4-Wheel/None
Tire Pressure Monitor	None

General Information

2004 Status	Unchanged
Series Started	2000
Where Made	US
Theft Rating	Very High
Twins	

Specifications

Fuel Econ. (city/hwy)	
Driving Range (mi.)	
Bumpers	Strong
Parking Index	Very Hard
Seating	7/8
Tow Rating	Very High-7600
Head/Leg Room (in.)	Roomy-41/42.3
Int. Space (cu. ft.)	
Cargo Space (cu. ft.)	Very Roomy-146.4

How the Competition Rates

Chevrolet Suburban	2	129
Dodge Durango		143
Toyota Sequoia	4	258

Ford Expedition/Lincoln Navigator — Large SUV

The Lincoln Navigator and the Ford Expedition remain unchanged. A new trim, the NBX, replaces the XLT FX4 trim model on the Expedition. The Navigator gets new exterior colors, a tire pressure monitoring system and an optional roll stability control system. A massive 4.6-liter V8 engine powers these full sized SUVs. There is a more powerful 5.4-liter V8 engine available as an option. The Expedition has cruise control, remote keyless entry and heated seats as standard equipment. The Navigator adds leather and wood trim to its list of standard features.

Ratings—10 Best, 1 Worst	2004	2003
Front Crash Tests	10	10
Side Crash Tests	—	—
Safety Features	8	8
Preventive Maintenance	4	4
Repair Costs	7	8
Warranty	2	2
Fuel Economy	1	1
Rollover	4	4
Complaints	—	5
Insurance Costs	10	10
OVERALL RATING	4	4

Price Range	Retail	Markup
Eddie Bauer 2WD	$37,890	14%
XLS 2WD	$31,940	14%
XLT 2WD	$33,765	14%
XLT 4WD	$36,520	14%

Last Year's Model

The Ford Expedition/Lincoln Navigator were redesigned in 2003. New 2003 features include power fold-down rear seats, independent rear suspension, and tire pressure monitors. The styling and dimensions changed minimally. The engine options for the Expedition are: a 4.6-liter V8 or a 5.4-liter V8. For those who like high-tech gadgets, a navigation and DVD entertainment system are available on both models.

Ford Expedition

2003

Ford Expedition

Lincoln Navigator

Safety Checklist

Frontal Crash Test	Very Good
Side Crash Test	
Airbags (Side/Head)	Front Opt. Rear Opt./Yes
Pretensioners/Impact Adjustors	None/Yes
Position/Weight Sensors	Yes/Yes
Seat/Head Adjustors	No
Roll Stability System	Yes
Child Seats Built-in	None
Antilock Brakes/Day Lamps	4-Wheel/None
Tire Pressure Monitor	Direct

General Information

2004 Status	Unchanged
Series Started	2003
Where Made	US
Theft Rating	Very High
Twins	

Specifications

Fuel Econ. (city/hwy)	Very Poor-14/19
Driving Range (mi.)	Very Long-444.7
Bumpers	Strong
Parking Index	Very Hard
Seating	9
Tow Rating	High-5564
Head/Leg Room (in.)	Cramped-39.7/41.2
Int. Space (cu. ft.)	
Cargo Space (cu. ft.)	Very Roomy-110.4

How the Competition Rates

	Rating	Pg.
Chevrolet Tahoe	3	130
Dodge Durango		143
Toyota Sequoia	4	258

Ford Explorer/Mercury Mountaineer — Mid-Size SUV

For 2004, the Ford Explorer/Mercury Mountaineer remain essentially unchanged with some minor improvements. These included a tire pressure monitoring system, a new stability control system, and new seating options for the second row seats. A 4.6-liter V6 engine powers the Explorer/Mountaineer and both SUVs have an automatic transmission. Consumers can also upgrade to a more powerful V8 engine. Safety features include dual stage airbags, side curtain airbags, and four-wheel antilock brakes.

Ford Explorer

Ratings—10 Best, 1 Worst	2004	2003
Front Crash Tests	9	9
Side Crash Tests*	10	10
Safety Features	10	8
Preventive Maintenance	5	5
Repair Costs	9	9
Warranty	2	2
Fuel Economy	1	1
Rollover	5	4
Complaints	—	—
Insurance Costs	10	10
OVERALL RATING	8	6

Mercury Mountaineer

Safety Checklist

Frontal Crash Test.... Very Good
Side Crash Test*.... Very Good
Airbags (Side/Head).... Front Standard/Yes
Pretensioners/Impact Adjustors.... Yes/Yes
Position/Weight Sensors.... Yes/Yes
Seat/Head Adjustors.... No
Roll Stability System.... Yes
Child Seats Built-in.... None
Antilock Brakes/Day Lamps.... 4-Wheel/None
Tire Pressure Monitor.... Direct

Price Range	Retail	Markup
Eddie Bauer 4WD	$35,325	11%
Limited AWD	$36,200	11%
XLS 2WD	$26,285	10%
XLS AWD	$28,510	10%

General Information

2004 Status.... Unchanged
Series Started.... 2002
Where Made.... US
Theft Rating.... Very High
Twins.... Mercury Mountaineer 2004

Last Year's Model

The Explorer/Mountaineer received minor improvements after its redesign in 2002. These included a rear seat entertainment system and new colors. The 2003 Explorer/Mountaineer is powered by a 4.6-liter V6. Safety systems include dual airbags and the new Ford safety canopy with side curtain air bags. A passenger weight sensor detects if a child is the front seat and will deactivate the passenger airbag.

Ford Explorer

Specifications

Fuel Econ. (city/hwy).... Very Poor-15/19
Driving Range (mi.).... Short-372.8
Bumpers.... Strong
Parking Index.... Average
Seating.... 5/7
Tow Rating.... Average-5400
Head/Leg Room (in.).... Roomy-39.9/42.4
Int. Space (cu. ft.)....
Cargo Space (cu. ft.).... Very Roomy-81.7

How the Competition Rates

	Rating	Pg.
Chevrolet Trail Blazer	3	132
Mitsubishi Endeavor	5	208
Toyota 4Runner	6	248

*Door became unlatched.

Ford Explorer Sport Trac

Large SUV

This year the Ford Explorer Sport Trac receives a revised instrument cluster and new standard equipment on its XLT trim model. The Sport Trac combines an SUV with the utility of a pick up. It is powered by 4.0-liter V6 engine and available in 2-wheel or 4-wheel drive versions. There is nearly 30 cubic feet of cargo room in the back bed. The Sport Trac comes with an AM/FM/CD player and bucket seats as standard equipment. Leather is available as an option. The Sport Trac is Ford's answer to GM's crossover SUV/trucks.

Ford Explorer Sport Trac

Ford Explorer Sport Track XLT

Ratings—10 Best, 1 Worst	2004	2003
Front Crash Tests	—	
Side Crash Tests	—	
Safety Features	8	
Preventive Maintenance	5	
Repair Costs	9	
Warranty	2	
Fuel Economy	2	
Rollover	3	
Complaints	—	
Insurance Costs	5	
OVERALL RATING	—	

Price Range	Retail	Markup
XLS 2WD	$23,045	10%
XLS 4WD	$25,815	10%
XLT 2WD	$24,560	10%
XLT 4WD	$27,390	10%

Last Year's Model

Ford Explorer Sport Trac 2003

Safety Checklist

Frontal Crash Test	Very Good
Side Crash Test	
Airbags (Side/Head)	Front Optional Rear Optional
Pretensioners/Impact Adjustors	Yes/Yes
Position/Weight Sensors	Yes/Yes
Seat/Head Adjustors	No
Roll Stability System	Yes
Child Seats Built-in	None
Antilock Brakes/Day Lamps	4-Wheel/Standard
Tire Pressure Monitor	None

General Information

2004 Status	Unchanged
Series Started	2001
Where Made	US
Theft Rating	Very High
Twins	

Specifications

Fuel Econ. (city/hwy)	Very Poor-16/20
Driving Range (mi.)	Average-395.6
Bumpers	
Parking Index	Very Hard
Seating	4
Tow Rating	Low-2740
Head/Leg Room (in.)	Average-39.4/42.4
Int. Space (cu. ft.)	
Cargo Space (cu. ft.)	Very Good/43.5

How the Competition Rates

	Rating	Pg.
Cadillac Escalade EXT	2	117
GMC Envoy XUV		159

Ford Focus — Compact

Except for minor improvements, the Focus remains unchanged. The ZX 3 now has leather seating, new struts and steering controls for improved handling. New colors choices are also available. A 2.0-liter inline 4-cylinder powers the Focus. There are two other engine choices including a new 2.3-liter 4-cylinder engine. Standard equipment includes an AM/FM cassette radio, power interior trunk release, and a passive anti-theft system. Options include an automatic transmission, 16-inch aluminum wheels and side airbags.

Ford Focus

Ratings—10 Best, 1 Worst	2004	2003
Front Crash Tests*	8	9
Side Crash Tests*	8	8
Safety Features	7	8
Preventive Maintenance	4	4
Repair Costs	10	10
Warranty	2	2
Fuel Economy	9	8
Rollover	7	7
Complaints	1	2
Insurance Costs	1	1
OVERALL RATING	8	7

Price Range	Retail	Markup
SE Sedan	$14,915	7%
ZTS	$15,535	7%
ZX3	$12,725	7%
ZX5	$15,035	7%

Last Year's Model

The 2003 Focus introduced a hatchback. The ZTS and ZX3 editions have the Advance Trac transmission, and manual transmission is now available in the wagon. With the most interior space in its class, the Focus is available in a three-door, four-door sedan, and wagon version. There are four trim models available: the ZX3, LX, SE, and ZTS. The Focus appeals to a broad cross section of buyers and is the best selling car in the world.

Ford Focus 2003

Ford SVT Focus

Safety Checklist

Frontal Crash Test* . . . Good
Side Crash Test* . . . Good
Airbags (Side/Head) . . . . Front Opt. Rear Optional/Head
Pretensioners/Impact Adjustors. . . . Yes/Yes
Position/Weight Sensors . . . Yes/Yes
Seat/Head Adjustors . . . No
Roll Stability System. . . . Optional
Child Seats Built-in . . . None
Antilock Brakes/Day Lamps . 2-Wheel (4-Whl. opt.)/None
Tire Pressure Monitor . . . None

General Information

2004 Status . . . Unchanged
Series Started. . . . 2000
Where Made. . . . US/Mexico
Theft Rating . . . Very High
Twins . . . .

Specifications

Fuel Econ. (city/hwy) . . . Very Good-27/33
Driving Range (mi.) . . . Long-411.7
Bumpers . . . Strong
Parking Index. . . . Very Easy
Seating. . . . 5
Tow Rating . . . Very Low-1000
Head/Leg Room (in.) . . . Very Cramped-39.1/40.8
Int. Space (cu. ft.). . . . Cramped-94
Cargo Space (cu. ft.) . . . Average-19

How the Competition Rates

	Rating	Pg.
Hyundai Elantra	10	169
Kia Optima	8	183
Nissan Sentra	8	221

*Ratings based on 4-door Focus. For 2-door crash results, see page 22.

Ford Freestar — Minivan

The Ford Freestar is all-new for 2004 and replaces the Windstar. It is available in five trim levels and is powered by either a 3.9-liter V6 or a 4.2-liter V6 engine mated to a four-speed automatic transmission. The interior volume is larger than the older Windstar. There are side curtain airbags on all three rows of seats to protect the passengers in a rollover. Standard equipment includes nine-cup holders, remote keyless entry, and power windows and locks. Options include leather seats and a Homelink garage door opener.

Ford Freestar

Ford Freestar

Ratings—10 Best, 1 Worst	2004	2003
Front Crash Tests	10	
Side Crash Tests	—	
Safety Features	7	
Preventive Maintenance	—	
Repair Costs	—	
Warranty	2	
Fuel Economy	2	
Rollover	6	
Complaints	—	
Insurance Costs	5	
OVERALL RATING	4	

Price Range

Limited	$32,945	11%
SE	$26,245	10%
SEL	$29,310	10%
SES	$28,065	10%

Last Year's Model

Model Not Produced in 2003

2003

Safety Checklist

Frontal Crash Test. . . . . Very Good
Side Crash Test . . . .
Airbags (Side/Head) . . . . Front Standard/Yes
Pretensioners/Impact Adjustors . . . . Standard/Yes
Position/Weight Sensors. . . . . Yes/No
Seat/Head Adjustors . . . . No
Roll Stability System. . . . . Yes
Child Seats Built-in . . . . None
Antilock Brakes/Day Lamps 4-Wheel/None
Tire Pressure Monitor . . . . None

General Information

2004 Status . . . . All New
Series Started . . . . No series indicated
Where Made. . . . .
Theft Rating . . . . Average
Twins. . . . . Mercury Monterey

Specifications

Fuel Econ. (city/hwy) . . . . Very Poor-17/23
Driving Range (mi.) . . . . Very Long-500.8
Bumpers . . . . Strong
Parking Index. . . . . Very Hard
Seating 7/8
Tow Rating Low-2000
Head/Leg Room (in.) . . . . Very Cramped-38.8/40.7
Int. Space (cu. ft.). . . . .
Cargo Space (cu. ft.) Average-25.8

How the Competition Rates

	Rating	Pg.
Dodge Caravan	10	141
Honda Odyssey	8	165
Mazda MPV	7	199

Ford F-Series — Standard Pickup

The Ford F-Series has been completely redesigned for 2004 with an interior unlike anything on previous F-Series models. The Regular cab and Super Cab models have been lengthened. There is now 13 extra inches of storage space on the Regular cab models. A new 5.4-liter V8 engine powers the F150 and there are three cab choices, three different box lengths, and nearly five series offerings. A new passenger sensing system deactivates the passenger airbag if there is no one sitting in the front seat.

Ford F-150

Ford F-250

Ratings—10 Best, 1 Worst	2004	2003
Front Crash Tests	—	9
Side Crash Tests	—	10
Safety Features	8	1
Preventive Maintenance	—	3
Repair Costs	—	9
Warranty	2	2
Fuel Economy	2	2
Rollover	6	6
Complaints	—	10
Insurance Costs	5	5
OVERALL RATING	—	5

Price Range	Retail	Markup
FX4 Supercrew	$34,185	15%
Lariat Supercrew	$32,115	14%
XL Reg Cab 4WD	$24,855	14%
XLT Styleside 4WD	$30,085	14%

Last Year's Model

Ford's best-selling truck was unchanged for 2003. The F-Series has dual airbags with a deactivation system for turning off the passenger side airbag when there is a rear-facing child seat present. (Be sure to turn the switch back on when an adult takes the seat.) Antilock bakes are optional and the F-Series is powered by a 4.2-liter V6, which delivers adequate horsepower. It has three cab choices, three box lengths and five different models.

Ford F-150 2003

Safety Checklist

Frontal Crash Test	
Side Crash Test	
Airbags (Side/Head)	Front Standard
Pretensioners/Impact Adjustors	Standard/Yes
Position/Weight Sensors	Yes/Yes
Seat/Head Adjustors	No
Roll Stability System	Yes
Child Seats Built-in	None
Antilock Brakes/Day Lamps	4-Wheel/Standard
Tire Pressure Monitor	None

General Information

2004 Status	All New
Series Started	No series indicated
Where Made	US
Theft Rating	Very High
Twins	

Specifications

Fuel Econ. (city/hwy)	Very Poor-16/19
Driving Range (mi.)	Very Long-447.8
Bumpers	Strong
Parking Index	Very Hard
Seating	3
Tow Rating	High-6500
Head/Leg Room (in.)	Roomy-40.9/41.3
Int. Space (cu. ft.)	
Cargo Space (cu. ft.)	

How the Competition Rates

	Rating	Pg.
Chevrolet Silverado	3	128
Dodge Ram Pickup	2	145
Toyota Tundra	3	222

Ford Mustang — Compact

The Mustang is unchanged for 2004. This is the Mustang's 40th anniversary and there is a new limited edition package available. It is powered by a 3.8-liter V6 engine and comes in coupe or convertible versions. Air conditioning, tinted glass, an AM/FM/CD stereo and power windows and locks are standard on the base Mustang. The deluxe package adds a rear spoiler and cruise control. The GT model has a more powerful 4.6-liter V8 engine. The Mustang is fitted with an emergency trunk release. The Mustang is due to be redesigned in 2005.

Ratings—10 Best, 1 Worst	2004	2003
Front Crash Tests	10	10
Side Crash Tests*	6	6
Safety Features	3	3
Preventive Maintenance	7	8
Repair Costs	9	9
Warranty	2	2
Fuel Economy	5	5
Rollover	10	10
Complaints	6	6
Insurance Costs	1	1
OVERALL RATING	7	7

Price Range	Retail	Markup
Base Convertible	$23,455	9%
Base Coupe	$17,720	9%
GT Convertible	$27,585	9%
GT Coupe	$23,245	9%

Last Year's Model

The 2003 Mustang is a carry forward from 2002 with the same powerful engines: the 3.8-liter V6 engine with 190 hp and the 4.6-liter V8 with 260 hp. The 3.8-liter engine actually meets low emission vehicle requirements. A traction control system helps to prevent wheel spin, and new chassis improvements give the Mustang a better ride. Coupes and convertible versions of the Mustang are available in 3 trim levels.

Ford Mustang Convertible

Ford SVTMustang Cobra Convertible

Ford SVTMustang Cobra Mystichrome

Safety Checklist

Frontal Crash Test	Very Good
Side Crash Test*	Average
Airbags (Side/Head)	No Side
Pretensioners/Impact Adjustors	Yes/Yes
Position/Weight Sensors	No/No
Seat/Head Adjustors	No
Roll Stability System	No
Child Seats Built-in	None
Antilock Brakes/Day Lamps	4-Wheel/None
Tire Pressure Monitor	None

General Information

2004 Status	Unchanged
Series Started	1994
Where Made	US
Theft Rating	Very High
Twins	

Specifications

Fuel Econ. (city/hwy)	Average-19/27
Driving Range (mi.)	Very Short-344.2
Bumpers	Strong
Parking Index	Easy
Seating	4
Tow Rating	Very Low-1000
Head/Leg Room (in.)	Cramped-38.1/42.6
Int. Space (cu. ft.)	Very Cramped-83
Cargo Space (cu. ft.)	Very Cramped-10.9

How the Competition Rates

	Rating	Pg.
Infiniti G35		175
Nissan 350Z	7	213
Toyota Solara		260

*For convertible crash results, see page 22.

Ford Ranger/Mazda Truck — Compact Pickup

For 2004 the Ford Ranger/Mazda Truck receives a new front grille and interior facelift. There is a new steering wheel on the Ranger and the Mazda Truck gets new leather seating options. A standard 2.3-liter 4-cylinder engine powers these compact pick-ups. You can upgrade to a V6 engine on both trucks. Dual airbags, and outboard seat belt pretensioners are some of the safety features found. A five-speed manual is standard on both models, but you can upgrade to a five-speed automatic transmission. An AM/FM stereo is standard.

Ford Ranger

Mazda Truck

Ratings—10 Best, 1 Worst	2004	2003
Front Crash Tests*	8	7
Side Crash Tests	7	—
Safety Features	2	2
Preventive Maintenance	8	6
Repair Costs	10	10
Warranty	2	2
Fuel Economy	7	7
Rollover	5	5
Complaints	7	5
Insurance Costs	1	1
OVERALL RATING	6	4

Price Range	Retail	Markup
Edge Supercab 4WD 4D	$22,205	11%
XL Reg. Cab 2WD SWB	$13,765	5%
XL Super Cab 2WD 4D	$18,785	10%
XLT Reg Cab LWB	$17,745	11%

Last Year's Model

The Ranger/Mazda Truck received only minor enhancements in 2003. There were new child safety anchor attachments available, the antilock brakes were improved, and there was a reduction noise levels in the cabin. The 2.5-liter engine on the 2WD models is strong, but you'll want to opt for the 4WD's 3.0-liter V6. There is a five-speed automatic transmission available. The Ranger/Mazda Truck performed well in frontal crash tests.

Ford Ranger 2003

Safety Checklist

Frontal Crash Test*	Good
Side Crash Test	Very Good
Airbags (Side/Head)	No Side
Pretensioners/Impact Adjustors	Yes/No
Position/Weight Sensors	No/No
Seat/Head Adjustors	No
Roll Stability System	No
Child Seats Built-in	None
Antilock Brakes/Day Lamps	4-Wheel/None
Tire Pressure Monitor	None

General Information

2004 Status	Unchanged
Series Started	1998
Where Made	US/Canada
Theft Rating	Very High
Twins	Mazda Truck 2004

Specifications

Fuel Econ. (city/hwy)	Good-23/26
Driving Range (mi.)	Long-412.4
Bumpers	Strong
Parking Index	Hard
Seating	2
Tow Rating	Very Low-1640
Head/Leg Room (in.)	Average-39.3/42.4
Int. Space (cu. ft.)	
Cargo Space (cu. ft.)	Roomy-37.3

How the Competition Rates

	Rating	Pg.
Chevrolet S Series	1	127
Dodge Dakota	7	142
Nissan Frontier	4	215

*For Ford Ranger/Mazda Truck Extended Cab crash results, see page 26-27.

Ford Taurus/Mercury Sable — Intermediate

The Taurus/Sable exterior receives a new grille, rear tail lamps, and a new front and rear facade. There is also an improved transmission and new exterior colors. While the exterior has changed, the basic mechanics are the same as the 2003 model. The Taurus/Sable is powered by a 3.0-liter V6, which delivers admirable performance, but is out classed by other V6 equipped sedans. There is a wagon version of each vehicle. The Sable has more luxury items as standard equipment than the Taurus.

Ford Taurus

Mercury Sable

Ratings—10 Best, 1 Worst	2004	2003
Front Crash Tests	10	10
Side Crash Tests	5	5
Safety Features	8	8
Preventive Maintenance	7	6
Repair Costs	9	9
Warranty	2	2
Fuel Economy	5	6
Rollover	9	9
Complaints	7	8
Insurance Costs	5	5
OVERALL RATING	9	9

Price Range	Retail	Markup
LX Sedan	$19,660	8%
SE Sedan	$20,195	9%
SEL Sedan	$23,305	9%
SEL Wagon	$23,445	9%

Last Year's Model

Ford's best-selling Taurus moved into 2003 unchanged. The 3.0-liter V6 remains standard and offers more power than the prior version. The four models range from the base LX to the SE, SES, and SEL. This year you can get power adjustable pedals, traction control, and side airbags. Other safety features include traction control and an emergency trunk release.

Ford Taurus

Safety Checklist

Frontal Crash Test	Very Good
Side Crash Test	Average
Airbags (Side/Head)	Front Standard/Yes
Pretensioners/Impact Adjustors	Yes/Yes
Position/Weight Sensors	Yes/Yes
Seat/Head Adjustors	No
Roll Stability System	No
Child Seats Built-in	None
Antilock Brakes/Day Lamps	4-Wheel (optional)/None
Tire Pressure Monitor	None

General Information

2004 Status	Minor Appearance Change
Series Started	1996
Where Made	US
Theft Rating	Very High
Twins	Mercury Sable 2004

Specifications

Fuel Econ. (city/hwy)	Average-20/28
Driving Range (mi.)	Long-413.1
Bumpers	Strong
Parking Index	Hard
Seating	5/6
Tow Rating	Very Low-1250
Head/Leg Room (in.)	Roomy-40/42.2
Int. Space (cu. ft.)	Average-102.5
Cargo Space (cu. ft.)	Average-17

How the Competition Rates

	Rating	Pg.
Chevrolet Malibu		126
Honda Accord	8	160
Hyundai Sonata	10	171

Ford Thunderbird — Compact

For 2004, the Thunderbird is unchanged, but it does get a new universal garage door opener, an improved map light, newly styled seats and new colors for the interior and exterior. A 3.9-liter V8 engine powers this "retro" looking coupe. The trunk is very small, but Ford claims you can fit two golf bags in it. The T-bird comes equipped with driver and passenger front and side airbags and an anti theft device. A six disc CD player is standard as is two-way power seating, cruise control, leather bucket seats, and antilock brakes.

Ford Thunderbird

Ford Thunderbird

Ratings—10 Best, 1 Worst	2004	2003
Front Crash Tests	10	10
Side Crash Tests	4	—
Safety Features	3	3
Preventive Maintenance	5	5
Repair Costs	7	7
Warranty	2	2
Fuel Economy	2	3
Rollover	10	10
Complaints	—	—
Insurance Costs	10	10
OVERALL RATING	5	5

Price Range	Retail	Markup
Convertible	$36,925	9%
Pacific Coast Roadster	$43,390	9%

Last Year's Model

Ford added a 3.9-liter 280 hp V8 engine in 2003. Traction control is standard and the classic egg-crate grille re-emerges on the 2003 model. Standard 17-inch wheels improve handling and a five-speed, clutchless, manual transmission adds engine control without learning to drive a manual transmission. Dual airbags, a child seat anchor system, and pretensioners on the seat belts are some of the safety features found on this coupe.

Ford Thunderbird 2003

Safety Checklist

Frontal Crash Test	Very Good
Side Crash Test	Poor
Airbags (Side/Head)	Front Standard
Pretensioners/Impact Adjustors	None/Yes
Position/Weight Sensors	No/No
Seat/Head Adjustors	No
Roll Stability System	No
Child Seats Built-in	None
Antilock Brakes/Day Lamps	4-Wheel/None
Tire Pressure Monitor	None

General Information

2004 Status	Unchanged
Series Started	2002
Where Made	US
Theft Rating	Average
Twins	

Specifications

Fuel Econ. (city/hwy)	Very Poor-17/23
Driving Range (mi.)	Very Short-346.7
Bumpers	Strong
Parking Index	Easy
Seating	2
Tow Rating	
Head/Leg Room (in.)	Cramped-37.2/43.7
Int. Space (cu. ft.)	Very Cramped-52.6
Cargo Space (cu. ft.)	Very Cramped-8.5

How the Competition Rates

	Rating	Pg.
Chrysler Sebring	10	138
Mitsubishi Eclipse	5	207
Mazda RX-8		201

GMC Envoy XL/XUV/Isuzu Ascender 7-pass. Large SUV

The Envoy XL/XUV is a versatile SUV capable of carrying large amounts of cargo. A power-sliding rear roof on the XUV allows tall items to stand upright in the cargo area which is waterproof and designed to be hosed out. A 275 horsepower 4.2L I-6 comes standard on the XL/XUV. The Isuzu Ascender shares the same platform. There are new electronic options this year as well. Cargo space is ample especially when the second and third row seats are folded and removed. The Ascender is powered by the same inline 6-cylinder as the XL/XUV.

GMC Envoy XUV

Ratings—10 Best, 1 Worst	2004	2003
Front Crash Tests	—	—
Side Crash Tests	—	—
Safety Features	6	5
Preventive Maintenance	—	—
Repair Costs	—	—
Warranty	2	9
Fuel Economy	1	2
Rollover	2	3
Complaints	—	—
Insurance Costs	5	5
OVERALL RATING	—	—

Price Range	Retail	Markup
SLE 2WD	$31,240	10%
SLE 4WD	$33,465	10%
SLT 2WD	$35,065	10%
SLT 4WD	$35,840	10%

Last Year's Model

The Isuzu Ascender was all-new for 2003 and, size-wise, falls in between a full sized and midsized SUV. It comes with two engines-a 4.2-liter inline six and a possible 5.3-liter V8 if you upgrade to the S trim level. Dual zone air conditioning, power windows and locks, and GM's OnStar communications system can be found as standard equipment. An anti-theft device, and daytime running lamps are standard as well.

Isuzu Ascender 7-pass. 2003

Isuzu Ascender 7-pass.

Safety Checklist

Frontal Crash Test	
Side Crash Test	
Airbags (Side/Head)	Fr. Std. Rear Opt.
Pretensioners/Impact Adjustors	None/Yes
Position/Weight Sensors	No/Yes
Seat/Head Adjustors	No
Roll Stability System	Yes
Child Seats Built-in	None
Antilock Brakes/Day Lamps	4-Wheel/None
Tire Pressure Monitor	None

General Information

2004 Status	Unchanged
Series Started	No series indicated
Where Made	
Theft Rating	Average
Twins	Trail Blazer EXT, Ascender 7-pass.

Specifications

Fuel Econ. (city/hwy)	Very Poor-15/20
Driving Range (mi.)	Long-422.5
Bumpers	
Parking Index	Very Hard
Seating	5
Tow Rating	High-5800
Head/Leg Room (in.)	Average-40.2/41.4
Int. Space (cu. ft.)	
Cargo Space (cu. ft.)	Very Roomy-49

How the Competition Rates

	Rating	Pg.
Cadillac Escalade EXT	2	117
Ford Explorer Sport Trac		151
Chevrolet Tahoe	3	130

*2004 Ratings for GMC Envoy XL/XUV; 2003 Ratings for Isuzu Ascender.

Honda Accord — Intermediate

For 2004, the Accord coupe and sedan get minor improvements. Side curtain airbags are now available on the EX 4-cylinder coupe and the EX V6 sedans and coupes. There are new exterior colors and a new seat belt reminder system added to both versions. There are two engine options: a 4-cylinder or a V6. Antilock brakes are standard. A satellite navigation system is available. The Accord comes with options such as power windows and locks, and keyless entry.

Honda Accord Coupe

Ratings—10 Best, 1 Worst	2004	2003
Front Crash Tests*	10	10
Side Crash Tests	9	—
Safety Features	6	7
Preventive Maintenance	—	—
Repair Costs	—	—
Warranty	1	1
Fuel Economy	8	8
Rollover	9	9
Complaints	—	—
Insurance Costs	10	5
OVERALL RATING	8	6

Price Range	Retail	Markup
DX Sedan	$15,900	11%
EX Sedan V6	$26,400	11%
LX Sedan 4-cyl	$20,100	11%
LX Sedan V6	$23,300	11%

Last Year's Model

All-new in 2003, the Accord continues as Honda's best selling sedan and coupe. A new 160 hp four-cylinder engine was offered as well as an optional 240 horsepower V6. Antilock brakes are standard. Side airbags and side curtain airbags are available EX V6 sedans. The coupe offers many of the same features as the sedan, but does not have the same interior volume. A satellite navigation system is also available.

Honda Accord 2003

Honda Accord Sedan

Safety Checklist

Frontal Crash Test*	Very Good
Side Crash Test	Very Good
Airbags (Side/Head)	Front Standard/Head
Pretensioners/Impact Adjustors	None/Yes
Position/Weight Sensors	Yes/Yes
Seat/Head Adjustors	No
Roll Stability System	No
Child Seats Built-in	None
Antilock Brakes/Day Lamps	4-Wheel/None
Tire Pressure Monitor	None

General Information

2004 Status	Unchanged
Series Started	2003
Where Made	US/Japan
Theft Rating	Very High
Twins	

Specifications

Fuel Econ. (city/hwy)	Good-24/33
Driving Range (mi.)	Very Long-467.8
Bumpers	Strong
Parking Index	Average
Seating	5
Tow Rating	
Head/Leg Room (in.)	Roomy-40.4/42.6
Int. Space (cu. ft.)	Average-102.7
Cargo Space (cu. ft.)	Cramped-14

How the Competition Rates

	Rating	Pg.
Chevrolet Malibu		126
Ford Taurus	9	157
Nissan Altima	9	214

*Ratings for 4-door Accord. For Coupe crash results, see page 24.

Honda Civic — Compact

For 2004, the Civic receives a major appearance update. There are new front and rear bumper designs, a new hood, and new headlights. The interior has also been improved in the Civic Hybrid and the coupe. There are also new option packages available. Keyless entry is now standard on the LX coupe and sedan models. A 115-horsepower, inline-4-cylinder engine powers the base model Civic. Dual airbags are standard and side impact airbags are optional. The hybrid version has one of the highest fuel economy ratings on the market.

Honda Civic Coupe

Ratings—10 Best, 1 Worst	2004	2003
Front Crash Tests*	10	10
Side Crash Tests*	9	9
Safety Features	5	6
Preventive Maintenance	10	7
Repair Costs	9	10
Warranty	1	1
Fuel Economy	10	9
Rollover	9	9
Complaints	5	3
Insurance Costs	1	1
OVERALL RATING	10	10

Honda Civic Sedan

Price Range	Retail	Markup
DX Coupe AT	$13,610	9%
EX Sedan	$18,060	9%
LX Coupe	$15,960	9%
LX Sedan	$16,410	9%

Safety Checklist

Frontal Crash Test*	Very Good
Side Crash Test*	Very Good
Airbags (Side/Head)	Front Optional Rear Optional
Pretensioners/Impact Adjustors	None/Yes
Position/Weight Sensors	Yes/Yes
Seat/Head Adjustors	No
Roll Stability System	No
Child Seats Built-in	None
Antilock Brakes/Day Lamps	4-Wheel/None
Tire Pressure Monitor	None

Last Year's Model

The 2003 Civic was a carryover from 2002, but the gas/electric hybrid engine option was introduced. The Civic performs very well in government front and in side crash tests. A 115 hp Inline 4-cylinder engine powers the Civic. Dual airbags are standard, but front side airbags remain optional. Impact door beams, and the new LATCH child seat tether are some of the safety features found in this vehicle.

General Information

2004 Status	Major Appearance Change
Series Started	2001
Where Made	US/Japan
Theft Rating	Very High
Twins	

Specifications

Fuel Econ. (city/hwy)	Very Good-29/38
Driving Range (mi.)	Long-428.5
Bumpers	Strong
Parking Index	Very Easy
Seating	5
Tow Rating	
Head/Leg Room (in.)	Average-39.8/42.2
Int. Space (cu. ft.)	Cramped-91.4
Cargo Space (cu. ft.)	Very Cramped-12.9

Honda Civic 2003

How the Competition Rates

	Rating	Pg.
Dodge Neon	8	144
Ford Focus	8	152
Hyundai Elantra	10	169

*Ratings based on 4-door model with side airbags. For other model ratings, see page 22-23.

Honda CR-V

Small SUV

For 2004, the CR-V remains unchanged. There is a new interior color available and a power door lock switch has been added to the front passenger side. The CR-V is one of the more popular compact SUVs available. A 2.4-liter 4-cylinder engine powers the CR-V. Cargo is ample and can be increased by folding the rear seats. Four-wheel antilock brakes are available. Dual stage airbags, side impact airbags, and pretensioners are some of the safety features found on this SUV.

Honda CR-V

Honda CR-V

Ratings—10 Best, 1 Worst	2004	2003
Front Crash Tests	10	10
Side Crash Tests	10	10
Safety Features	5	6
Preventive Maintenance	10	8
Repair Costs	7	4
Warranty	1	1
Fuel Economy	6	6
Rollover	5	5
Complaints	—	—
Insurance Costs	10	10
OVERALL RATING	9	7

Price Range	Retail	Markup
EX 4WD	$22,550	8%
LX 2WD	$19,000	8%
LX 2WD w/side airbags	$19,250	8%
LX 4WD w/side airbags	$20,450	8%

Last Year's Model

The 2003 CR-V received minor improvements since its redesign in 2002. The 160-hp, 2.4-liter four-cylinder engine provides excellent horsepower. Cargo space has grown by 3.8 inches An AM/FM/CD player is now standard. Four-wheel disc antilock brakes were added this year. On the EX model, side-impact airbags are standard, but on the LX they are optional. Most models will have an automatic transmission and four-wheel drive.

Honda CR-V

Safety Checklist

Frontal Crash Test	Very Good
Side Crash Test	Very Good
Airbags (Side/Head)	Front Standard
Pretensioners/Impact Adjustors	None/Yes
Position/Weight Sensors	Yes/Yes
Seat/Head Adjustors	No
Roll Stability System	No
Child Seats Built-in	None
Antilock Brakes/Day Lamps	4-Wheel/None
Tire Pressure Monitor	None

General Information

2004 Status	Unchanged
Series Started	2001
Where Made	Japan
Theft Rating	Very Low
Twins	

Specifications

Fuel Econ. (city/hwy)	Average-22/26
Driving Range (mi.)	Short-361.6
Bumpers	Strong
Parking Index	Very Easy
Seating	5
Tow Rating	Very Low-1500
Head/Leg Room (in.)	Roomy-40.9/41.3
Int. Space (cu. ft.)	Roomy-106
Cargo Space (cu. ft.)	Roomy-33.5

How the Competition Rates

	Rating	Pg.
Ford Escape	8	147
Jeep Liberty	10	180
Subaru Forester	6	239

Honda Element

Small SUV

The 2004, Element does not change after its introduction last year. The EX model gets new passenger seat armrests and keyless entry has been added. Bungee cords have been added to the driver side front and rear seats to help you secure items on the roof rack. There are also new color choices. The Element is targeted at younger buyers. The same 2.4-liter, 4-cylinder engine that powers the CR-V, powers the Element. An AM/FM/CD player is standard. Cargo space is ample, and there is even rubber-flooring for easy clean up.

Honda Element

Honda Element

Ratings—10 Best, 1 Worst	2004	2003
Front Crash Tests	10	10
Side Crash Tests*	10	10
Safety Features	2	2
Preventive Maintenance	—	—
Repair Costs	—	—
Warranty	1	1
Fuel Economy	6	6
Rollover	4	4
Complaints	—	—
Insurance Costs	5	5
OVERALL RATING	4	4

Price Range	Retail	Markup
2WD DX	$16,100	9%
2WD LX	$17,100	9%
4WD LX	$18,500	9%
4WD EX	$20,300	9%

Last Year's Model

The Honda Element was all-new in 2003. A pillar-less side door configuration allows for easy loading and unloading. Front-wheel drive and four-wheel drive options are available. An AM/FM/CD player with additional electronic outlets is optional. The Element is powered by the CR-V's 2.4-liter I-Vetec four-cylinder engine. Despite its boxy look, the element has a smooth suspension and easy handling.

Honda Element 2003

Safety Checklist

Frontal Crash Test	Very Good
Side Crash Test	Very Good*
Airbags (Side/Head)	No Side
Pretensioners/Impact Adjustors	Yes/NA
Position/Weight Sensors	NA/NA
Seat/Head Adjustors	NA
Roll Stability System	NA
Child Seats Built-in	None
Antilock Brakes/Day Lamps	4-Wheel/None
Tire Pressure Monitor	None

General Information

2004 Status	Unchanged
Series Started	2003
Where Made	
Theft Rating	Average
Twins	

Specifications

Fuel Econ. (city/hwy)	Average-22/26
Driving Range (mi.)	Short-375.8
Bumpers	Strong
Parking Index	Very Easy
Seating	5
Tow Rating	Very Low-1500
Head/Leg Room (in.)	Very Roomy-43.3/41
Int. Space (cu. ft.)	Average-103.6
Cargo Space (cu. ft.)	Average-25.1

How the Competition Rates

	Rating	Pg.
Chevrolet Tracker	1	131
Jeep Wrangler	7	181
Isuzu Rodeo	4	178

*Higher likelihood of head injury.

Honda Insight — Subcompact

For 2004, the Insight gets a new CD player with four speakers as standard equipment and a new interior color option: beige. The Insight's hybrid power system gives it the highest miles per gallon rating in the market. A 1.0-liter 3-cylinder engine and an electronic motor power this little subcompact. Cargo room is almost non-existent, it fits only two people, and comes with a manual or an automatic transmission. The fuel consumption and seat belt reminder lights have been jazzed up.

Honda Insight

Honda Insight

Ratings—10 Best, 1 Worst	2004	2003
Front Crash Tests	7	7
Side Crash Tests	5	—
Safety Features	1	1
Preventive Maintenance	—	—
Repair Costs	—	—
Warranty	1	1
Fuel Economy	10	10
Rollover	8	8
Complaints	2	6
Insurance Costs	1	1
OVERALL RATING	2	4

Price Range	Retail	Markup
Hatchback Base	$19,180	7%
Hatchback CVT	$21,380	7%

Last Year's Model

Unchanged in 2003, some versions of the Insight get 61 miles per gallon in the city and 68 mpg on the highway. Amazing fuel economy is generated by Honda's Integrated Motor Assist system which combines a 1.0-liter 3-cylinder gasoline engine with an electric motor. The only competition in this class of vehicles is the Toyota Prius. The most dramatic difference with these vehicles is the style of the Insight and its limited passenger capacity.

Honda Insight 2003

Safety Checklist

Frontal Crash Test	Good
Side Crash Test	Average
Airbags (Side/Head)	None
Pretensioners/Impact Adjustors	None/No
Position/Weight Sensors	No/No
Seat/Head Adjustors	No
Roll Stability System	No
Child Seats Built-in	None
Antilock Brakes/Day Lamps	4-Wheel/None
Tire Pressure Monitor	None

General Information

2004 Status	Minor Appearance Change
Series Started	2000
Where Made	Japan
Theft Rating	Average
Twins	

Specifications

Fuel Econ. (city/hwy)	Very Good-57/56
Driving Range (mi.)	Very Long-599.4
Bumpers	Strong
Parking Index	Very Easy
Seating	2
Tow Rating	
Head/Leg Room (in.)	Average-38.8/42.9
Int. Space (cu. ft.)	Very Cramped-47.7
Cargo Space (cu. ft.)	Cramped-16.3

How the Competition Rates

	Rating	Pg.
Honda Civic (Hybrid)	10	161
Toyota Prius		256

Honda Odyssey — Minivan

For 2004, the Odyssey remains unchanged. Honda no longer offers evergreen pearl as an exterior color and the navigation system has also been improved. A 3.5-liter V6 engine powers the Odyssey. The EX trim model has power rear doors, and automatic climate control. Cargo room is ample and the seats fold flat. A rear seat DVD entertainment system is available as an option. Dual stage airbags, and side curtain impact airbags are some of the safety features found on the Odyssey. Traction control is available on the EX and should improve road stability.

Ratings—10 Best, 1 Worst	2004	2003
Front Crash Tests	**10**	10
Side Crash Tests	**10**	10
Safety Features	**7**	6
Preventive Maintenance	**8**	7
Repair Costs	**3**	2
Warranty	**1**	1
Fuel Economy	**4**	4
Rollover	**7**	7
Complaints	**4**	4
Insurance Costs	**10**	10
OVERALL RATING	**7**	7

Price Range	Retail	Markup
EX	$26,990	11%
EX (w/Leather & Nav. Sys.)	$30,490	11%
EX (Leather)	$28,490	11%
LX	$24,490	11%

Last Year's Model

The popular Odyssey was unchanged in 2003. An extended version is available with two sliding doors and a longer wheelbase. Traction control comes standard on the EX. The 3.5-liter 240 hp V6 engine is one of the most powerful engines found on a minivan. The EX model has power rear doors, automatic climate control, a security system, and an upgraded stereo as standard features. A rear seat DVD entertainment system is optional.

Honda Odyssey 2003

Honda Odyssey

Honda Odyssey

Safety Checklist

Frontal Crash Test	Very Good
Side Crash Test	Very Good
Airbags (Side/Head)	Front Standard/Yes
Pretensioners/Impact Adjustors	None/Yes
Position/Weight Sensors	Yes/Yes
Seat/Head Adjustors	No
Roll Stability System	No
Child Seats Built-in	None
Antilock Brakes/Day Lamps	4-Wheel/None
Tire Pressure Monitor	None

General Information

2004 Status	Unchanged
Series Started	2000
Where Made	Canada/Japan
Theft Rating	Very Low
Twins	

Specifications

Fuel Econ. (city/hwy)	Poor-18/25
Driving Range (mi.)	Long-411.9
Bumpers	Strong
Parking Index	Hard
Seating	7
Tow Rating	Average-3500
Head/Leg Room (in.)	Roomy-41.2/41
Int. Space (cu. ft.)	Very Roomy-170.1
Cargo Space (cu. ft.)	Very Roomy-88.5

How the Competition Rates

	Rating	Pg.
Chevrolet Venture	6	133
Dodge Caravan	10	141
Nissan Quest	6	220

Honda Pilot

Mid-Size SUV

For 2004, the Pilot receives a few minor improvements since its introduction in 2003. The EX now has heated seats and side mirrors. There are new interior and exterior colors to choose from as well. A 3.5-liter V6 engine powers the Pilot and full time 4-wheel drive is standard. A five-speed automatic transmission is available. Options include a rear seat DVD entertainment system and a navigation system which has a variety of improvements. Dual stage airbags, side impact airbags, and seat belt pretensioners are some of the safety features found on this SUV.

Honda Pilot

Ratings—10 Best, 1 Worst	2004	2003
Front Crash Tests	**10**	10
Side Crash Tests	**10**	10
Safety Features	**7**	8
Preventive Maintenance	—	—
Repair Costs	—	—
Warranty	**1**	1
Fuel Economy	**2**	3
Rollover	**7**	6
Complaints	—	—
Insurance Costs	**5**	5
OVERALL RATING	**6**	6

Honda Pilot

Safety Checklist

Frontal Crash Test. . . . . Very Good
Side Crash Test. . . . . Very Good
Airbags (Side/Head). . . . . Front Standard
Pretensioners/Impact Adjustors. . . . . Yes/Yes
Position/Weight Sensors . . . . Yes/Yes
Seat/Head Adjustors . . . . No
Roll Stability System. . . . . Yes
Child Seats Built-in . . . . None
Antilock Brakes/Day Lamps 4-Wheel/None
Tire Pressure Monitor . . . . None

Price Range	Retail	Markup
EX	$29,470	11%
EX (w/Leather & Nav. Sys.)	$32,870	11%
EX (Leather)	$30,870	11%
LX	$27,100	11%

General Information

2004 Status . . . . Unchanged
Series Started. 2003
Where Made . . . . Canada/Japan
Theft Rating . . . . Average
Twins . . . .

Last Year's Model

All-new in 203, the Pilot has a unique style and 8-inches of ground clearance. Eight passengers can fit into this SUV. A 3.5 V6 engine and full time 4-wheel drive is standard. The Pilot has a standard five -speed automatic transmission. Options include a satellite-linked DVD navigation system and a rear seat DVD entertainment system. Seat belt pretensioners and headrests are installed in all eight seating positions.

Honda Pilot 2003

Specifications

Fuel Econ. (city/hwy) . . . . Very Poor-17/22
Driving Range (mi.) Short-363.6
Bumpers . . . . Strong
Parking Index . . . . Hard
Seating. 5
Tow Rating. Average-3500
Head/Leg Room (in.) Roomy-41.9/41.4
Int. Space (cu. ft.). . . . . Very Roomy-128.2
Cargo Space (cu. ft.) . . . . Very Roomy-48.7

How the Competition Rates

	Rating	Pg.
Chevrolet Trail Blazer	2	132
Ford Explorer	8	150
Mitsubishi Endeavor	5	208

Honda S2000 — Subcompact

For 2004, the S2000 is refreshed, but not totally redesigned. There is a new 2.2-liter engine and transmission. The suspension has been improved and there are new front and rear bumper designs. The amount of shoulder and elbowroom has been increased. The S2000 handles like a sports car. The soft top automatically raises and lowers in less than six seconds. Air conditioning and leather seating are standard features in this convertible. Dual airbags and side impact airbags are also standard.

Honda S2000

Ratings—10 Best, 1 Worst	2004	2003
Front Crash Tests	9	9
Side Crash Tests	7	—
Safety Features	3	3
Preventive Maintenance	10	10
Repair Costs	7	1
Warranty	1	1
Fuel Economy	5	5
Rollover	10	10
Complaints	3	10
Insurance Costs	1	1
OVERALL RATING	7	4

Price Range	Retail	Markup
Base Model	$32,800	7%

Last Year's Model

The S2000 was unchanged in 2003. It is powered by a 4-cylinder, 240-horsepower engine. Although performance is the focus of this sports car, it has many safety features. Dual airbags and seat belt pretensioners are standard. The controls are positioned where the driver will intuitively seek them out, so he or she can focus on the road. The top raises and lowers in six seconds. Air conditioning and leather are standard features on this roadster.

Honda S2000 2003

Honda S2000

Safety Checklist

Frontal Crash Test	Very Good
Side Crash Test	Good
Airbags (Side/Head)	None
Pretensioners/Impact Adjustors	None/Yes
Position/Weight Sensors	No/No
Seat/Head Adjustors	No
Roll Stability System	No
Child Seats Built-in	None
Antilock Brakes/Day Lamps	4-Wheel/Optional
Tire Pressure Monitor	None

General Information

2004 Status	Minor Appearance Change
Series Started	2000
Where Made	Japan
Theft Rating	Very High
Twins	

Specifications

Fuel Econ. (city/hwy)	Average-20/26
Driving Range (mi.)	Very Short-294.6
Bumpers	Strong
Parking Index	Very Easy
Seating	2
Tow Rating	
Head/Leg Room (in.)	Very Cramped-34.6/44.3
Int. Space (cu. ft.)	Very Cramped-48.4
Cargo Space (cu. ft.)	Very Cramped-5

How the Competition Rates

	Rating	Pg.
Ford Thunderbird	5	158
Mazda MX-5 Miata	4	200
Chrysler Crossfire		135

Hyundai Accent

Subcompact

For 2004, the Accent remains unchanged after being restyled last year. A 1.6-liter 4-cylinder engine powers the Accent. Side impact airbags are standard. The mid range GT trim model offers cloth seats, front fog lamps, and a rear body spoiler. Air conditioning is standard on the GL trim model, but is an option on the base Accent. The Hyundai Accent is one of the least expensive automobiles on the road. It provides solid, reliable transportation, not a lot of flare, and good crash test performance.

Hyundai Accent

Ratings—10 Best, 1 Worst	2004	2003
Front Crash Tests	9	9
Side Crash Tests	5	—
Safety Features	2	2
Preventive Maintenance	8	7
Repair Costs	10	10
Warranty	10	10
Fuel Economy	9	9
Rollover	9	9
Complaints	10	4
Insurance Costs	5	5
OVERALL RATING	10	10

Price Range	Retail	Markup
3 Door Hatchback Coupe	$9,999	5%
GL Hatchback Coupe AT	$11,699	7%
GL Sedan AT	$12,099	7%
GT Hatchback Coupe AT	$12,199	7%

Last Year's Model

The low-priced Accent moved into 2003 with a major face-lift. There have been improvements to the front façade, fenders, headlamps and the tail-lights. A 1.6-liter 4-cylinder engine powers the Accent. There are three trim levels: the L and GS hatchback and the 4-door GL sedan. Air conditioning is now standard and the Accent has safety belt pretensioners to help keep you safe. The Accent was one of 2003's least expensive new cars.

Hyundai Accent

Hyundai Accent

Safety Checklist

Frontal Crash Test	Very Good
Side Crash Test	
Airbags (Side/Head)	None
Pretensioners/Impact Adjustors	Standard/No
Position/Weight Sensors	No/No
Seat/Head Adjustors	No
Roll Stability System	No
Child Seats Built-in	None
Antilock Brakes/Day Lamps	4-Wheel (optional)/None
Tire Pressure Monitor	None

General Information

2004 Status	Minor Appearance Change
Series Started	2001
Where Made	South Korea
Theft Rating	Very High
Twins	

Specifications

Fuel Econ. (city/hwy)	Very Good-27/35
Driving Range (mi.)	Very Short-358.1
Bumpers	Strong
Parking Index	Very Easy
Seating	5
Tow Rating	
Head/Leg Room (in.)	Average-38.9/42.6
Int. Space (cu. ft.)	Very Cramped-88
Cargo Space (cu. ft.)	Average-16.9

How the Competition Rates

	Rating	Pg.
Dodge Neon	8	144
Kia Spectra	9	187
Scion xA		236

Hyundai Elantra — Compact

For 2004, the Elantra receives a major restyling, but mechanically remains the same. The hood, grille, front bumpers, headlamps, and rear assemblies have all been changed. Interior upgrades include a new instrument cluster, and new air conditioning vents and controls. The engine remains the same. A 2.0-liter 4-cylinder engine powers the Elantra. Front and side airbags are standard. Leather seats are standard on the GT model. The Elantra is considered a low emissions vehicle.

Hyundai Elantra GLS

Ratings—10 Best, 1 Worst	2004	2003
Front Crash Tests	10	10
Side Crash Tests	9	9
Safety Features	2	2
Preventive Maintenance	7	7
Repair Costs	10	10
Warranty	10	10
Fuel Economy	8	8
Rollover	8	8
Complaints	10	6
Insurance Costs	1	1
OVERALL RATING	10	10

Price Range	Retail	Markup
5 Door GT AT	$15,649	9%
GLS AT	$14,099	9%
GLS Man	$13,299	9%
GT AT	$15,649	9%

Last Year's Model

In 2003, Elantra added a new trim model to its line up: the GT hatchback. Side impact airbags are standard. Air conditiong, power locks/windows/mirrors, and a tilted steering column are also standard. The 2.0-liter engine provides peppy power to this aerodynamically shaped vehicle. Seat belt pretensioners standard. The GT includes leather seats, purple gauges, a CD player, and keyless entry.

Hyundai Elantra 2003

Hyundai Elantra GLS

Safety Checklist

Frontal Crash Test	Very Good
Side Crash Test	Very Good
Airbags (Side/Head)	Front Standard
Pretensioners/Impact Adjustors	Yes/No
Position/Weight Sensors	No/No
Seat/Head Adjustors	No
Roll Stability System	No
Child Seats Built-in	None
Antilock Brakes/Day Lamps	4-Wheel (optional)/None
Tire Pressure Monitor	None

General Information

2004 Status	Minor Appearance Change
Series Started	2001
Where Made	South Korea
Theft Rating	Very High
Twins	

Specifications

Fuel Econ. (city/hwy)	Good-24/33
Driving Range (mi.)	Average-396.7
Bumpers	Strong
Parking Index	Very Easy
Seating	5
Tow Rating	Very Low-1500
Head/Leg Room (in.)	Roomy-39.6/43.2
Int. Space (cu. ft.)	Cramped-94
Cargo Space (cu. ft.)	Very Cramped-12.9

How the Competition Rates

	Rating	Pg.
Chevrolet Cavalier	3	123
Honda Civic	10	161
Toyota Corolla	7	252

Hyundai Santa Fe — Small SUV

The Santa Fe remains unchanged for 2004. In late 2003, the Santa Fe got a new 3.5-liter V6 engine which becomes the standard engine on the LX model. There are four trim levels to choose from. The LX model has a modified suspension this year. A power-sliding sunroof and leather seating are optional and a CD player is standard. Antilock brakes and traction control are options on some of the trim models, but standard on the others so compare the different trim levels carefully. The Santa Fe comes in two-wheel and four-wheel drive versions.

Hyundai Santa Fe

Hyundai Santa Fe

Ratings—10 Best, 1 Worst	2004	2003
Front Crash Tests	8	8
Side Crash Tests*	7	—
Safety Features	2	2
Preventive Maintenance	7	7
Repair Costs	7	8
Warranty	10	10
Fuel Economy	5	5
Rollover	6	5
Complaints	10	10
Insurance Costs	5	5
OVERALL RATING	9	8

Price Range	Retail	Markup
2.4L Man	$17,999	7%
GLS 3.5L FWD	$21,999	7%
GLS FWD	$20,999	7%
LX 4WD	$25,499	7%

Last Year's Model

The Hyundai Santa Fe did not change for the 2003 year. Built on a version of the Sonata platform, it has a choice of front wheel drive or full-time 4WD. There are three engine choices available: a 4-cylinder and two V6 engines. Leather seats, ABS, and traction control are options. A/C, power windows, a roof rack, and privacy glass are standard. 16-inch wheels are standard as well.

Hyundai Santa Fe

Safety Checklist

Frontal Crash Test	Good
Side Crash Test*	Good
Airbags (Side/Head)	Front Standard
Pretensioners/Impact Adjustors	Yes/No
Position/Weight Sensors	No/No
Seat/Head Adjustors	No
Roll Stability System	No
Child Seats Built-in	None
Antilock Brakes/Day Lamps	4-Wheel (optional)/None
Tire Pressure Monitor	None

General Information

2004 Status	Unchanged
Series Started	2001
Where Made	South Korea
Theft Rating	Very Low
Twins	

Specifications

Fuel Econ. (city/hwy)	Average-20/27
Driving Range (mi.)	Average-389.4
Bumpers	Weak
Parking Index	Easy
Seating	5
Tow Rating	Low-2700
Head/Leg Room (in.)	Average-39.6/41.6
Int. Space (cu. ft.)	Average-100.7
Cargo Space (cu. ft.)	Roomy-29.4

How the Competition Rates

	Rating	Pg.
Ford Escape	8	147
Honda CR-V	9	162
Jeep Liberty	10	180

*Side ratings for front occupant. Data missing for rear occupant.

Hyundai Sonata — Intermediate

Hyundai's mid-sized sedan rolls into 2004 unchanged. The Sonata comes with a 2.4-liter 4-cylinder as its standard engine or you an upgrade to an optional 2.7-liter V6. The interior is well equipped for the price of the Sonata. The LX model comes with leather, side impact airbags, and automatic climate control. In the standard base model, leather is optional. A manual transmission is standard with the upgrade being a four-speed automatic. All models of the Sonata are equipped with a keyless entry system.

Hyundai Sonata

Ratings—10 Best, 1 Worst	2004	2003
Front Crash Tests	8	8
Side Crash Tests	9	9
Safety Features	3	3
Preventive Maintenance	7	7
Repair Costs	8	7
Warranty	10	10
Fuel Economy	7	7
Rollover	10	10
Complaints	10	5
Insurance Costs	1	1
OVERALL RATING	9	10

Hyundai Sonata

Price Range

Model	Price	%
2.4 AT	$16,799	10%
GLS	$18,799	10%
LX	$19,799	11%
V6 AT	$17,649	10%

Safety Checklist

Frontal Crash Test	Good
Side Crash Test	Very Good
Airbags (Side/Head)	Front Standard
Pretensioners/Impact Adjustors	Yes/No
Position/Weight Sensors	No/No
Seat/Head Adjustors	No
Roll Stability System	Yes
Child Seats Built-in	None
Antilock Brakes/Day Lamps	4-Wheel/None
Tire Pressure Monitor	None

Last Year's Model

The 2003 Sonata has minor improvements over the year before. There are three versions: the base, the LX and the GLS. The LX sedan comes with a leather interior, automatic temperature control, and side-impact airbags. The dual stage airbags detect if there is a passenger in the front seat. The optional V6 engine increases to 2.7 liters producing 181 hp, versus the standard four-cylinder rated at 149 hp. A manual transmission is standard.

Hyundai Sonata 2003

General Information

2004 Status	Unchanged
Series Started	1995
Where Made	South Korea
Theft Rating	Very High
Twins	

Specifications

Fuel Econ. (city/hwy)	Good-22/30
Driving Range (mi.)	Long-430.0
Bumpers	Strong
Parking Index	Easy
Seating	5
Tow Rating	
Head/Leg Room (in.)	Roomy-39.3/43.3
Int. Space (cu. ft.)	Average-100
Cargo Space (cu. ft.)	Cramped-14.1

How the Competition Rates

	Rating	Pg.
Buick Regal	6	112
Chevrolet Malibu		126
Honda Accord	8	160

Hyundai Tiburon

Compact

Since the Tiburon was all new last year, it only receives minor trim upgrades and changes in option packages for 2004. There is a new spoiler on both trim models. There are also new tire and wheel packages available. The Tiburon is powered by a 2.0-liter 4-cylinder engine, but for added performance upgrade to the V6. A manual transmission is standard, but you can upgrade to an automatic. There is a 6-speed manual transmission option on the fully loaded Tiburon. Legroom is average. Dual stage airbags and side impact airbags are standard safety features.

Ratings—10 Best, 1 Worst	2004	2003
Front Crash Tests	—	—
Side Crash Tests	—	—
Safety Features	2	2
Preventive Maintenance	—	6
Repair Costs	—	7
Warranty	10	10
Fuel Economy	7	7
Rollover	10	10
Complaints	—	—
Insurance Costs	5	5
OVERALL RATING	—	—

Price Range	Retail	Markup
Base AT	$17,899	10%
GT 6-man	$19,149	10%
GT AT	$19,099	10%
GT MAN	$18,199	10%

Last Year's Model

The Hyundai Tiburon was all-new in 2003 and provided the compact sports car market with a low price contender. A 2.0-liter 4-cylinder or a 2.7-liter V6 engine power the Tiburon. You have a choice between a five or six-speed manual transmission or a four-speed automatic. The headroom and legroom have been improved and the sides of the car have been reinforced with steel protection beams. Dual front and side airbags are standard.

Hyundai Tiburon

Hyundai Tiburon

Hyundai Tiburon

Safety Checklist

Frontal Crash Test	
Side Crash Test	
Airbags (Side/Head)	Front Standard
Pretensioners/Impact Adjustors	Yes/No
Position/Weight Sensors	No/No
Seat/Head Adjustors	No
Roll Stability System	No
Child Seats Built-in	None
Antilock Brakes/Day Lamps	4-Wheel/None
Tire Pressure Monitor	None

General Information

2004 Status	Unchanged
Series Started	2003
Where Made	South Korea
Theft Rating	Average
Twins	

Specifications

Fuel Econ. (city/hwy)	Good-23/30
Driving Range (mi.)	Short-364.9
Bumpers	Weak
Parking Index	Easy
Seating	4
Tow Rating	
Head/Leg Room (in.)	Average-38/43
Int. Space (cu. ft.)	Very Cramped-81.9
Cargo Space (cu. ft.)	Cramped-14.7

How the Competition Rates

	Rating	Pg.
Acura RSX	7	98
Mitsubishi Eclipse	5	207
Toyota Celica	8	251

Hyundai XG350 — Intermediate

The 2004 version of the XG350 has gone through a minor restyling. There is a new headlight design, a new front bumper, and front air dam. A new electronic braking system has also been added and the interior controls have also been improved. For its price and size, the XG350 is well equipped. A 3.5-liter V6 is the standard engine. Leather seating, traction control, keyless entry, and side impact airbags are standard. Other comfort features include an AM/FM/CD stereo system, a trip computer, and heated mirrors.

Hyundai XG350

Ratings—10 Best, 1 Worst	2004	2003
Front Crash Tests	—	—
Side Crash Tests	9	—
Safety Features	2	2
Preventive Maintenance	7	7
Repair Costs	7	7
Warranty	10	10
Fuel Economy	3	3
Rollover	9	9
Complaints	10	—
Insurance Costs	1	1
OVERALL RATING	—	—

Price Range	Retail	Markup
Sedan	$23,999	12%
Sedan L	$25,599	12%

Last Year's Model

The 2003 XG350 was a carryover from 2002. A 194 hp 3.5-liter V6 engine powers this sedan. Some of the standard features include antilock brakes, air-conditioning, cruise control, remote keyless entry, and front and side airbags. Other features include heated mirrors, power seats, and a trip computer. There are two trim levels: the base and the L model.

Hyundai XG350 2003

Hyundai XG350

Safety Checklist

- Frontal Crash Test ...
- Side Crash Test ... Very Good
- Airbags (Side/Head) ... Front Standard
- Pretensioners/Impact Adjustors ... Yes/No
- Position/Weight Sensors ... No/No
- Seat/Head Adjustors ... No
- Roll Stability System ... No
- Child Seats Built-in ... None
- Antilock Brakes/Day Lamps ... 4-Wheel/None
- Tire Pressure Monitor ... None

General Information

- 2004 Status ... Minor Appearance Change
- Series Started ... 2001
- Where Made ... South Korea
- Theft Rating ... Average
- Twins ...

Specifications

- Fuel Econ. (city/hwy) ... Poor-17/26
- Driving Range (mi.) ... Short-372.5
- Bumpers ... Strong
- Parking Index ... Average
- Seating ... 5
- Tow Rating ...
- Head/Leg Room (in.) ... Roomy-39.7/43.3
- Int. Space (cu. ft.) ... Average-102
- Cargo Space (cu. ft.) ... Very Cramped-12

How the Competition Rates

	Rating	Pg.
Buick Century	6	108
Ford Taurus	9	157
Suzuki Verona		246

Infiniti FX — Small SUV

The 2004 FX 35/45 crossover SUV's got only minor improvements since being introduced in late 2003. Some of the enhancements include refinements in the suspension, a new power passenger seat, and aluminum roof rails. There are new option packages as well. The FX 35 is powered by a V6 and the 45 is powered by a massive 4.5-liter V8. A tire monitor and cruise control are standard. The FX models are well equipped with leather seats and several electronic options, including a rear view monitor and a navigation system.

Infinti FX35

Infiniti FX45

Ratings—10 Best, 1 Worst	2004	2003
Front Crash Tests	—	
Side Crash Tests	—	
Safety Features	9	
Preventive Maintenance	—	
Repair Costs	—	
Warranty	9	
Fuel Economy	1	
Rollover	7	
Complaints	—	
Insurance Costs	5	
OVERALL RATING	—	

Price Range	Retail	Markup
FX35 2WD	$34,350	10%
FX35 AWD	$35,850	10%
FX45 AWD	$44,375	11%

Last Year's Model

All new in late 2003, the FX gave Infiniti the ability to successfully compete in the luxury SUV market dominated by the Lexus RX300. The two trim models, the 35 and the 45, are styled like a sport sedan rather than a SUV. 4-way powered leather seats, a rear view monitor, and the "Intelligent Key" locking systems are standard. A 3.5-liter V6 powers the FX 35. The better-equipped FX 45 is available with a V8. All-wheel drive is available on both models.

Model Not Produced in 2003

2003

Safety Checklist

Frontal Crash Test	
Side Crash Test	
Airbags (Side/Head)	Fr. Std. Rear Opt./Yes
Pretensioners/Impact Adjustors	Standard/Yes
Position/Weight Sensors	Yes/Yes
Seat/Head Adjustors	No
Roll Stability System	Yes
Child Seats Built-in	None
Antilock Brakes/Day Lamps	4-Wheel/None
Tire Pressure Monitor	Direct

General Information

2004 Status	All New
Series Started	No series indicated
Where Made	Japan
Theft Rating	Average
Twins	

Specifications

Fuel Econ. (city/hwy)	Very Poor-15/19
Driving Range (mi.)	Average-394.4
Bumpers	
Parking Index	Hard
Seating	5
Tow Rating	Average-3500
Head/Leg Room (in.)	Very Roomy-40.8/43.9
Int. Space (cu. ft.)	Roomy-105.1
Cargo Space (cu. ft.)	Roomy-28.5

How the Competition Rates

	Rating	Pg.
Acura MDX	10	96
BMW X5	8	106
Lexus RX 330	9	194

Infiniti G35 — Compact

These high performance luxury vehicles receive only minor improvements since their introduction last year. The sport coupe gets a new center console, an improved 6-disc CD changer, and a standard tire pressure monitor. The sedan gains heated mirrors, heated seats, and a tire pressure monitoring system. A 260 horsepower 3.5-liter V6 engine powers both versions of the G35. Dual stage airbags, 4-wheel ABS, and side impact airbags are standard. A manual transmission is available on both models, but most cars will come with a 5-speed automatic transmission.

Infiniti G35 Sedan

Infiniti G35 Sport Coupe

Ratings—10 Best, 1 Worst	2004	2003
Front Crash Tests	—	—
Side Crash Tests	—	—
Safety Features	7	7
Preventive Maintenance	—	—
Repair Costs	—	—
Warranty	9	8
Fuel Economy	4	5
Rollover	10	10
Complaints	—	—
Insurance Costs	5	5
OVERALL RATING	—	—

Price Range	Retail	Markup
Coupe 5sp aut	$29,250	9%
Coupe with Leather	$31,550	10%
Sedan 3.5 V6	$30,100	10%
Sedan V6 3.5	$27,950	9%

Last Year's Model

The G35 sport sedan and coupe were all new in 2003. A 3.5-liter V6 engine powers G35. The styling and curves are similar to the Nissan 350Z. A five-speed automatic is standard, but on the coupe you can get a six-speed manual as an option. Power seats, windows and power door locks are standard. A six-disc CD changer is available. A DVD navigation system is an option. XM and Sirius satellite radio packages are optional.

Infiniti G35 2003

Safety Checklist

Frontal Crash Test	
Side Crash Test	
Airbags (Side/Head)	Front Standard/Yes
Pretensioners/Impact Adjustors	Yes/Yes
Position/Weight Sensors	No/No
Seat/Head Adjustors	Yes
Roll Stability System	No
Child Seats Built-in	None
Antilock Brakes/Day Lamps	4-Wheel/None
Tire Pressure Monitor	None

General Information

2004 Status	Unchanged
Series Started	2003
Where Made	Japan
Theft Rating	Average
Twins	

Specifications

Fuel Econ. (city/hwy)	Poor-19/26
Driving Range (mi.)	Long-432.4
Bumpers	
Parking Index	Easy
Seating	4
Tow Rating	
Head/Leg Room (in.)	Roomy-39.2/43.8
Int. Space (cu. ft.)	Average-101.4
Cargo Space (cu. ft.)	Very Cramped-7.8

How the Competition Rates

	Rating	Pg.
Audi A4	10	101
BMW 3 Series	9	104
Nissan Altima	9	214

Infiniti I35 — Large

For 2004, Infiniti's luxury sport sedan receives only minor improvements. These include a standard sunroof, a power rear sunshade and new body moldings. A 3.5-liter V6 engine powers the I35. A 4-speed automatic transmission with traction control is standard. Side impact airbags and 4-wheel antilock brakes are some of the standard safety systems found on this sedan. Active head restraints prevent injuries to the head and neck during an accident. The interior is well equipped with electronic features and modern styling.

Infiniti I35

Infiniti I35

Ratings—10 Best, 1 Worst	2004	2003
Front Crash Tests	9	9
Side Crash Tests	10	10
Safety Features	7	7
Preventive Maintenance	8	—
Repair Costs	2	1
Warranty	9	8
Fuel Economy	5	5
Rollover	8	8
Complaints	1	—
Insurance Costs	10	10
OVERALL RATING	10	9

Price Range	Retail	Markup
Infiniti I35	TBA	

Last Year's Model

The Infiniti I35 remained unchanged in 2003. Five occupants can listen to a six-disc CD changer and a cassette player while sitting in leather seats. Side-impact airbags and active head restraints for the front seats are standard and reduce the chance of whiplash injuries. A 24-valve V6 engine propels this sedan and traction control, ABS, and side impact airbags are standard. An electronic stabilization system is an option.

Infiniti I35

Safety Checklist

Frontal Crash Test	Very Good
Side Crash Test	Very Good
Airbags (Side/Head)	Front Standard/Head Opt.
Pretensioners/Impact Adjustors	Yes/Yes
Position/Weight Sensors	No/No
Seat/Head Adjustors	Yes
Roll Stability System	No
Child Seats Built-in	None
Antilock Brakes/Day Lamps	4-Wheel/None
Tire Pressure Monitor	None

General Information

2004 Status	Unchanged
Series Started	2000
Where Made	Japan
Theft Rating	Average
Twins	

Specifications

Fuel Econ. (city/hwy)	Average-20/26
Driving Range (mi.)	Long-412.9
Bumpers	
Parking Index	Hard
Seating	5
Tow Rating	Very Low-1000
Head/Leg Room (in.)	Very Roomy-40.5/43.9
Int. Space (cu. ft.)	Average-102.5
Cargo Space (cu. ft.)	Cramped-14.9

How the Competition Rates

	Rating	Pg.
Acura TL	10	99
Chrysler 300M	10	134
Ford Crown Victoria	10	146

Isuzu Axiom

Mid-Size SUV

While there are some new features on the 2004 Axiom, it stays mechanically unchanged. A new direct injection 3.5-liter V6 engine is available which improves the fuel economy over the previous V6 engine models. A new six-speaker stereo is also available and other options include a moon roof, leather upholstery, automatic climate control, and a digital compass. Dual airbags are standard on the Axiom. Due to a drop in Axiom sales, 2004 is expected to be the last year for the Axiom.

Isuzu Axiom

Ratings—10 Best, 1 Worst	2004	2003
Front Crash Tests	7	7
Side Crash Tests	10	10
Safety Features	5	5
Preventive Maintenance	1	—
Repair Costs	7	—
Warranty	8	9
Fuel Economy	2	3
Rollover	6	6
Complaints	—	—
Insurance Costs	10	10
OVERALL RATING	6	7

Isuzu Axiom

Price Range	Retail	Markup
S 2WD	$24,849	6%
S 4WD	$27,499	6%
XS 2WD	$28,499	6%
XS 4WD	$30,499	6%

Last Year's Model

First introduced in 2002, the Axiom received minor improvements. The same engine immobilizer (an anti-theft device) that is on the Ascender was added in 2003. Options include a moon roof, leather upholstery, automatic climate control, and other gadgets such as a digital compass. The engine is a 230-hp 3.5-liter V6 engine with a four-speed automatic transmission. Dual front airbags, and four-wheel antilock brakes are standard.

Isuzu Axiom 2003

Safety Checklist

Frontal Crash Test	Good
Side Crash Test	Very Good
Airbags (Side/Head)	No Side/Yes
Pretensioners/Impact Adjustors	None/No
Position/Weight Sensors	Yes/No
Seat/Head Adjustors	No
Roll Stability System	Yes
Child Seats Built-in	None
Antilock Brakes/Day Lamps	4-Wheel (optional)/None
Tire Pressure Monitor	None

General Information

2004 Status	Unchanged
Series Started	2002
Where Made	US
Theft Rating	Average
Twins	

Specifications

Fuel Econ. (city/hwy)	Very Poor-17/21
Driving Range (mi.)	Short-362.6
Bumpers	Weak
Parking Index	Hard
Seating	5
Tow Rating	Average-4500
Head/Leg Room (in.)	Average-39.9/42.1
Int. Space (cu. ft.)	
Cargo Space (cu. ft.)	Roomy-35.2

How the Competition Rates

	Rating	Pg.
Chevrolet Blazer	1	122
Honda Pilot	6	166
Kia Sorento	5	186

Isuzu Rodeo — Mid-Size SUV

The Rodeo is unchanged for 2004 except for new engine options. The 4-cylinder engine has been dropped and the 3.2-liter V6 is now standard on all models. A new sound package includes a six-CD changer and a tire pressure monitoring system has been added. Antilock brakes are standard on RWD models and all-disc antilock brakes are standard on 4WD versions. Side-impact airbags are not available yet. Moving up to the LS model ads air conditioning, remote keyless entry, power windows, door locks and heated mirrors to the list of standard features.

Isuzu Rodeo

Ratings—10 Best, 1 Worst	2004	2003
Front Crash Tests	5	5
Side Crash Tests	10	10
Safety Features	3	3
Preventive Maintenance	1	1
Repair Costs	3	8
Warranty	8	9
Fuel Economy	3	3
Rollover	5	5
Complaints	4	10
Insurance Costs	5	5
OVERALL RATING	3	5

Isuzu Rodeo

Price Range	Retail	Markup
S 2WD 4A	$23,699	6%
S 2WD 4A	$20,949	6%
S 4WD 4A	$25,699	6%
S 4WD 4A	$22,829	6%

Last Year's Model

In 2003 the Rodeo received some front end restyling, but was essentially unchanged. A keyless entry system was introduced as a standard feature and engine choices were a 4-cylinder or V6 engine, depending on the model. The Rodeo seats five, has a cassette stereo, tachometer and intermittent wipers as standard features, but air conditioning is optional. Antilock brakes are standard, but no side impact airbags are available.

Isuzu Rodeo

Safety Checklist

Frontal Crash Test	Average
Side Crash Test	Very Good
Airbags (Side/Head)	No Side/Yes
Pretensioners/Impact Adjustors	None/No
Position/Weight Sensors	No/No
Seat/Head Adjustors	No
Roll Stability System	No
Child Seats Built-in	None
Antilock Brakes/Day Lamps	4-Wheel/None
Tire Pressure Monitor	Indirect

General Information

2004 Status	Unchanged
Series Started	1998
Where Made	US
Theft Rating	Very High
Twins	

Specifications

Fuel Econ. (city/hwy)	Poor-18/23
Driving Range (mi.)	Average-399.0
Bumpers	Weak
Parking Index	Average
Seating	7
Tow Rating	Low-2500
Head/Leg Room (in.)	Average-38.9/42.1
Int. Space (cu. ft.)	
Cargo Space (cu. ft.)	Roomy-33

How the Competition Rates

	Rating	Pg.
Chevrolet Blazer	1	122
Kia Sorento	5	186
Nissan Xterra	6	223

Jeep Grand Cherokee — Mid-Size SUV

For 2004, the Grand Cherokee receives an appearance change. The front facades and fog lamps have been redesigned. Two new option packages have been added to the Laredo and Limited models. The rear lift gate features a window that swings up separately. A roof rack is standard. A 4.0-liter Inline 6-cylinder engine powers the Grand Cherokee and all-disc antilock brakes are standard. Side curtain-type airbags are standard in the Overland trim model but optional in the other models. Four-wheel and two-wheel drives are available.

Jeep Grand Cherokee

Ratings—10 Best, 1 Worst	2004	2003
Front Crash Tests	4	4
Side Crash Tests	10	10
Safety Features	4	4
Preventive Maintenance	10	10
Repair Costs	9	9
Warranty	8	6
Fuel Economy	2	3
Rollover	4	4
Complaints	3	2
Insurance Costs	10	10
OVERALL RATING	8	6

Jeep Grand Cherokee

Safety Checklist

Frontal Crash Test	Poor
Side Crash Test	Very Good
Airbags (Side/Head)	Fr. Std. Rear Opt.
Pretensioners/Impact Adjustors	None/No
Position/Weight Sensors	No/No
Seat/Head Adjustors	No
Roll Stability System	Yes
Child Seats Built-in	None
Antilock Brakes/Day Lamps	4-Wheel/None
Tire Pressure Monitor	Direct

Price Range

Laredo 2WD	$26,980	9%
Limited 2WD	$31,910	9%
Limited 4WD	$34,340	9%
Overland 4WD	$38,995	10%

General Information

2004 Status	Minor Appearance Change
Series Started	1993
Where Made	US
Theft Rating	Very High
Twins	

Last Year's Model

Looks-wise, the Grand Cherokee was unchanged for 2003. A new 4.7-liter V8 was standard and a more powerful 5.2-liter engine was an option. Improvements to the Grand Cherokee included the LATCH child safety system, ceiling mounted side curtain airbags, tire pressure monitors, and rain sensing wipers. You can choose between two-and four-wheel drive models. Handling is good for a SUV. Cargo room is adequate.

Jeep Grand Cherokee 2003

Specifications

Fuel Econ. (city/hwy)	Very Poor-16/21
Driving Range (mi.)	Short-367.4
Bumpers	
Parking Index	Average
Seating	5
Tow Rating	Average-5000
Head/Leg Room (in.)	Average-39.7/41.7
Int. Space (cu. ft.)	Very Roomy-128.6
Cargo Space (cu. ft.)	

How the Competition Rates

	Rating	Pg.
Chevrolet Trail Blazer	2	132
Ford Explorer	8	150
Nissan Pathfinder	7	218

Jeep Liberty — Mid-Size SUV

For 2004, the Jeep Liberty receives minor improvements. A new hands free communication system is available as a factory installed option. There are new color options, a new seat belt reminder system, and a tire pressure monitor. A 3.7-liter V6 powers the base line Liberty. There is a 2.4-liter inline 4-cylinder option on the Liberty Sport. An organizer is available to help manage the cargo. An AM/FM/CD radio is standard. Multi stage driver and passenger airbags are also standard features on the Liberty as are 4-wheel antilock brakes.

Jeep Liberty

Jeep Liberty

Ratings—10 Best, 1 Worst	2004	2003
Front Crash Tests	8	8
Side Crash Tests	10	10
Safety Features	3	3
Preventive Maintenance	9	9
Repair Costs	8	10
Warranty	8	6
Fuel Economy	4	4
Rollover	5	4
Complaints	2	—
Insurance Costs	10	10
OVERALL RATING	10	10

Price Range	Retail	Markup
4x2 Limited Edition	$22,700	7%
4x2 Renegade	$22,860	7%
4x2 Sport	$18,010	6%
4x4 Limited Edition	$24,210	7%

Last Year's Model

Keeping the same body lines, new features on the 2003 Liberty included multistage driver and passenger airbags, an improved suspension, and the new Renegade trim model. The standard engine is a 3.7-liter V6 which was new for 2003. Dual front airbags come standard, but antilock brakes are optional. The Liberty replaced the former Jeep Cherokee with a modern looking, smoother riding, and more luxurious vehicle.

Jeep Liberty 2003

Safety Checklist

Frontal Crash Test	Good
Side Crash Test	Very Good
Airbags (Side/Head)	Fr. Std. Rear Opt.
Pretensioners/Impact Adjustors	None/No
Position/Weight Sensors	No/No
Seat/Head Adjustors	No
Roll Stability System	Yes
Child Seats Built-in	None
Antilock Brakes/Day Lamps	4-Wheel/None
Tire Pressure Monitor	Direct

General Information

2004 Status	Unchanged
Series Started	2002
Where Made	US
Theft Rating	Very High
Twins	

Specifications

Fuel Econ. (city/hwy)	Poor-19/23
Driving Range (mi.)	Average-381.3
Bumpers	
Parking Index	Easy
Seating	5
Tow Rating	Low-2000
Head/Leg Room (in.)	Average-40.7/40.8
Int. Space (cu. ft.)	Average-101.7
Cargo Space (cu. ft.)	Roomy-29

How the Competition Rates

	Rating	Pg.
Ford Escape	8	147
Honda CR-V	9	162
Isuzu Rodeo	4	178

Jeep Wrangler

Small SUV

Redesigned last year, the 2004 Jeep Wrangler remains unchanged. It does however, receive new wheel choices and new option packages. The Wrangler lineup includes the SE, Sport, X, Sahara, and Rubicon editions. The 2.4-liter Inline 4-cylinder engine powers the Wrangler. There is the option of upgrading to a more powerful 4.0-liter Inline 6-cylinder rated at 190 horsepower. Dual front airbags are standard and a hard top is available as an option.

Jeep Wrangler Sport

Jeep Wrangler Rubicon

Ratings—10 Best, 1 Worst	2004	2003
Front Crash Tests	7	7
Side Crash Tests	—	—
Safety Features	2	2
Preventive Maintenance	10	9
Repair Costs	10	9
Warranty	8	6
Fuel Economy	2	3
Rollover	5	5
Complaints	7	4
Insurance Costs	5	5
OVERALL RATING	7	6

Price Range	Retail	Markup
Rubicon	$25,085	10%
Sahara	$22,665	9%
SE	$16,270	7%
Sport	$20,253	7%

Last Year's Model

Redesigned for 2003, the Wrangler got a new front, end design, interior, engine options and improved suspension. The Rubicon trim level was added last year for those needing more off road performance. This 4-wheel drive off-road vehicle is a top seller for Jeep. Dual de-powered airbags are standard and 4-wheel antilock brakes are optional.

Jeep Wrangler 2003

Safety Checklist

Frontal Crash Test . . . . . Good
Side Crash Test . . . . .
Airbags (Side/Head) . . . . . Front Optional Rear Optional
Pretensioners/Impact Adjustors . . . . . None/No
Position/Weight Sensors . . . . . No/No
Seat/Head Adjustors . . . . . No
Roll Stability System . . . . . Yes
Child Seats Built-in . . . . . None
Antilock Brakes/Day Lamps . . . 4-Wheel (optional)/None
Tire Pressure Monitor . . . . . None

General Information

2004 Status . . . . . Unchanged
Series Started 1993
Where Made . . . . . US
Theft Rating . . . . . Very High
Twins . . . . .

Specifications

Fuel Econ. (city/hwy) . . . . . Very Poor-19/20
Driving Range (mi.) Short-369.3
Bumpers . . . . .
Parking Index . . . . . Very Easy
Seating 4
Tow Rating . . . . . Very Low-1000
Head/Leg Room (in.) Average-40.9/41.1
Int. Space (cu. ft.) Cramped-92.4
Cargo Space (cu. ft.) . . . . . Very Cramped-9.1

How the Competition Rates

	Rating	Pg.
Chevrolet Tracker	1	131
Honda Element	4	163
Subaru Baja		238

Kia Amanti Compact

The all-new Amanti is Kia's first large automobile. The Amanti is based on the Hyundai XG350, but is nearly 4 inches longer and has a 3.5-liter V6 engine that produces nearly 195 horsepower. A five-speed automatic transmission is available. A powered sunroof is standard as is dual climate control, an in-dash six CD changer, cruise control and a lockable glove box. Front and rear seat mounted side airbags and side curtain airbags are available. A new electronic stability system improves braking and handling.

Kia Amanti

Kia Amanti

Ratings—10 Best, 1 Worst	2004	2003
Front Crash Tests	—	
Side Crash Tests	—	
Safety Features	6	
Preventive Maintenance	—	
Repair Costs	—	
Warranty	10	
Fuel Economy	3	
Rollover	—	
Complaints	—	
Insurance Costs	5	
OVERALL RATING	—	

Price Range	Retail	Markup
Kia Amanti	$24,995	9%

Last Year's Model

Model Not Produced in 2003

2003

Safety Checklist

Frontal Crash Test ....
Side Crash Test ....
Airbags (Side/Head) .... Front Standard/Yes
Pretensioners/Impact Adjustors .... None/Yes
Position/Weight Sensors .... No/No
Seat/Head Adjustors .... Yes
Roll Stability System.......... Yes
Child Seats Built-in .... None
Antilock Brakes/Day Lamps.......... 4-Wheel/
Tire Pressure Monitor .... None

General Information

2004 Status .... All New
Series Started .... No series indicated
Where Made .... South Korea
Theft Rating .... Average
Twins ....

Specifications

Fuel Econ. (city/hwy) Poor-17/25
Driving Range (mi.) ....
Bumpers..........
Parking Index..........
Seating.......... 5
Tow Rating ....
Head/Leg Room (in.).......... Very Roomy-40/43.7
Int. Space (cu. ft.)..........
Cargo Space (cu. ft.) ....

How the Competition Rates

	Rating	Pg.
Hyundai XG350		173
Pontiac Bonneville	7	226
Buick Century	6	108

Kia Optima

Compact

For 2004, the Optima receives a new horizontally styled grille and improvements to the wheel and tire packages. A 2.7-liter V6 is standard on this mid-size sedan as is an automatic transmission. An AM/FM/CD player is standard on all models, but you can upgrade to a stereo with a CD/cassette player. Dual stage front airbags are standard. Side impact airbags are standard on all trims. Keyless entry can be found on the higher end SE and SE V6 models. Power windows and doors are standard on all models as well.

Kia Optima

Ratings—10 Best, 1 Worst	2004	2003
Front Crash Tests	8	8
Side Crash Tests	—	—
Safety Features	1	1
Preventive Maintenance	7	—
Repair Costs	7	—
Warranty	10	10
Fuel Economy	7	7
Rollover	10	9
Complaints	—	—
Insurance Costs	1	1
OVERALL RATING	8	6

Kia Optima

Price Range	Retail	Markup
EX	$18,095	9%
EX V6	$19,495	10%
LX	$15,500	8%
LX V6	$17,895	10%

Last Year's Model

For 2003, the Kia Optima remained unchanged, except for some styling tweaks. The 2.7-liter V6 engine is available as an option on most models. The standard engine is a 4-cylinder. An automatic transmission is standard on all models. The SE manual transmission sedan has been dropped from the line up. The LX and SE models got additional option packages and improved equipment. Power windows and door locks are standard.

Kia Optima

Safety Checklist

Frontal Crash Test	Good
Side Crash Test	
Airbags (Side/Head)	No Side
Pretensioners/Impact Adjustors	None/No
Position/Weight Sensors	No/No
Seat/Head Adjustors	No
Roll Stability System	No
Child Seats Built-in	None
Antilock Brakes/Day Lamps	4-Wheel (optional)/None
Tire Pressure Monitor	None

General Information

2004 Status	Unchanged
Series Started	2002
Where Made	South Korea
Theft Rating	Very High
Twins	

Specifications

Fuel Econ. (city/hwy)	Good-22/30
Driving Range (mi.)	Long-430.0
Bumpers	Weak
Parking Index	Easy
Seating	4
Tow Rating	
Head/Leg Room (in.)	Roomy-39/43.3
Int. Space (cu. ft.)	Average-100
Cargo Space (cu. ft.)	Cramped-13.6

How the Competition Rates

	Rating	Pg.
Chevrolet Cavalier	3	123
Mitsubishi Galant		209
Pontiac Grand Am	4	227

Kia Rio Subcompact

For 2004, the Kia Rio remains unchanged. This is one of the least expensive cars you can buy. It has a 1.6-liter, four-cylinder engine. Air conditioning, power windows, and four-wheel antilock brakes are optional. A manual transmission is standard, but you can upgrade to an automatic. The Rio also comes in a wagon version. The upgrade package provides a map light, power steering, a tachometer and vanity mirrors. An AM/FM stereo with CD player is also optional.

Kia Rio

Ratings—10 Best, 1 Worst	2004	2003
Front Crash Tests	8	8
Side Crash Tests	3	3
Safety Features	1	1
Preventive Maintenance	7	6
Repair Costs	7	8
Warranty	10	10
Fuel Economy	8	8
Rollover	8	8
Complaints	—	—
Insurance Costs	5	5
OVERALL RATING	7	7

Kia Rio

Safety Checklist

Frontal Crash Test . . . . Good
Side Crash Test . . . . Poor
Airbags (Side/Head) . . . . No Side
Pretensioners/Impact Adjustors . . . . None/No
Position/Weight Sensors . . . . No/No
Seat/Head Adjustors . . . . No
Roll Stability System . . . . No
Child Seats Built-in . . . . None
Antilock Brakes/Day Lamps . . . 4-Wheel (optional)/None
Tire Pressure Monitor . . . . None

Price Range	Retail	Markup
Base Sedan	$9,740	4%
Cinco Wagon	$11,365	5%

General Information

2004 Status . . . . Unchanged
Series Started. 2001
Where Made . . . . South Korea
Theft Rating . . . . Very High
Twins . . . .

Last Year's Model

The Kia Rio was restyled and received a more powerful engine in 2003. Designed to compete with the Hyundai Accent, the Rio offers very basic, but solid transportation. A 1.6-liter four-cylinder engine powers the Rio. There are automatic off headlights and optional front fog lamps available. The interior console has been improved, an AM/FM/CD radio is available and ABS is optional. Side impact airbags are not available on the Rio.

Kia Rio

Specifications

Fuel Econ. (city/hwy). Good-25/32
Driving Range (mi.). . . . . Very Short-330.0
Bumpers . . . . Weak
Parking Index. . . . . Very Easy
Seating. 5
Tow Rating . . . .
Head/Leg Room (in.) Roomy-39.4/42.8
Int. Space (cu. ft.) . . . . Very Cramped-88.3
Cargo Space (cu. ft.). . . . . Very Cramped-9.2

How the Competition Rates

	Rating	Pg.
Dodge Neon	8	144
Hyundai Accent	10	168
Mitsubishi Lancer	7	210

Kia Sedona **Minivan**

For 2004, the Sedona receives a minor appearance change which includes a new front grille and larger Kia logo design. There are new wheels and wheel covers. There are also new colors and fabric choices as well. A 3.5-liter V6 engine powers the Sedona. An automatic transmission is standard. The Sedona has seating for seven passengers and cargo room is ample. Antilock brakes are optional on the EX version. Remote keyless entry is found on all models except the base version and a sunroof is available as an option.

Kia Sedona

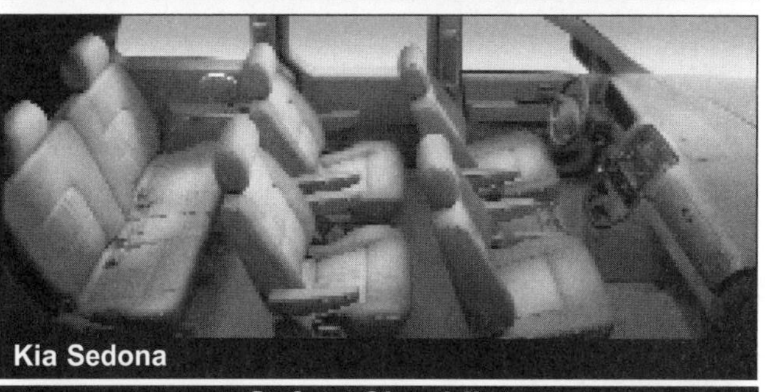
Kia Sedona

Ratings—10 Best, 1 Worst	2004	2003
Front Crash Tests	10	10
Side Crash Tests	10	10
Safety Features	2	2
Preventive Maintenance	5	—
Repair Costs	4	—
Warranty	10	10
Fuel Economy	1	2
Rollover	7	7
Complaints	—	—
Insurance Costs	5	5
OVERALL RATING	6	6

Price Range	Retail	Markup
EX	$22,085	9%
LX	$19,975	6%

Last Year's Model

The Kia Sedona was unchanged in 2003. The Sedona stresses price and value over its competitors. It comes in two trim models: the base LX and the upscale EX. Seating for seven is standard and the interior space is very roomy. A 195-hp. 3.5 liter V6 engine includes a five-speed-automatic transmission. Antilock brakes are optional only on the EX version.

Kia Sedona

Safety Checklist

Frontal Crash Test . . . Very Good
Side Crash Test . . . Very Good
Airbags (Side/Head) . . . No Side
Pretensioners/Impact Adjustors . . . Yes/No
Position/Weight Sensors . . . No/No
Seat/Head Adjustors . . . No
Roll Stability System . . . No
Child Seats Built-in . . . None
Antilock Brakes/Day Lamps . . . 4-Wheel (optional)/None
Tire Pressure Monitor . . . None

General Information

2004 Status . . . Unchanged
Series Started . . . 2002
Where Made . . . South Korea
Theft Rating . . . Average
Twins . . .

Specifications

Fuel Econ. (city/hwy) . . . Very Poor-15/20
Driving Range (mi.) . . . Very Short-334.6
Bumpers . . . Weak
Parking Index . . . Very Hard
Seating . . . 7
Tow Rating . . . Average-3500
Head/Leg Room (in.) . . . Cramped-39.4/40.6
Int. Space (cu. ft.) . . . Very Roomy-150.5
Cargo Space (cu. ft.) . . . Average-21.8

How the Competition Rates

	Rating	Pg.
Dodge Caravan	10	141
Ford Freestar	4	153
Honda Odyssey	8	165

Kia Sorento Mid-Size SUV

For 2004, the Kia Sorento gets a few improvements since its introduction last year. There is an available 5-speed manual transmission and a new sport package that has alloy wheels, a roof rack, and keyless entry. There are new exterior colors. A 3.5-liter V6 engine that produces nearly 192 hp powers the Sorento. Dual stage front airbags, antilock brakes, and side curtain airbags provide a high degree of safety. There are two trim levels: LX and EX versions. The Sorento has rear-wheel drive.

Kia Sorento

Kia Sorento

Ratings—10 Best, 1 Worst	2004	2003
Front Crash Tests	8	8
Side Crash Tests	10	10
Safety Features	2	2
Preventive Maintenance	—	—
Repair Costs	—	—
Warranty	10	10
Fuel Economy	1	2
Rollover	5	5
Complaints	—	—
Insurance Costs	5	5
OVERALL RATING	5	5

Price Range	Retail	Markup
EX 4X2	$23,050	8%
EX 4X4	$24,850	8%
LX 4X2	$18,995	6%
LX 4X4	$20,800	6%

Last Year's Model

The Kia Sorento was all-new for 2003. Rear-wheel and four-wheel drive versions are available. A 3.5-liter V6 engine that produces nearly 192 hp powers the Sorento. An automatic transmission is standard. The LX base model has air conditioning, cruise control, and power windows as standard equipment. Side curtain airbags are standard as well. Additional options included a CD player, air conditioning, and leather seating.

Kia Sorento

Safety Checklist

Frontal Crash Test	Good
Side Crash Test	Very Good
Airbags (Side/Head)	Front Standard
Pretensioners/Impact Adjustors	None/No
Position/Weight Sensors	No/No
Seat/Head Adjustors	No
Roll Stability System	No
Child Seats Built-in	None
Antilock Brakes/Day Lamps	4-Wheel (optional)/None
Tire Pressure Monitor	None

General Information

2004 Status	Unchanged
Series Started	2003
Where Made	South Korea
Theft Rating	Average
Twins	

Specifications

Fuel Econ. (city/hwy)	Very Poor-15/20
Driving Range (mi.)	Very Short-356.6
Bumpers	
Parking Index	Easy
Seating	5
Tow Rating	Average-3500
Head/Leg Room (in.)	Roomy-39.7/42.6
Int. Space (cu. ft.)	Very Roomy-138.4
Cargo Space (cu. ft.)	Roomy-31.4

How the Competition Rates

	Rating	Pg.
Honda Pilot	6	166
Nissan Murano	7	217
Saturn VUE	9	235

Kia Spectra — Subcompact

For 2004, the Spectra is unchanged. A tachometer has been added to the base 4-door model and there are two types of Spectras available: a hatchback and a sedan. The only engine is a 1.8-liter 4-cylinder engine. Remote control mirrors, a tachometer, and an AM/FM/CD stereo are standard features. Front and rear independent suspension improves the ride and the available front disc brakes are powered assisted. The Spectra is also a low cost automobile with limited options. Dual stage airbags are standard.

Kia Spectra 4 Door

Kia Spectra 5 Door

Ratings—10 Best, 1 Worst	2004	2003
Front Crash Tests	9	9
Side Crash Tests	7	7
Safety Features	1	1
Preventive Maintenance	7	6
Repair Costs	9	8
Warranty	10	10
Fuel Economy	7	7
Rollover	9	9
Complaints	—	—
Insurance Costs	1	1
OVERALL RATING	9	8

Price Range	Retail	Markup
GS Hatchback	$13,040	6%
GSX Hatchback	$14,090	6%
LS Sedan	$13,050	7%
Sedan	$11,820	7%

Last Year's Model

The Spectra was unchanged for 2003. This four door, five-passenger car comes with two trim levels, the GS and GSX which are a sedan and a hatchback. The only engine is a 1.8-liter 4-cylinder model. Alloy wheels and fog lamps are optional on the sedan. A rear window defroster is standard on both trim models. Cruise control is optional on the sedan version.

Kia Spectra 2003

Safety Checklist

Frontal Crash Test	Very Good
Side Crash Test	Good
Airbags (Side/Head)	No Side
Pretensioners/Impact Adjustors	None/No
Position/Weight Sensors	No/No
Seat/Head Adjustors	No
Roll Stability System	No
Child Seats Built-in	None
Antilock Brakes/Day Lamps	4-Wheel (optional)/None
Tire Pressure Monitor	None

General Information

2004 Status	Unchanged
Series Started	2001
Where Made	South Korea
Theft Rating	Very High
Twins	

Specifications

Fuel Econ. (city/hwy)	Good-22/30
Driving Range (mi.)	Very Short-330.0
Bumpers	Strong
Parking Index	Very Easy
Seating	4/5
Tow Rating	
Head/Leg Room (in.)	Roomy-39.6/43.1
Int. Space (cu. ft.)	Cramped-94.1
Cargo Space (cu. ft.)	Very Cramped-10.4

How the Competition Rates

	Rating	Pg.
Chevrolet Aveo		121
Scion xB		237
Ford Focus	8	152

Land Rover Discovery — Mid-Size SUV

After a series of improvements in 2003 the Discovery remains unchanged for 2004. The Discovery comes with a 217 horsepower V8 engine, 4-wheel disc brakes, and automatic electronic brake distribution is standard. The interior is average for its size class, but the rear legroom is tight, especially in the third row seats. All seating positions feature head restraints and three-point seatbelts-even on the optional third-row seats. The Discovery does have a very good suspension system, but still has a rollover rating.

Land Rover Discovery

Ratings—10 Best, 1 Worst	2004	2003
Front Crash Tests	9	9
Side Crash Tests	—	—
Safety Features	3	4
Preventive Maintenance	1	1
Repair Costs	5	4
Warranty	7	6
Fuel Economy	1	1
Rollover	2	2
Complaints	5	8
Insurance Costs	1	1
OVERALL RATING	1	1

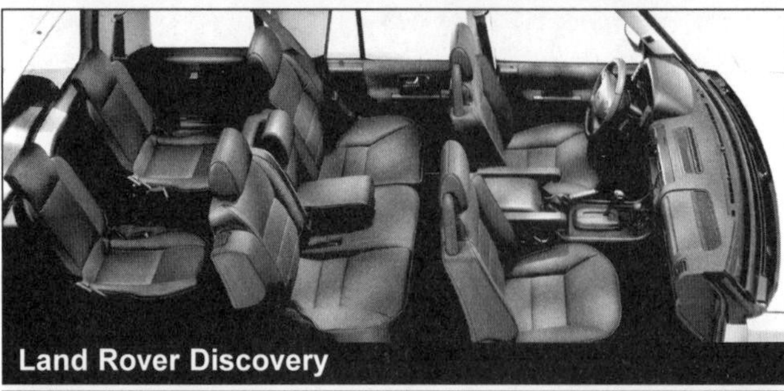
Land Rover Discovery

Safety Checklist

Frontal Crash Test. . . . . Very Good
Side Crash Test . . . .
Airbags (Side/Head) . . . . No Side
Pretensioners/Impact Adjustors. . . . . Yes/Yes
Position/Weight Sensors . . . . No/No
Seat/Head Adjustors . . . . No
Roll Stability System . . . . No
Child Seats Built-in . . . . None
Antilock Brakes/Day Lamps 4-Wheel/Optional
Tire Pressure Monitor . . . . None

Price Range	Retail	Markup
G4 Limited Edition	$39,995	10%
HSE	$41,250	10%
S	$34,995	10%
SE	$39,250	10%

General Information

2004 Status . . . . Unchanged
Series Started. 1994
Where Made. . . . . United Kingdom
Theft Rating . . . . Very High
Twins . . . .

Last Year's Model

The Discovery received a new engine and some other improvements in 2003. Permanent four-wheel drive is standard. Power adjustable driver seats, dual zone automatic climate control, a DVD entertainment system, and auto dimming rearview mirrors are standard features. The three different trim levels of the Discovery ensure that a customer can get just about anything they want in this vehicle.

Specifications

Fuel Econ. (city/hwy) . . . . Very Poor-13/17
Driving Range (mi.). . . . . Very Short-357.7
Bumpers. . . . .
Parking Index . . . . Hard
Seating. 5
Tow Rating . . . . Very Low-1650
Head/Leg Room (in.) Roomy-40.4/42.3
Int. Space (cu. ft.). . . . .
Cargo Space (cu. ft.) . . . . Very Roomy-40.5

Land Rover Discovery

How the Competition Rates

	Rating	Pg.
Acura MDX	10	96
Buick Rainier	4	111
Mercedes-Benz M-Class		204

Land Rover Freelander — Small SUV

The only small SUV in Land Rover's line up, receives some new additions, but remains essentially unchanged from 2003. A new Freestyle option package allows the driver to have a soft-top convertible. The Freelander is equipped with dual front airbags and seatbelts with pre-tensioners for the front-seat occupants. The SE3 comes with air conditioning, power front windows, cruise control, power steering, and heated front windscreen as standard equipment. Cargo room is average for its class.

Land Rover Freelander

Land Rover Freelander

Ratings—10 Best, 1 Worst	2004	2003
Front Crash Tests	—	—
Side Crash Tests	—	—
Safety Features	2	3
Preventive Maintenance	7	—
Repair Costs	2	—
Warranty	7	6
Fuel Economy	2	3
Rollover	5	5
Complaints	3	10
Insurance Costs	10	10
OVERALL RATING	—	—

Price Range	Retail	Markup
HSE	$28,995	11%
SE	$25,995	11%
SE3	$26,995	12%

Safety Checklist

Frontal Crash Test	
Side Crash Test	
Airbags (Side/Head)	No Side
Pretensioners/Impact Adjustors	None/Yes
Position/Weight Sensors	No/No
Seat/Head Adjustors	No
Roll Stability System	No
Child Seats Built-in	None
Antilock Brakes/Day Lamps	4-Wheel/None
Tire Pressure Monitor	None

General Information

2004 Status	Unchanged
Series Started	2001
Where Made	United Kingdom
Theft Rating	Average
Twins	

Last Year's Model

The 2003 Freelander was a carryover from 2002. A new power train was added as well as chassis improvements that reduced noise levels, vibration and harshness in the frame. The interior has bucket seats up front and a 60/40 split folding rear seat. There are three trim levels available: the S, SE, and the HSE. The Freelander has cloth or leather seating options and a new V6 engine was added in 2003. Antilock brakes are standard

Land Rover Freelander

Specifications

Fuel Econ. (city/hwy)	Very Poor-17/21
Driving Range (mi.)	Very Short-293.8
Bumpers	
Parking Index	Average
Seating	5
Tow Rating	Average-3562
Head/Leg Room (in.)	Cramped-38.4/41.8
Int. Space (cu. ft.)	
Cargo Space (cu. ft.)	Average-19.3

How the Competition Rates

	Rating	Pg.
Buick Rendezvous	5	113
Mitsubishi Endeavor	5	208
Kia Sorento	5	186

Lexus ES 330 — Intermediate

For 2004, the ES300 becomes the ES330 with the introduction of a new 3.3-liter V6 as the standard engine. There are upgrades to the transmission and new side impact airbags. Cruise control and a multi-information display with trip computer are standard. The display can also be fitted with a Lexus DVD-based navigation system. Some of the luxury features found on the more expensive LS430 are also found on the ES330. Dual zone climate control and a stability system are standard as is a built-in, Homelink garage door opener.

Lexus ES 330

Lexus ES 330

Ratings—10 Best, 1 Worst	2004	2003
Front Crash Tests	—	10
Side Crash Tests	—	9
Safety Features	10	10
Preventive Maintenance	—	4
Repair Costs	—	3
Warranty	9	8
Fuel Economy	3	6
Rollover	6	8
Complaints	—	—
Insurance Costs	5	10
OVERALL RATING	—	9

Price Range	Retail	Markup
Sedan	$31,725	13%

Last Year's Model

Since the ES 300 was redesigned in 2002, there were few changes to the 2003 model. Power adjustable-accelerator and brake pedals were added. Luxury features such as dual zone climate control, powerful audio systems, and leather seats, make this car an attractive option for higher end buyers. The 3.0-liter V6 engine provides adequate power for this luxury sedan. A built-in garage door opener is standard.

Lexus ES 300 — 2003

Safety Checklist

Frontal Crash Test	
Side Crash Test	
Airbags (Side/Head)	Front Standard/Yes
Pretensioners/Impact Adjustors	Yes/Yes
Position/Weight Sensors	Yes/Yes
Seat/Head Adjustors	Yes
Roll Stability System	Yes
Child Seats Built-in	None
Antilock Brakes/Day Lamps	4-Wheel/Standard
Tire Pressure Monitor	None

General Information

2004 Status	All New
Series Started	No series indicated
Where Made	Japan
Theft Rating	Very High
Twins	

Specifications

Fuel Econ. (city/hwy)	Poor-18/24
Driving Range (mi.)	Average-395.5
Bumpers	
Parking Index	Average
Seating	5
Tow Rating	Average-3500
Head/Leg Room (in.)	Average-39.3/42.5
Int. Space (cu. ft.)	Very Roomy-140.8
Cargo Space (cu. ft.)	Roomy-38.3

How the Competition Rates

	Rating	Pg.
Acura TL	10	99
Nissan Maxima	9	216
Saab 9-5	10	232

Lexus GS 300/GS 430

For 2004, the GS300/430 remain unchanged. Both sedans compete with European sport sedans such as the Audi A6 and Volvo 80 Series. A 4.3-liter V8 engine powers the GS 430. An inline 6-cylinder engine powers the GS 300. The GS300/430 comes equipped with dual stage airbags, side curtain airbags, and a vehicle stability control system. A power moon roof, power door locks, and 10-way powered leather memory seats are standard. The GS430 has heated front seats as standard equipment. A Mark Lenvison sound system is available as an option.

Ratings—10 Best, 1 Worst	2004	2003
Front Crash Tests	—	—
Side Crash Tests	—	—
Safety Features	10	9
Preventive Maintenance	4	4
Repair Costs	2	2
Warranty	9	8
Fuel Economy	4	4
Rollover	9	9
Complaints	10	—
Insurance Costs	5	5
OVERALL RATING	—	—

Price Range	Retail	Markup
4D Luxury Sedan	$38,605	14%

Last Year's Model

The GS sedans zipped into 2003 with some minor changes. The GS sedans had improved engines, a better suspension, and an aggressive exterior design. The GS300 has a 3.0-liter 225 hp engine. A bigger 4.3-liter V8 engine is found on the GS430. These are well built, thoughtfully appointed luxury cars that compete well against their European counterparts. Options include a moon roof, a DVD navigation system and multi-CD changer.

Lexus GS 300 2003

Lexus GS 300

Lexus GS430

Safety Checklist

Frontal Crash Test	
Side Crash Test	
Airbags (Side/Head)	Front Standard/Yes
Pretensioners/Impact Adjustors	Yes/Yes
Position/Weight Sensors	Yes/Yes
Seat/Head Adjustors	No
Roll Stability System	Yes
Child Seats Built-in	None
Antilock Brakes/Day Lamps	4-Wheel/Standard
Tire Pressure Monitor	None

General Information

2004 Status	Unchanged
Series Started	1998
Where Made	Japan
Theft Rating	Very High
Twins	

Specifications

Fuel Econ. (city/hwy)	Poor-18/25
Driving Range (mi.)	Long-407.8
Bumpers	
Parking Index	Average
Seating	5
Tow Rating	Low-2000
Head/Leg Room (in.)	Roomy-39/44.5
Int. Space (cu. ft.)	Average-100
Cargo Space (cu. ft.)	Cramped-14.8

How the Competition Rates

	Rating	Pg.
Audi A6		102
Cadillac CTS	7	114
Volvo 80 Series	9	270

Intermediate

...nains unchanged. There is a ...m alloy wheel option available. ...ylinder engine powers the IS300. ...equipment includes dual stage ...e stability control system, and side ... An optional DVD-based Lexus naviga- ...s located on a pop-up screen in the front ...ory seats are available, but only for the driv- ... windows, cruise control and automatic cli- ...ontrol are standard equipment.

Lexus IS 300

Lexus IS 300

...atings—10 Best, 1 Worst	2004	2003
Front Crash Tests	—	—
Side Crash Tests	10	10
Safety Features	10	9
Preventive Maintenance	4	5
Repair Costs	4	2
Warranty	9	8
Fuel Economy	3	4
Rollover	10	9
Complaints	10	10
Insurance Costs	1	1
OVERALL RATING	—	—

Price Range	Retail	Markup
Sedan	$29,435	14%
SportCross	$30,805	14%

Last Year's Model

One of the few rear wheel drive vehicles available, the IS300 has many of the design features of the larger GS300. The console contains gauges designed to look like sport watches rather than traditional instruments. A six-disc CD changer, side impact airbags and a trunk safety release handle are standard. Heated mirrors and a tilting steering wheel are also standard. The IS 300 is designed to compete with the A4 and BMW 328i.

Lexus IS 300

2003

Safety Checklist

Frontal Crash Test ....
Side Crash Test. .... Very Good
Airbags (Side/Head) .... Front Standard/Yes
Pretensioners/Impact Adjustors .... Standard/Yes
Position/Weight Sensors .... Yes/Yes
Seat/Head Adjustors .... No
Roll Stability System.......................... Yes
Child Seats Built-in .... None
Antilock Brakes/Day Lamps 4-Wheel/Standard
Tire Pressure Monitor .... Direct

General Information

2004 Status .... Minor Appearance Change
Series Started............................... 2000
Where Made............................... Japan
Theft Rating .... Very High
Twins ....

Specifications

Fuel Econ. (city/hwy) Poor-18/24
Driving Range (mi.)............... Very Short-354.9
Bumpers.......................................
Parking Index........................ Very Easy
Seating 5
Tow Rating Low-2000
Head/Leg Room (in.) Average-39.1/42.7
Int. Space (cu. ft.) Cramped-89.2
Cargo Space (cu. ft.)............ Very Cramped-10.1

How the Competition Rates

	Rating	Pg.
Audi A4	10	101
BMW 3 Series	9	104
Volkswagen Passat	8	265

Lexus LS 430 — Large

For 2004, the LS430 goes through a major restyling of the exterior. There is a new 6-speed automatic transmission and new advanced driver and front passenger airbags are available. New safety features include a tire pressure monitor and a pre-collision automatic safety system that analyzes a crash before it happens. A powerful 4.3-liter V8 engine is standard. The LS430 is wired for XM satellite radio and a DVD-based navigation system is optional.

Lexus LS 430

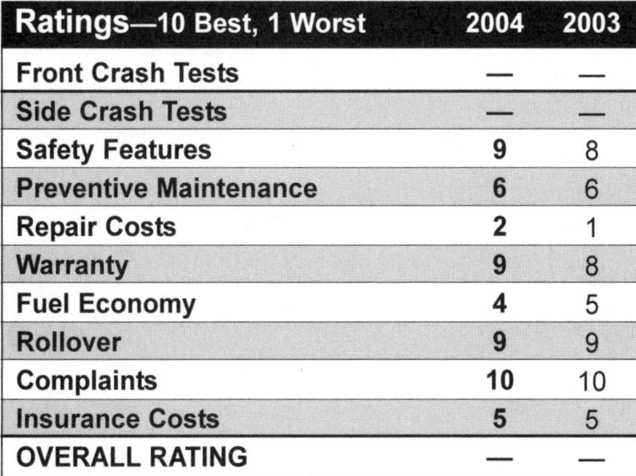

Ratings—10 Best, 1 Worst	2004	2003
Front Crash Tests	—	—
Side Crash Tests	—	—
Safety Features	9	8
Preventive Maintenance	6	6
Repair Costs	2	1
Warranty	9	8
Fuel Economy	4	5
Rollover	9	9
Complaints	10	10
Insurance Costs	5	5
OVERALL RATING	—	—

Lexus LS 430

Safety Checklist

Frontal Crash Test	
Side Crash Test	
Airbags (Side/Head)	Front Standard/Yes
Pretensioners/Impact Adjustors	Standard/Yes
Position/Weight Sensors	Yes/Yes
Seat/Head Adjustors	No
Roll Stability System	Yes
Child Seats Built-in	None
Antilock Brakes/Day Lamps	4-Wheel/None
Tire Pressure Monitor	Direct

Price Range	Retail	Markup
Sedan	$55,125	15%

General Information

2004 Status	Major Appearance Change
Series Started	2001
Where Made	Japan
Theft Rating	Very High
Twins	

Last Year's Model

In 2003 the LS 430 was a carryover from the previous year and only received minor enhancements. The LS430 engine has what Lexus calls VVTi, Variable Valve Timing. This system provides better performance, improves fuel economy, and reduces overall emissions output. The cruise control system has a feature that senses vehicles in front of you and warns about obstacles. A DVD navigation system is an option.

Lexus LS 430 2003

Specifications

Fuel Econ. (city/hwy)	Poor-18/25
Driving Range (mi.)	Very Long-457.2
Bumpers	
Parking Index	Average
Seating	5
Tow Rating	
Head/Leg Room (in.)	Very Roomy-39.6/44
Int. Space (cu. ft.)	Roomy-107.2
Cargo Space (cu. ft.)	Average-20.2

How the Competition Rates

	Rating	Pg.
Ford Crown Victoria	10	146
Lincoln Town Car	10	197
Acura TL	10	99

Lexus RX 330 — Mid-Size SUV

The RX330 is all-new for 2004 and includes a 3.3-liter V6 engine and a multi-panel moon roof as standard. Options include a power lift gate, high-intensity discharge headlights and a laser-based adaptive cruise control. A back seat DVD entertainment system, a navigation system, and rear camera to help back up are also available. Multistage front airbags, side impact airbags, and side curtain airbags are all standard. The rear seat splits three ways.

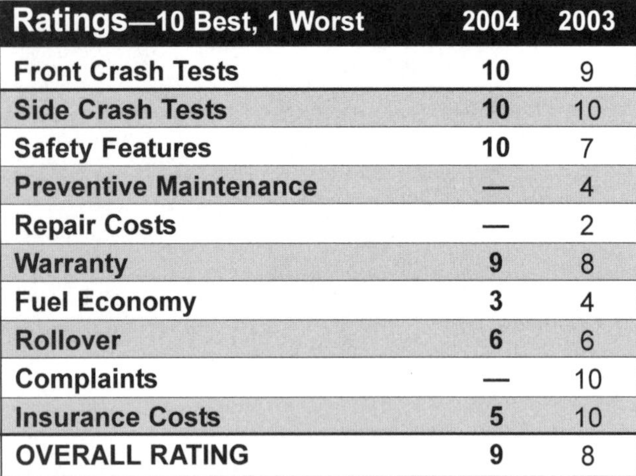

Ratings—10 Best, 1 Worst	2004	2003
Front Crash Tests	10	9
Side Crash Tests	10	10
Safety Features	10	7
Preventive Maintenance	—	4
Repair Costs	—	2
Warranty	9	8
Fuel Economy	3	4
Rollover	6	6
Complaints	—	10
Insurance Costs	5	10
OVERALL RATING	9	8

Price Range	Retail	Markup
AWD	$36,425	13%
FWD	$35,025	13%

Last Year's Model

The RX300, which was unchanged in 2003, handles more like a car than a SUV. It comes equipped with heated outside mirrors, cruise control and a moon roof. Seat belt height adjusters, pretensioners, side impact airbags and 4-wheel ABS are standard safety features on the RX. Under the hood, a 3.0-liter V6 engine that meets California Low Emission Vehicle standards, powers the RX300.

Lexus RX 300

Lexus RX 330

Lexus RX 330

Safety Checklist

Frontal Crash Test. . . . . Very Good
Side Crash Test. . . . . Very Good
Airbags (Side/Head) . . . . Fr. Std. Rear Opt./Yes
Pretensioners/Impact Adjustors . . . . Standard/Yes
Position/Weight Sensors . . . . Yes/Yes
Seat/Head Adjustors . . . . Yes
Roll Stability System. . . . . Yes
Child Seats Built-in . . . . None
Antilock Brakes/Day Lamps 4-Wheel/Standard
Tire Pressure Monitor . . . . Direct

General Information

2004 Status . . . . All New
Series Started . . . . No series indicated
Where Made. . . . . Japan
Theft Rating . . . . Average
Twins . . . .

Specifications

Fuel Econ. (city/hwy) Poor-18/24
Driving Range (mi.) Average-389.4
Bumpers. . . . .
Parking Index . . . . Average
Seating. 5
Tow Rating. Average-3500
Head/Leg Room (in.) Average-39.3/42.5
Int. Space (cu. ft.). . . . . Very Roomy-140.8
Cargo Space (cu. ft.) Roomy-38.3

How the Competition Rates

	Rating	Pg.
Acura MDX	10	96
Chrysler Pacifica	8	136
Infiniti FX		174

Lincoln Aviator

Mid-Size SUV

For 2004, the Aviator receives only minor improvements since its introduction last year. A new tire pressure monitoring system is now standard. There are new exterior and interior colors this year, as well as an upgraded DVD based navigation system with an in dash six-disc CD changer. A 4.6-liter V8 engine powers the Aviator. A 5-speed automatic transmission is standard for all trim models. Side curtain airbags, and a roll stability control system are some of the safety features found on this SUV.

Lincoln Aviator

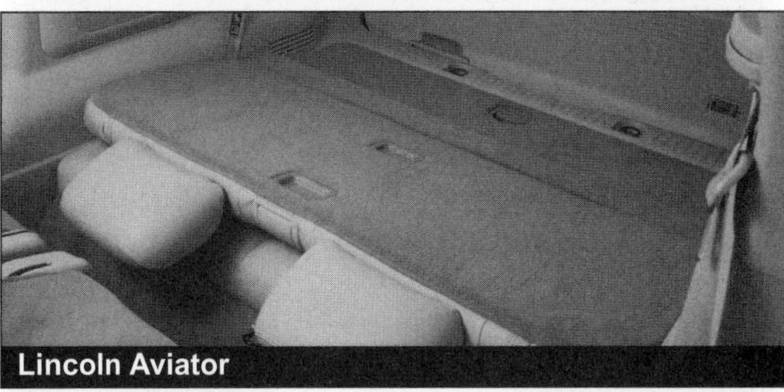

Lincoln Aviator

Ratings—10 Best, 1 Worst	2004	2003
Front Crash Tests	—	—
Side Crash Tests	—	—
Safety Features	8	8
Preventive Maintenance	8	—
Repair Costs	10	—
Warranty	6	5
Fuel Economy	1	1
Rollover	4	4
Complaints	—	—
Insurance Costs	5	5
OVERALL RATING	—	4

Price Range	Retail	Markup
2WD	$39,710	9%
4WD	$42,660	9%

Last Year's Model

The Aviator was brand new in 2003. This variation of the Ford Explorer gave Lincoln a smaller SUV to compliment its large Navigator. An all-aluminum 4.6-liter V8 provides nearly 302 horsepower. Dual front airbags, standard ABS, and a built-in anti-theft device are standard features as are dual zone climate control, and heated and power adjusted mirrors. A DVD entertainment system is available on the Premium trim model.

Lincoln Aviator 2003

Safety Checklist

Frontal Crash Test	
Side Crash Test	
Airbags (Side/Head)	Front Standard/Yes
Pretensioners/Impact Adjustors	Yes/Yes
Position/Weight Sensors	No/No
Seat/Head Adjustors	No
Roll Stability System	Yes
Child Seats Built-in	None
Antilock Brakes/Day Lamps	4-Wheel/None
Tire Pressure Monitor	Direct

General Information

2004 Status	Unchanged
Series Started	2003
Where Made	US
Theft Rating	Average
Twins	

Specifications

Fuel Econ. (city/hwy)	Very Poor-13/19
Driving Range (mi.)	Very Short-341.0
Bumpers	
Parking Index	Very Hard
Seating	5/7
Tow Rating	High-7100
Head/Leg Room (in.)	Roomy-39.9/42.4
Int. Space (cu. ft.)	
Cargo Space (cu. ft.)	Very Roomy-77.3

How the Competition Rates

	Rating	Pg.
BMW X5	8	106
Buick Rainier	4	111
Mitsubishi Endeavor	5	208

Lincoln LS

Large

For 2004, the LS receives an improved transmission, new exterior and interior colors, and Sirius satellite radio. The LS is powered by a 3.0-liter V6 or a 3.9-liter V8 depending on the model. All LS models have a five-speed automatic transmission. Antilock brakes, AdvanceTrac stability systems, and an electronic braking system improve stability. Dual stage airbags, as well as occupant position and weight sensors provide additional safety. A DVD navigation system, heated rear seats and rear park assist are also available.

Lincoln LS

Ratings—10 Best, 1 Worst	2004	2003
Front Crash Tests	—	9
Side Crash Tests	9	9
Safety Features	6	7
Preventive Maintenance	4	—
Repair Costs	8	9
Warranty	6	5
Fuel Economy	4	4
Rollover	10	10
Complaints	4	2
Insurance Costs	5	5
OVERALL RATING	—	8

Price Range	Retail	Markup
4D Sedan V6	$31,860	9%
4D Sedan V8	$39,460	9%

Last Year's Model

The Lincoln LS received a major appearance change in 2003 and a list of improvements that included a more modern looking front facade, an improved standard 3.0-liter V6, an optional 3.9-liter V8, and available DVD navigation. The standard LS comes with an automatic transmission, front mounted side airbags and 4-wheel ABS.

Lincoln LS

Lincoln LS

Safety Checklist

Frontal Crash Test	
Side Crash Test	Very Good
Airbags (Side/Head)	Front Standard/Yes
Pretensioners/Impact Adjustors	None/Yes
Position/Weight Sensors	NA/NA
Seat/Head Adjustors	No
Roll Stability System	Yes
Child Seats Built-in	None
Antilock Brakes/Day Lamps	4-Wheel/None
Tire Pressure Monitor	None

General Information

2004 Status	Unchanged
Series Started	1999
Where Made	US
Theft Rating	Very High
Twins	Jaguar S-Type 2004

Specifications

Fuel Econ. (city/hwy)	Poor-18/25
Driving Range (mi.)	Short-370.7
Bumpers	Strong
Parking Index	Hard
Seating	5
Tow Rating	
Head/Leg Room (in.)	Roomy-40.5/42.8
Int. Space (cu. ft.)	Roomy-103.9
Cargo Space (cu. ft.)	Cramped-13.5

How the Competition Rates

	Rating	Pg.
Acura RL	7	97
BMW 5 Series		105
Pontiac Bonneville	7	226

Lincoln Town Car — Large

For 2004, the Town Car adds Sirius satellite radio as an option and a navigation system. A 4.6-liter V8 engine mated to a 4-speed automatic transmission powers the Town Car. Dual stage airbags and safety belts with pretensioners are standard safety features. Leather seats, eight-way power driver and passenger seats, and dual zone climate control are standard equipment. There is an automatic anti-theft system as well.

Lincoln Town Car

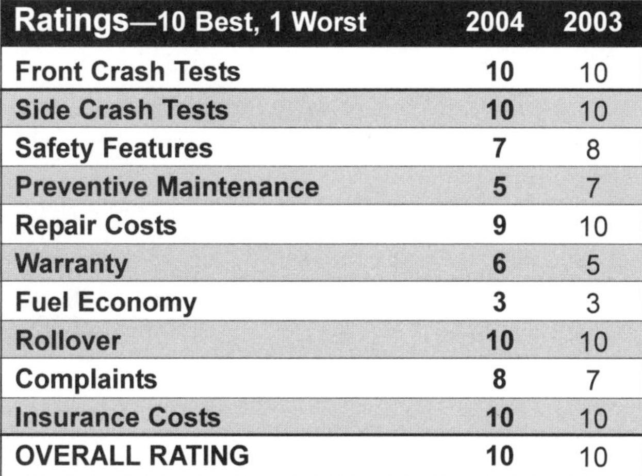

Ratings—10 Best, 1 Worst	2004	2003
Front Crash Tests	10	10
Side Crash Tests	10	10
Safety Features	7	8
Preventive Maintenance	5	7
Repair Costs	9	10
Warranty	6	5
Fuel Economy	3	3
Rollover	10	10
Complaints	8	7
Insurance Costs	10	10
OVERALL RATING	10	10

Lincoln Town Car

Safety Checklist

Frontal Crash Test . . . . . Very Good
Side Crash Test . . . . . Very Good
Airbags (Side/Head) . . . . . Front Standard/Yes
Pretensioners/Impact Adjustors . . . . . None/Yes
Position/Weight Sensors . . . . . Yes/Yes
Seat/Head Adjustors . . . . . No
Roll Stability System . . . . . No
Child Seats Built-in . . . . . None
Antilock Brakes/Day Lamps 4-Wheel/None
Tire Pressure Monitor . . . . . None

Price Range	Retail	Markup
Executive	$41,360	9%
Signature	$41,020	9%
Ultimate	$44,130	9%

General Information

2004 Status . . . . . Unchanged
Series Started 1998
Where Made . . . . . US
Theft Rating . . . . . Very High
Twins . . . . .

Last Year's Model

The Town Car received a major appearance change in 2003. Some of the improvements included 17-inch tires, restyled interior consoles and a new front facade. Holding up to six passengers, the Town Car is powered by a new 4.6-liter V8 that delivers nearly 239 hp. A four-speed automatic transmission is standard. Dual stage front airbags and antilock brakes are standard as well. Leather seats and wood-like trim are also available.

Lincoln Town Car — 2003

Specifications

Fuel Econ. (city/hwy) Poor-17/25
Driving Range (mi.) Short-377.3
Bumpers . . . . . Strong
Parking Index . . . . . Very Hard
Seating 6
Tow Rating Low-2000
Head/Leg Room (in.) . . . . . Very Roomy-39.3/45.8
Int. Space (cu. ft.) Roomy-112.7
Cargo Space (cu. ft.) Average-21

How the Competition Rates

	Rating	Pg.
Lexus LS 430		193
Ford Crown Victoria	10	146
Mercedes-Benz E-Class	9	203

Mazda 6 — Compact

For 2004, the Mazda 6 remains unchanged since its introduction last year. There are two models, the I and S. The I is powered by a 2.3-liter inline 4-cylinder engine and the S has a more powerful V6 engine. The Mazda 6 is designed as a sport sedan. The suspension is taut and a 4-speed automatic transmission with overdrive comes standard. You can choose between a 5-speed automatic or 5-speed manual transmission. Leather seating is optional on both models of the 6.

Mazda 6

Ratings—10 Best, 1 Worst	2004	2003
Front Crash Tests	10	10
Side Crash Tests	8	8
Safety Features	6	6
Preventive Maintenance	—	—
Repair Costs	—	—
Warranty	1	4
Fuel Economy	7	7
Rollover	10	9
Complaints	—	—
Insurance Costs	5	5
OVERALL RATING	7	8

Mazda 6

Price Range	Retail	Markup
Sedan I	$18,750	8%
Sedan S	$21,345	8%

Safety Checklist

Frontal Crash Test. . . . . Very Good
Side Crash Test. . . . . Good
Airbags (Side/Head). . . . . Front Optional/Yes
Pretensioners/Impact Adjustors . . . . None/Yes
Position/Weight Sensors. . . . . Yes/No
Seat/Head Adjustors . . . . No
Roll Stability System . . . . No
Child Seats Built-in . . . . None
Antilock Brakes/Day Lamps 4-Wheel/None
Tire Pressure Monitor . . . . None

General Information

2004 Status . . . . Unchanged
Series Started. 2003
Where Made . . . . US
Theft Rating . . . . Average
Twins . . . .

Last Year's Model

The Mazda 6 was brand new in 2003 with two trim levels offering different engine choices. The base line I has a 2.3 four-cylinder engine, and the S has a V6. The interior comfortably seats five adults. A five-speed manual is standard. Antilock brakes are standard on all trim models and so are dual stage front airbags. A 6-CD changer option and a three-year roadside assistance package were offered in 2003 on this sports sedan.

Mazda 6 2003

Specifications

Fuel Econ. (city/hwy). Good-23/29
Driving Range (mi.) . . . . Very Long-456.5
Bumpers . . . . Weak
Parking Index . . . . Hard
Seating. 5
Tow Rating . . . .
Head/Leg Room (in.) Average-38.7/42.3
Int. Space (cu. ft.) Cramped-96.1
Cargo Space (cu. ft.). Cramped-15.2

How the Competition Rates

	Rating	Pg.
Honda Accord	8	160
Infiniti I35	10	176
Nissan Maxima	9	216

Mazda MPV — Minivan

For 2004, the Mazda MPV remains unchanged after its midlife restyling last year. The MPV is available in two trims models: the LX and ES. Both are powered by a 3.0-liter V6 engine and have a five-speed automatic transmission. There is no all-wheel drive option available. Front bucket seats with four-way passenger seating adjustments are standard. Four-wheel antilock brakes, dual stage front impact airbags, and a panic alarm are standard. You can even get an optional "winged" spoiler. An in dash AM/FM 6-disc changer is also available as an option.

Mazda MPV

Mazda MPV

Ratings—10 Best, 1 Worst	2004	2003
Front Crash Tests	10	10
Side Crash Tests	10	10
Safety Features	4	4
Preventive Maintenance	6	6
Repair Costs	3	5
Warranty	1	4
Fuel Economy	4	4
Rollover	6	6
Complaints	10	6
Insurance Costs	10	10
OVERALL RATING	6	8

Price Range	Retail	Markup
ES	$28,230	8%
LX	$23,260	8%

Last Year's Model

The MPV remains mechanically unchanged for 2003, but it did get a sportier look. Improvements included a new 3.0-liter 6-cylinder engine, 17-inch alloy wheels, and a new suspension. Creature comforts include a DVD entertainment system and four folding captain's chairs. Four-wheel antilock brakes, reinforced side impact beams, and dual side airbags round are some of the safety features. There are only two interior colors to choose from.

Mazda MPV

Safety Checklist

Frontal Crash Test	Very Good
Side Crash Test	Very Good
Airbags (Side/Head)	Front Optional Rear Optional
Pretensioners/Impact Adjustors	Yes/Yes
Position/Weight Sensors	Yes/No
Seat/Head Adjustors	No
Roll Stability System	No
Child Seats Built-in	None
Antilock Brakes/Day Lamps	4-Wheel/None
Tire Pressure Monitor	None

General Information

2004 Status	Unchanged
Series Started	1999
Where Made	Japan
Theft Rating	Very High
Twins	

Specifications

Fuel Econ. (city/hwy)	Poor-18/25
Driving Range (mi.)	Long-407.8
Bumpers	Weak
Parking Index	Average
Seating	7
Tow Rating	Low-2000
Head/Leg Room (in.)	Average-41/40.8
Int. Space (cu. ft.)	Very Roomy-127
Cargo Space (cu. ft.)	Average-17.2

How the Competition Rates

	Rating	Pg.
Chevrolet Venture	6	133
Dodge Caravan	10	141
Honda Odyssey	8	165

Mazda MX-5 Miata — Compact

For 2004, the Mazda MX-5 Miata remains unchanged. A five-speed manual transmission is standard on the base line model, but you can upgrade to an optional 4-speed automatic. The bucket seats both come with power adjustments. Leather seating is optional. Some of the safety features include an optional security system and panic alarm. Dual airbags and an ignition disable device are standard. Remote keyless entry, front fog lights and power windows are standard as well.

Mazda MX-5 Miata

Ratings—10 Best, 1 Worst	2004	2003
Front Crash Tests	9	9
Side Crash Tests	4	—
Safety Features	2	2
Preventive Maintenance	7	6
Repair Costs	3	3
Warranty	1	4
Fuel Economy	7	7
Rollover	10	10
Complaints	5	5
Insurance Costs	5	5
OVERALL RATING	4	5

Mazda MX-5 Miata

Price Range	Retail	Markup
Base Model	$21,868	8%
LS	$24,673	8%

Last Year's Model

This classic roadster remained unchanged in 2003. Minor additions improved the suspension, performance and comfort level of the Miata. The MX-5 is powered by the standard 1.8-liter 4-cylinder engine. ABS brakes improve the stopping ability and transmission choices include a five or six-speed manual or a four-speed automatic.

Mazda Miata

2003

Safety Checklist

Frontal Crash Test . . . . . Very Good
Side Crash Test . . . . . Poor
Airbags (Side/Head) . . . . . No Side
Pretensioners/Impact Adjustors . . . . . Yes/No
Position/Weight Sensors . . . . . No/No
Seat/Head Adjustors . . . . . No
Roll Stability System . . . . . No
Child Seats Built-in . . . . . None
Antilock Brakes/Day Lamps . . . 4-Wheel (optional)/None
Tire Pressure Monitor . . . . . None

General Information

2004 Status . . . . . Unchanged
Series Started 1993
Where Made . . . . . Japan
Theft Rating . . . . . Very High
Twins . . . . .

Specifications

Fuel Econ. (city/hwy) Good-22/28
Driving Range (mi.) . . . . . Very Short-309.2
Bumpers . . . . . Weak
Parking Index . . . . . Very Easy
Seating 2
Tow Rating . . . . .
Head/Leg Room (in.) . . . . . Very Cramped-37.1/42.75
Int. Space (cu. ft.) . . . . . Very Cramped-46
Cargo Space (cu. ft.) . . . . . Very Cramped-5.1

How the Competition Rates

	Rating	Pg.
BMW Z4	9	107
Ford Thunderbird	5	158
Honda S2000	7	167

Mazda RX-8 — Compact

The all-new Mazda RX-8 marks the return of Mazda's high performance rotary powered sports car. A 210 horsepower 1.3-liter engine powers the RX-8 or you can upgrade to a more powerful 250-horsepower rotary engine. A 4-speed automatic transmission is standard, but you can select a six-speed manual. There are rear-opening doors for the backseat. The RX-8 is designed for four people in its snug cockpit. Antilock brakes are standard and a stability control system is included to help prevent skidding.

Mazda RX-8

Mazda RX-8

Ratings—10 Best, 1 Worst	2004	2003
Front Crash Tests	—	
Side Crash Tests	—	
Safety Features	8	
Preventive Maintenance	—	
Repair Costs	—	
Warranty	1	
Fuel Economy	4	
Rollover	10	
Complaints	—	
Insurance Costs	5	
OVERALL RATING	—	

Price Range	Retail	Markup
Coupe 6-sp. man.	$26,680	8%
Coupe auto.	$25,180	8%

Last Year's Model

Model Not Produced in 2003

2003

Safety Checklist

Frontal Crash Test	
Side Crash Test	
Airbags (Side/Head)	Front Standard/Yes
Pretensioners/Impact Adjustors	Standard/Yes
Position/Weight Sensors	Yes/No
Seat/Head Adjustors	No
Roll Stability System	Yes
Child Seats Built-in	None
Antilock Brakes/Day Lamps	4-Wheel/None
Tire Pressure Monitor	None

General Information

2004 Status	All New
Series Started	No series indicated
Where Made	US
Theft Rating	Average
Twins	

Specifications

Fuel Econ. (city/hwy)	Poor-18/25
Driving Range (mi.)	Very Short-327.5
Bumpers	
Parking Index	Easy
Seating	4
Tow Rating	
Head/Leg Room (in.)	Very Cramped-35.8/43
Int. Space (cu. ft.)	
Cargo Space (cu. ft.)	Very Cramped-7.6

How the Competition Rates

	Rating	Pg.
BMW Z4	9	107
Honda S2000	7	167
Nissan 350Z	7	213

Mercedes-Benz C-Class — Intermediate

For 2004, the Mercedes C-Class gets heated front seats, new tires for the sport coupes, and a new all-wheel drive option on the C240 and C320 wagons. There are three different body styles in the C-Class family: coupes, sedans and wagons. Dual zone climate control and computer aided stability control systems are standard features. All-wheel drive is available on most models. A sport shift manual transmission is available on the coupes. There is a driver's information display and navigation system.

Mercedes-Benz C-Class Sports Coupe

Mercedes-Benz C-Class Sports Coupe

Ratings—10 Best, 1 Worst	2004	2003
Front Crash Tests	8	8
Side Crash Tests	10	10
Safety Features	8	8
Preventive Maintenance	10	10
Repair Costs	1	2
Warranty	1	1
Fuel Economy	4	5
Rollover	8	9
Complaints	10	10
Insurance Costs	10	10
OVERALL RATING	9	9

Price Range	Retail	Markup
C230 Kompressor Sedan	$28,710	10%
C240 Sedan	$32,280	10%
C240 Wagon	$33,780	10%
C320 Wagon	$39,130	10%

Last Year's Model

Mercedes' entry level C-Class received some minor changes and a new C240 wagon. The C230 sport coupe received a more efficient 189-horsepower engine. Dual front airbags, side impact airbags, rollover curtains, and stability control are standard features. Dual-zone climate control and a driver adapted five-speed automatic transmission are also standard. All-wheel drive has been added as an option to most models.

Mercedes-Benz C-Class 2003

Safety Checklist

Frontal Crash Test	Good
Side Crash Test	Very Good
Airbags (Side/Head)	Fr. Std. Rear Opt./Yes
Pretensioners/Impact Adjustors	Yes/Yes
Position/Weight Sensors	No/No
Seat/Head Adjustors	No
Roll Stability System	Yes
Child Seats Built-in	None
Antilock Brakes/Day Lamps	4-Wheel/Standard
Tire Pressure Monitor	None

General Information

2004 Status	Unchanged
Series Started	2001
Where Made	Germany
Theft Rating	Very High
Twins	

Specifications

Fuel Econ. (city/hwy)	Poor-19/25
Driving Range (mi.)	Very Short-349.3
Bumpers	Weak
Parking Index	Easy
Seating	5
Tow Rating	
Head/Leg Room (in.)	Cramped-38.9/41.7
Int. Space (cu. ft.)	Very Cramped-85.5
Cargo Space (cu. ft.)	Very Cramped-12.2

How the Competition Rates

	Rating	Pg.
Audi A4	10	101
BMW 3 Series	9	104
Infiniti G35		175

Mercedes-Benz E-Class — Large

For 2004, the E-Class changes little since its redesign last year. There is a new four-wheel drive system available on the sedan and wagon and a V8 is now offered on the wagon. The E320 is powered by a 3.6-liter V6. The E500 sedan is powered by a massive 5.0-liter V8. There is a high performance 5.5-liter V8 on the E55 AMG sport sedan. Safety features include dual state airbags, side impact and side curtain airbags, and crash sensors. Luxury features include dual-zone automatic climate control and a navigation system.

Mercedes-Benz E500 Sedan

Ratings—10 Best, 1 Worst	2004	2003
Front Crash Tests	9	9
Side Crash Tests	10	10
Safety Features	10	9
Preventive Maintenance	—	—
Repair Costs	—	—
Warranty	1	1
Fuel Economy	5	5
Rollover	10	9
Complaints	—	—
Insurance Costs	10	10
OVERALL RATING	9	9

Price Range	Retail	Markup
E320 sedan	$48,170	9%
E320 wagon	$50,670	9%
E500 sedan	$56,270	9%
E500 wagon	$60,670	9%

Last Year's Model

All-new in 2003, a 3.2-liter V6 engine powers the E320 and a new 5.0-liter V8 engine powers the E500 sedan. The suspension has been improved with a new air suspension system and larger tires. The frame has been strengthened while, at the same time, reducing weight. Crash sensors, rollover sensors, and seat belt pretensioners are all standard. Luxury features include dual-zone automatic climate control, and parking assist systems.

Mercedes-Benz E-Class 2003

Mercedes-Benz E500 Sedan

Safety Checklist

Frontal Crash Test	Very Good
Side Crash Test	Very Good
Airbags (Side/Head)	Fr. Std. Rear Opt./Yes
Pretensioners/Impact Adjustors	Yes/Yes
Position/Weight Sensors	Yes/Yes
Seat/Head Adjustors	No
Roll Stability System	Yes
Child Seats Built-in	None
Antilock Brakes/Day Lamps	4-Wheel/None
Tire Pressure Monitor	Direct

General Information

2004 Status	Unchanged
Series Started	2003
Where Made	Germany
Theft Rating	Very High
Twins	

Specifications

Fuel Econ. (city/hwy)	Average-19/27
Driving Range (mi.)	Very Long-451.6
Bumpers	Weak
Parking Index	Hard
Seating	5
Tow Rating	
Head/Leg Room (in.)	Very Cramped-37.4/41.9
Int. Space (cu. ft.)	Cramped-97.2
Cargo Space (cu. ft.)	Cramped-15.9

How the Competition Rates

	Rating	Pg.
Audi A6		102
Cadillac CTS	7	114
Volvo 80 Series	9	270

Mercedes-Benz M-Class — Mid-Size SUV

For 2004, the M-class receives only minor changes. The ML55 AMG has been discontinued and the ML350 model replaces the ML320 trim model. There are two engine choices: a V6 on the ML 350 or a V8 found on the ML500. A DVD based navigation is standard on the ML500. Luxury features include a leather steering wheel, dual heated power windows, and footwell lights. The Mercedes "Tele-Aid" communications system is standard on all models.

Mercedes-Benz ML500

Mercedes-Benz ML500

Ratings—10 Best, 1 Worst	2004	2003
Front Crash Tests	—	—
Side Crash Tests	—	—
Safety Features	9	9
Preventive Maintenance	4	3
Repair Costs	2	1
Warranty	1	1
Fuel Economy	2	3
Rollover	4	4
Complaints	9	7
Insurance Costs	10	10
OVERALL RATING	—	—

Price Range	Retail	Markup
ML350	$38,020	10%
ML500	$46,070	8%

Last Year's Model

There were few changes to the Mercedes SUV in 2003. A new DVD based navigation system was standard on the ML400 and ML55 AMG models. The engine choices include a V6 on the ML320 base line model, a V8 on the ML500 and the very powerful 342-hp. V8 engine on the ML55 AMG. All vehicles have a five-speed automatic transmission and the "Tele-Aid" communications system was standard.

Mercedes-Benz M-Class

Safety Checklist

Frontal Crash Test	
Side Crash Test	
Airbags (Side/Head)	Fr. Std. Rear Opt./Yes
Pretensioners/Impact Adjustors	Yes/Yes
Position/Weight Sensors	Yes/Yes
Seat/Head Adjustors	No
Roll Stability System	Yes
Child Seats Built-in	None
Antilock Brakes/Day Lamps	4-Wheel/None
Tire Pressure Monitor	None

General Information

2004 Status	Unchanged
Series Started	1998
Where Made	US
Theft Rating	Very High
Twins	

Specifications

Fuel Econ. (city/hwy)	Very Poor-17/21
Driving Range (mi.)	Long-420.2
Bumpers	Weak
Parking Index	Average
Seating	5
Tow Rating	Average-5000
Head/Leg Room (in.)	Cramped-39.8/40.3
Int. Space (cu. ft.)	
Cargo Space (cu. ft.)	Roomy-34.7

How the Competition Rates

	Rating	Pg.
Acura MDX	10	96
Buick Rainier	4	111
Volvo XC90	8	271

Mercury Monterey — Minivan

The all-new 2004 Monterey marks Mercury's return to the luxury minivan market since it ended production of the Villager in 2003. A 4.2-liter V6 engine powers the Monterey. Dual-zone climate control, first row console storage, and power-sliding doors are standard. A DVD rear seat entertainment system is offered as an option. Heated and cooled front seats and a fold-into-floor third row seat are standard. AdvanceTrak, an automated stability control system, is available on all models.

Mercury Monterey

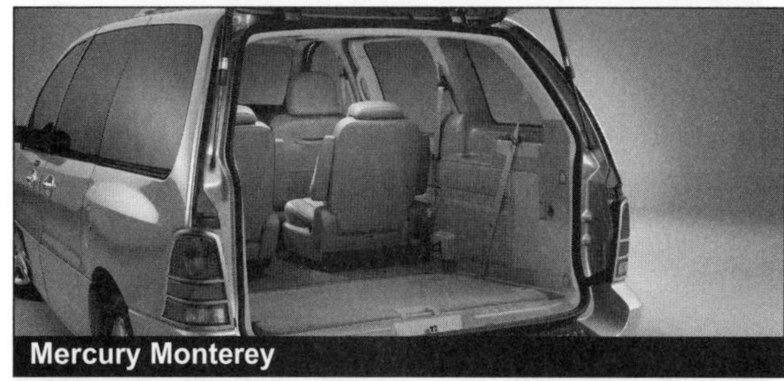

Mercury Monterey

Ratings—10 Best, 1 Worst	2004	2003
Front Crash Tests	10	
Side Crash Tests	—	
Safety Features	8	
Preventive Maintenance	—	
Repair Costs	—	
Warranty	2	
Fuel Economy	2	
Rollover	6	
Complaints	—	
Insurance Costs	5	
OVERALL RATING	4	

Price Range	Retail	Markup
Convenience	$29,995	13%
Luxury	$33,995	13%
Premier	$35,525	13%

Last Year's Model

Model Not Produced in 2003

2003

Safety Checklist

Frontal Crash Test. . . . . Very Good
Side Crash Test . . . .
Airbags (Side/Head) . . . . Fr. Std. Rear Opt./Yes
Pretensioners/Impact Adjustors . . . . Standard/Yes
Position/Weight Sensors . . . . Yes/Yes
Seat/Head Adjustors . . . . No
Roll Stability System. . . . . Yes
Child Seats Built-in . . . . None
Antilock Brakes/Day Lamps. 4-Wheel/
Tire Pressure Monitor . . . . None

General Information

2004 Status . . . . All New
Series Started . . . . No series indicated
Where Made . . . . US
Theft Rating . . . . Average
Twins . . . . Ford Freestar

Specifications

Fuel Econ. (city/hwy) . . . . Very Poor-16/22
Driving Range (mi.) . . . . Very Long-474.2
Bumpers. . . . .
Parking Index. . . . . Very Hard
Seating. 7
Tow Rating . . . .
Head/Leg Room (in.) . . . . Very Cramped-38.8/40.7
Int. Space (cu. ft.). . . . .
Cargo Space (cu. ft.) Average-25.9

How the Competition Rates

	Rating	Pg.
Chrysler Town and Country	10	140
Chevrolet Venture	6	133
Nissan Quest	6	220

Mini Cooper — Compact

For 2004, the Mini Cooper remains unchanged. A 1.6-liter 4-cylinder engine powers the Cooper. The interior is well equipped for vehicle of its size. Leather, side airbags, and a sunroof are all available. The more powerful Cooper S comes with a 163-horsepowered engine. Most Coopers have contrasting roof colors. The ride is smooth despite being so low to the ground. Option packages provide additional features including upgraded audio systems and a navigation system.

Mini Cooper

Mini Cooper S

Ratings—10 Best, 1 Worst	2004	2003
Front Crash Tests	8	8
Side Crash Tests*	6	—
Safety Features	9	8
Preventive Maintenance	10	—
Repair Costs	7	—
Warranty	4	6
Fuel Economy	8	8
Rollover	9	9
Complaints	—	—
Insurance Costs	1	1
OVERALL RATING	10	7

Price Range	Retail	Markup
Cooper	$16,449	10%
Cooper S	$19,449	11%

Safety Checklist

Frontal Crash Test . . . Good
Side Crash Test* . . . Average
Airbags (Side/Head) . . . Front Standard/Yes
Pretensioners/Impact Adjustors . . . Yes/Yes
Position/Weight Sensors . . . Yes/Yes
Seat/Head Adjustors . . . No
Roll Stability System . . . Yes
Child Seats Built-in . . . None
Antilock Brakes/Day Lamps . . . 4-Wheel (optional)/None
Tire Pressure Monitor . . . Direct

General Information

2004 Status . . . Unchanged
Series Started . . . 2002
Where Made . . .
Theft Rating . . . Average
Twins . . .

Last Year's Model

The 2003 model of the Mini was a carryover from 2002. This car became an instant hit, and dealers originally had a hard time keeping them in stock. A 1.6-liter 4-cylinder engine powers this subcompact and a "drive-by-wire" throttle system to enhance responsiveness. The Mini comes in two trims: the Cooper and the Cooper S. The Cooper S has a more powerful engine and extra options.

Mini Cooper 2003

Specifications

Fuel Econ. (city/hwy) . . . Good-25/32
Driving Range (mi.) . . . Short-366.0
Bumpers . . .
Parking Index . . . Very Easy
Seating . . . 4
Tow Rating . . . Very Low-1433
Head/Leg Room (in.) . . . Cramped-38.8/41.3
Int. Space (cu. ft.) . . . Very Cramped-77
Cargo Space (cu. ft.) . . . Very Cramped-5.3

How the Competition Rates

	Rating	Pg.
Ford Focus	8	152
Chrysler PT Cruiser	9	137
Honda Civic	10	161

*Applies to front occupant only. Rear seat too small for test.

Mitsubishi Eclipse — Compact

For 2004, the Eclipse remains unchanged. There are new exterior colors, improvements to the stereo system, new power side view mirrors and a seatbelt reminder system. The dashboard of the Eclipse Spyder convertible also gets a new look. The Eclipse is powered by a standard 2.4-liter inline 4-cylinder. There is the option of upgrading to a 3.0-liter V6 when you buy the GT. Dual airbags are standard. Manual and automatic transmissions are available. Antilock brakes are available as well and leather seating is an option.

Mitsubishi Eclipse GTS

Mitsubishi Eclipse Spyder

Ratings—10 Best, 1 Worst	2004	2003
Front Crash Tests	8	8
Side Crash Tests*	5	—
Safety Features	2	2
Preventive Maintenance	8	8
Repair Costs	6	5
Warranty	5	5
Fuel Economy	6	6
Rollover	10	10
Complaints	2	2
Insurance Costs	1	1
OVERALL RATING	5	5

Price Range	Retail	Markup
GT	$21,497	7%
RS	$18,297	7%
Spyder GS	$24,297	7%
Spyder GTS	$28,777	7%

Last Year's Model

Mitsubishi's sporty compact received some minor improvements to the exterior in 2003. The inside of the RS, GS and GT received new seat fabrics, and the GTS has leather seating. The 2.4-liter 4-cylinder engine provides ample performance, at the same time improving the emissions quality of the vehicle in the RS and GS models. The Eclipse offers expensive sport car performance at an entry-level car's price.

Mitsubishi Eclipse 2003

Safety Checklist

Frontal Crash Test . . . Good
Side Crash Test . . . Average
Airbags (Side/Head) . . . Front Standard
Pretensioners/Impact Adjustors . . . None/No
Position/Weight Sensors . . . No/No
Seat/Head Adjustors . . . No
Roll Stability System . . . No
Child Seats Built-in . . . None
Antilock Brakes/Day Lamps . . . 4-Wheel/None
Tire Pressure Monitor . . . None

General Information

2004 Status . . . Unchanged
Series Started . . . 2000
Where Made . . . USA/Japan
Theft Rating . . . Very High
Twins . . .

Specifications

Fuel Econ. (city/hwy) . . . Average-21/28
Driving Range (mi.) . . . Average-388.1
Bumpers . . . Strong
Parking Index . . . Easy
Seating . . . 4
Tow Rating . . .
Head/Leg Room (in.) . . . Cramped-37.9/42.3
Int. Space (cu. ft.) . . . Very Cramped-75.2
Cargo Space (cu. ft.) . . . Very Cramped-7.2

How the Competition Rates

	Rating	Pg.
Acura RSX	7	98
Mazda RX-8		201
Subaru Impreza	4	240

*Applies to front occupant only. Rear seat too small for test.

Mitsubishi Endeavor — Large SUV

The all-new 2004 Mitsubishi Endeavor falls in between the Montero and the smaller Montero sport. It is designed for bad weather, not for trails. There are three trim models available: the LS, XLS and the Limited. Antilock brakes are optional on the front-wheel drive XLS and standard on the Limited. Side impact airbags are optional on the XLS. A 3.8-liter V6 engine powers the Endeavor, which comes equipped with either front-wheel drive or all-wheel drive. A power sunroof is optional. An automatic transmission is standard.

Ratings—10 Best, 1 Worst	2004	2003
Front Crash Tests	10	
Side Crash Tests	10	
Safety Features	3	
Preventive Maintenance	—	
Repair Costs	—	
Warranty	5	
Fuel Economy	2	
Rollover	5	
Complaints	—	
Insurance Costs	5	
OVERALL RATING	5	

Price Range	Retail	Markup
Limited 2WD	$31,697	8%
Limited 4WD	$33,197	8%
LS AWD	$27,597	8%
XLS 2WD	$27,897	8%

Last Year's Model

Model Not Produced in 2003

2003

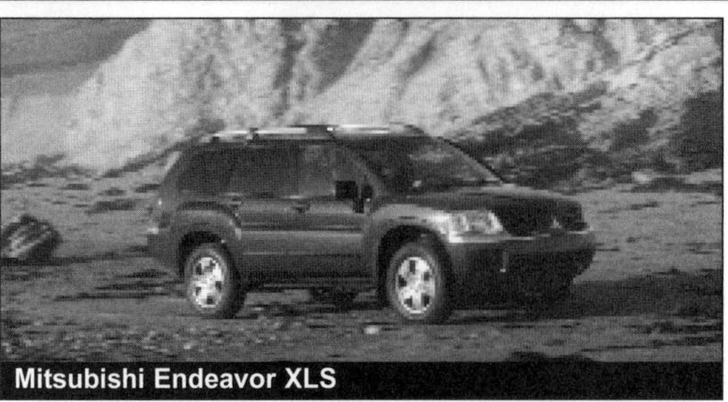

Mitsubishi Endeavor XLS

Mitsubishi Endeavor XLS

Safety Checklist

Frontal Crash Test	Very Good
Side Crash Test	Very Good
Airbags (Side/Head)	No Side
Pretensioners/Impact Adjustors	Standard/Yes
Position/Weight Sensors	No/No
Seat/Head Adjustors	No
Roll Stability System	No
Child Seats Built-in	None
Antilock Brakes/Day Lamps	4-Wheel/None
Tire Pressure Monitor	None

General Information

2004 Status	All New
Series Started	No series indicated
Where Made	USA
Theft Rating	Average
Twins	

Specifications

Fuel Econ. (city/hwy)	Very Poor-17/23
Driving Range (mi.)	Long-412.2
Bumpers	Strong
Parking Index	Hard
Seating	5
Tow Rating	
Head/Leg Room (in.)	Average-39.6/41.4
Int. Space (cu. ft.)	Roomy-106.7
Cargo Space (cu. ft.)	Very Roomy-40.7

How the Competition Rates

	Rating	Pg.
Chevrolet Tahoe	3	130
Chrysler Pacifica	8	136
Ford Expedition	4	149

Mitsubishi Galant — Compact

The Galant has been redesigned for 2004 and now offers a 3.8-liter V6 and an interior volume increase of nearly 100 cubic feet. The stance is wider and longer as well. Four trim models are available and each provides a variety of options to choose from. A 2.4-liter 4-cylinder powers the base model DX. The GTS offers more luxury features as standard equipment including leather, a premium audio system, a sunroof and standard side airbags. The mid model LS is expected to be under $22,000.

Ratings—10 Best, 1 Worst	2004	2003
Front Crash Tests	—	5
Side Crash Tests	—	5
Safety Features	1	3
Preventive Maintenance	—	9
Repair Costs	—	7
Warranty	5	5
Fuel Economy	5	6
Rollover	—	9
Complaints	—	7
Insurance Costs	1	1
OVERALL RATING	—	8

Price Range	Retail	Markup
ES	$18,717	8%
GTZ-V6	$24,637	8%
LS	$21,317	8%
LS-V6	$23,347	8%

Last Year's Model

Unchanged in 2003, the Galant is powered by a 2.4-liter engine, which is standard in the DE, ES, and LS models. An optional V6 engine is offered on the ES and LS. On the GTZ the V6 engine is standard. An all-weather options package has been added on all models. The Galant comes in four trim levels. Leather seating is optional. The Galant comes with a 5-speed manual transmission, but you can upgrade to a 4-speed automatic.

Mitsubishi Galant 2003

Mitsubishi Galant ES

Mitsubishi Galant GTS

Safety Checklist

Frontal Crash Test. . . . . Good
Side Crash Test. . . . . Very Good
Airbags (Side/Head) . . . . . Front Optional Rear Optional
Pretensioners/Impact Adjustors. . . . . /Yes
Position/Weight Sensors . . . . /
Seat/Head Adjustors . . . .
Roll Stability System . . . . No
Child Seats Built-in. . . . .
Antilock Brakes/Day Lamps . . . . /
Tire Pressure Monitor . . . . None

General Information

2004 Status . . . . All New
Series Started . . . . No series indicated
Where Made . . . . USA
Theft Rating . . . . Very High
Twins . . . .

Specifications

Fuel Econ. (city/hwy) Average-19/27
Driving Range (mi.) Average-388.0
Bumpers . . . . Strong
Parking Index . . . .
Seating. 5
Tow Rating . . . .
Head/Leg Room (in.) Roomy-39.6/42.6
Int. Space (cu. ft.) Average-101.3
Cargo Space (cu. ft.). Cramped-13.3

How the Competition Rates

	Rating	Pg.
Chevrolet Cavalier	3	123
Ford Focus	8	152
Kia Optima	8	183

Mitsubishi Lancer — Compact

For 2004, the sedan version of the Lancer remains unchanged. The big news is the introduction of the Lancer Sportback wagon, which is all-new for 2004, and designed to help Mitsubishi compete with the new breed of hatchbacks, which are becoming more popular with younger buyers. A 2.0-liter 4-cylinder engine powers the base model Lancer. Power windows and locks, AM/FM/CD stereo system, and dual airbags are standard. Each trim model offers its own options packages. There is also a turbocharged trim model called the Evolution.

Ratings—10 Best, 1 Worst	2004	2003
Front Crash Tests	9	9
Side Crash Tests	6	6
Safety Features	3	3
Preventive Maintenance	9	—
Repair Costs	5	—
Warranty	5	5
Fuel Economy	8	8
Rollover	9	8
Complaints	—	—
Insurance Costs	1	1
OVERALL RATING	7	5

Price Range	Retail	Markup
ES	$13,597	7%
LS	$15,997	7%
Ralliant	$17,997	7%
Sportback Ralliant	$19,197	7%

Last Year's Model

The 2003 Lancer was unchanged. The base model ES comes with a 2.0-liter 16-value 4-cylinder engine, power windows and locks, as well as a 140-watt AM/FM/CD stereo system. The LS and OZ-RALLY models offer additional features such as remote keyless entry, redesigned gauges on the dashboard, and embroidered floor mates. Standard safety features include dual airbags. Antilock brakes are optional on the LS model.

Mitsubishi Lancer — 2003

Mitsubishi Lancer LS

Mitsubishi Lancer Sportback

Safety Checklist

Frontal Crash Test	Very Good
Side Crash Test	Average
Airbags (Side/Head)	Front Standard
Pretensioners/Impact Adjustors	Yes/No
Position/Weight Sensors	No/No
Seat/Head Adjustors	No
Roll Stability System	No
Child Seats Built-in	None
Antilock Brakes/Day Lamps	4-Wheel/None
Tire Pressure Monitor	None

General Information

2004 Status	Major Appearance Change
Series Started	2002
Where Made	Japan
Theft Rating	Average
Twins	

Specifications

Fuel Econ. (city/hwy)	Good-24/29
Driving Range (mi.)	Very Short-343.4
Bumpers	Strong
Parking Index	Very Easy
Seating	5
Tow Rating	
Head/Leg Room (in.)	Average-38.8/43.2
Int. Space (cu. ft.)	Cramped-93.9
Cargo Space (cu. ft.)	Very Cramped-11.3

How the Competition Rates

	Rating	Pg.
Chevrolet Cavalier	3	123
Hyundai Elantra	10	169
Suzuki Aerio		243

Mitsubishi Montero Sport — Small SUV

For 2004, the Montero Sport is unchanged and is powered by the same 3.5-liter V6 as last year. Antilock brakes are standard on its 4x4 versions and there is a new tire pressure monitoring system. Cruise control, remote keyless entry, and privacy glass are available as options. The only transmission is a four-speed automatic. The Montero Sport has excellent side crash test results, but suffers from very poor gas mileage.

Mitsubishi Montero Sport

Ratings—10 Best, 1 Worst	2004	2003
Front Crash Tests	5	5
Side Crash Tests	10	10
Safety Features	3	3
Preventive Maintenance	1	1
Repair Costs	3	2
Warranty	5	5
Fuel Economy	1	3
Rollover	4	4
Complaints	10	9
Insurance Costs	5	5
OVERALL RATING	4	2

Mitsubishi Montero Sport

Safety Checklist

Frontal Crash Test	
Side Crash Test	
Airbags (Side/Head)	Front Standard
Pretensioners/Impact Adjustors	None/No
Position/Weight Sensors	No/No
Seat/Head Adjustors	No
Roll Stability System	No
Child Seats Built-in	None
Antilock Brakes/Day Lamps	4-Wheel/None
Tire Pressure Monitor	Direct

Price Range	Retail	Markup
CS 2WD	$22,907	8%
Limited 2WD	$31,317	8%
LS 4WD	$27,777	8%
Limited 4WD	$32,887	8%

General Information

2004 Status	Unchanged
Series Started	2002
Where Made	Japan
Theft Rating	Very High
Twins	

Last Year's Model

The Montero Sport received a minor appearance change in 2003. A 3.5-liter V6 engine is the only choice. The ES model has air conditioning, halogen lamps, folding power mirrors and 15-inch wheels as standard equipment. Dual stage airbags, side impact and head airbags and 4-wheel anti lock brakes are some of the standard safety features. The Montero Sport suffers from a high theft rating and poor fuel economy.

Mitsubishi Montero

Specifications

Fuel Econ. (city/hwy)	Very Poor-15/19
Driving Range (mi.)	Average-394.4
Bumpers	Strong
Parking Index	Average
Seating	7
Tow Rating	Average-5000
Head/Leg Room (in.)	Very Roomy-41.5/42.3
Int. Space (cu. ft.)	
Cargo Space (cu. ft.)	Very Roomy-96.4

How the Competition Rates

	Rating	Pg.
Chevrolet Blazer	1	122
Ford Explorer	8	150
Kia Sorento	5	186

Mitsubishi Outlander — Mid-Size SUV

The 2004 Outlander has only minor changes since its introduction last year. The 2.4-liter engine has 20 more horsepower and is more fuel-efficient. There is a new anti-theft engine immobilizer and new color choices. Two-wheel and all wheel drive models are available. Driver and front passenger airbags are standard on all models, but side airbags and ABS are options on the XLS. An AM/FM/CD player is standard. The Outlander comes in two trims levels.

Mitsubishi Outlander XLS

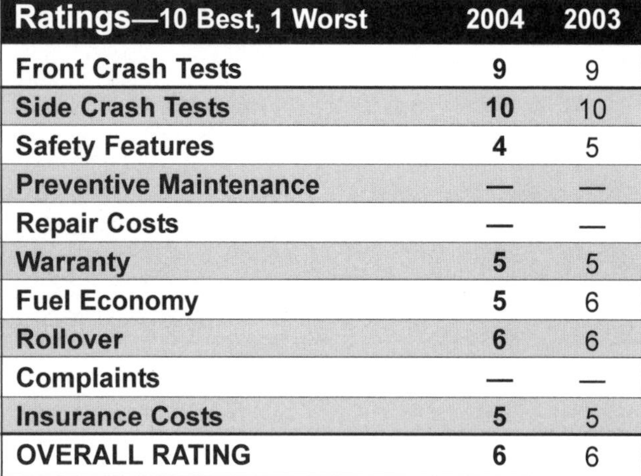

Ratings—10 Best, 1 Worst	2004	2003
Front Crash Tests	9	9
Side Crash Tests	10	10
Safety Features	4	5
Preventive Maintenance	—	—
Repair Costs	—	—
Warranty	5	5
Fuel Economy	5	6
Rollover	6	6
Complaints	—	—
Insurance Costs	5	5
OVERALL RATING	6	6

Price Range	Retail	Markup
AWD	$22,197	8%
AWD LS	$20,097	8%
FWD LS	$18,297	8%
FWD XLS	$19,797	8%

Last Year's Model

Based on the Lancer, this entry level SUV was all new for 2003. There are two trim models available: LS and XLS. A 2.4-liter 16-valve engine rated at 140 horsepower powers both models. A Sportronic automatic transmission allows the driver the option of clutchless shifting. Two-wheel and all-wheel drive models are available. Driver and front passenger airbags are standard. Side airbags and antilock brakes are options on the XLS.

2003

Mitsubishi Outlander XLS

Safety Checklist

Frontal Crash Test	Very Good
Side Crash Test	Very Good
Airbags (Side/Head)	Front Standard
Pretensioners/Impact Adjustors	Yes/No
Position/Weight Sensors	No/No
Seat/Head Adjustors	No
Roll Stability System	Yes
Child Seats Built-in	None
Antilock Brakes/Day Lamps	4-Wheel/None
Tire Pressure Monitor	None

General Information

2004 Status	Unchanged
Series Started	2003
Where Made	Japan
Theft Rating	Average
Twins	

Specifications

Fuel Econ. (city/hwy)	Average-21/26
Driving Range (mi.)	Short-360.9
Bumpers	Strong
Parking Index	Average
Seating	5
Tow Rating	Very Low-1500
Head/Leg Room (in.)	Average-38.9/42.3
Int. Space (cu. ft.)	Cramped-96.1
Cargo Space (cu. ft.)	Average-24.4

How the Competition Rates

	Rating	Pg.
Kia Sorento	5	186
Nissan Murano	7	217
Subaru Forester	6	239

Nissan 350Z — Compact

The big news for the 2004 350Z is the introduction of the much-anticipated Roadster model. A fully automatic soft top stows compactly under a lightweight cover between the cabin and the rear quarter. Additional enhancements for the Z coupe include an automatically opening cover for the navigation system, new colors, and pre-wiring for a satellite radio system. Dual stage front airbags, 4-wheel antilock brakes and new driver and passenger kneepads are some of the safety features. Currently, the Z is the best-selling sports car in the Untied States.

Nissan 350Z Coupe

Ratings—10 Best, 1 Worst	2004	2003
Front Crash Tests	9	9
Side Crash Tests	7	—
Safety Features	6	6
Preventive Maintenance	—	—
Repair Costs	—	—
Warranty	4	3
Fuel Economy	4	5
Rollover	10	8
Complaints	—	—
Insurance Costs	5	5
OVERALL RATING	7	5

Nissan 350Z Roadster

Safety Checklist

Frontal Crash Test . . . . . Very Good
Side Crash Test . . . . . Good
Airbags (Side/Head) . . . . . Front Standard/Yes
Pretensioners/Impact Adjustors . . . . . Yes/Yes
Position/Weight Sensors . . . . . No/No
Seat/Head Adjustors . . . . . No
Roll Stability System . . . . . No
Child Seats Built-in . . . . . None
Antilock Brakes/Day Lamps 4-Wheel/None
Tire Pressure Monitor . . . . . Direct

Price Range	Retail	Markup
Base Coupe 6sp	$26,370	7%
Enthusiast Roadster 6sp	$33,850	8%
Performance Coupe 6sp	$30,530	8%
Touring Roadster at	$37,190	8%

General Information

2004 Status . . . . . Unchanged
Series Started 2003
Where Made . . . . . Japan
Theft Rating . . . . . Average
Twins . . . . .

Last Year's Model

Nissan brought back this "cultural icon" in 2003. A 287 hp V6 engine powers the 350Z. The body maintains the wide front stance of previous generations of the Z. Dual-stage front airbags and antilock brakes with Brake Assist are standard. Side-impact airbags and inflatable side curtain airbags are optional. The Z is a powerful contender in the compact sports car market and fills the gap between inexpensive and luxury sport cars.

Nissan 350Z 2003

Specifications

Fuel Econ. (city/hwy) Poor-19/26
Driving Range (mi.) Long-432.4
Bumpers . . . . . Strong
Parking Index . . . . . Easy
Seating 2
Tow Rating . . . . .
Head/Leg Room (in.) Cramped-38.2/42.6
Int. Space (cu. ft.) . . . . . Very Cramped-50.5
Cargo Space (cu. ft.) . . . . . Very Cramped-6.8

How the Competition Rates

	Rating	Pg.
Chrysler Crossfire		135
Ford Mustang	7	155
Mazda RX-8		201

Nissan Altima

Intermediate

For 2004 the Nissan Altima remains unchanged. A 2.5-liter 4-cylinder remains the standard engine, but you can upgrade to a V6. Automatic transmission-equipped V6 Altimas offer an available traction control system. Braking is provided by standard 4-wheel disc brakes. The interior is comfortable, with cloth as the standard material, but with leather optional. The Altima comes with dual-stage supplemental air bags that sense the collision severity and deploy accordingly.

Nissan Altima

Ratings—10 Best, 1 Worst	2004	2003
Front Crash Tests	10	10
Side Crash Tests	7	7
Safety Features	7	7
Preventive Maintenance	7	9
Repair Costs	8	6
Warranty	4	3
Fuel Economy	7	7
Rollover	9	9
Complaints	6	—
Insurance Costs	1	1
OVERALL RATING	9	10

Nissan Altima

Safety Checklist

Frontal Crash Test	Very Good
Side Crash Test	Good
Airbags (Side/Head)	Front Opt. Rear Opt./Yes
Pretensioners/Impact Adjustors	Yes/Yes
Position/Weight Sensors	Yes/Yes
Seat/Head Adjustors	No
Roll Stability System	No
Child Seats Built-in	None
Antilock Brakes/Day Lamps	4-Wheel (optional)/None
Tire Pressure Monitor	None

Price Range	Retail	Markup
2.5 AT	$17,350	2%
2.5 S AT	$19,200	7%
2.5 SL AT	$23,200	8%
3.5 SE	$23,250	8%

General Information

2004 Status	Unchanged
Series Started	2002
Where Made	US/Japan
Theft Rating	Very High
Twins	

Last Year's Model

The 2003 Altima was a carryover from 2002. The base engine is a 2.5-liter four-cylinder with the Maxima's 3.0-liter V6 as an option on most models. Both engines come with a four-speed automatic or five-speed manual transmission. Antilock brakes and side impact airbags are standard. Side curtain airbags are optional on the Altima. Cloth seating is standard and leather is optional.

Nissan Altima

Specifications

Fuel Econ. (city/hwy)	Good-23/29
Driving Range (mi.)	Average-383.0
Bumpers	Strong
Parking Index	Hard
Seating	5
Tow Rating	
Head/Leg Room (in.)	Very Roomy-40.5/43.9
Int. Space (cu. ft.)	Average-102.5
Cargo Space (cu. ft.)	Cramped-15.1

How the Competition Rates

	Rating	Pg.
Ford Taurus	9	157
Hyundai XG350		173
Oldsmobile Alero	6	224

Nissan Frontier

Compact Pickup

The 2004 Frontier, Nissan's only compact pick-up, remains unchanged. A 3.3-liter V6 engine is standard on all models. There is a new options package available on the King Cab model. A tire pressure monitoring system is a standard feature. The King Cab has seating for 5, and has the one of the largest interiors in the industry. Driver and passenger dual stage airbags and pretensions in the seat belt are standard. A 6-disc CD changer is available in many of the option packages.

Nissan Frontier

Nissan Frontier

Ratings—10 Best, 1 Worst	2004	2003
Front Crash Tests	7	7
Side Crash Tests	10	10
Safety Features	3	3
Preventive Maintenance	3	3
Repair Costs	7	10
Warranty	4	3
Fuel Economy	4	4
Rollover	5	5
Complaints	6	—
Insurance Costs	1	1
OVERALL RATING	4	5

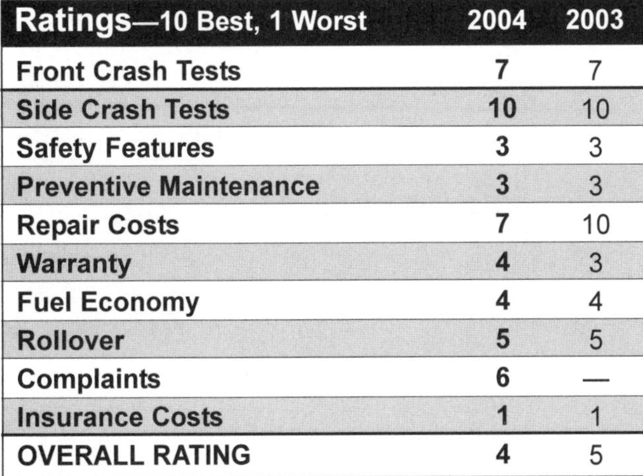

Price Range	Retail	Markup
SC V6 KC 4x4	$24,890	10%
SVE-V6 KC 4X4	$22,880	10%
XE KC 4x2	$15,490	10%
XE-V6 CC 4x2 Standard Bed	$19,970	10%

Last Year's Model

For 2003 the Frontier offered the first powered sunroof on a compact pick up. A tire pressure monitor is also available. The 3.3-liter V6 engine has been upgraded to provide more power. Like most pick up trucks, there are a variety of options, cab sizes, and wheelbases to choose from. Crew cab pick-ups have conventional sized back doors. Dual stage airbags are available, but side impact airbags are not.

Nissan Frontier 2003

Safety Checklist

Frontal Crash Test	Good
Side Crash Test	Very Good
Airbags (Side/Head)	No Side
Pretensioners/Impact Adjustors	Yes/Yes
Position/Weight Sensors	No/No
Seat/Head Adjustors	No
Roll Stability System	No
Child Seats Built-in	None
Antilock Brakes/Day Lamps	2-Wheel (4-Whl. opt.)/None
Tire Pressure Monitor	Direct

General Information

2004 Status	Unchanged
Series Started	2002
Where Made	US/Other
Theft Rating	Very High
Twins	

Specifications

Fuel Econ. (city/hwy)	Poor-20/23
Driving Range (mi.)	Long-412.2
Bumpers	
Parking Index	Very Hard
Seating	2
Tow Rating	Average-3500
Head/Leg Room (in.)	Cramped-39.3/41.4
Int. Space (cu. ft.)	Very Cramped-75
Cargo Space (cu. ft.)	Roomy-33

How the Competition Rates

	Rating	Pg.
Chevrolet Colorado		124
Dodge Dakota	7	142
Ford Ranger	6	156

Nissan Maxima

Intermediate

The Nissan Maxima has been redesigned for 2004 and has a new 3.5-liter, 265 horsepower V6 engine with an available 6-speed manual transmission option. The frame is nearly 3 inches longer than the 2003 model and the suspension is firmer. This gives the car the feel of a luxury sport sedan. There are a number of option packages available that provide traction control, an 8-speaker stereo system, and a powered glass sunroof. Dual stage airbags and side curtain airbags are some of the advanced safety features found in this sedan.

Ratings—10 Best, 1 Worst	2004	2003
Front Crash Tests	10	9
Side Crash Tests	9	9
Safety Features	9	5
Preventive Maintenance	—	6
Repair Costs	—	1
Warranty	4	3
Fuel Economy	5	5
Rollover	9	8
Complaints		10
Insurance Costs	5	5
OVERALL RATING	9	6

Price Range	Retail	Markup
SE 6sp	$26,950	9%
SE at	$26,950	9%
SL	$28,900	9%

Last Year's Model

The Maxima moved into 2003 unchanged, but there was the addition of a new Titanium Edition package option. The Maxima is powered by a 3.5-liter V6. Antilock brakes are standard and there are optional side-impact airbags available. The Maxima has child seat anchors, special headlights, and tail lamps. A navigation system is an option. Most sedans will have an automatic transmission, but an optional, five-speed manual is available.

Nissan Maxima 2003

Nissan Maxima SL

Nissan Maxima SL

Safety Checklist

Frontal Crash Test	Very Good
Side Crash Test	Very Good
Airbags (Side/Head)	Front Standard/Yes
Pretensioners/Impact Adjustors	Standard/Yes
Position/Weight Sensors	Yes/No
Seat/Head Adjustors	Yes
Roll Stability System	Yes
Child Seats Built-in	None
Antilock Brakes/Day Lamps	4-Wheel/None
Tire Pressure Monitor	None

General Information

2004 Status	All New
Series Started	2003
Where Made	Japan/US
Theft Rating	Very High
Twins	

Specifications

Fuel Econ. (city/hwy)	Average-20/28
Driving Range (mi.)	Very Long-459.0
Bumpers	Strong
Parking Index	Hard
Seating	5
Tow Rating	
Head/Leg Room (in.)	Very Roomy-40.1/43.9
Int. Space (cu. ft.)	Average-103.6
Cargo Space (cu. ft.)	Cramped-15.5

How the Competition Rates

	Rating	Pg.
Ford Taurus	9	157
Honda Accord	8	160
Pontiac Grand Am	4	227

Nissan Murano

Mid-Size SUV

The Murano was first introduced in 2003, and it gets some minor enhancements for 2004. There is a new manual shift mode found in the transmission of the SE model. A sunroof is now available as option and the Murano comes pre-wired for satellite radio. It is powered by a 3.5 liter V6 giving it nearly 240-horse power. The Murano comes with many standard safety features such as dual-stage front air bags with seat belt sensors, side-impact air bags and side curtain air bags. The Murano handles more like a car than a SUV.

Nissan Murano

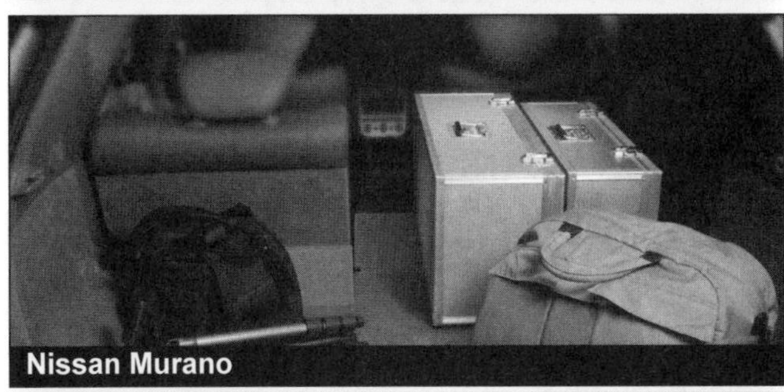

Nissan Murano

Ratings—10 Best, 1 Worst	2004	2003
Front Crash Tests	8	8
Side Crash Tests	10	10
Safety Features	7	7
Preventive Maintenance	—	—
Repair Costs	—	—
Warranty	4	3
Fuel Economy	5	5
Rollover	7	7
Complaints	—	—
Insurance Costs	5	5
OVERALL RATING	7	6

Price Range	Retail	Markup
SE 2WD	$29,800	11%
SE AWD	$31,400	11%
SL 2WD	$28,850	11%
SL AWD	$30,450	11%

Last Year's Model

The Murano was introduced in 2003 as a 5 passenger SUV with a split folding rear seat. It is powered by a 3.5 liter V6 engine and has the same CVT transmission shared with other Nissan models. Standard features include dual front airbags, seat mounted side airbags. Options include leather seating and 6-disc CD player.

Nissan Murano 2003

Safety Checklist

Frontal Crash Test	Good
Side Crash Test	Very Good
Airbags (Side/Head)	Front Standard/Yes
Pretensioners/Impact Adjustors	Yes/Yes
Position/Weight Sensors	No/No
Seat/Head Adjustors	Yes
Roll Stability System	No
Child Seats Built-in	None
Antilock Brakes/Day Lamps	4-Wheel/None
Tire Pressure Monitor	Direct

General Information

2004 Status	Unchanged
Series Started	2003
Where Made	Canada/US
Theft Rating	Average
Twins	

Specifications

Fuel Econ. (city/hwy)	Average-20/25
Driving Range (mi.)	Very Long-476.9
Bumpers	
Parking Index	Average
Seating	5
Tow Rating	Average-3500
Head/Leg Room (in.)	Very Roomy-40.7/43.4
Int. Space (cu. ft.)	Roomy-109.9
Cargo Space (cu. ft.)	Roomy-32.6

How the Competition Rates

	Rating	Pg.
Honda Pilot	6	166
Jeep Liberty	10	180
Saturn VUE	9	235

Nissan Pathfinder — Mid-Size SUV

Nissan's mid sized SUV returns unchanged. There are some new interior option packages and three new exterior colors. This year, Pathfinder is offered in both 4x2 and 4x4 drive configurations and in two models. It is powered by a 3.3-liter V6. Leather seats are available on the LE model as is satellite radio. Dual stage airbags are standard on both trim models. Side impact airbags and side curtain airbags are standard on the LE, but optional on SE. A vehicle security system with immobilizer and remote keyless entry is standard

Nissan Pathfinder

Nissan Pathfinder

Ratings—10 Best, 1 Worst	2004	2003
Front Crash Tests	8	8
Side Crash Tests	10	10
Safety Features	4	3
Preventive Maintenance	4	5
Repair Costs	6	4
Warranty	4	3
Fuel Economy	2	2
Rollover	5	5
Complaints	9	9
Insurance Costs	5	5
OVERALL RATING	7	6

Price Range	Retail	Markup
4x2 SE	$26,900	10%
4x2 LE	$31,500	10%
4x4 SE	$28,900	10%
4x4 LE	$34,550	10%

Last Year's Model

The Pathfinder debuted in 1996 and continued into 2003 with few changes. XM Satellite radio was added and there is a new leather option. Dual airbags and 4-wheel ABS are standard. A 3.3-liter V6 is the only engine choice on the Pathfinder. The base XE and mid-level SE models come with either a manual or automatic transmission. The LE comes only with an automatic transmission.

Nissan Pathfinder 2003

Safety Checklist

Frontal Crash Test	Average
Side Crash Test	Very Good
Airbags (Side/Head)	None/Yes
Pretensioners/Impact Adjustors	Yes/Yes
Position/Weight Sensors	No/No
Seat/Head Adjustors	No
Roll Stability System	No
Child Seats Built-in	None
Antilock Brakes/Day Lamps	4-Wheel/None
Tire Pressure Monitor	Direct

General Information

2004 Status	Unchanged
Series Started	1996
Where Made	Japan/Canada
Theft Rating	Very High
Twins	

Specifications

Fuel Econ. (city/hwy)	Very Poor-16/21
Driving Range (mi.)	Short-378.1
Bumpers	
Parking Index	Average
Seating	5
Tow Rating	Average-3500
Head/Leg Room (in.)	Average-39.5/41.7
Int. Space (cu. ft.)	Very Roomy-138.9
Cargo Space (cu. ft.)	Roomy-38

How the Competition Rates

	Rating	Pg.
Chevrolet Trail Blazer	2	132
Ford Explorer	8	150
Honda Pilot	6	166

Nissan Pathfinder Armada

Large SUV

The all-new 2004 Pathfinder Armada marks Nissan's entry into the full sized SUV market. It is longer than the standard Pathfinder and it has a more powerful engine: a massive 5.6-liter V8. The Armada has a 9,100 lbs towing capacity. The interior has fold flat 2nd and 3rd row bench seats for extra storage capacity. Captain's chairs are also available. A DVD entertainment system with wireless headphones is available as an option. The Armada comes equipped with dual stage airbags. Front side impact airbags are optional on the SE model, but standard on the LE.

Nissan Pathfinder Armada

Nissan Pathfinder Armada

Ratings—10 Best, 1 Worst	2004	2003
Front Crash Tests	—	
Side Crash Tests	—	
Safety Features	9	
Preventive Maintenance	—	
Repair Costs		
Warranty	4	
Fuel Economy	1	
Rollover	5	
Complaints	—	
Insurance Costs	5	
OVERALL RATING	—	

Price Range	Retail	Markup
2WD LE	$37,800	10%
2WD SE	$33,300	10%
4WD LE	$40,600	10%
4WD SE Off Road	$39,250	10%

Last Year's Model

Model Not Produced in 2003

2003

Safety Checklist

Frontal Crash Test . . . .
Side Crash Test . . . .
Airbags (Side/Head) . . . . Fr. Std. Rear Opt./Yes
Pretensioners/Impact Adjustors . . . . Standard/Yes
Position/Weight Sensors. Yes/No
Seat/Head Adjustors . . . . Yes
Roll Stability System. . . . . Yes
Child Seats Built-in . . . . None
Antilock Brakes/Day Lamps 4-Wheel/None
Tire Pressure Monitor . . . . Direct

General Information

2004 Status . . . . All New
Series Started . . . . No series indicated
Where Made. . . . . Japan
Theft Rating . . . . Average
Twins . . . .

Specifications

Fuel Econ. (city/hwy) . . . . Very Poor-13/19
Driving Range (mi.) Long-424.3
Bumpers. . . . .
Parking Index. . . . . Very Hard
Seating 7/8
Tow Rating . . . . Very High-9000
Head/Leg Room (in.) Roomy-40.9/41.8
Int. Space (cu. ft.). . . . .
Cargo Space (cu. ft.) Average-19.5

How the Competition Rates

	Rating	Pg.
Ford Expedition	5	149
Dodge Durango		143
Chevrolet Tahoe	3	130

Nissan Quest — Minivan

The Nissan Quest is all-new for 2004. Its design is a radical departure from the stereotypical minivan. The Quest combines the styling aspects of a sports car with the practicality of a minivan. The standard engine is a 3.5-liter V6. The sliding doors are the largest found on any minivan and the roof contains some unique skylights. This gives the Quest a sense of openness. It is loaded with electronic features including a 10 speaker Bose audio system and a DVD entertainment system. The Quest also has standard side curtain airbags to protect all three rows of passengers.

Nissan Quest

Nissan Quest

Ratings—10 Best, 1 Worst	2004	2003
Front Crash Tests	10	
Side Crash Tests	—	
Safety Features	9	
Preventive Maintenance	—	
Repair Costs	—	
Warranty	4	
Fuel Economy	4	
Rollover	7	
Complaints	—	
Insurance Costs	5	
OVERALL RATING	6	

Price Range	Retail	Markup
S	$24,240	8%
SE	$32,240	9%
SL	$26,740	9%

Last Year's Model

Model Not Produced in 2003

2003

Safety Checklist

Frontal Crash Test	Very Good
Side Crash Test	
Airbags (Side/Head)	Fr. Std. Rear Opt./Yes
Pretensioners/Impact Adjustors	Standard/Yes
Position/Weight Sensors	Yes/Yes
Seat/Head Adjustors	Yes
Roll Stability System	Yes
Child Seats Built-in	None
Antilock Brakes/Day Lamps	4-Wheel/None
Tire Pressure Monitor	None

General Information

2004 Status	All New
Series Started	No series indicated
Where Made	Japan
Theft Rating	Very High
Twins	

Specifications

Fuel Econ. (city/hwy)	Poor-18/25
Driving Range (mi.)	Long-411.9
Bumpers	
Parking Index	Very Hard
Seating	7
Tow Rating	Average-3500
Head/Leg Room (in.)	Roomy-41.9/41.6
Int. Space (cu. ft.)	
Cargo Space (cu. ft.)	

How the Competition Rates

	Rating	Pg.
Chrysler Town and Country	10	140
Mercury Monterey	4	205
Honda Odyssey	8	165

Nissan Sentra — Subcompact

The Sentra enters 2004 with a major appearance change. The front and rear fascias have been redesigned and there is a new look to the hood. The Sentra is offered with two engines, a 1.8-liter 4-cylinder and a 2.5-liter 4-cylinder. The interior has been upgraded, and there is a new braking option package on the SE-R model. A remote keyless entry system, power locks and windows are available. Dual front airbags are standard. The Sentra offers a solid blend safety, fuel economy, performance and economics.

Nissan Sentra SE-R

Nissan Sentra SE-R

Ratings—10 Best, 1 Worst	2004	2003
Front Crash Tests	9	9
Side Crash Tests*	2	—
Safety Features	3	3
Preventive Maintenance	10	10
Repair Costs	8	4
Warranty	4	3
Fuel Economy	9	9
Rollover	8	8
Complaints	9	9
Insurance Costs	1	1
OVERALL RATING	8	7

Price Range	Retail	Markup
Base at	$13,000	5%
S 2.5	$16,700	8%
S at	$15,000	8%
SE-R	$17,100	8%

Last Year's Model

For 2003, the Sentra got a new trim level, the sporty SE-R, which competes with the Neon R/T. A 1.8-liter four-cylinder engine powers the XE and GRE sedans. The new SE-R has a 165 hp, 2.5-liter 4-cylinder engine. Front seat side impact airbags are optional. A five-speed manual transmission is standard on the Sentra, but most consumers will purchase the optional four-speed automatic. Cloth seats are standard as well.

Nissan Sentra 2003

Safety Checklist

Frontal Crash Test	Very Good
Side Crash Test*	Very Poor
Airbags (Side/Head)	Front Standard
Pretensioners/Impact Adjustors	Yes/Yes
Position/Weight Sensors	No/No
Seat/Head Adjustors	No
Roll Stability System	No
Child Seats Built-in	None
Antilock Brakes/Day Lamps	4-Wheel (optional)/None
Tire Pressure Monitor	None

General Information

2004 Status	Major Appearance Change
Series Started	1995
Where Made	Mexico/US
Theft Rating	Very High
Twins	

Specifications

Fuel Econ. (city/hwy)	Very Good-28/35
Driving Range (mi.)	Average-400.0
Bumpers	Strong
Parking Index	Very Easy
Seating	5
Tow Rating	
Head/Leg Room (in.)	Average-39.9/41.6
Int. Space (cu. ft.)	Cramped-88.5
Cargo Space (cu. ft.)	Very Cramped-11.6

How the Competition Rates

	Rating	Pg.
Dodge Neon	8	144
Ford Focus	8	152
Honda Civic	10	161

*Side ratings are for front occupant only. Data missing for rear occupant.

Nissan Titan — Standard Pickup

The all-new 2004 Titan is Nissan's first standard sized pickup. It is powered by a massive 5.6-liter V8 engine that generates nearly 300 hp. The Titan has the highest towing capacity of its class- 9400lbs. It will be available in King and Crew Cab versions with either two-or four-wheel drive. A front bench seat is standard and power-adjusting captain's chairs are optional on SE and LE models. Front dual stage, side impact and side curtain airbags are standard on the Titan.

Nissan Titan

Ratings—10 Best, 1 Worst	2004	2003
Front Crash Tests	—	
Side Crash Tests	—	
Safety Features	8	
Preventive Maintenance	—	
Repair Costs	—	
Warranty	4	
Fuel Economy	1	
Rollover	5	
Complaints	—	
Insurance Costs	5	
OVERALL RATING	—	

Price Range	Retail	Markup
SE King Cab 4x2	$24,400	9%
LE King Cab 4x2	$28,800	9%
SE Crew Cab 4x2	$26,700	9%
LE Crew Cab 4x4	$34,200	9%

Last Year's Model

Model Not Produced in 2003

2003

Nissan Titan

Safety Checklist

Frontal Crash Test . . . . .
Side Crash Test . . . . .
Airbags (Side/Head) . . . . . Front Standard/Yes
Pretensioners/Impact Adjustors . . . . . Standard/Yes
Position/Weight Sensors. . . . . Yes/No
Seat/Head Adjustors . . . . . No
Roll Stability System. . . . . Yes
Child Seats Built-in . . . . . None
Antilock Brakes/Day Lamps 4-Wheel/None
Tire Pressure Monitor. . . . . Direct

General Information

2004 Status . . . . . All New
Series Started . . . . . No series indicated
Where Made. . . . .
Theft Rating . . . . . Average
Twins . . . . .

Specifications

Fuel Econ. (city/hwy) . . . . . Very Poor-14/19
Driving Range (mi.) . . . . . Very Long-444.7
Bumpers. . . . .
Parking Index. . . . . Very Hard
Seating. 5
Tow Rating . . . . . Very High-9400
Head/Leg Room (in.) Roomy-40.9/41.8
Int. Space (cu. ft.). . . . .
Cargo Space (cu. ft.) . . . . .

How the Competition Rates

	Rating	Pg.
Chevrolet Silverado	3	128
Dodge Ram Pickup	3	145
Ford F-Series		154

Nissan Xterra

Mid-Size SUV

For 2004, the Xterra remains unchanged. There are new wheel options for 2004 and new exterior colors. The Xterra is powered by a 3.3-liter V6 engine and an optional supercharged version produces nearly 240-horse power. Dual stage airbags are standard and side impact airbags are a stand-alone option. Cruise control is optional on base models. The Xterra comes equipped with little extras that most SUVs don't have, like a first aid kit and is roomy enough to seat 5 adults.

Nissan Xterra

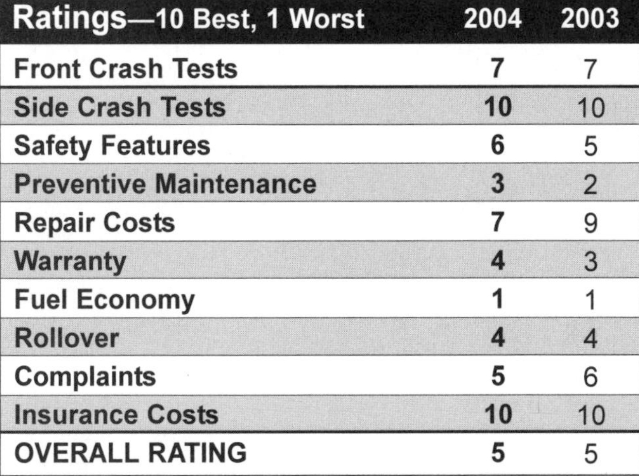

Ratings—10 Best, 1 Worst	2004	2003
Front Crash Tests	7	7
Side Crash Tests	10	10
Safety Features	6	5
Preventive Maintenance	3	2
Repair Costs	7	9
Warranty	4	3
Fuel Economy	1	1
Rollover	4	4
Complaints	5	6
Insurance Costs	10	10
OVERALL RATING	5	5

Nissan Xterra

Price Range	Retail	Markup
4x2 XE V6	$20,400	8%
4x2 SE	$24,700	2%
4x4 XE	$22,400	2%
4x4 SE V6	$26,700	8%

Last Year's Model

Nissan's Xterra rolled into 2003 with the same design but it did receive some important improvements. There is a new Dynamic Control system, which aids in tight turns. The 3.3-liter V-6 engine produces 180 hp, which is 10hp more than the 2002 versions. There are five engine/drive/trim configurations and standard 4-wheel antilock brakes. This is a youth oriented vehicle with lots of options for young buyers with active life styles.

Nissan Xterra 2003

Safety Checklist

Frontal Crash Test . . . . . Good
Side Crash Test . . . . . Very Good
Airbags (Side/Head) . . . . . No Side/Yes
Pretensioners/Impact Adjustors . . . . . Yes/Yes
Position/Weight Sensors . . . . . No/No
Seat/Head Adjustors . . . . . No
Roll Stability System . . . . . No
Child Seats Built-in . . . . . None
Antilock Brakes/Day Lamps 4-Wheel/None
Tire Pressure Monitor . . . . . Direct

General Information

2004 Status . . . . . Unchanged
Series Started 2000
Where Made . . . . . US/Japan
Theft Rating . . . . . Very High
Twins . . . . .

Specifications

Fuel Econ. (city/hwy) . . . . . Very Poor-15/19
Driving Range (mi.) . . . . . Very Short-321.5
Bumpers . . . . .
Parking Index . . . . . Easy
Seating 5
Tow Rating Average-3500
Head/Leg Room (in.) Cramped-38.6/41.4
Int. Space (cu. ft.) . . . . .
Cargo Space (cu. ft.) . . . . . Very Roomy-44.5

How the Competition Rates

	Rating	Pg.
Ford Escape	8	147
Isuzu Axiom	6	177
Hyundai Santa Fe	9	170

Oldsmobile Alero — Compact

The Alero remains completely unchanged for 2004. Antilock brakes are optional, daytime running lights and side impact bars are standard. An anti theft device disables the engine if there is tampering detected. A 2.2-liter inline 4-cylinder is standard, a 3.4-liter V-6 is optional and the standard transmission is a 4-speed automatic. XM radio is offered and leather seats are an option on most models. Safety features include dual airbags and antilock brakes. The Alero offers excellent fuel economy with 24 mpg in the city and 32 mpg on the highway.

Oldsmobile Alero

Oldsmobile Alero

Ratings—10 Best, 1 Worst	2004	2003
Front Crash Tests*	9	9
Side Crash Tests*	5	5
Safety Features	3	3
Preventive Maintenance	4	3
Repair Costs	4	5
Warranty	—	7
Fuel Economy	8	8
Rollover	9	9
Complaints	4	5
Insurance Costs	1	1
OVERALL RATING	6	4

Price Range	Retail	Markup
GL1 Sedan	$20,150	9%
GL2 Sedan	$21,700	9%
GLS Sedan	$22,800	10%
GX 2D	$18,200	7%

Last Year's Model

There were no changes to the compact Alero except some new exterior colors and XM Satellite Radio as an option. The car still uses the 2.2-liter inline 4-cylinder, but you can upgrade to the 3.4-liter V6. The rearrangement of the alternator, compressor, and power steering pump has reduced noise. Safety features include dual airbags and antilock brakes. With great crash test scores, the Alero competes with the Taurus/Accord/Camry trio.

Oldsmobile Alero 2003

Safety Checklist

Frontal Crash Test*	Very Good
Side Crash Test*	Average
Airbags (Side/Head)	Front Standard
Pretensioners/Impact Adjustors	None/No
Position/Weight Sensors	No/No
Seat/Head Adjustors	No
Roll Stability System	No
Child Seats Built-in	None
Antilock Brakes/Day Lamps	4-Wheel/Standard
Tire Pressure Monitor	Indirect

General Information

2004 Status	Unchanged
Series Started	1999
Where Made	US
Theft Rating	Very High
Twins	

Specifications

Fuel Econ. (city/hwy)	Good-24/33
Driving Range (mi.)	Average-385.7
Bumpers	Weak
Parking Index	Easy
Seating	5
Tow Rating	Very Low-1000
Head/Leg Room (in.)	Cramped-38.3/42.1
Int. Space (cu. ft.)	Cramped-91.2
Cargo Space (cu. ft.)	Cramped-14.6

How the Competition Rates

	Rating	Pg.
Chevrolet Malibu		126
Honda Accord	8	160
Volkswagen Passat	8	265

*Ratings based on 4-door model. For 2-door crash results, see page 24.

Pontiac Aztek

Mid-Size SUV

For 2004, the Aztec has a few changes and is available in front-wheel and all-wheel drive versions. Antilock brakes, traction control, side impact airbags, driver head protection, and a vehicle tracker system to find your vehicle if it's stolen are optional. A 3.4-liter V-6 engine provides 185 horsepower. A Rally Edition is available with lowered front suspension and a cargo area speaker system. A camping package is also offered, which includes a tent and awning that fits onto the rear of the vehicle.

Ratings—10 Best, 1 Worst	2004	2003
Front Crash Tests	7	7
Side Crash Tests	9	9
Safety Features	3	3
Preventive Maintenance	6	—
Repair Costs	3	3
Warranty	2	3
Fuel Economy	4	5
Rollover	7	7
Complaints	5	2
Insurance Costs	10	10
OVERALL RATING	5	5

Price Range	Retail	Markup
AWD	$23,895	9%
FWD	$20,995	9%

Last Year's Model

For 2003, the Aztek remained unchanged on the outside, but the inside was a different story. There were new seating fabrics and new interior colors. Pontiac has loaded their unconventional vehicle with a DVD entertainment system and XM Satellite Radio. A 3.4-liter V6 engine powers the Aztek. Other improvements come in the form of a tire pressure monitoring system and new exterior colors. The Aztek was on of the first car based SUVs.

Pontiac Aztek

Pontiac Aztek Rally

Pontiac Aztek Rally

Safety Checklist

Frontal Crash Test	Good
Side Crash Test	Very Good
Airbags (Side/Head)	Front Standard
Pretensioners/Impact Adjustors	None/No
Position/Weight Sensors	No/No
Seat/Head Adjustors	No
Roll Stability System	No
Child Seats Built-in	None
Antilock Brakes/Day Lamps	4-Wheel/Standard
Tire Pressure Monitor	Indirect

General Information

2004 Status	Unchanged
Series Started	2001
Where Made	Canada
Theft Rating	Very Low
Twins	

Specifications

Fuel Econ. (city/hwy)	Poor-19/26
Driving Range (mi.)	Average-389.1
Bumpers	Strong
Parking Index	Easy
Seating	5
Tow Rating	Average-3500
Head/Leg Room (in.)	Cramped-39.7/40.5
Int. Space (cu. ft.)	Roomy-105.1
Cargo Space (cu. ft.)	Very Roomy-93.5

How the Competition Rates

	Rating	Pg.
Honda Pilot	6	166
Isuzu Axiom	6	177
Nissan Murano	7	217

Pontiac Bonneville — Large

For 2004, the Bonneville has a new model called the GPX, which replaces the SSEi. The GPX comes with a 275 horsepower 4.6-liter V-8 engine and GM's StabiliTrak stability control system as standard equipment. A high quality audio system is also standard. The unchanged SE and SLE models have a 3.8-liter V6 as their standard engine. Other features include keyless entry, an alarm system, and a tire pressure monitor. XM satellite radio is optional on most models.

Pontiac Bonneville GXP

Pontiac Bonneville GXP

Ratings—10 Best, 1 Worst	2004	2003
Front Crash Tests	9	9
Side Crash Tests	9	9
Safety Features	4	4
Preventive Maintenance	4	4
Repair Costs	5	6
Warranty	2	3
Fuel Economy	3	4
Rollover	10	10
Complaints	6	8
Insurance Costs	10	10
OVERALL RATING	7	8

Price Range	Retail	Markup
SE	$26,845	9%
SLE	$29,695	9%

Last Year's Model

In 2003, there were minor improvements on the Bonneville, particularly to the bucket seats, which are standard. XM Satellite Radio is optional on all models. The SSEi has a 3.8-liter supercharged V6. The entry and mid-range Bonnevilles have a 3.8-liter V6 without the supercharger. All models have an automatic transmission as standard. The SSEi version has an improved suspension, a driver's heads-up display, and optional leather seating.

Pontiac Bonneville 2003

Safety Checklist

Frontal Crash Test	Very Good
Side Crash Test	Very Good
Airbags (Side/Head)	Front Standard
Pretensioners/Impact Adjustors	None/No
Position/Weight Sensors	No/No
Seat/Head Adjustors	No
Roll Stability System	Yes
Child Seats Built-in	None
Antilock Brakes/Day Lamps	4-Wheel/Standard
Tire Pressure Monitor	Indirect

General Information

2004 Status	Minor Appearance Change
Series Started	2000
Where Made	US
Theft Rating	Very Low
Twins	Buick LeSabre, Cadillac Seville 2004

Specifications

Fuel Econ. (city/hwy)	Poor-17/27
Driving Range (mi.)	Short-377.4
Bumpers	Strong
Parking Index	Very Hard
Seating	5/6
Tow Rating	Very Low-1000
Head/Leg Room (in.)	Average-38.7/42.6
Int. Space (cu. ft.)	Very Roomy-121.8
Cargo Space (cu. ft.)	Average-18

How the Competition Rates

	Rating	Pg.
Buick LeSabre	7	109
Cadillac CTS	7	110
Chrysler 300M	10	134

Pontiac Grand Am — Intermediate

The only changes implemented in the 2004 Grand AM have to do with the audio system. A four-speaker sound system is now standard with an optional MP3 player. Depending on the model, there is a choice of three engines: a 2.2L I-4, a 170 horsepower 3.4L V-6, or a 175 horsepower 3.4L Ram-Air V-6. The standard features on the 2004 Grand Am include a CD player, a leather-wrapped steering wheel with integrated radio controls, and a remote keyless entry system.

Pontiac Grand Am

Ratings—10 Best, 1 Worst	2004	2003
Front Crash Tests*	9	9
Side Crash Tests*	5	5
Safety Features	2	2
Preventive Maintenance	4	3
Repair Costs	5	4
Warranty	2	3
Fuel Economy	8	8
Rollover	9	9
Complaints	—	—
Insurance Costs	1	1
OVERALL RATING	4	3

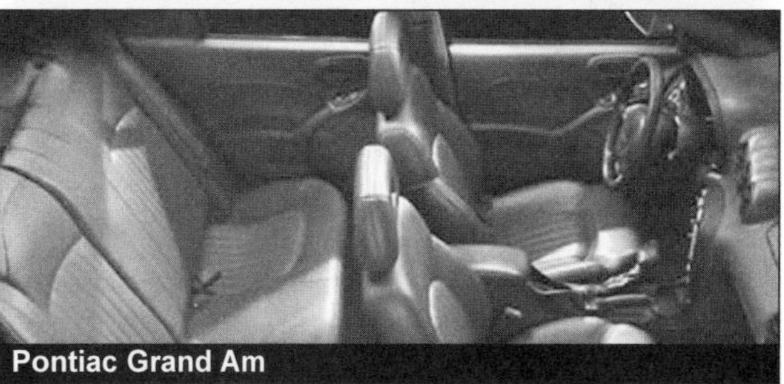
Pontiac Grand Am

Safety Checklist

Frontal Crash Test*	Very Good
Side Crash Test*	Average
Airbags (Side/Head)	No Side
Pretensioners/Impact Adjustors	None/No
Position/Weight Sensors	No/No
Seat/Head Adjustors	No
Roll Stability System	No
Child Seats Built-in	None
Antilock Brakes/Day Lamps	4-Wheel/Standard
Tire Pressure Monitor	None

Price Range	Retail	Markup
GT Coupe	$21,825	9%
GT1 Sedan	$23,075	9%
SE	$17,070	9%
SE2	$21,375	9%

General Information

2004 Status	Unchanged
Series Started	2002
Where Made	US
Theft Rating	Very High
Twins	

Last Year's Model

The Grand AM received minor exterior changes, a new trim level, and exterior color options in 2003. OnStar is now standard in all models except the base SE model. The coupe version SE has been dropped. The GT/GT1 coupes remain unchanged. A 4-cylinder engine is more fuel-efficient than last year's model but with the same power. ABS, tilt steering wheel, air conditioning, and an anti-theft system are standard.

Specifications

Fuel Econ. (city/hwy)	Good-24/33
Driving Range (mi.)	Average-385.7
Bumpers	Strong
Parking Index	Easy
Seating	5
Tow Rating	Very Low-1000
Head/Leg Room (in.)	Cramped-38.3/42.1
Int. Space (cu. ft.)	Cramped-92.2
Cargo Space (cu. ft.)	Cramped-14.6

Pontiac Grand Am

How the Competition Rates

	Rating	Pg.
Chrysler Sebring	10	138
Ford Taurus	9	157
Oldsmobile Alero	6	224

*Ratings based on 4-door model. For 2-door crash results, see page 24.

Pontiac Grand Prix — Large

The all-new 2004 Grand Prix has a number of improvements designed to help it stay competitive in the intermediate sport sedan market. It has a new 260 horsepower 3.8-liter V-6 engine. The Comp G package offers a supercharged version of this engine along with an improved suspension system. Another option is the heads up display that allows the car to be operated with the instrument lights off. Additional improvements include antilock brakes a vehicle stability enhancement system, wider opening doors, and a bigger trunk.

Ratings—10 Best, 1 Worst	2004	2003
Front Crash Tests	7	7
Side Crash Tests	6	5
Safety Features	4	2
Preventive Maintenance	—	5
Repair Costs	—	8
Warranty	2	3
Fuel Economy	6	6
Rollover	10	10
Complaints	6	7
Insurance Costs	5	5
OVERALL RATING	6	6

Price Range	Retail	Markup
GT1	$21,760	9%
GT2	$23,660	9%
GTP	$25,860	9%

Last Year's Model

There were no major changes for the Grand Prix in 2003. It comes in coupe or sedan versions and three trim levels. You can choose from the base SE, sporty GT or the GTP with a high performance engine. In addition to the standard 3.1-liter V6 engine, you have the choice of a powerful 3.8-liter 175 hp V6. The interior is comfortable and the headroom is average. GM'S OnStar system is available as an option.

Pontiac Grand Prix 2003

Pontiac Grand Prix GTP

Pontiac Grand Prix GTP

Safety Checklist

Frontal Crash Test	Good
Side Crash Test	Average
Airbags (Side/Head)	No Side/Yes
Pretensioners/Impact Adjustors	None/No
Position/Weight Sensors	No/No
Seat/Head Adjustors	No
Roll Stability System	No
Child Seats Built-in	None
Antilock Brakes/Day Lamps	4-Wheel/Standard
Tire Pressure Monitor	None

General Information

2004 Status	All New
Series Started	1997
Where Made	US
Theft Rating	Very High
Twins	Chevrolet Impala, Chevrolet Monte Carlo 2004

Specifications

Fuel Econ. (city/hwy)	Average-20/30
Driving Range (mi.)	Average-400.0
Bumpers	
Parking Index	Hard
Seating	5
Tow Rating	
Head/Leg Room (in.)	Cramped-38.5/42.4
Int. Space (cu. ft.)	Roomy-114
Cargo Space (cu. ft.)	Cramped-16

How the Competition Rates

	Rating	Pg.
Chrysler 300M	10	134
Cadillac CTS	7	114
Lincoln LS		196

Pontiac GTO — Compact

Pontiac brings back the GTO in 2004. This high-powered "muscle" car comes equipped with a massive 5.7-liter V8 which is also used on the Corvette. The driver has a choice of a six-speed manual or a four-speed automatic transmission. Four-wheel antilock brakes and bucket seats are standard. Dual stage front airbags, three point safety belts, and an Emergency Mode system, which deactivates the engine and fuel pump in the event of an accident, are standard. A six-speaker audio system, keyless entry, and a multi-functional driver information display are also available.

Ratings—10 Best, 1 Worst	2004	2003
Front Crash Tests	—	
Side Crash Tests	—	
Safety Features	3	
Preventive Maintenance	—	
Repair Costs	—	
Warranty	2	
Fuel Economy	2	
Rollover	10	
Complaints	—	
Insurance Costs	5	
OVERALL RATING	—	

Price Range	Retail	Markup
Base Coupe	$31,795	8%

Last Year's Model

Model Not Produced in 2003

2003

Pontiac GTO

Pontiac GTO

Safety Checklist

Frontal Crash Test	
Side Crash Test	
Airbags (Side/Head)	Front Standard
Pretensioners/Impact Adjustors	Standard/Yes
Position/Weight Sensors	No/No
Seat/Head Adjustors	No
Roll Stability System	No
Child Seats Built-in	None
Antilock Brakes/Day Lamps	4-Wheel/Standard
Tire Pressure Monitor	None

General Information

2004 Status	All New
Series Started	No series indicated
Where Made	US
Theft Rating	Average
Twins	

Specifications

Fuel Econ. (city/hwy)	Very Poor-16/21
Driving Range (mi.)	Very Short-331.5
Bumpers	
Parking Index	Average
Seating	4
Tow Rating	Very Low-1000
Head/Leg Room (in.)	Very Cramped-37.3/42.2
Int. Space (cu. ft.)	
Cargo Space (cu. ft.)	

How the Competition Rates

	Rating	Pg.
Mazda RX-8		201
Infiniti G35		175
Nissan 350Z	7	213

Pontiac Vibe/Toyota Matrix — Compact

For 2004, the Pontiac Vibe/Toyota Matrix remains unchanged. Both are built on the same platform and are powered by the same engine. The standard 1.8-liter engine can be upgraded to the more powerful engine found on the Celica. The Vibe now offers XM Satellite Radio as an option. The Matrix comes equally equipped with a keyless entry system, cruise control and an advance audio system. A DVD based navigation system is offered as an option in both vehicles. Both are targeted at younger buyers needing the utility of an SUV at the price of a car.

Pontiac Vibe

Ratings—10 Best, 1 Worst	2004	2003
Front Crash Tests	10	10
Side Crash Tests	10	10
Safety Features	4	4
Preventive Maintenance	10	—
Repair Costs	6	—
Warranty	2	3
Fuel Economy	9	9
Rollover	7	7
Complaints	—	—
Insurance Costs	5	5
OVERALL RATING	9	7

Toyota Matrix

Price Range	Retail	Markup
4D Utility Base	$16,485	7%
4D Utility AWD	$19,785	7%
GT Utility	$19,435	7%

Safety Checklist

Frontal Crash Test	Very Good
Side Crash Test	Very Good
Airbags (Side/Head)	Front Standard
Pretensioners/Impact Adjustors	/Yes
Position/Weight Sensors	No/No
Seat/Head Adjustors	No
Roll Stability System	No
Child Seats Built-in	None
Antilock Brakes/Day Lamps	4-Wheel/Standard
Tire Pressure Monitor	None

General Information

2004 Status	Unchanged
Series Started	2003
Where Made	US
Theft Rating	Average
Twins	Toyota Matrix 2004

Last Year's Model

Brand new for 2003, these compact hatchbacks, have a 1.5 liter 180 hp engine. Targeted at younger buyers, the Vibe/Matrix offers a roomy interior and several electronic packages including an optional DVD based navigation system. Safety features such as daytime running lamps, delay-entry lighting and all-wheel drive are available on these hatchbacks. The Vibe/Matrix has excellent crash test results.

Pontiac Vibe 2003

Specifications

Fuel Econ. (city/hwy)	Very Good-28/33
Driving Range (mi.)	Average-396.6
Bumpers	
Parking Index	Easy
Seating	5
Tow Rating	Very Low-1500
Head/Leg Room (in.)	Roomy-40.6/41.8
Int. Space (cu. ft.)	Roomy-111.5
Cargo Space (cu. ft.)	Average-19.3

How the Competition Rates

	Rating	Pg.
Honda Element	4	163
Chrysler PT Cruiser	9	137
Subaru Outback	9	242

*Ratings are for Pontiac Vibe.

Saab 9-3 | Compact

The 2004 Saab 9-3 now offers a convertible. Saab has introduced a number of safety features including four layers of steel reinforcement on the windshield frame and cabin. There are automatic pop-up roll bars on the rear seats to help protect the passengers and the front seats quickly power forward to let back seat passengers in. A number of braking and stability control systems come standard on the sedan and convertible. Aimed at younger buyers, the sedan and convertible are powered by the same 2.4-liter turbo charged four-cylinder engine.

Saab 9-3 Sedan

Ratings—10 Best, 1 Worst	2004	2003
Front Crash Tests	—	—
Side Crash Tests	—	—
Safety Features	10	9
Preventive Maintenance	—	3
Repair Costs	—	4
Warranty	7	7
Fuel Economy	7	7
Rollover	9	9
Complaints	—	—
Insurance Costs	5	5
OVERALL RATING	—	—

Saab 9-3 Convertible

Price Range	Retail	Markup
Convertible Arc	$39,995	6%
Sport Sedan Arc	$30,185	6%
Sport Sedan Linear	$26,090	6%

Safety Checklist

Frontal Crash Test	
Side Crash Test	
Airbags (Side/Head)	Front Standard/Yes
Pretensioners/Impact Adjustors	Yes/Yes
Position/Weight Sensors	Yes/Yes
Seat/Head Adjustors	Yes
Roll Stability System	Yes
Child Seats Built-in	None
Antilock Brakes/Day Lamps	4-Wheel/Standard
Tire Pressure Monitor	None

General Information

2004 Status	Unchanged
Series Started	2003
Where Made	Sweden
Theft Rating	Very Low
Twins	

Last Year's Model

The Saab 9-3 was completely redesigned for 2003. It has a longer wheelbase and new 5-speed automatic and 6-speed manual transmissions that improve the performance of the standard 2.0-liter inline turbo engine. Safety features include: second-generation active head restraints, load-limiting seatbelts, dual and side curtain airbags. A driver's heads up display is also available which displays key instruments right on the windshield.

Saab 9-3 2003

Specifications

Fuel Econ. (city/hwy)	Good-22/31
Driving Range (mi.)	Long-415.0
Bumpers	Strong
Parking Index	Easy
Seating	5
Tow Rating	Average-4340
Head/Leg Room (in.)	Average-38.9/42.3
Int. Space (cu. ft.)	Cramped-90
Cargo Space (cu. ft.)	Cramped-15

How the Competition Rates

	Rating	Pg.
BMW 3 Series	9	104
Infiniti G35		175
Volvo 40 Series		267

Saab 9-5 — Intermediate

The 2004 Saab 9-5 is available in Linear, Arc, and Aero models. Safety features include an electronic stabilization system, dual airbags, and side impact airbags. There is extensive head protection including Saab's new active head restraints and side curtain airbags. A 2.3-liter inline turbo charged engine is standard. New bi-xenon headlamps are optional on the Arc and Aero models. A five-speed manual transmission is standard, but you can upgrade to a five-speed automatic. The 9-5 performed well in government crash tests.

Saab 9-5 Sedan

Ratings—10 Best, 1 Worst	2004	2003
Front Crash Tests	10	10
Side Crash Tests	10	10
Safety Features	8	8
Preventive Maintenance	5	3
Repair Costs	2	3
Warranty	7	7
Fuel Economy	5	6
Rollover	8	9
Complaints	8	7
Insurance Costs	10	10
OVERALL RATING	**10**	10

Saab 9-5 Sport Wagon

Price Range	Retail	Markup
Sedan Aero	$39,465	7%
Sedan Arc	$34,430	7%
Sport Wagon Arc	$35,140	7%
Sport Wagon Linear	$32,200	6%

Last Year's Model

The 9-5 received improvements to its electronics in 2003, which included an electronic stability system and a Homelink garage door opener. The 2.3-liter inline turbo is standard for the Linear wagon and the Arc. The five-speed manual transmission comes with a hydraulic clutch to aid shifting. Antilock brakes, dual airbags and side impact airbags provide protection in the event of an accident. The 9-5 did well in government crash tests.

Saab 9-5 2003

Safety Checklist

Frontal Crash Test	Very Good
Side Crash Test	Very Good
Airbags (Side/Head)	Front Standard/Yes
Pretensioners/Impact Adjustors	Yes/Yes
Position/Weight Sensors	No/No
Seat/Head Adjustors	Yes
Roll Stability System	Yes
Child Seats Built-in	None
Antilock Brakes/Day Lamps	4-Wheel/Standard
Tire Pressure Monitor	None

General Information

2004 Status	Unchanged
Series Started	1999
Where Made	Sweden
Theft Rating	Very Low
Twins	

Specifications

Fuel Econ. (city/hwy)	A verage-20/29
Driving Range (mi.)	Long-430.1
Bumpers	Strong
Parking Index	Average
Seating	5
Tow Rating	
Head/Leg Room (in.)	Average-38.7/42.4
Int. Space (cu. ft.)	Cramped-96.2
Cargo Space (cu. ft.)	Cramped-15.9

How the Competition Rates

	Rating	Pg.
Honda Accord	8	160
Nissan Maxima	9	216
Volkswagen Passat	8	265

Saturn ION — Compact

Unchanged on the outside, the 2004 ION's interior has been freshened-up. A new Red Line trim model has been introduced as a sportier version of the ION. It comes with a 200 horsepower 2.0-liter supercharged 4-cylinder engine, and better handling than standard ION models. The ION's safety features are average for a car of its size and side curtain airbags are optional. An engine immobilizer, standard on every ION, provides basic theft prevention.

Saturn ION

Ratings—10 Best, 1 Worst	2004	2003
Front Crash Tests	10	10
Side Crash Tests*	4	—
Safety Features	7	5
Preventive Maintenance	8	—
Repair Costs	9	—
Warranty	2	3
Fuel Economy	8	8
Rollover	8	8
Complaints	—	—
Insurance Costs	5	5
OVERALL RATING	9	6

Price Range	Retail	Markup
Coupe 3	$16,685	7%
Sedan 1	$10,430	8%
Sedan 2	$13,735	8%
Sedan 3	$15,260	8%

Last Year's Model

The ION was all-new in 2003. Powered by a 137 hp, 2.2-liter four-cylinder engine, the ION is geared toward younger buyers. The control console is tilted toward the driver, an anti theft device is standard, and a remote keyless entry system is optional. An In-dash CD player, automatic dimming mirrors, programmable automatic locks, and GM's OnStar are some of the electronic options available on the ION

Saturn ION — 2003

Saturn ION Quad Coupe

Safety Checklist

Frontal Crash Test	Very Good
Side Crash Test*	Poor
Airbags (Side/Head)	Front Standard/Yes
Pretensioners/Impact Adjustors	Yes/Yes
Position/Weight Sensors	NA/NA
Seat/Head Adjustors	No
Roll Stability System	Yes
Child Seats Built-in	None
Antilock Brakes/Day Lamps	4-Wheel (opt.)/Standard
Tire Pressure Monitor	None

General Information

2004 Status	Unchanged
Series Started	2003
Where Made	US
Theft Rating	Average
Twins	

Specifications

Fuel Econ. (city/hwy)	Good-24/32
Driving Range (mi.)	Short-365.1
Bumpers	
Parking Index	Easy
Seating	5
Tow Rating	Very Low-1000
Head/Leg Room (in.)	Roomy-40/42.2
Int. Space (cu. ft.)	Cramped-93
Cargo Space (cu. ft.)	Cramped-14.7

How the Competition Rates

	Rating	Pg.
Dodge Neon	8	144
Honda Civic	10	161
Kia Optima	8	183

*Side rating for rear occupant only.

Saturn L/LW — Intermediate

The Saturn L/LW series has been limited to the L300 sedan and wagon models for 2004. Antilock brakes, traction control, side curtain airbags and automatic headlamps are standard on all models. The base sedan and wagon is equipped with a 140 horsepower 2.2-liter inline four-cylinder. The upgraded versions of the sedan and wagon have a 182 horsepower 3.0L V-6. L300 wagon has a DVD entertainment system and OnStar as an option and the sedan has an optional sunroof. A manual transmission is no longer offered. All models come with a 4-speed automatic transmission.

Saturn L300

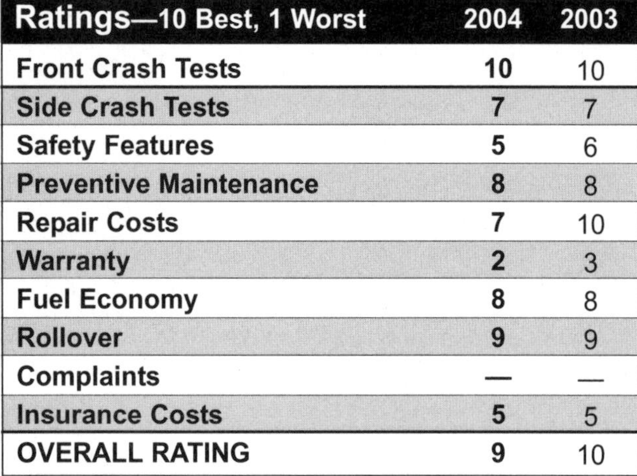

Ratings—10 Best, 1 Worst	2004	2003
Front Crash Tests	10	10
Side Crash Tests	7	7
Safety Features	5	6
Preventive Maintenance	8	8
Repair Costs	7	10
Warranty	2	3
Fuel Economy	8	8
Rollover	9	9
Complaints	—	—
Insurance Costs	5	5
OVERALL RATING	9	10

Price Range	Retail	Markup
Sedan 1	$16,370	9%
Sedan 2	$20,785	9%
Station Wagon 1	$18,420	9%
Station Wagon 2	$22,935	9%

Last Year's Model

The L Series received new styling for the interior and exterior in 2003. These improvements included wrap around headlamps, an optional fog lamp, and a raised hood and brush nickeled finish on the control surfaces. New electronic upgrades include DVD entertainment system as an option. New safety systems included a new child seat restraint system and center rear three point seatbelt. OnStar is now available as an option.

Saturn L 2003

Saturn LW300

Safety Checklist

Frontal Crash Test	Very Good
Side Crash Test	Good
Airbags (Side/Head)	Front Standard/Yes
Pretensioners/Impact Adjustors	None/Yes
Position/Weight Sensors	No/No
Seat/Head Adjustors	No
Roll Stability System	No
Child Seats Built-in	None
Antilock Brakes/Day Lamps	4-Wheel (opt.)/Standard
Tire Pressure Monitor	None

General Information

2004 Status	Unchanged
Series Started	2000
Where Made	US
Theft Rating	Very Low
Twins	

Specifications

Fuel Econ. (city/hwy)	Good-24/32
Driving Range (mi.)	Long-424.6
Bumpers	
Parking Index	Average
Seating	5
Tow Rating	Very Low-1000
Head/Leg Room (in.)	Average-39.3/42.3
Int. Space (cu. ft.)	Cramped-96.9
Cargo Space (cu. ft.)	Average-17.5

How the Competition Rates

	Rating	Pg.
Chevrolet Malibu		126
Honda Accord	8	160
Hyundai Elantra	10	169

Saturn VUE

Mid-Size SUV

Only minor changes were implemented for the 2004 VUE. Dual-stage front air bags, which deploy at a lower velocity for less severe crashes, have been introduced along with front seat-belt pretensioners. The fuel tank is larger this year. A CD player, DVD entertainment system and XM satellite radio are available. Heated seats and lumbar supports are optional. A sport version called Red Line has also been introduced this year. A more powerful 250 horsepower 3.5L-liter V-6 engine replaces the 3.0-liter V6 engine as an option.

Saturn VUE

Saturn VUE

Ratings—10 Best, 1 Worst	2004	2003
Front Crash Tests	9	9
Side Crash Tests	10	10
Safety Features	6	4
Preventive Maintenance	7	—
Repair Costs	7	—
Warranty	2	3
Fuel Economy	7	7
Rollover	6	6
Complaints	—	—
Insurance Costs	10	10
OVERALL RATING	9	6

Price Range	Retail	Markup
AWD 4-cyl.	$20,010	7%
AWD V6	$23,610	7%
FWD 4-cyl.	$16,775	7%
FWD V6	$21,960	7%

Last Year's Model

In 2003 the Saturn Vue received some minor changes. These included optional heated leather seats, advanced audio systems, new exterior colors and a V6 option for these front wheel drive vehicles. Head curtain side airbags as well as, standard dual stage airbags are among the safety features. An automatic transmission is standard on V6 powered VUE models. The interior space is average for this midsized SUV.

Saturn VUE 2003

Safety Checklist

Frontal Crash Test	Very Good
Side Crash Test	Very Good
Airbags (Side/Head)	Front Standard/Yes
Pretensioners/Impact Adjustors	None/No
Position/Weight Sensors	No/No
Seat/Head Adjustors	No
Roll Stability System	Yes
Child Seats Built-in	None
Antilock Brakes/Day Lamps	4-Wheel (opt.)/Standard
Tire Pressure Monitor	None

General Information

2004 Status	Minor Appearance Change
Series Started	2002
Where Made	US
Theft Rating	Average
Twins	

Specifications

Fuel Econ. (city/hwy)	Good-22/28
Driving Range (mi.)	Short-377.4
Bumpers	
Parking Index	Hard
Seating	5
Tow Rating	Very Low-1500
Head/Leg Room (in.)	Average-40.4/41.2
Int. Space (cu. ft.)	Average-100
Cargo Space (cu. ft.)	Roomy-30.8

How the Competition Rates

	Rating	Pg.
Honda Pilot	6	166
Jeep Liberty	10	180
Nissan Xterra	5	223

Scion xA — Subcompact

The Scion is a youth oriented division of Toyota. The all-new xA is a subcompact hatchback designed to give affordable, practical transportation to young, first time buyers. A 108 horsepower, 1.5-liter four-cylinder engine powers the xA. About 40 different accessories including fog lamps, a front-end mask, rear spoiler and audio equipment will be available. A manual transmission is standard, but an automatic is optional. Some of the standard safety equipment includes antilock brakes and dual stage front airbags Side airbags are not offered.

Scion xA

Scion xA

Ratings—10 Best, 1 Worst	2004	2003
Front Crash Tests	—	
Side Crash Tests	—	
Safety Features	7	
Preventive Maintenance	—	
Repair Costs	—	
Warranty	3	
Fuel Economy	10	
Rollover	7	
Complaints	—	
Insurance Costs	5	
OVERALL RATING	—	

Price Range	Retail	Markup
XA 5M	$12,480	5%
XA LE 4ECTi	$13,280	5%

Last Year's Model

Model Not Produced in 2003

2003

Safety Checklist

Frontal Crash Test	
Side Crash Test	
Airbags (Side/Head)	No Side/Yes
Pretensioners/Impact Adjustors	Standard/Yes
Position/Weight Sensors	Yes/No
Seat/Head Adjustors	No
Roll Stability System	Yes
Child Seats Built-in	None
Antilock Brakes/Day Lamps	4-Wheel/None
Tire Pressure Monitor	None

General Information

2004 Status	All New
Series Started	No series indicated
Where Made	
Theft Rating	Average
Twins	

Specifications

Fuel Econ. (city/hwy)	Very Good-32/38
Driving Range (mi.)	Long-409.9
Bumpers	
Parking Index	Very Easy
Seating	5
Tow Rating	
Head/Leg Room (in.)	Cramped-39.6/41.3
Int. Space (cu. ft.)	Very Cramped-86
Cargo Space (cu. ft.)	Very Cramped-11.7

How the Competition Rates

	Rating	Pg.
Chevrolet Aveo		121
Ford Focus	8	152
Mitsubishi Lancer	7	210

Scion xB — Subcompact

The Scion xB is all-new for 2004. This subcompact van is designed to attracted younger buyers with its practicality and hip image. The same 1.5-liter, 4-cylinder engine that powers its cousin, the xA, powers the xB. The second row seats can fold flat or be removed. Standard features include air conditioning, keyless entry, and power windows and locks. There is a CD player with MP3 capability as well. Safety features included antilock brakes and a stability control system. Side impact airbags are not available.

Scion xB

Scion xB

Ratings—10 Best, 1 Worst	2004	2003
Front Crash Tests	—	
Side Crash Tests	—	
Safety Features	7	
Preventive Maintenance	—	
Repair Costs	—	
Warranty	3	
Fuel Economy	10	
Rollover	5	
Complaints	—	
Insurance Costs	5	
OVERALL RATING	—	

Price Range	Retail	Markup
xB 5-sp.	$13,680	5%
xB AT	$14,480	5%

Last Year's Model

Model Not Produced in 2003

2003

Safety Checklist

Frontal Crash Test	
Side Crash Test	
Airbags (Side/Head)	No Side/Yes
Pretensioners/Impact Adjustors	Standard/Yes
Position/Weight Sensors	Yes/No
Seat/Head Adjustors	No
Roll Stability System	Yes
Child Seats Built-in	None
Antilock Brakes/Day Lamps	4-Wheel/None
Tire Pressure Monitor	None

General Information

2004 Status	All New
Series Started	No series indicated
Where Made	
Theft Rating	Average
Twins	

Specifications

Fuel Econ. (city/hwy)	Very Good-31/35
Driving Range (mi.)	Average-388.9
Bumpers	Weak
Parking Index	Very Easy
Seating	5
Tow Rating	
Head/Leg Room (in.)	Very Roomy-46.1/45.3
Int. Space (cu. ft.)	Cramped-90.2
Cargo Space (cu. ft.)	Average-21.2

How the Competition Rates

	Rating	Pg.
Honda Element	4	163
Hyundai Accent	10	168
Kia Rio	7	184

Subaru Baja

Mid-Size SUV

For 2004, the Baja gets a new Turbo version in its line up which has a new front hood scope for the engine. The Baja is configured to be a four-passenger vehicle. The cargo bed can hold two full sized mountain bikes with a special bed extension in place. A 2.5-liter 4-cylinder engine powers the baseline Baja. All-wheel drive is standard. Fog lamps and power door locks are also available. The Turbo offers 6-way power driver's seats with manual lumbar support. Cruise control is standard. Subaru's warranty includes roadside assistance.

Ratings—10 Best, 1 Worst	2004	2003
Front Crash Tests	—	—
Side Crash Tests	—	—
Safety Features	5	4
Preventive Maintenance	—	—
Repair Costs	—	—
Warranty	3	4
Fuel Economy	5	6
Rollover	6	6
Complaints	—	—
Insurance Costs	5	5
OVERALL RATING	—	—

Price Range	Retail	Markup
Subaru Baja	TBA	

Last Year's Model

The Baja crossover vehicle was all-new in 2003. The Baja's interior is similar to Legacy's and can seat four passengers. The expandable cargo bed is designed to hold such equipment as mountain bikes, so there is plenty of room in the back for just about anything. Subaru's 2.5-liter 4-cylinder engine powers the Baja. All-wheel drive is standard as are dual stage front airbags.

Subaru Baja 2003

Subaru Baja Turbo

Subaru Baja Turbo

Safety Checklist

Frontal Crash Test	
Side Crash Test	
Airbags (Side/Head)	Front Standard
Pretensioners/Impact Adjustors	Yes/Yes
Position/Weight Sensors	No/No
Seat/Head Adjustors	No
Roll Stability System	No
Child Seats Built-in	None
Antilock Brakes/Day Lamps	4-Wheel/Standard
Tire Pressure Monitor	None

General Information

2004 Status	Unchanged
Series Started	2003
Where Made	US
Theft Rating	Average
Twins	

Specifications

Fuel Econ. (city/hwy)	Average-21/26
Driving Range (mi.)	Average-388.5
Bumpers	Strong
Parking Index	Average
Seating	5
Tow Rating	Low-2400
Head/Leg Room (in.)	Average-38.3/43.3
Int. Space (cu. ft.)	Cramped-90.5
Cargo Space (cu. ft.)	Average-17.7

How the Competition Rates

	Rating	Pg.
Honda Element	4	163
Jeep Wrangler	7	181
Nissan Xterra	5	223

Subaru Forester

Small SUV

For 2004, the Forester gets a new turbo charged trim model called the 2.5 XT. This model has new hood mounted air intakes, all-wheel drive, and a fully independent suspension system. All Foresters come with an AM/FM/CD stereo. Several option packages are available which include automatic climate control and a leather wrapped steering wheel. Antilock brakes, dual stage front airbags, and side impact airbags are standard equipment. The Forester is smaller than most SUVs, but most find it easier to drive. The Forester has good cargo room once the rear seat is folded down.

Ratings—10 Best, 1 Worst	2004	2003
Front Crash Tests	**10**	—
Side Crash Tests	**10**	10
Safety Features	**6**	7
Preventive Maintenance	—	6
Repair Costs	—	6
Warranty	**3**	4
Fuel Economy	**4**	5
Rollover	**7**	6
Complaints	**4**	3
Insurance Costs	**1**	1
OVERALL RATING	**6**	—

Price Range		
AWD 2.5 X	$20,895	9%
AWD 2.5 XS	$23,145	10%
AWD 2.5 XT	$24,970	10%

Last Year's Model

The Forester was redesigned for 2003. The body structure has been strengthened and there are improvements to the front and rear facade. The interior has a new layout with a new console design and newly styled bucket seats. A 2.5-liter 4-cylinder engine, rated at 165 hp, powers the Forester. A five-speed manual transmission and all-wheel drive are standard. Dual front airbags, side impact airbags, and antilock brakes are standard.

Subaru Forester

Subaru Forester XS

Subaru Forester XT

Safety Checklist

Frontal Crash Test	Very Good
Side Crash Test	Very Good
Airbags (Side/Head)	Front Standard/Yes
Pretensioners/Impact Adjustors	Yes/Yes
Position/Weight Sensors	No/No
Seat/Head Adjustors	No
Roll Stability System	No
Child Seats Built-in	None
Antilock Brakes/Day Lamps	4-Wheel/Standard
Tire Pressure Monitor	None

General Information

2004 Status	Unchanged
Series Started	1997
Where Made	Japan
Theft Rating	Very Low
Twins	

Specifications

Fuel Econ. (city/hwy)	Poor-19/26
Driving Range (mi.)	Very Short-343.7
Bumpers	Strong
Parking Index	Very Easy
Seating	5
Tow Rating	Low-2400
Head/Leg Room (in.)	Very Cramped-39.8/33.7
Int. Space (cu. ft.)	Cramped-93.5
Cargo Space (cu. ft.)	Roomy-32

How the Competition Rates

	Rating	Pg.
Ford Escape	8	147
Honda CR-V	9	162
Hyundai Santa Fe	9	170

Subaru Impreza — Subcompact

For 2004, the Impreza gets a face-lift on the front fenders, headlights, grille, bumpers and taillights. There is also a new high performance model, the WRX STI. Antilock brakes and all-wheel drive come standard on all Imprezas. A 2.5-liter four-cylinder engine powers the standard Impreza. A five-speed manual transmission is standard with a four-speed automatic as optional. Daytime running lights are standard. Side airbags can be found on the new WRX STI model, but they are not available on standard Impreza models. Remote keyless entry is also standard.

Ratings—10 Best, 1 Worst	2004	2003
Front Crash Tests	9	9
Side Crash Tests*	6	—
Safety Features	3	3
Preventive Maintenance	7	6
Repair Costs	5	5
Warranty	3	4
Fuel Economy	4	5
Rollover	8	8
Complaints	1	—
Insurance Costs	1	1
OVERALL RATING	3	4

Price Range	Retail	Markup
2.5 RS	$19,395	9%
Wagon 2.5 TS	$17,895	9%
Wagon WRX	$23,995	9%
WRX	$24,495	9%

Last Year's Model

The Impreza was unchanged for 2003 except for some minor improvements. There are 4 trim models in the Impreza line up. They include the WRX, TS Sport wagon, RS sedan and Outback sport wagon. The base engine is the 2.5-liter 4-cylinder. A five-speed manual transmission is standard on all models, but there is an optional four-speed automatic available. Antilock brakes are standard, but side impact airbags are not.

Subaru Impreza 2003

Subaru Impreza WRX Sport Wagon

Subaru Impreza WRX STi

Safety Checklist

Frontal Crash Test	Very Good
Side Crash Test*	Average
Airbags (Side/Head)	Front Standard
Pretensioners/Impact Adjustors	Yes/No
Position/Weight Sensors	No/No
Seat/Head Adjustors	No
Roll Stability System	No
Child Seats Built-in	None
Antilock Brakes/Day Lamps	4-Wheel/Standard
Tire Pressure Monitor	None

General Information

2004 Status	Major Appearance Change
Series Started	2002
Where Made	Japan
Theft Rating	Average
Twins	

Specifications

Fuel Econ. (city/hwy)	Poor-19/26
Driving Range (mi.)	Very Short-343.7
Bumpers	Strong
Parking Index	Easy
Seating	5
Tow Rating	Low-2000
Head/Leg Room (in.)	Average-38.6/42.9
Int. Space (cu. ft.)	Very Cramped-87.6
Cargo Space (cu. ft.)	Very Cramped-11

How the Competition Rates

	Rating	Pg.
Acura RSX	7	98
Dodge Neon	8	144
Suzuki Aerio		243

*Rating for front occupant only.

Subaru Legacy — Compact

For 2004, the Legacy receives new standard features, and a new 35th Anniversary edition trim model. A 2.5-liter 4-cylinder engine powers all Legacies. A five-speed manual transmission is standard, but you can have a 4-speed automatic as an option. Standard safety features include antilock brakes, pre-tensioners and dual front airbags. Power doors and locks are standard. Cargo room is ample, especially in the wagon trim models. The 35th Anniversary Edition has a six-way powered driver's seat.

Subaru Legacy GT Sedan

Subaru Legacy L Sport Wagon

Ratings—10 Best, 1 Worst	2004	2003
Front Crash Tests	9	9
Side Crash Tests*	8	8
Safety Features	5	5
Preventive Maintenance	7	6
Repair Costs	5	7
Warranty	3	4
Fuel Economy	7	7
Rollover	9	9
Complaints	4	2
Insurance Costs	1	1
OVERALL RATING	8	8

Price Range	Retail	Markup
2.5 GT AWD	$26,995	10%
2.5 GT AWD	$26,095	10%
35th Anniversary Edition	$21,495	10%
L AWD	$21,395	10%

Last Year's Model

The 2003 Legacy remained unchanged for 2003 except GM's OnStar is now standard on all Legacy models. The interior has room for five passengers. Air conditioning, power doors and locks, and leather seats are available. A standard five-speed manual transmission can found on the 2.5-liter engine models. Antilock brakes are standard and side airbags are available.

Subaru Legacy 2003

Safety Checklist

Frontal Crash Test	Very Good
Side Crash Test*	Good
Airbags (Side/Head)	Front Standard
Pretensioners/Impact Adjustors	Yes/Yes
Position/Weight Sensors	No/No
Seat/Head Adjustors	No
Roll Stability System	No
Child Seats Built-in	None
Antilock Brakes/Day Lamps	4-Wheel/Standard
Tire Pressure Monitor	None

General Information

2004 Status	Unchanged
Series Started	2000
Where Made	US
Theft Rating	Very Low
Twins	

Specifications

Fuel Econ. (city/hwy)	Good-22/27
Driving Range (mi.)	Long-405.6
Bumpers	Strong
Parking Index	Easy
Seating	5
Tow Rating	Low-2000
Head/Leg Room (in.)	Roomy-38.9/43.3
Int. Space (cu. ft.)	Cramped-91.4
Cargo Space (cu. ft.)	Very Cramped-12.45

How the Competition Rates

	Rating	Pg.
Hyundai Elantra	10	169
Mitsubishi Galant		209
Pontiac Vibe	9	230

*Ratings based on 4-door sedan model. For wagon crash results, see page 23.

Subaru Outback

Compact

The Outback is a quasi-SUV developed from the Legacy. It moves into 2004 unchanged. The standard engine is a 2.5-liter high performance 4-cylinder, but a more powerful 3.0-liter 6-cylinder engine is available. The maximum seating capacity is five passengers, but the seats can be folded and removed to meet many cargo needs. Daytime running lights and 4-wheel antilock brakes are available. Dual stage driver and passenger airbags are standard. A powered sliding glass sunroof is standard.

Ratings—10 Best, 1 Worst	2004	2003
Front Crash Tests	**9**	9
Side Crash Tests	**10**	10
Safety Features	**5**	5
Preventive Maintenance	**7**	6
Repair Costs	**5**	8
Warranty	**3**	4
Fuel Economy	**7**	7
Rollover	**7**	7
Complaints	**7**	5
Insurance Costs	**10**	10
OVERALL RATING	**9**	8

Price Range	Retail	Markup
H6 3.0 Sedan	$28,795	10%
L.L. Bean Edition	$30,295	10%
Wagon AWD	$24,145	10%
Wagon Limited	$27,695	10%

Last Year's Model

This Subaru model continued into 2003 with few changes. OnStar is standard and the front facade got some restyling. A 2.5-liter engine is standard and a manual transmission comes standard. There are a variety of models available. The optional 3.0-liter 212 hp engine makes this a peppy vehicle. The top of the line model is the VDC version and has an electronic stability system and traction control. All models have standard antilock brakes.

Subaru Outback

Subaru Outback Sedan

Subaru Outback Wagon

Safety Checklist

Frontal Crash Test . . . .
Side Crash Test. . . . . Very Good
Airbags (Side/Head). . . . . Front Standard
Pretensioners/Impact Adjustors. . . . . Yes/Yes
Position/Weight Sensors . . . . No/No
Seat/Head Adjustors . . . . No
Roll Stability System . . . . No
Child Seats Built-in . . . . None
Antilock Brakes/Day Lamps 4-Wheel/Standard
Tire Pressure Monitor . . . . None

General Information

2004 Status . . . . Unchanged
Series Started. 2000
Where Made . . . . US
Theft Rating. . . . . Very Low
Twins . . . .

Specifications

Fuel Econ. (city/hwy). Good-22/28
Driving Range (mi.) Long-413.9
Bumpers . . . . Strong
Parking Index. . . . . Easy
Seating. 5
Tow Rating Low-2000
Head/Leg Room (in.) Average-38.1/43.3
Int. Space (cu. ft.) Cramped-91.4
Cargo Space (cu. ft.). . . . . Very Cramped-12.4

How the Competition Rates

	Rating	Pg.
Pontiac Vibe	9	230
Volkswagen Golf	9	264
Ford Focus	8	152

Suzuki Aerio — Subcompact

For 2004, the Suzuki Aerio remains unchanged except the base engine gets 10 more horsepower. The Sedan S is powered by a 2.3-liter inline 4-cylinder. A manual transmission is standard on all models, but you can opt for an automatic transmission. All-wheel drive is available. Standard equipment includes an AM/FM/CD player, a remote trunk release, daytime running lights and power mirrors. The SX and LX models add cruise control, power locks, a remote keyless entry system and a chrome muffler to their list of standard features. Seatbelt pretensioners are standard.

Suzuki Aerio SX

Ratings—10 Best, 1 Worst	2004	2003
Front Crash Tests	—	—
Side Crash Tests	—	—
Safety Features	3	3
Preventive Maintenance	2	—
Repair Costs	4	—
Warranty	5	5
Fuel Economy	9	9
Rollover	7	7
Complaints	10	—
Insurance Costs	1	1
OVERALL RATING	—	—

Price Range	Retail	Markup
LX AT	$15,999	10%
S AT	$14,299	10%
SX AT	$16,299	10%
SX AWD	$17,299	10%

Last Year's Model

The Aerio remained unchanged in 2003. There is a four-door sedan, wagon, and sports wagon. All vehicles are targeted at the younger buyer. A 2.0-liter four cylinder produces 141hp and drives with either a manual or automatic transmission. All wheel drive is available as an option. Standard equipment includes AC, power windows and locks and a CD player. The sedan is roomy for its size and the trunk is easy to load.

Suzuki Aerio
2003

Suzuki Aerio SX

Safety Checklist

Frontal Crash Test . . . .
Side Crash Test . . . .
Airbags (Side/Head) . . . . No Side
Pretensioners/Impact Adjustors . . . . Yes/No
Position/Weight Sensors . . . . No/No
Seat/Head Adjustors . . . . No
Roll Stability System . . . . No
Child Seats Built-in . . . . None
Antilock Brakes/Day Lamps. . . . 4-Wheel (opt.)/Standard
Tire Pressure Monitor . . . . None

General Information

2004 Status . . . . Unchanged
Series Started. 2002
Where Made. . . . . Japan
Theft Rating . . . . Average
Twins . . . .

Specifications

Fuel Econ. (city/hwy) . . . . Very Good-26/31
Driving Range (mi.) Short-370.1
Bumpers. . . . .
Parking Index. . . . . Very Easy
Seating. 5
Tow Rating . . . .
Head/Leg Room (in.) Average-40.6/41.4
Int. Space (cu. ft.). Roomy-104.7
Cargo Space (cu. ft.). Cramped-14.6

How the Competition Rates

	Rating	Pg.
Ford Focus	8	152
Kia Rio	7	184
Scion xA		236

Suzuki Forenza **Compact**

The Forenza is Suzuki's all new compact sedan. Suzuki plans for this car to compete with the Civic, Sentra and Corolla. A 2.0-liter 4-cylinder engine powers the Forenza. Power steering and all disc brakes are standard. Fog lamps and a powered sunroof are options. Standard features include heated mirrors, power windows and locks, and an in-dash CD/cassette stereo. Side impact airbags are not available. You have a choice between a five-speed manual and an optional four-speed automatic transmission.

Suzuki Forenza

Ratings—10 Best, 1 Worst	2004	2003
Front Crash Tests	—	
Side Crash Tests	—	
Safety Features	4	
Preventive Maintenance	—	
Repair Costs	—	
Warranty	5	
Fuel Economy	7	
Rollover	8	
Complaints	—	
Insurance Costs	5	
OVERALL RATING	—	

Price Range	Retail	Markup
EX AT	$16,499	9%
LX AT	$15,699	9%
S AT	$13,799	9%
S MT	$12,999	9%

Last Year's Model

Model Not Produced in 2003

2003

Suzuki Forenza

Safety Checklist

Frontal Crash Test . . . .
Side Crash Test . . . .
Airbags (Side/Head) . . . . Fr. Std. Rear Opt.
Pretensioners/Impact Adjustors. . . . . /Yes
Position/Weight Sensors . . . . No/No
Seat/Head Adjustors . . . . No
Roll Stability System. . . . . Yes
Child Seats Built-in . . . . None
Antilock Brakes/Day Lamps. . . . 4-Wheel (opt.)/Standard
Tire Pressure Monitor . . . . None

General Information

2004 Status . . . . All New
Series Started . . . . No series indicated
Where Made. . . . . Japan
Theft Rating . . . . Average
Twins . . . .

Specifications

Fuel Econ. (city/hwy). Good-22/30
Driving Range (mi.) Short-362.5
Bumpers. . . . .
Parking Index . . . .
Seating 5
Tow Rating . . . .
Head/Leg Room (in.). Average-39.1/42
Int. Space (cu. ft.). . . . .
Cargo Space (cu. ft.). . . . . Very Cramped-12.4

How the Competition Rates

	Rating	Pg.
Dodge Neon	8	144
Hyundai Elantra	10	169
Kia Optima	8	183

Suzuki Grand Vitara Small SUV

For 2004, the Grand Vitara remains essentially unchanged, but it does receive a new spare tire, roof rails and rear light designs. The Grand Vitara comes in two versions: the LX and the EX. Automatic climate control and an in-dash CD player are standard. There are 4-wheel and 2-wheel drive versions available. Cruise control is standard on the EX version. A 2.5-liter 6-cylinder engine is standard. Dual airbags and ABS are standard as are chrome interior door handles and privacy glass on all trim models.

Suzuki Grand Vitara

Ratings—10 Best, 1 Worst	2004	2003
Front Crash Tests	7	7
Side Crash Tests*	10	—
Safety Features	4	4
Preventive Maintenance	2	—
Repair Costs	1	1
Warranty	5	5
Fuel Economy	3	3
Rollover	5	5
Complaints	2	2
Insurance Costs	1	1
OVERALL RATING	1	2

Price Range		
2WD LX AT	$18,999	9%
2WD LX MT	$17,999	9%
4WD EX AT	$22,499	6%
4WD LX AT	$20,499	6%

Last Year's Model

The Grand Vitara rolled into 2003 unchanged. This SUV comes in three trim levels. The JLS, midrange JLX, and the Limited. Each trim level offers an increase in options and in performance. The Grand Vitara is powered by a 2.5 liter, 165hp V6 engine. Standard equipment includes a CD player, rear privacy mirrors, visor mirrors, cruise control, and remote keyless entry. Antilock brakes are standard on the Limited and optional on the JLX.

Suzuki Grand Vitara 2003

Suzuki Grand Vitara

Safety Checklist

Frontal Crash Test	Good
Side Crash Test*	Very Good
Airbags (Side/Head)	No Side
Pretensioners/Impact Adjustors	Yes/No
Position/Weight Sensors	No/No
Seat/Head Adjustors	No
Roll Stability System	Yes
Child Seats Built-in	None
Antilock Brakes/Day Lamps	4-Wheel (opt.)/Standard
Tire Pressure Monitor	None

General Information

2004 Status	Unchanged
Series Started	1999
Where Made	Japan
Theft Rating	Very High
Twins	

Specifications

Fuel Econ. (city/hwy)	Poor-19/21
Driving Range (mi.)	Very Short-335.5
Bumpers	
Parking Index	Very Easy
Seating	5
Tow Rating	Very Low-1500
Head/Leg Room (in.)	Average-39.9/41.4
Int. Space (cu. ft.)	Roomy-106.3
Cargo Space (cu. ft.)	Average-23.4

How the Competition Rates

	Rating	Pg.
Chevrolet Blazer	1	122
Honda Element	4	163
Hyundai Santa Fe	9	170

*Higher likelihood of head injury.

Suzuki Verona — Intermediate

The all-new 2004 Verona is designed to give Suzuki a competitor to the Accord and Camry. A 2.5-liter inline six-cylinder engine powers this front wheel drive sedan. Fog lamps are standard and there is a powered sunroof available on the higher priced models. Power windows and doors locks are standard. Cruise control, a four-speed automatic transmission, and dual stage airbags are also standard. Antilock brakes and a traction control system are optional on the Verona. Side impact air bags are not available.

Suzuki Verona

Ratings—10 Best, 1 Worst	2004	2003
Front Crash Tests	—	
Side Crash Tests	—	
Safety Features	4	
Preventive Maintenance	—	
Repair Costs	—	
Warranty	5	
Fuel Economy	5	
Rollover	9	
Complaints	—	
Insurance Costs	5	
OVERALL RATING	—	

Price Range	Retail	Markup
EX	$19,999	10%
LX	$18,299	11%
S	$16,999	11%

Last Year's Model

Model Not Produced in 2003

2003

Suzuki Verona

Safety Checklist

Frontal Crash Test	
Side Crash Test	
Airbags (Side/Head)	No Side
Pretensioners/Impact Adjustors	Standard/No
Position/Weight Sensors	No/No
Seat/Head Adjustors	No
Roll Stability System	Yes
Child Seats Built-in	None
Antilock Brakes/Day Lamps	4-Wheel (opt.)/Standard
Tire Pressure Monitor	None

General Information

2004 Status	All New
Series Started	No series indicated
Where Made	
Theft Rating	Average
Twins	

Specifications

Fuel Econ. (city/hwy)	Average-20/28
Driving Range (mi.)	Average-394.8
Bumpers	
Parking Index	
Seating	5
Tow Rating	
Head/Leg Room (in.)	Average-39.1/42.2
Int. Space (cu. ft.)	
Cargo Space (cu. ft.)	Cramped-13.4

How the Competition Rates

	Rating	Pg.
Chevrolet Malibu		126
Ford Taurus	9	157
Hyundai Sonata	10	171

Suzuki XL-7 — Mid-Size SUV

For 2004, the XL-7 gets a major face-lift. There is a new front grille design, fog lamps and new front and rear bumpers. There is also a new four-wheel drive system, new front passenger airbags, and a new panic button on the keyless entry remote. Heated front seats are available, but only the EX models. The XL-7 comes in either a 5 or 7-passenger models. A manual or automatic transmission is available. A 2.7-liter V6 engine powers the XL-7. The XL-7 has a six-disc in-dash CD changer and a sunroof. Leather is available on the LX model.

Ratings—10 Best, 1 Worst	2004	2003
Front Crash Tests	—	—
Side Crash Tests	—	—
Safety Features	5	2
Preventive Maintenance	2	—
Repair Costs	1	1
Warranty	5	5
Fuel Economy	2	2
Rollover	5	5
Complaints	10	10
Insurance Costs	5	5
OVERALL RATING	—	—

Price Range	Retail	Markup
2WD EX AT	$23,699	9%
2WD LX AT	$20,999	9%
4WD EX III	$27,399	8%
4WD LX AT	$22,899	9%

Last Year's Model

The XL-7 was unchanged in 2003. Cloth upholstery is standard, but the Limited has leather. Standard equipment includes air conditioning, remote keyless entry, and a CD player. Antilock brakes are standard on the Touring and Limited models, but optional on other trim levels. Side-impact airbags are not available. A 2.7-liter V 6 engine powers the XL-7. A five-speed manual transmission is standard, but automatic is available.

Suzuki XL-7

Suzuki XL-7

Suzuki XL-7

Safety Checklist

Frontal Crash Test . . . .
Side Crash Test . . . .
Airbags (Side/Head) . . . . No Side
Pretensioners/Impact Adjustors . . . . None/Yes
Position/Weight Sensors. . . . . Yes/No
Seat/Head Adjustors . . . . No
Roll Stability System. . . . . Yes
Child Seats Built-in . . . . None
Antilock Brakes/Day Lamps 4-Wheel/Standard
Tire Pressure Monitor . . . . None

General Information

2004 Status. . . . . Major Appearance Change
Series Started. 2001
Where Made. . . . . Japan
Theft Rating . . . . Average
Twins . . . .

Specifications

Fuel Econ. (city/hwy) . . . . Very Poor-17/22
Driving Range (mi.). . . . . Very Short-320.0
Bumpers. . . . .
Parking Index . . . . Hard
Seating 5/7
Tow Rating Low-3000
Head/Leg Room (in.). Average-40/41.4
Int. Space (cu. ft.) Roomy-118.2
Cargo Space (cu. ft.) . . . . Very Roomy-40.3

How the Competition Rates

	Rating	Pg.
Ford Explorer	8	150
Isuzu Axiom	6	177
Mitsubishi Montero Sport	4	211

Toyota 4Runner

Mid-Size SUV

Only minor changes have been made to the 4Runner in 2004. To improve safety, a roll sensing system has been installed. A third row seat is now available on the Limited and SR5 models. A rear camera option is available with the DVD entertainment system option. A 4.0-liter V6 engine is standard and a more powerful 4.7-liter V8 is offered as an option on all models. The transmission is a four-speed automatic. Standard safety features include: Four-channel antilock brakes, dual-stage front airbags, and child door locks.

Toyota 4Runner

Ratings—10 Best, 1 Worst	2004	2003
Front Crash Tests	9	9
Side Crash Tests	10	10
Safety Features	6	6
Preventive Maintenance	—	4
Repair Costs	—	3
Warranty	3	3
Fuel Economy	2	2
Rollover	5	5
Complaints	—	—
Insurance Costs	10	10
OVERALL RATING	6	4

Price Range	Retail	Markup
Limited 4x2 V6	$33,445	12%
Limited 4X4 V8	$36,970	12%
SR5 4x2 V6	$27,170	12%
SR5 4x4 V8	$27,170	12%

Last Year's Model

Toyota's midsize SUV was redesigned for 2003 and increased in both power and size over previous models. The 2003 changes increased the length of the vehicle by nearly six inches and the widened wheelbase. The result is a roomier interior than in previous models, but fuel economy is very poor and the bumpers are weak. A roll stability system comes standard, along with four-wheel antilock brakes. Daytime running lights are optional.

Toyota 4Runner

Toyota 4Runner

Safety Checklist

Frontal Crash Test . . . . Very Good
Side Crash Test . . . . Very Good
Airbags (Side/Head) . . . . Front Standard
Pretensioners/Impact Adjustors . . . . Yes/Yes
Position/Weight Sensors . . . . No/No
Seat/Head Adjustors . . . . No
Roll Stability System . . . . Yes
Child Seats Built-in . . . . None
Antilock Brakes/Day Lamps 4-Wheel/Optional
Tire Pressure Monitor . . . . None

General Information

2004 Status . . . . Unchanged
Series Started 2003
Where Made . . . . US
Theft Rating . . . . Very High
Twins . . . .

Specifications

Fuel Econ. (city/hwy) . . . . Very Poor-16/20
Driving Range (mi.) Long-404.4
Bumpers . . . . Weak
Parking Index . . . . Average
Seating 5
Tow Rating Average-5000
Head/Leg Room (in.) Average-39.7/41.7
Int. Space (cu. ft.) Average-103.1
Cargo Space (cu. ft.) . . . . Very Roomy-42.2

How the Competition Rates

	Rating	Pg.
Chevrolet Trail Blazer	2	132
Ford Explorer	8	150
Jeep Grand Cherokee	8	179

Toyota Avalon — Intermediate

The 2004 Avalon remains unchanged. A new vehicle stability control system is now available on the XL model. A 3.0-liter V6 engine rated at 210 horsepower powers the Avalon. Rain sensing wipers are available and a DVD entertainment system is available for the rear passengers. Power windows and locks, cruise control and a five-speed automatic transmission are standard. ABS, dual stage airbags, and optional side curtain airbags are some of the safety features found on this vehicle. The design and feel of the Avalon is similar to vehicles under the Lexus nameplate.

Toyota Avalon XLS

Ratings—10 Best, 1 Worst	2004	2003
Front Crash Tests	10	10
Side Crash Tests	9	9
Safety Features	6	7
Preventive Maintenance	10	9
Repair Costs	4	4
Warranty	3	3
Fuel Economy	6	6
Rollover	9	9
Complaints	9	7
Insurance Costs	10	10
OVERALL RATING	10	10

Toyota Avalon XLS

Safety Checklist

Frontal Crash Test. . . . . Very Good
Side Crash Test. . . . . Very Good
Airbags (Side/Head) . . . . . Fr. Std. Rear Opt.
Pretensioners/Impact Adjustors. . . . . Yes/Yes
Position/Weight Sensors . . . . . No/No
Seat/Head Adjustors . . . . . No
Roll Stability System. . . . . Yes
Child Seats Built-in . . . . . None
Antilock Brakes/Day Lamps 4-Wheel/Standard
Tire Pressure Monitor . . . . . None

Price Range	Retail	Markup
XL	$26,865	12%
XLS	$30,405	14%

General Information

2004 Status . . . . . Unchanged
Series Started. 1996
Where Made . . . . . US
Theft Rating . . . . . Very High
Twins . . . . .

Last Year's Model

In 2003 the Avalon went through minor changes mainly to the front facade and interior. Multi-stage front passenger airbags, 16-inch alloy wheels, and rain sensing windshield wipers are standard on the XLS. The powerful 3.0-liter 210 horsepower V6 engine powers the Avalon. The two trim levels are the XL and XLS. Standard features include a CD player, power everything, cruise control, automatic transmission, and dual zone air conditioning.

Toyota Avalon 2003

Specifications

Fuel Econ. (city/hwy) Average-21/29
Driving Range (mi.) . . . . . Very Long-443.6
Bumpers . . . . . Weak
Parking Index . . . . . Hard
Seating 5
Tow Rating Low-2000
Head/Leg Room (in.). Cramped-38.7/41.7
Int. Space (cu. ft.). Roomy-106.6
Cargo Space (cu. ft.). Cramped-15.9

How the Competition Rates

	Rating	Pg.
Ford Taurus	9	157
Lexus ES 330		190
Infiniti I35	10	176

Toyota Camry

Intermediate

For 2004, the Limited Edition Camry gets a unique front grille, fog lamps, and other improvements to the exterior and interior. The SE model gets a new 3.3-liter V6 engine. There is also a new transmission available on the XLE and SE models. A 2.4-liter 4-cylinder engine powers the base model Camry. Safety features include dual stage airbags, 4-wheel ABS, and side curtain airbags. Other features include a remote keyless entry system, cruise control and day running lights. A multifunctional display is available on the XLE model.

Toyota Camry XLE

Toyota Camry XLE

Ratings—10 Best, 1 Worst	2004	2003
Front Crash Tests	10	—
Side Crash Tests	9	4
Safety Features	8	8
Preventive Maintenance	10	10
Repair Costs	3	3
Warranty	3	3
Fuel Economy	8	8
Rollover	9	9
Complaints	7	—
Insurance Costs	5	5
OVERALL RATING	10	—

Price Range	Retail	Markup
LE V6	$22,260	12%
SE	$23,315	12%
XLE	$22,295	12%
XLE V6	$25,405	12%

Last Year's Model

The 2003 Camry was a carryover from the redesign of 2002. Fog lamps are standard on the 2003 Camry XLE and power adjustable pedals are available as an option on all models. The Camry comes with a 2.4-liter four-cylinder engine and a standard five-speed manual transmission is available. An automatic transmission is optional, but you have to upgrade to the 3.0-liter V6 engine. There are three trim levels: LE, XLE, and the sporty SE.

Toyota Camry 2003

Safety Checklist

Frontal Crash Test	Very Good
Side Crash Test	Very Good
Airbags (Side/Head)	Front & Back/Head
Pretensioners/Impact Adjustors	Yes/Yes
Position/Weight Sensors	No/No
Seat/Head Adjustors	No
Roll Stability System	Yes
Child Seats Built-in	None
Antilock Brakes/Day Lamps	4-Wheel/Standard
Tire Pressure Monitor	None

General Information

2004 Status	Minor Appearance Change
Series Started	2001
Where Made	US/Japan
Theft Rating	Very High
Twins	

Specifications

Fuel Econ. (city/hwy)	Good-23/32
Driving Range (mi.)	Very Long-487.2
Bumpers	Weak
Parking Index	Easy
Seating	5
Tow Rating	
Head/Leg Room (in.)	Cramped-39.2/41.6
Int. Space (cu. ft.)	Average-101.7
Cargo Space (cu. ft.)	Average-16.7

How the Competition Rates

	Rating	Pg.
Ford Taurus	9	157
Honda Accord	8	160
Mazda 6	7	198

Toyota Celica — Compact

For 2004, the Toyota Celica remains unchanged, but it does get new high intensity discharge headlamps on the GT Model. A 1.8-liter 4-cylinder engine powers this sport coupe. A five speed manual transmission is standard, but you can upgrade to an automatic transmission. A cold weather starter package is standard on the GTS version of the Celica. Daytime running lamps are also standard. Remote keyless entry, leather trimmed seats, and rear spoilers are some of the options available on the Celica.

Toyota Celica GTS

Ratings—10 Best, 1 Worst	2004	2003
Front Crash Tests	9	9
Side Crash Tests*	3	—
Safety Features	3	3
Preventive Maintenance	8	7
Repair Costs	5	4
Warranty	3	3
Fuel Economy	10	9
Rollover	10	10
Complaints	8	8
Insurance Costs	1	1
OVERALL RATING	7	7

Price Range	Retail	Markup
GT Automatic	$18,190	11%
GT Manual	$17,390	11%
GT-S Automatic	$22,755	11%
GT-S Manual	$22,055	11%

Last Year's Model

The Celica received a major appearance change in 2003, but mechanically it is still the same as the 2002 model. The designers have revised the lower air intake, added new headlights, and have redesigned the interior instrument gauges. The coupe comes in two models the GT and GTS. The GT is powered by a 1.8liter 4-cylinder that provides 140 horsepower. A 5-speed manual transmission is standard, but you can opt for an automatic.

Toyota Celica 2003

Toyota Celica GTS

Safety Checklist

Frontal Crash Test	Very Good
Side Crash Test*	Poor
Airbags (Side/Head)	Front Optional
Pretensioners/Impact Adjustors	Yes/No
Position/Weight Sensors	No/No
Seat/Head Adjustors	No
Roll Stability System	No
Child Seats Built-in	None
Antilock Brakes/Day Lamps	4-Wheel (optional)/None
Tire Pressure Monitor	None

General Information

2004 Status	Unchanged
Series Started	2000
Where Made	Japan
Theft Rating	Very High
Twins	

Specifications

Fuel Econ. (city/hwy)	Very Good-29/36
Driving Range (mi.)	Very Long-460.8
Bumpers	Weak
Parking Index	Easy
Seating	4
Tow Rating	Low-2000
Head/Leg Room (in.)	Average-38.4/43.6
Int. Space (cu. ft.)	Very Cramped-76.3
Cargo Space (cu. ft.)	Very Cramped-12.9

How the Competition Rates

	Rating	Pg.
Acura RSX	7	98
Ford Mustang	7	155
Mazda RX-8		201

*Applies to front occupant only. Rear seat too small for test.

Toyota Corolla — Compact

The Corolla is unchanged for 2004. A 1.8-liter 4-cylinder engine powers the Corolla. An all-weather guard package that includes a heavy-duty heater system is available. With a manual transmission, gas mileage is very good for a car of its class, and the Corolla has low emissions. However, it has a cramped interior and weak bumpers. A conventional ABS system and a 3-channel ABS system are both optional. Side impact bars, height adjustable front seat belts, and a three-point rear center seat belt are among the standard safety features found on this compact.

Toyota Corolla S

Ratings—10 Best, 1 Worst	2004	2003
Front Crash Tests	10	10
Side Crash Tests	8	8
Safety Features	3	3
Preventive Maintenance	—	10
Repair Costs	—	5
Warranty	3	3
Fuel Economy	10	9
Rollover	8	8
Complaints	—	—
Insurance Costs	1	1
OVERALL RATING	7	7

Toyota Corolla S

Safety Checklist

- Frontal Crash Test. . . . . Very Good
- Side Crash Test. . . . . Good
- Airbags (Side/Head) . . . . . Front Optional
- Pretensioners/Impact Adjustors . . . . . Yes/No
- Position/Weight Sensors . . . . . No/No
- Seat/Head Adjustors . . . . . No
- Roll Stability System. . . . . Yes
- Child Seats Built-in . . . . . None
- Antilock Brakes/Day Lamps. . . . 4-Wheel (opt.)/Standard
- Tire Pressure Monitor . . . . . None

Price Range	Retail	Markup
CE Sedan 5-sp.	$13,570	8%
CE Sedan AT	$14,370	8%
LE Sedan AT	$15,580	11%
S Sedan AT	$15,315	11%

General Information

- 2004 Status . . . . . Unchanged
- Series Started. 2003
- Where Made . . . . . US/Canada
- Theft Rating . . . . . Very High
- Twins . . . . .

Last Year's Model

The Corolla was redesigned in 2003 and is larger and heavier than the 2002 model. However, there is only 90 cubic feet of space in the interior cabin that still makes it feel cramped. There is a new suspension system that gives the Corolla better handling. The Corolla performed very well on frontal crash tests. Some of the safety features found include dual stage airbags and safety belt pretensioners. A-1.8-liter 4-cylinder engine is standard.

Toyota Corolla 2003

Specifications

- Fuel Econ. (city/hwy) . . . . . Very Good-29/38
- Driving Range (mi.) Long-428.5
- Bumpers . . . . . Weak
- Parking Index. . . . . Very Easy
- Seating. 5
- Tow Rating . . . . . Very Low-1500
- Head/Leg Room (in.). Cramped-39.1/41.3
- Int. Space (cu. ft.) Cramped-90.3
- Cargo Space (cu. ft.). Cramped-13.6

How the Competition Rates

	Rating	Pg.
Chevrolet Cavalier	3	123
Dodge Neon	8	144
Honda Civic	10	161

Toyota ECHO — Subcompact

The 2004 ECHO remains unchanged from 2003's model. The ECHO's 1.5-liter 4-cylinder engine with variable valve timing is one of the highest mileage engines ever offered. All five seats have three point seatbelts with emergency locking retractors and pretensioners. The rear seats fold down to make more room for cargo and a tilt steering wheel is standard. An AM/FM stereo is standard, but you can upgrade to a deluxe AM/FM/CD stereo that has six speakers. Keyless entry is an option.

Toyota ECHO

Toyota ECHO

Ratings—10 Best, 1 Worst	2004	2003
Front Crash Tests	8	8
Side Crash Tests	8	8
Safety Features	1	1
Preventive Maintenance	7	6
Repair Costs	6	6
Warranty	3	3
Fuel Economy	10	9
Rollover	7	7
Complaints	8	—
Insurance Costs	1	1
OVERALL RATING	8	6

Price Range	Retail	Markup
2 DR AT	$11,045	6%
2 DR M/T	$10,245	6%
4 DR AT	$11,575	6%
4 DR M/T	$10,775	6%

Last Year's Model

This small sedan received a major appearance change in 2003 and was lengthened by half an inch. The front and rear areas were completely redesigned and there are new power options for the doors and windows. The interior received new fabrics and colors. It is equipped with dual airbags and a child restraint top tether anchors. The 2003 ECHO had good crash test results. A 1.5-liter 4-cyclinder engine powers the ECHO.

Toyota ECHO 2003

Safety Checklist

Frontal Crash Test	Good
Side Crash Test	Good
Airbags (Side/Head)	Front Optional
Pretensioners/Impact Adjustors	Yes/No
Position/Weight Sensors	No/No
Seat/Head Adjustors	No
Roll Stability System	No
Child Seats Built-in	None
Antilock Brakes/Day Lamps	4-Wheel (optional)/None
Tire Pressure Monitor	None

General Information

2004 Status	Unchanged
Series Started	2002
Where Made	Japan
Theft Rating	Very High
Twins	

Specifications

Fuel Econ. (city/hwy)	Very Good-33/39
Driving Range (mi.)	Long-421.9
Bumpers	Weak
Parking Index	Very Easy
Seating	5
Tow Rating	
Head/Leg Room (in.)	Average-39.9/41.1
Int. Space (cu. ft.)	Very Cramped-88
Cargo Space (cu. ft.)	Cramped-13.6

How the Competition Rates

	Rating	Pg.
Hyundai Accent	10	168
Kia Spectra	9	187
Mini Cooper	10	206

Toyota Highlander — Mid-Size SUV

The Highlander has received a minor appearance change for 2004. The grille, headlamps, tail lamps, fog lamps, and skid plate have all been given a new look and the interior has been freshened-up. A third row seat and a DVD player are both optional. The standard engine is a 2.4 liter four cylinder. A more powerful option is a 3.3L V-6. ABS and Brake Assist are standard. Seat mounted side impact airbags and skid control are available in certain option packages.

Toyota Highlander

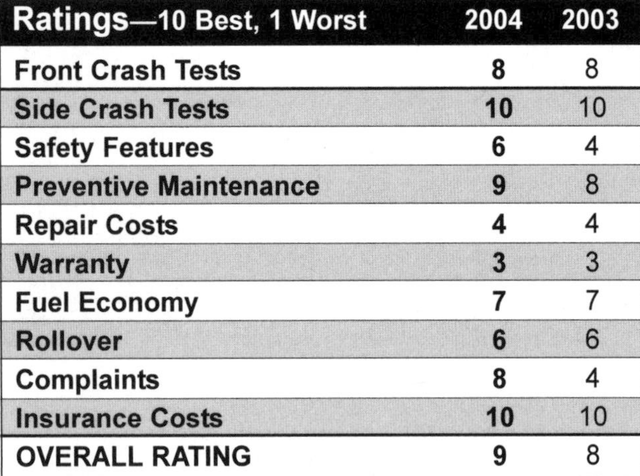

Ratings—10 Best, 1 Worst	2004	2003
Front Crash Tests	8	8
Side Crash Tests	10	10
Safety Features	6	4
Preventive Maintenance	9	8
Repair Costs	4	4
Warranty	3	3
Fuel Economy	7	7
Rollover	6	6
Complaints	8	4
Insurance Costs	10	10
OVERALL RATING	9	8

Toyota Highlander

Safety Checklist

Frontal Crash Test........................Good
Side Crash Test......................Very Good
Airbags (Side/Head)...........Fr. Std. Rear Opt./Yes
Pretensioners/Impact Adjustors..............Yes/NA
Position/Weight Sensors...................No/Yes
Seat/Head Adjustors........................Yes
Roll Stability System.........................NA
Child Seats Built-in........................None
Antilock Brakes/Day Lamps.........4-Wheel/Optional
Tire Pressure Monitor.......................None

Price Range	Retail	Markup
2WD V6	$25,140	12%
4WD 4-cyl.	$25,480	12%
4WD V6	$27,390	12%
Limited 4WD	$31,380	12%

General Information

2004 Status.............Minor Appearance Change
Series Started...........................2001
Where Made.............................Japan
Theft Rating.........................Very Low
Twins.......................................

Last Year's Model

The 2003 Highlander is a carryover from 2002. The same engine that powers the Camry powers the Highlander. An automatic transmission is standard. Front seat-mounted side impact airbags are optional. The Highlander performed slightly above average in the government's crash tests. Standard features include cruise control, antilock brakes, and a map light. Dual stage airbags are standard on all models.

Toyota Highlander

Specifications

Fuel Econ. (city/hwy)..................Good-22/27
Driving Range (mi.)...............Very Long-456.0
Bumpers..................................Weak
Parking Index...........................Average
Seating.....................................5
Tow Rating.........................Very Low-1500
Head/Leg Room (in.)..............Cramped-40/40.7
Int. Space (cu. ft.)...................Roomy-105.7
Cargo Space (cu. ft.)..................Roomy-38.5

How the Competition Rates

	Rating	Pg.
Ford Escape	8	147
Jeep Liberty	10	180
Hyundai Santa Fe	9	170

Toyota MR2 Spyder

Subcompact

The 2004 MR2 Spyder is unchanged from 2003. It is equipped with a 138 horsepower 16 valve 1.8L I-4 engine and independent strut suspension. For added safety, the MR2 Spyder has front and rear crumple zones, dual air bags, safety belt pretensioners and emergency locking retractors. Antilock brakes are standard. A full size spare is included and a CD player with 4 speakers comes standard. There are very few optional features on the MR2 Spyder.

Toyota MR2 Spyder

Ratings—10 Best, 1 Worst	2004	2003
Front Crash Tests	—	—
Side Crash Tests	—	—
Safety Features	3	3
Preventive Maintenance	7	7
Repair Costs	3	2
Warranty	3	3
Fuel Economy	9	9
Rollover	10	10
Complaints	3	—
Insurance Costs	1	1
OVERALL RATING	—	—

Toyota MR2 Spyder

Safety Checklist

Frontal Crash Test	
Side Crash Test	
Airbags (Side/Head)	Front Standard
Pretensioners/Impact Adjustors	Yes/No
Position/Weight Sensors	No/No
Seat/Head Adjustors	No
Roll Stability System	No
Child Seats Built-in	None
Antilock Brakes/Day Lamps	4-Wheel (standard)
Tire Pressure Monitor	None

Price Range	Retail	Markup
5M	$24,645	11%
6SMT	$25,645	11%

General Information

2004 Status	Unchanged
Series Started	2000
Where Made	
Theft Rating	Average
Twins	

Last Year's Model

Toyota's roadster received some minor changes to its exterior and to its mechanical components, but it was unchanged in 2003. There was a new headlight configuration and fog lamps are now standard. The interior has a new instrument panel and black leather seating is available as an option. The semi manual transmission is now a six-speed version. A CD player is standard on all models. A 1.8-liter inline four-cylinder engine powers the Spyder.

Specifications

Fuel Econ. (city/hwy)	Very Good-26/32
Driving Range (mi.)	Short-360.6
Bumpers	Weak
Parking Index	Very Easy
Seating	2
Tow Rating	
Head/Leg Room (in.)	Very Cramped-37/42.2
Int. Space (cu. ft.)	Very Cramped-48
Cargo Space (cu. ft.)	Very Cramped-1.5

Toyota MR2 Spyder 2003

How the Competition Rates

	Rating	Pg.
Ford Thunderbird	5	158
Honda S2000	7	167
Mazda RX-8		201

Toyota Prius — Intermediate

For 2004, the Toyota Prius has been completely redesigned. It's now the same size class as the Camry. The car now has a higher rear window similar to a hatchback and the wheelbase is now 5.4 inches longer. Five people can fit inside the Prius and the cargo volume has increased. The Prius has a 1.5 four-cylinder engine rated at 78 horsepower. A new battery system increases energy output over the previous generation's battery. Antilock brakes and dual airbags are standard features. Nearly 120,000 of these vehicles have been sold worldwide.

Toyota Prius

Ratings—10 Best, 1 Worst	2004	2003
Front Crash Tests	—	7
Side Crash Tests	—	6
Safety Features	**4**	3
Preventive Maintenance	—	—
Repair Costs	—	—
Warranty	**3**	3
Fuel Economy	**10**	10
Rollover	**8**	8
Complaints	—	1
Insurance Costs	**1**	1
OVERALL RATING	—	5

Toyota Prius

Safety Checklist

Frontal Crash Test ....
Side Crash Test ....
Airbags (Side/Head) .... Fr. Std. Rear Opt.
Pretensioners/Impact Adjustors .... Standard/Yes
Position/Weight Sensors .... No/No
Seat/Head Adjustors .... No
Roll Stability System.......... Yes
Child Seats Built-in .... None
Antilock Brakes/Day Lamps 4-Wheel/None
Tire Pressure Monitor .... None

Price Range	Retail	Markup
Base Model	$19,995	6%

General Information

2004 Status .... All New
Series Started .... No series indicated
Where Made.......... Japan
Theft Rating .... Average
Twins ....

Last Year's Model

Toyota's Prius was unchanged in 2003. The Prius has a hybrid engine which runs on either electricity or gasoline alone, or a combination of both. It is equipped with a 1.5-liter gasoline engine and an electric motor with permanent magnet design. Fuel economy is very good. Antilock brakes and dual airbags are standard safety features. The Prius has cruise control, a navigation system, and side airbags as optional features.

Toyota Prius 2003

Specifications

Fuel Econ. (city/hwy) .... Very Good-59/51
Driving Range (mi.) .... Very Long-655.8
Bumpers .... Weak
Parking Index.......... Very Easy
Seating.......... 5
Tow Rating ....
Head/Leg Room (in.) Average-39.1/41.9
Int. Space (cu. ft.) Average-99
Cargo Space (cu. ft.).......... Cramped-16.1

How the Competition Rates

	Rating	Pg.
Honda Civic (Hybrid)	10	161
Honda Insight	2	164

Toyota RAV4 — Small SUV

The RAV4 goes through a series of changes in 2004. A new, more powerful 2.0-liter inline 4-cylinder engine has been added, along with traction control and brake assist. The front airbags have been upgraded with a better design. Improvements have been made to increase the comfort and convenience on the RAV4. The RAV4 is now features steering wheel audio controls, power mirrors, a scheduled maintenance light, and a battery access panel. The front bumper, headlights, grille, and taillights have been restyled as well to give the RAV4 a new look.

Toyota RAV4

Ratings—10 Best, 1 Worst	2004	2003
Front Crash Tests	7	7
Side Crash Tests	10	10
Safety Features	4	3
Preventive Maintenance	9	9
Repair Costs	4	2
Warranty	3	3
Fuel Economy	8	8
Rollover	6	6
Complaints	7	3
Insurance Costs	1	1
OVERALL RATING	7	6

Toyota RAV4

Safety Checklist

Frontal Crash Test . . . . . Good
Side Crash Test . . . . . Very Good
Airbags (Side/Head) . . . . . Front Optional Rear Optional
Pretensioners/Impact Adjustors . . . . . Yes/No
Position/Weight Sensors . . . . . No/No
Seat/Head Adjustors . . . . . No
Roll Stability System . . . . . Yes
Child Seats Built-in . . . . . None
Antilock Brakes/Day Lamps . . . . 4-Wheel (opt.)/Optional
Tire Pressure Monitor . . . . . Direct

Price Range	Retail	Markup
4X2 4ECT	$19,400	8%
4X2 5M	$18,350	8%
4X4 4ECT	$20,800	10%
4X4 5M	$19,750	10%

General Information

2004 Status . . . . . Minor Appearance Change
Series Started 2001
Where Made . . . . . US
Theft Rating . . . . . Very High
Twins . . . . .

Last Year's Model

For 2003, the RAV4 got a new trim model. The Sports Package trim level has a new sport grille façade, tubular roof rack, air conditioning, cruise control, and a 3-in-1 audio system. A 2.0-liter 4-cylinder engine powers the base model RAV4. There are 2WD and 4WD options. ABS is optional. Because of its narrow stance, rollover is more likely in this vehicle than in standard passenger cars.

Specifications

Fuel Econ. (city/hwy) Good-24/29
Driving Range (mi.) Average-382.5
Bumpers . . . . . Weak
Parking Index . . . . . Very Easy
Seating 5
Tow Rating . . . . . Very Low-680
Head/Leg Room (in.) . . . . . Very Roomy-41.3/42.4
Int. Space (cu. ft.) Roomy-113.8
Cargo Space (cu. ft.) Roomy-29.2

Toyota RAV4 2003

How the Competition Rates

	Rating	Pg.
Chevrolet Tracker	1	131
Honda CR-V	9	162
Honda Element	4	163

Toyota Sequoia — Large SUV

A carryover from 2003, the Sequoia remains Toyota's largest SUV. The standard engine is a 4.7-liter 240hp V8. Gas mileage is low on this SUV. Cargo room is ample, beating out the Expedition. The Sequoia performed well on frontal crash tests, but it has few advanced safety features. Side and head airbags are optional. The rear window is electric and retracts into the hatch. The third row seat splits in half and removes easily. Steering wheel audio controls are standard. The two trim options, the SR5 and the Limited offer different luxury packages.

Toyota Sequoia

Ratings—10 Best, 1 Worst	2004	2003
Front Crash Tests	10	10
Side Crash Tests	—	—
Safety Features	2	2
Preventive Maintenance	4	4
Repair Costs	4	2
Warranty	3	3
Fuel Economy	1	1
Rollover	5	5
Complaints	10	10
Insurance Costs	10	10
OVERALL RATING	3	3

Toyota Sequoia

Safety Checklist

Frontal Crash Test	Very Good
Side Crash Test	
Airbags (Side/Head)	Front Optional/Head
Pretensioners/Impact Adjustors	/No
Position/Weight Sensors	No/No
Seat/Head Adjustors	No
Roll Stability System	No
Child Seats Built-in	None
Antilock Brakes/Day Lamps	4-Wheel/Optional
Tire Pressure Monitor	None

Price Range	Retail	Markup
LTD 4X2	$40,900	12%
LTD 4X4	$44,220	13%
SR5 2WD	$31,625	12%
SR5 4WD	$44,220	13%

General Information

2004 Status	Unchanged
Series Started	2001
Where Made	US
Theft Rating	Very High
Twins	

Last Year's Model

For 2003, the suspension on the Sequoia received improvements as did the interior. A factory available DVD rear seat entertainment system is an option. Fuel economy is very poor, but the Sequoia has a large gas tank. The 2003 Sequoia performed well on frontal crash tests, but has weak bumpers. The standard engine on the Sequoia is the massive 4.7-liter V8 engine. An automatic transmission is standard.

Toyota Sequoia 2003

Specifications

Fuel Econ. (city/hwy)	Very Poor-14/18
Driving Range (mi.)	Long-406.0
Bumpers	Weak
Parking Index	Very Hard
Seating	8
Tow Rating	High-6500
Head/Leg Room (in.)	Roomy-41.1/41.6
Int. Space (cu. ft.)	
Cargo Space (cu. ft.)	Roomy-27.8

How the Competition Rates

	Rating	Pg.
Chevrolet Tahoe	3	130
Dodge Durango		143
Ford Expedition	4	149

Toyota Sienna | Minivan

For 2004, the Toyota Sienna is all-new. The standard V6 engine comes with a 5-speed automatic transmission. An all-wheel drive system is available on all trims. A laser cruise control system comes standard. The exterior glass shields 94 percent of UV rays, according to Toyota. Third row sunshades have been added to this ultra-low emissions vehicle. An optional tow package provides a 3,500-pound towing capability. There are 10-cup holders, four coat hooks, and door-mounted storage compartments.

Toyota Sienna XLE Ltd.

Ratings—10 Best, 1 Worst	2004	2003
Front Crash Tests	10	10
Side Crash Tests	10	9
Safety Features	6	2
Preventive Maintenance	—	6
Repair Costs	—	3
Warranty	3	3
Fuel Economy	5	4
Rollover	6	7
Complaints	—	5
Insurance Costs	10	10
OVERALL RATING	7	6

Price Range	Retail	Markup
CE 8-Pass. FWD	$23,575	11%
LE 7-Pass. AWD	$27,875	11%
Ltd 7-Pass. AWD	$36,930	12%
XLE 7-Pass. AWD	$31,465	12%

Last Year's Model

For 2003, the Sienna received a new right hand sliding door, dual power sliding doors on the LE model, and captain chairs for the interior. Safety features include dual airbags, 4-wheel antilock brakes, and an optional built-in child seat. There are three models: CE, LE, and XLE. A tire pressure monitor is standard as is a V6 engine and CD player. You can also get a DVD entertainment system for the rear passengers.

Toyota Sienna 2003

Toyota Sienna XLE Ltd.

Safety Checklist

Frontal Crash Test	Very Good
Side Crash Test	Very Good
Airbags (Side/Head)	Front Optional/Head
Pretensioners/Impact Adjustors	Yes/Yes
Position/Weight Sensors	No/No
Seat/Head Adjustors	No
Roll Stability System	Yes
Child Seats Built-in	None
Antilock Brakes/Day Lamps	4-Wheel/Standard
Tire Pressure Monitor	Direct

General Information

2004 Status	All New
Series Started	No series indicated
Where Made	US
Theft Rating	Very High
Twins	

Specifications

Fuel Econ. (city/hwy)	Average-19/27
Driving Range (mi.)	Very Long-438.5
Bumpers	Weak
Parking Index	Hard
Seating	7
Tow Rating	Average-3500
Head/Leg Room (in.)	Very Roomy-42/42.9
Int. Space (cu. ft.)	Very Roomy-177.4
Cargo Space (cu. ft.)	Very Roomy-43.9

How the Competition Rates

	Rating	Pg.
Chrysler Town and Country	10	140
Honda Odyssey	8	165
Mercury Monterey	4	205

Toyota Solara — Intermediate

The all-new 2004 Toyota Solara received a number of changes. The convertible has been eliminated from this year's model lineup. The 2004 Solara includes 20 percent more interior space than the 2003 model. All models are equipped with either 2.4-liter four-cylinder engine or a 3.3-liter V-6. A full size spare tire and side airbags are both standard. Side curtain airbags provide excellent head and neck protection.

Toyota Solara

Ratings—10 Best, 1 Worst	2004	2003
Front Crash Tests	—	—
Side Crash Tests	—	8
Safety Features	8	2
Preventive Maintenance	—	—
Repair Costs	—	6
Warranty	3	3
Fuel Economy	5	8
Rollover	9	10
Complaints	—	10
Insurance Costs	10	5
OVERALL RATING	—	—

Price Range	Retail	Markup
SE 4-aut.	$19,950	11%
SE Sport 4-aut.	$21,445	11%
SLE 4-cyl.	$22,995	11%
SLE V6	$25,995	11%

Last Year's Model

The Toyota Solara was unchanged in 2003. The Solara comes with either a 2.2-liter inline 4-cylinder or a 3.0-liter V6 engine. A five-speed manual transmission comes standard, but you can get a four-speed automatic transmission as an option for both engines. Safety features include standard front dual stage airbags, seat belt pretensioners, ABS and daytime running lamps. Front side airbags and traction control are optional for the SLE model.

Toyota Solara

Toyota Solara

Safety Checklist

Frontal Crash Test	
Side Crash Test	
Airbags (Side/Head)	Fr. Std. Rear Opt./Yes
Pretensioners/Impact Adjustors	Standard/Yes
Position/Weight Sensors	Yes/No
Seat/Head Adjustors	No
Roll Stability System	Yes
Child Seats Built-in	None
Antilock Brakes/Day Lamps	4-Wheel/Standard
Tire Pressure Monitor	None

General Information

2004 Status	All New
Series Started	No series indicated
Where Made	Canada
Theft Rating	Very High
Twins	

Specifications

Fuel Econ. (city/hwy)	Average-20/29
Driving Range (mi.)	Long-430.1
Bumpers	Weak
Parking Index	Average
Seating	4
Tow Rating	
Head/Leg Room (in.)	Cramped-38/42
Int. Space (cu. ft.)	Cramped-92.1
Cargo Space (cu. ft.)	Cramped-13.8

How the Competition Rates

	Rating	Pg.
Chrysler Sebring	10	138
Ford Mustang	7	155
Infiniti G35		175

Toyota Tacoma — Compact Pickup

Though the appearance remains unchanged, the Tacoma has a few mechanical upgrades in 2004. The PreRunner 4x4 model has a new vehicle skid control system. A 2.4-liter 4-cylinder provides adequate power and there are two additional engine options including a V6. Creature comforts are numerous and give this truck a car like feel. The 2004 Tacoma has dual stage airbags with a passenger airbag cutoff switch and side impact door beams for added safety.

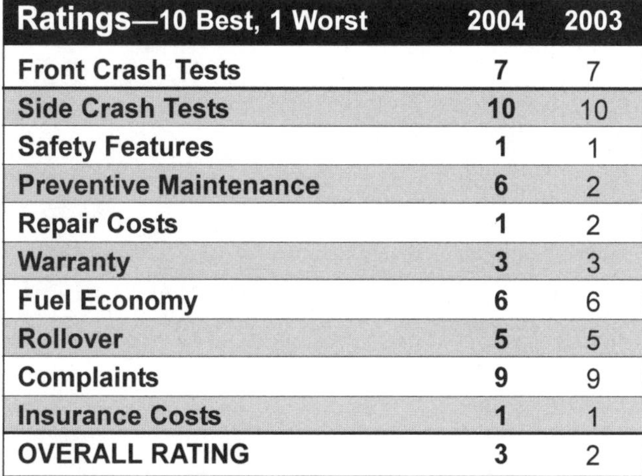

Ratings—10 Best, 1 Worst	2004	2003
Front Crash Tests	7	7
Side Crash Tests	10	10
Safety Features	1	1
Preventive Maintenance	6	2
Repair Costs	1	2
Warranty	3	3
Fuel Economy	6	6
Rollover	5	5
Complaints	9	9
Insurance Costs	1	1
OVERALL RATING	3	2

Price Range	Retail	Markup
4X2 Reg Cab	$12,260	8%
4x2 Xtracab V6	$20,160	9%
4X4 Reg Cab	$17,570	11%
PreRunner Double Cab V6	$19,350	9%

Last Year's Model

After its redesign in 2001, the Tacoma was unchanged in 2003. ABS is standard. A new child restraint system for the front passenger seat and rear outboard seats were introduced last year. There are nearly 17 model configurations available. A 4-door double cab and an S-Runner sport truck are available. Leather seating is available as an option. The Tacoma has high insurance costs.

Toyota Tacoma

Toyota Tacoma Double Cab

Toyota Tacoma Xtra Cab

Safety Checklist

Frontal Crash Test	Good
Side Crash Test	Very Good
Airbags (Side/Head)	No Side
Pretensioners/Impact Adjustors	Yes/No
Position/Weight Sensors	No/No
Seat/Head Adjustors	No
Roll Stability System	No
Child Seats Built-in	None
Antilock Brakes/Day Lamps	4-Wheel/None
Tire Pressure Monitor	None

General Information

2004 Status	Unchanged
Series Started	1995
Where Made	US
Theft Rating	Very High
Twins	

Specifications

Fuel Econ. (city/hwy)	Average-22/25
Driving Range (mi.)	Short-367.4
Bumpers	Weak
Parking Index	Easy
Seating	3
Tow Rating	Average-3500
Head/Leg Room (in.)	Cramped-38.5/41.7
Int. Space (cu. ft.)	
Cargo Space (cu. ft.)	Roomy-39.6

How the Competition Rates

	Rating	Pg.
Chevrolet Colorado		124
Dodge Dakota	5	142
Ford Ranger	5	156

Toyota Tundra — Standard Pickup

The 2004 Tundra comes with a V8 engine and a new towing package. The 4x2 model has an available Sport Package. Antilock brakes come standard. Rear seat air-conditioning ducts, rear seat audio, and a rear seat entertainment system are all-new to the Tundra. A JBL audio system is available. On the exterior, the taillights have been redesigned and a moon roof and a power vertical sliding rear window with defroster have been added.

Toyota Tundra Double Cab

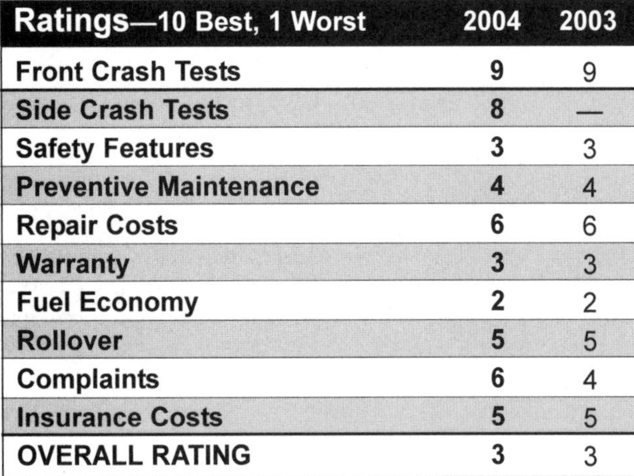

Ratings—10 Best, 1 Worst	2004	2003
Front Crash Tests	9	9
Side Crash Tests	8	—
Safety Features	3	3
Preventive Maintenance	4	4
Repair Costs	6	6
Warranty	3	3
Fuel Economy	2	2
Rollover	5	5
Complaints	6	4
Insurance Costs	5	5
OVERALL RATING	3	3

Toyota Tundra Double Cab

Price Range	Retail	Markup
4x2 V8 Access Cab Limited	$27,075	11%
4x4 Stepside Cab Limited 4A	$31,165	11%
Reg Cab 5M	$15,955	11%
Reg Cab V6 4A	$16,795	11%

Last Year's Model

In 2003, the Tundra pickup received a new V8 trim model called Access Cab Sidestep, a new grille, front end design, heated mirrors, and new fabrics for the interior. The 4.7-liter V8 on the Access Cab produces 240hp. An automatic transmission is standard, but a manual transmission is available. Dual airbags are standard. Typical of pickups, the Tundra has a large number of cab/bed sizes and drive train configurations available.

Toyota Tundra 2003

Safety Checklist

Frontal Crash Test	Very Good
Side Crash Test	Good
Airbags (Side/Head)	No Side
Pretensioners/Impact Adjustors	Yes/No
Position/Weight Sensors	No/No
Seat/Head Adjustors	No
Roll Stability System	No
Child Seats Built-in	None
Antilock Brakes/Day Lamps	4-Wheel/Optional
Tire Pressure Monitor	None

General Information

2004 Status	Unchanged
Series Started	2000
Where Made	US
Theft Rating	Very High
Twins	

Specifications

Fuel Econ. (city/hwy)	Very Poor-16/19
Driving Range (mi.)	Very Long-454.7
Bumpers	Weak
Parking Index	Very Hard
Seating	3
Tow Rating	Average-5000
Head/Leg Room (in.)	Average-40.3/41.5
Int. Space (cu. ft.)	Very Cramped-60
Cargo Space (cu. ft.)	Very Roomy-171

How the Competition Rates

	Rating	Pg.
Dodge Ram Pickup	3	145
Ford F-Series		154
Chevrolet Silverado	3	128

Volkswagen Beetle   Subcompact

There are only minor changes to the Volkswagen Beetle in 2004. The GLX trim model is no longer in production. There are new wheel options on all GL and GLS models and a new, improved 1.9-liter turbo engine is offered. Later in the model year an advanced airbag with dual stage deployment will be added. Other improvements include active safety headrests that help protect against whiplash. The 2004 model also has a fuel cap seal indicator that tells you if the fuel cap is loose.

Volkswagen New Beetle GLS

Ratings—10 Best, 1 Worst	2004	2003
Front Crash Tests	9	9
Side Crash Tests	8	8
Safety Features	3	3
Preventive Maintenance	5	8
Repair Costs	6	7
Warranty	7	10
Fuel Economy	7	7
Rollover	8	7
Complaints	10	10
Insurance Costs	5	5
OVERALL RATING	8	10

Volkswagen New Beetle Convertible

Safety Checklist

Frontal Crash Test. . . . . Very Good
Side Crash Test. . . . . Good
Airbags (Side/Head). . . . . Front Standard
Pretensioners/Impact Adjustors . . . . Yes/No
Position/Weight Sensors . . . . No/No
Seat/Head Adjustors . . . . No
Roll Stability System . . . . No
Child Seats Built-in . . . . None
Antilock Brakes/Day Lamps 4-Wheel/Standard
Tire Pressure Monitor . . . . None

Price Range	Retail	Markup
GL 5-sp.	$16,330	5%
GL Convertible	$20,900	5%
GLS	$19,395	7%
GLS 1.8 Turbo	$25.995	7%

General Information

2004 Status . . . . Minor Appearance Change
Series Started. 1998
Where Made . . . . Mexico
Theft Rating. . . . . Very Low
Twins . . . .

Last Year's Model

In 2003, the Beetle convertible was a new addition to the hot selling Beetle family. The convertible is powered by the same 115 hp 2.0-liter 4-cylinder found in the base line Beetle model. The standard engine is a 2.0 liter four cylinder found on the GL model. Front and side airbags are standard. Fuel economy is good at 23/29 mpg. The Beetle has also preformed well in government crash tests.

Volkswagen Beetle 2003

Specifications

Fuel Econ. (city/hwy). Good-23/29
Driving Range (mi.) Short-367.7
Bumpers . . . . Strong
Parking Index. . . . . Very Easy
Seating. 4
Tow Rating . . . .
Head/Leg Room (in.). Cramped-41.3/39.4
Int. Space (cu. ft.). . . . . Very Cramped-85
Cargo Space (cu. ft.) . . . . Very Cramped-12

How the Competition Rates

	Rating	Pg.
Chrysler PT Cruiser	9	137
Mini Cooper	10	206
Pontiac Vibe	9	230

Volkswagen Golf/Jetta — Compact

There have been some minor improvements to the 2004 Jetta and Golf. The high performance R32 model has been added to the Golf line up, while the Jetta GLX is no more. New exterior colors have been added, as well as new alloy wheel options. The Golf and Jetta have very low fuel economy and repair costs. Also both cars have done well in government crash tests-both scoring a very good.

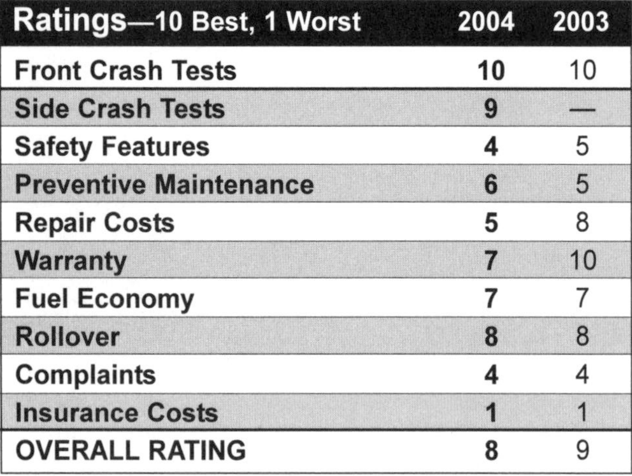

Ratings—10 Best, 1 Worst	2004	2003
Front Crash Tests	**10**	10
Side Crash Tests	**9**	—
Safety Features	**4**	5
Preventive Maintenance	**6**	5
Repair Costs	**5**	8
Warranty	**7**	10
Fuel Economy	**7**	7
Rollover	**8**	8
Complaints	**4**	4
Insurance Costs	**1**	1
OVERALL RATING	**8**	9

Price Range	Retail	Markup
2 DR GL	$15,580	7%
4 DR GL	$15,780	7%
4 DR GLS	$18,140	7%
GL TDI	$17,200	7%

Last Year's Model

Unchanged in 2003, the Golf and the Jetta came with 4-year/50,000 miles 24-hour roadside assistance. Antilock brakes are standard and come with the choice of a 5-speed manual or automatic transmission with overdrive. Dual airbags, daytime running lights and front seat belt pretensions are standard. A 2.0-liter 4-cylinder engine powers the base line Golf and Jetta. A turbo diesel version is available and gets nearly 42 mpg in city driving.

Volkswagen Jetta

2003

Volkswagen Golf GL

Volkswagen Jetta GLI

Safety Checklist

Frontal Crash Test	Very Good
Side Crash Test	Very Good
Airbags (Side/Head)	Front Standard/Yes
Pretensioners/Impact Adjustors	Yes/No
Position/Weight Sensors	No/No
Seat/Head Adjustors	No
Roll Stability System	No
Child Seats Built-in	None
Antilock Brakes/Day Lamps	4-Wheel/Standard
Tire Pressure Monitor	None

General Information

2004 Status	Unchanged
Series Started	1999
Where Made	Brazil
Theft Rating	Very High
Twins	Volkswagen Jetta 2004

Specifications

Fuel Econ. (city/hwy)	Good-23/29
Driving Range (mi.)	Short-367.7
Bumpers	Weak
Parking Index	Very Easy
Seating	5
Tow Rating	
Head/Leg Room (in.)	Cramped-38.6/41.5
Int. Space (cu. ft.)	Very Cramped-88
Cargo Space (cu. ft.)	Average-18

How the Competition Rates

	Rating	Pg.
Chevrolet Cavalier	3	123
Ford Focus	8	152
Honda Civic	10	161

Volkswagen Passat

Intermediate

For 2004, the Passat receives a host of electronic improvements. A new 2.0-liter TDI engine has been added to the line up, but it won't appear until well into the 2004 model year. There are new exterior color options, but the greatest improvements are in electronic options. The same system is standard on the GLX and W8 models. There is now a new Homelink garage door system and a light to warn you if your fuel cap is loose.

Volkswagen Passat GLX

Ratings—10 Best, 1 Worst	2004	2003
Front Crash Tests	10	10
Side Crash Tests	8	8
Safety Features	9	8
Preventive Maintenance	3	4
Repair Costs	2	8
Warranty	7	10
Fuel Economy	4	5
Rollover	9	8
Complaints	2	2
Insurance Costs	5	5
OVERALL RATING	8	10

Price Range	Retail	Markup
AWD GLX	$32,605	9%
GL	$21,780	10%
GLS	$23,380	10%
GLS Wagon	$24,380	10%

Last Year's Model

The 2003 Passat carried forward from 2002 with a few additions. These changes included a new 170 hp, 1.8-liter engine on the GL trim model. There is a V6 option on some models. A new suspension stabilization system option, new wheels, and a new sunroof were also added in 2003. Front, side, and curtain airbags, are standard. Antilock brakes, and daytime running lights are just some of the many safety features found on the Passat.

Volkswagen Passat

Volkswagen Passat GLX Wagon

Safety Checklist

Frontal Crash Test	Very Good
Side Crash Test	Good
Airbags (Side/Head)	Front Standard/Yes
Pretensioners/Impact Adjustors	Yes/Yes
Position/Weight Sensors	Yes/No
Seat/Head Adjustors	No
Roll Stability System	Yes
Child Seats Built-in	None
Antilock Brakes/Day Lamps	4-Wheel/Standard
Tire Pressure Monitor	None

General Information

2004 Status	Unchanged
Series Started	1998
Where Made	Germany
Theft Rating	Very High
Twins	

Specifications

Fuel Econ. (city/hwy)	Poor-19/26
Driving Range (mi.)	Very Short-354.6
Bumpers	Strong
Parking Index	Average
Seating	5
Tow Rating	
Head/Leg Room (in.)	Very Cramped-37.8/41.5
Int. Space (cu. ft.)	Cramped-93
Cargo Space (cu. ft.)	Roomy-39

How the Competition Rates

	Rating	Pg.
BMW 3 Series	9	104
Nissan Maxima	9	216
Volvo 60 Series	10	268

Volkswagen Touareg — Mid-Size SUV

The Touareg is all-new for 2004 and marks Volkswagen's entry into the SUV market. The standard Touareg is powered by a 3.2 liter, 220 horsepower V6 engine. A 4.2-liter V8 is optional. Electronic stabilization systems and 4-wheel antilock brakes, help handle the road. The interior comes equipped with dual zone climate control, and a telemetrics system that will notify police and emergency response units if you get into an accident. The Touareg has a built in theft deterrent system. A six-speed automatic transmission is standard. A navigation system is available as an option.

Volkswagen Touareg

Volkswagen Touareg

Ratings—10 Best, 1 Worst	2004	2003
Front Crash Tests	—	
Side Crash Tests	—	
Safety Features	9	
Preventive Maintenance	—	
Repair Costs	—	
Warranty	7	
Fuel Economy	1	
Rollover	—	
Complaints	—	
Insurance Costs	5	
OVERALL RATING	—	

Price Range	Retail	Markup
V6	$34,900	10%
V8	$40,700	10%
V8x	$45,550	10%

Last Year's Model

Model Not Produced in 2003

2003

Safety Checklist

Frontal Crash Test	
Side Crash Test	
Airbags (Side/Head)	Fr. Std. Rear Opt./Yes
Pretensioners/Impact Adjustors	Standard/Yes
Position/Weight Sensors	Yes/Yes
Seat/Head Adjustors	No
Roll Stability System	Yes
Child Seats Built-in	None
Antilock Brakes/Day Lamps	4-Wheel/None
Tire Pressure Monitor	None

General Information

2004 Status	All New
Series Started	No series indicated
Where Made	Germany
Theft Rating	Average
Twins	Porsche Cayenne

Specifications

Fuel Econ. (city/hwy)	Very Poor-15/20
Driving Range (mi.)	Very Long-446.2
Bumpers	
Parking Index	Hard
Seating	5
Tow Rating	Very High-7716
Head/Leg Room (in.)	Cramped-38.7/41.3
Int. Space (cu. ft.)	Average-99
Cargo Space (cu. ft.)	Roomy-31

How the Competition Rates

	Rating	Pg.
BMW X5	8	106
Acura MDX	10	96
Lincoln Aviator		195

Volvo 40 Series — Compact

For 2004, the Volvo 40 series gains a new Limited Edition for the sedan and wagon and the side mirrors have been changed to reduce wind noise. The Limited Sport Package offered on the wagon and sedan gives you a moon roof, a power driver's seat, and rear spoilers. Leather seating, stainless-steel scuff plates and front fog lamps are also new this year. The engine is a perfectly adequate 1.8-liter 4-cylinder. Standard equipment includes keyless entry, cruise control and a seven-speaker AM/FM CD player.

Volvo S40

Volvo S40 Limited Sport

Ratings—10 Best, 1 Worst	2004	2003
Front Crash Tests	—	—
Side Crash Tests	—	—
Safety Features	8	8
Preventive Maintenance	3	2
Repair Costs	6	1
Warranty	6	8
Fuel Economy	7	7
Rollover	8	8
Complaints	—	—
Insurance Costs	5	5
OVERALL RATING	—	—

Price Range

Model	Price	
S40 Base	$24,450	2%
S40 LSE	$28,545	6%
V40 Base	$25,450	6%
V40 LSE	$29,545	6%

Last Year's Model

Volvo's compact sedan and wagon got a mild life face-lift in 2003. The improvements include a new grille design, headlights, and moldings. A standard 1.8-liter, 4-cylinder 160 hp engine powers these front wheel drive vehicles. Safety features are impressive, as should be expected in a Volvo. Dual deployment front airbags, side airbags, a whiplash protection system, seat belt pretensioners, and antilock brakes are all standard.

Volvo 40 Series — 2003

Safety Checklist

Frontal Crash Test	
Side Crash Test	
Airbags (Side/Head)	Fr. Std. Rear Opt./Yes
Pretensioners/Impact Adjustors	Yes/Yes
Position/Weight Sensors	No/No
Seat/Head Adjustors	Yes
Roll Stability System	No
Child Seats Built-in	Optional
Antilock Brakes/Day Lamps	4-Wheel/Standard
Tire Pressure Monitor	None

General Information

2004 Status	Minor Appearance Change
Series Started	2001
Where Made	Netherlands
Theft Rating	Very High
Twins	

Specifications

Fuel Econ. (city/hwy)	Good-22/30
Driving Range (mi.)	Average-397.5
Bumpers	Weak
Parking Index	Easy
Seating	5
Tow Rating	Low-2000
Head/Leg Room (in.)	Very Cramped-38.7/41.1
Int. Space (cu. ft.)	Very Cramped-88
Cargo Space (cu. ft.)	Roomy-33.5

How the Competition Rates

	Rating	Pg.
Audi A4	10	101
BMW 3 Series	9	104
Infiniti G35		175

Volvo 60 Series — Intermediate

For 2004, the Volvo S60 gets minor improvements to the side mirrors and a new model, the sporty S60 R. There is a new 2.5-liter turbo engine available as well. Dual stage airbags, side impact airbags and antilock brakes are standard. A keyless entry system, seats with a three-position memory, and a navigation system are available. Cruise control is standard. Leather seating and a new stability control system are available.

Ratings—10 Best, 1 Worst	2004	2003
Front Crash Tests	**8**	8
Side Crash Tests	**10**	10
Safety Features	**10**	9
Preventive Maintenance	**3**	2
Repair Costs	**5**	5
Warranty	**6**	8
Fuel Economy	**7**	6
Rollover	**10**	9
Complaints	—	—
Insurance Costs	**5**	5
OVERALL RATING	**10**	9

Price Range	Retail	Markup
2.5T	$29,310	6%
2.5T AWD	$31,060	6%
R	$36,875	6%
T5	$32,960	6%

Last Year's Model

For 2003, a 2.4-liter five-cylinder engine powers the S60. Rear passengers have their own climate controls and the more aerodynamic shape reduces road noise. The 60 Series comes with dual stage front airbags, side impact and side curtain airbags. The 60 Series also comes with Volvo's whiplash protection system. Traction control is available. There are three engine choices and antilock brakes are standard.

Volvo 60 Series

Volvo S60 AWD

Volvo S60 AWD

Safety Checklist

Frontal Crash Test	Good
Side Crash Test	Very Good
Airbags (Side/Head)	Front & Back/Yes
Pretensioners/Impact Adjustors	Yes/Yes
Position/Weight Sensors	No/No
Seat/Head Adjustors	Yes
Roll Stability System	Yes
Child Seats Built-in	Optional
Antilock Brakes/Day Lamps	4-Wheel/Standard
Tire Pressure Monitor	None

General Information

2004 Status	Minor Appearance Change
Series Started	2000
Where Made	Belgium
Theft Rating	Very High
Twins	

Specifications

Fuel Econ. (city/hwy)	Good-22/31
Driving Range (mi.)	Very Long-468.2
Bumpers	Weak
Parking Index	Very Hard
Seating	5
Tow Rating	Average-3300
Head/Leg Room (in.)	Average-38.9/42.6
Int. Space (cu. ft.)	Cramped-94
Cargo Space (cu. ft.)	Roomy-36.5

How the Competition Rates

	Rating	Pg.
Audi A6		102
Buick Regal	6	112
Toyota Avalon	10	249

Volvo 70 Series — Intermediate

For 2004, the Volvo 70 Series-the C70 convertible, the V70, and XC70 wagons-got a minor appearance change. The V70 wagon adds a new sport version called the V70 R. The XC70's mirrors have been redesigned to reduce wind noise and new 15-inch alloy wheels have been added. Two new colors are available on the C70 convertible. The 70 Series vehicles come equipped with such features as an available navigation system, keyless entry and dual stage airbags. A 2.4-liter turbo remains the base engine in most models. The XC70 has AWD.

Volvo C70 Convertible

Ratings—10 Best, 1 Worst	2004	2003
Front Crash Tests	—	—
Side Crash Tests	—	—
Safety Features	10	9
Preventive Maintenance	5	3
Repair Costs	3	5
Warranty	6	8
Fuel Economy	5	5
Rollover	9	9
Complaints	—	—
Insurance Costs	10	10
OVERALL RATING	—	—

Volvo V70 Wagon

Price Range	Retail	Markup
2.5 T Wagon	$31,460	6%
R	$38,375	6%
T5 Wagon	$34,460	6%
XC Cross Country	$34,460	6%

Last Year's Model

Unchanged for 2003, the wagon (V70) isn't radically different from the previous 850. However, the C70 convertible's aggressive and sporty styling is a departure for Volvo. The coupe was dropped in 2003. Safety is still Volvo's strength. Dual airbags, side impact airbags, daytime running lamps, pretensioners, and ABS are all standard. This Volvo did very well in the government's crash tests. The standard engine is a 2.3-liter 236 hp model.

Volvo 70 Series

Safety Checklist

Frontal Crash Test	
Side Crash Test	
Airbags (Side/Head)	Front & Back/Yes
Pretensioners/Impact Adjustors	Yes/Yes
Position/Weight Sensors	No/No
Seat/Head Adjustors	Yes
Roll Stability System	Yes
Child Seats Built-in	Optional
Antilock Brakes/Day Lamps	4-Wheel/Standard
Tire Pressure Monitor	None

General Information

2004 Status	Minor Appearance Change
Series Started	1998
Where Made	Sweden/Belgium
Theft Rating	Very Low
Twins	

Specifications

Fuel Econ. (city/hwy)	Average-20/26
Driving Range (mi.)	Long-412.9
Bumpers	Weak
Parking Index	Hard
Seating	5
Tow Rating	Average-3300
Head/Leg Room (in.)	Average-39.3/42.6
Int. Space (cu. ft.)	
Cargo Space (cu. ft.)	Roomy-37.5

How the Competition Rates

	Rating	Pg.
Audi Allroad Quattro		103
Saab 9-5	10	232
Lexus ES 330		190

Information is for the V70 Wagon.

Volvo 80 Series

Large

For 2004, Volvo's flagship sedan receives a major appearance change. The front headlights and front fascia have been reworked, and the side mirrors have been redesigned to reduce noise. The interior features new gauges and a three-spoke wood steering wheel. The standard engine is a 2.9-liter inline six-cylinder engine, but there is also an inline six-cylinder turbo available. This large car is loaded with an available navigation system, dual climate control, and a rain sensor. Dual stage airbags, and side curtain impact airbags are standard.

Volvo S80

Volvo S80

Ratings—10 Best, 1 Worst	2004	2003
Front Crash Tests	10	10
Side Crash Tests	10	10
Safety Features	10	9
Preventive Maintenance	2	2
Repair Costs	3	4
Warranty	6	8
Fuel Economy	5	6
Rollover	10	9
Complaints	—	—
Insurance Costs	10	10
OVERALL RATING	9	10

Price Range	Retail	Markup
2.9	$37,045	6%
T-6	$44,525	6%
T-6 Elite	$48,515	6%

Last Year's Model

Unchanged in 2003, the S80 came with a 2.9-liter 6-cylinder engine or 6-cylinder twin turbo as an option. The list of safety features is impressive: de-powered airbags for driver and front passenger, side impact inflatable curtains, side impact airbags in all seats, safety belt pretensioners, daytime running lamps, and antilock brakes. The interior is well equipped with leather and wood panel trim. Dual climate control is also standard on all models.

Volvo 80 Series

Safety Checklist

Frontal Crash Test. . . . . . Very Good
Side Crash Test. . . . . . Very Good
Airbags (Side/Head). . . . . . Front & Back/Yes
Pretensioners/Impact Adjustors. . . . . . Yes/Yes
Position/Weight Sensors . . . . . . No/No
Seat/Head Adjustors . . . . . . Yes
Roll Stability System. . . . . . Yes
Child Seats Built-in . . . . . . Optional
Antilock Brakes/Day Lamps 4-Wheel/Standard
Tire Pressure Monitor . . . . . . None

General Information

2004 Status. . . . . . Major Appearance Change
Series Started. 1999
Where Made . . . . . . Sweden
Theft Rating. . . . . . Very Low
Twins . . . . . .

Specifications

Fuel Econ. (city/hwy) Average-20/28
Driving Range (mi.) . . . . . . Very Long-482.0
Bumpers . . . . . . Weak
Parking Index . . . . . . Hard
Seating. 5
Tow Rating. Average-3300
Head/Leg Room (in.) Average-38.9/42.2
Int. Space (cu. ft.) Average-99
Cargo Space (cu. ft.) Roomy-39.8

How the Competition Rates

	Rating	Pg.
Buick Park Avenue	7	110
Cadillac CTS	7	114
Lincoln LS		196

Volvo XC90

Mid-Size SUV

The XC90 remains unchanged for 2004. A standard turbo-charged five-cylinder engine powers the XC90. It is loaded with lots of electronic features including a DVD based entertainment system, a remote garage door opener, power windows and sunroof. The XC90 has some of the best safety features of its class. Dual stage airbags, Boron steel roof frame, pretensioners, front and side curtain airbags are just some of the features. Options include heated seats, a second row child seat booster and leather seating surfaces.

Volvo XC90

Volvo XC90

Ratings—10 Best, 1 Worst	2004	2003
Front Crash Tests	9	—
Side Crash Tests	10	—
Safety Features	10	8
Preventive Maintenance	—	—
Repair Costs	—	—
Warranty	6	8
Fuel Economy	3	4
Rollover	5	6
Complaints	—	—
Insurance Costs	5	5
OVERALL RATING	8	—

Price Range	Retail	Markup
2.5T	$34,440	6%
2.5T AWD	$36,190	7%
T6	$40,565	6%

Last Year's Model

The 2003 XC90 was Volvo's first SUV to hit the market. There is seating for five or seven depending on the trim model. A turbo-charged five-cylinder engine produces nearly 208 horsepower. A roll stability control system automatically detects any change in the vehicles angle and will automatically correct it so that the XC90 will not roll over. Side airbags are standard. A DVD entertainment system is optional.

Volvo XC90 2003

Safety Checklist

Frontal Crash Test	Very Good
Side Crash Test	Very Good
Airbags (Side/Head)	Front Standard/Yes
Pretensioners/Impact Adjustors	Yes/Yes
Position/Weight Sensors	Yes/Yes
Seat/Head Adjustors	Yes
Roll Stability System	Yes
Child Seats Built-in	Optional
Antilock Brakes/Day Lamps	4-Wheel/Standard
Tire Pressure Monitor	None

General Information

2004 Status	Unchanged
Series Started	2003
Where Made	Sweden
Theft Rating	Average
Twins	

Specifications

Fuel Econ. (city/hwy)	Poor-18/24
Driving Range (mi.)	Average-385.4
Bumpers	
Parking Index	Hard
Seating	7
Tow Rating	Average-5000
Head/Leg Room (in.)	Average-40.1/41
Int. Space (cu. ft.)	
Cargo Space (cu. ft.)	Very Roomy-85.1

How the Competition Rates

	Rating	Pg.
Acura MDX	10	96
Buick Rendezvous	5	113
Lexus RX 330	9	194